TOWNLANDS
in Ulster

TOWNLANDS
in Ulster

LOCAL HISTORY STUDIES

◆

Edited by
W.H. CRAWFORD
& R.H. FOY

ULSTER HISTORICAL FOUNDATION
IN ASSOCIATION
WITH THE
FEDERATION FOR ULSTER LOCAL STUDIES

First published 1998
by the Ulster Historical Foundation
12 College Square East, Belfast, BT1 6DD
in association with
The Federation for Ulster Local Studies,
18 May Street, Belfast, BT1 4NL

All rights reserved. No part of this publication may be reproduced, stored in
a retrieval system or transmitted in any form or by any means, mechanical
or otherwise without permission of the publisher

© Ulster Historical Foundation, 1998

ISBN 0-901905-84-4

Typset by the Ulster Historical Foundation
Printed by ColourBooks Ltd
Cover and Design by Dunbar Design

CONTENTS

PREFACE — vii

INTRODUCTION — 1

Creating the Framework — 6
WILLIAM H. CRAWFORD

Forttown, County Antrim — 35
WILLIAM MACAFEE

Scolbow, County Antrim — 67
ROBERT H. FOY

Ballymagee, County Down — 95
SANDRA A. MILLSOP

Cranfield, County Down — 111
HUGH S. IRVINE

Drumskinney & Montiaghroe, County Fermanagh — 135
JOHN B. CUNNINGHAM

Gallon, County Tyrone — 155
W. JOHN BRADLEY

Hollyhill, County Tyrone — 189
JOHN DOOHER

Owenreagh, County Londonderry — 215
GRAHAM MAWHINNEY

INDEX — 237

PREFACE

In 1991 the Federation for Ulster Local Studies published *Every Stoney Acre has a Name: a celebration of the townland in Ulster* (edited by Tony Canavan). This was a weapon in its long-running campaign to maintain the use of townland names when the Post Office was pressuring rural dwellers to abandon them in favour of new ill-devised road names and numbered houses. The Federation affirmed the popular belief that the townland still represents a vital element in rural life and, as such, has to be preserved for posterity. As Seamus Heaney pointed out in his preface:

> The Townlands Campaign is manifestly something more than resistance to change for its own sake…Whether one is studying the townland as an administrative unit, or a locus of linguistic and topographical evidence, or a site of genealogical and historical revelation, one is in every case testifying to the valency and carrying power of the nomenclature itself.

In general, townspeople find it difficult to understand why country people should resent the replacement of this archaic tradition of townlands by the modern system of road names with numbered houses. Many fail to appreciate the importance that country people attach to the term 'tradition'. Only when their own personal traditions comes under attack do they begin to realise the vital part that tradition plays in our emotional life. Then they are forced to reassess its importance and value in their lives.

We in the Federation for Ulster Local Studies were forced to try to justify our campaign to preserve not only townland names but the very concept of townlands. We have discussed the history of that concept and its value in helping us to understand our own past. In this publication several individuals have tried to relate their knowledge of individuals, families and communities to the official records that have survived for townlands that they know well. We have placed their stories in the context of the documents to demonstrate that there is much to be gained by consulting them. The evidence from the documents, however, often challenged or complicated tradition so much that the essays had to be revised, sometimes several times. We are very grateful to each of our contributors for completing and revising their essays in these circumstances.

We could not have contemplated a publication on these lines if the Public Record Office of Northern Ireland had not been engaged on a major ongoing project to make its resources accessible to a much wider public. It has published many findings aids including archives of landed estates, of the Encumbered and Landed Estates Courts, and of Land Registry. Of especial relevance to this publication is its new Geographical Index of townlands in Northern Ireland available on the web. Over the past few years the staff of PRONI have encouraged us to organise local history seminars using their resources and facilities. We are grateful to them also for providing copies of relevant maps and documents as well as permitting us to quote from documents in their possession. We should like to thank Dr Anthony Malcolmson, Deputy Keeper and Chief Executive, Dr David Lammey, Dr Roger Strong, and Mrs Heather Stanley.

The library of the Ulster Folk and Transport Musuem at Cultra, Holywood, encourages students of local history to use its specialist resources and we are grateful for the ready help of the Librarian, Mr Roger Dixon and his assistant, Mrs Sally Skilling.

At an important stage in the development of this publication the Ulster Local History Trust agreed to grant aid the very specialist map preparation in this volume. This publication should convince everyone that such maps are essential to townland studies because they enable the reader to concentrate on the townland under review.

We wish to thank Mr Ian Wilson, curator of the North Down Heritage Centre in Bangor, for permitting us to reproduce three items from the Clandeboye estate maps prepared by Thomas Raven in 1625.

This book has also received support from both the Rural Development Council and the Cultural Traditions Programme of the Community Relations Council which aims to encourage acceptance and understanding of cultural diversity.

W. H. Crawford

Key to townland maps

▭	Building
—·—	Townland line
——	Field boundary
═══	Fenced road/path
······	Unfenced path
· · · ·	Track
6	Valuation boundary
▨	Wood
▢	Lake

PREFACE

PUBLIC RECORD OFFICE OF NORTHERN IRELAND
GEOGRAPHICAL INDICES

There are almost 9,500 townlands in Northern Ireland. PRONI has collected together all the townland names found in the six counties of Northern Ireland and presented them in a number of useful ways on the PRONI web-site (the web-site address is: http://proni.nics.gov.uk/geogindx/geogindx.htm).

Using a combination of colour-coded and numerical reference maps, and straight-forward tables, Northern Ireland is broken down into Counties, Baronies, Poor Law Unions, Parishes, Diocese and Townlands. There is even a glossary to explain exactly what a gneeve is – or was!

For those interested in townlands, the information is presented in four different ways: by County, by Parish, within Major Estates, and Alphabetically. The list of townlands by county is, due to the sheer volume of information, currently presented as an alphabetical list in a simple table format while the parish index gives the names of all the townlands within that parish, the county in which they are situated (parishes frequently straddled county borders), the electoral divisions, and an Ordnance Survey map reference number.

The townlands by Major Estate are listed by landowner. As landowners frequently held land in more than one area, there are sub-divisions within this grouping. For example, the Duke of Abercorn held land in the Manors of Strabane, Cloghhogle, Donelong and Dirrigoon, while the Annesley family owned estates in Castlewellan, Banfield, Newcastle and Dunlady. Each townland is therefore listed under the estate or manor in which it lies, but under the general heading of the landowner.

In the alphabetical index clicking on a letter will bring up all townlands starting with that letter and the list will also show the county in which the townland is situated.

The indices are searchable: each page can be searched using the normal 'FIND' command on your browser, or for a very general search, use the search engine on the PRONI Home page. A dedicated search engine is currently under construction within the Geographical Index page.

Anyone interested in the geography of Northern Ireland will find PRONI's new Geographical Indices of immense benefit. Suggestions and queries to mcveiga.proni@doeni.gov.uk.

INTRODUCTION

W. H. CRAWFORD

To appreciate the value of the concept of the townland the best course for us is to examine in detail every aspect of one or more of them in terms of our own experience. We can all appreciate the deep knowledge about their townlands that many people possess: as John Mogey wrote in *Rural Life in Northern Ireland* (Oxford, 1947), 'they know every tree, every rock, every field and house and most of the tales and legends associated with them.' (p.228) If we wish, however, to relate this traditional knowledge to the histories of our communities, we have to try also to explain the important historical changes that have occurred, in terms that readers can understand.

In local history studies we concentrate on the community that has lived in the townland. We want to fathom the culture that evolved in the context of the landscape and in the community's response to change imposed from beyond its boundaries. This exercise must be even more significant today when local communities are being pressed to assess their potential for social and economic development. All communities could benefit from an audit of their historical assets and an analysis of their presentation for visitors. We need all the documentary, artifactual, and oral evidence that we can find in order to fix our townland in its historical and geographical context.

We wish to encourage people throughout the province to undertake the study of the history of either their own townland or one that they know well. This publication will introduce them to the documentary sources that survive in archives and explain how they can be related to the traditions, the artefacts, and the oral evidence that they are so jealous of preserving. Such studies will make us all much more aware of our heritage and its significance. The very richness of the evidence will stimulate new creative writing. From such publications teaching materials and methods will be devised to transmit the findings for future generations.

BASIC SOURCES AVAILABLE FOR THE STUDY OF ALL TOWNLANDS
IN THE PUBLIC RECORD OFFICE OF NORTHERN IRELAND

Ordnance Survey maps (OS)
Townland Valuation (VAL/1B) with map (VAL/1A)
Tenement Valuation (VAL/2B or printed) with map (VAL/2A or VAL/12D)

Valuation Revision Lists (VAL/12B & /12F) updating the Tenement Valuation between 1865 and 1935.

The records of the First Northern Ireland General Revaluation from 1935 to 1954 (VAL/3), the Second from 1956-72 (VAL/4), and the Third since 1976 (VAL/14).

Census figures 1841-1991 (published townland figures 1841-1926: after this they are held by the Census Office)

Census returns for 1901 (MIC/354)

Tithe Composition Applotment books 1823-37 (FIN/5): see *Guide to Tithe Records.*

N.B. Information about the most valuable supplementary sources may be found in the two volumes entitled *Guide to Landed Estate Records.*

As more people, also, learn how to find and apply documentary evidence to studies of their own locality, they will augment and refine our comprehension of the documents themselves and the circumstances in which they were created. In the long term these case studies and others that are bound to follow, should help us to generalise anew about historical trends and the factors that have affected Ulster history. They will provide us with new concepts and introduce us to fresh sources that will inform future surveys of our landscape and culture. At the same time they should help us to isolate local and peculiar factors that have affected the characters of individual districts ranging from single townlands to whole districts, such as estates.

In doing this, however, we shall become more and more aware that we need to compare the history of our townland with that of many others, if we wish to gain a more accurate understanding of the factors involved. Indeed, it has been observed that a local historian cannot confine his study to a single district or locality because the essence of local history is the problem of regional variation within societies. Although it is likely that we will end up with as many questions as answers, we should come, during the exercise, to appreciate the significance of the townland in Irish local history.

For this publication we invited several individuals to write about the history of a townland or group of townlands of their choice. Some responded almost immediately with drafts but they differed so widely in both focus and content that we decided to try to devise a 'framework' that would encompass the topics that we hoped to cover and present them in a logical sequence. In due time every contributor received not only this framework but also a collection of 'basic sources', copies of documents and transcripts that are available for each and every townland in the country. Of course it was not possible for the contributors to make a fresh start but several of them did incorporate much of the material into their essays and one of the editors has made comments on various sources.

The major problem with this publication was reproduction of the early Ordnance Survey and Valuation maps. Our experience has convinced us that the OS maps are essential for understanding the changes in the landscape over the past two centuries while the Valuation records provide much vital evidence. There are, however, problems with reproducing them. As the boundaries on the Valuation maps are marked in red, photocopies print them out in black, making them

INTRODUCTION

indistinguishable from other boundaries on the OS maps. Many of the original Valuation maps, too, had sustained blemishes during their service life. We therefore obtained xerox copies of the OS revised edition (which marks field boundaries) from the OS headquarters, ran off extra copies and then marked these up in red pencil from the original Valuation maps in the Public Record Office. To reproduce them for this publication we sent the marked-up copies at first to Brian MacDonald but later, at his suggestion, to Matthew Stout, both professional cartographers who had collaborated in the production of the wonderful *Atlas of the Irish Rural Landscape* (Cork, 1997), of which Stout had been one of the three editors. While we have to admit that we have taken the maps of individual townlands out of their original context, we believe that their clarity of reproduction will enable readers to concentrate better on each study.

Although whole books could be written about individual townlands, we were concerned to present studies of a variety of townlands throughout the province. We had to draw the line at twelve to limit the amount of preparatory work required. Of the original twelve, eight scripts have been completed and are published here. We suggested a maximum of five thousand words for each essay and encouraged our authors to concentrate on those aspects they found most interesting. We hope that our readers will browse through the volume, enjoy the essays, and reflect on the significant characteristics of their own townlands. Consider the variety and range of concepts, ideas, and observations placed before you.

> FORTTOWN, near Ballymoney in north Antrim, was one of the townlands that was formed out of the ancient ecclesiastical district of Tullaghgore which contained seven quarterlands. It lay on the eastern slope of the fertile Seacon esker running down to the Garry Bog. In time the inhabitants reclaimed a considerable quantity of bog. Bill Macafee, who grew up in the townland, relates the family histories of the farmers and cottiers against the background of the wider Seacon community.

> SCOLBOW or SCOLBOA, on a hilltop in mid Antrim, had belonged to the Abbey of Kells but was leased in the seventeenth century from the Bishop of Connor by the Clotworthy family who became Lord Massereene. Now uninhabited, it was occupied by both British and Irish farmers as early as the mid-seventeenth century. Bob Foy has used oral tradition and documentary sources to trace the history of the several families who lived there and of relations between them.

> BALLYMAGEE, now part of the town of Bangor in north Down, represents cultivated monastic land acquired from the Crown in the early seventeenth century by Sir James Hamilton, first Viscount Clandeboye. Maps of the estate drawn by Thomas Raven in 1625, suggest that the property was ripe for development. Sandra Millsopp has concentrated on sorting out the property in the townland leased by three families of minor gentry and on searching through a wide variety of sources to trace the tenant-farmers. She has also uncovered links with the 1798 Rebellion.

> CRANFIELD, occupying the most southerly point in County Down at the mouth of Carlingford Lough, has a distinctive community of small farmers and fishermen. Hugh Irvine from Kilkeel has married his study of the

documentary evidence to the reminiscences of some of the older inhabitants.

DRUMSKINN(E)Y & MONTIAGHROE are two neighbouring townlands in the remote countryside of north-west Fermanagh. Drumskinny stone circle is the most famous archaeological site in the district. John Cunningham, who taught for a time in Montiagh school, relates the community to the landscape.

GALLON or GALLAN was the name once applied to a mountain side used for grazing on the western flank of the Sperrins opposite Newtownstewart in Tyrone. By the early eighteenth century part of it was defined as the three townlands of Upper Gallan, Lower Gallan and the Sessagh of Gallan. John Bradley, who was the last master of Gallan school and whose family has lived there for two centuries, has always been interested in the history of his district. Here is the essence of the fruits of his research.

HOLLYHILL or HOLLY-HILL was a Plantation freehold on the Abercorn estate near Strabane. The government had recommended landlords to settle on their estates substantial tenants who would support their landlords and provide an element of both stability and security within their districts. The Rev John Sinclair acquired the property in 1683 and his family built the big house and laid out trees and parkland in the demesne around it. John Dooher's especial interest lies in James Sinclair's scheme after the Napoleonic Wars to lay out compact farms on the slopes of the high hill above the big house. He traces the subsequent fortunes of this community up to recent years.

OWENREAGH is one of The Sixtowns in the mountainous parish of Ballinascreen in south Londonderry. Its present landscape of ladderback farms reflects the reforms of John Stevenson of Tobermore who bought the Sixtowns from the Church of Ireland in 1835. Graham Mawhinney, whose family has lived there for more than two centuries, perpetuates the local history tradition there established by Geordie Barnett (1876-1965), whose reputation for learning was province wide.

The preparation and revision of the framework has subjected to fresh examination many of the current concepts about the social and cultural history of rural Ulster. Our opening chapter introduces certain key concepts based on the current state of our knowledge and explains our reasons for recommending sources that can be examined in the Public Record Office of Northern Ireland.

THE REGISTRY OF DEEDS in Henrietta Street, Dublin is the other very valuable source for eighteenth century Ulster local history. Soon after it opened in 1708 registration of deeds of all kinds of property became the rule rather than the exception. Memorials of these deeds in the form of either a complete transcript or a fairly full abstract of the original document, were copied into huge volumes and indexed both by the names of the grantors and by placenames. In the placename index each county is indexed separately with townland names in alphabetical order (volume number, page number, and memorial number). For further information see P. Roebuck, 'The Irish Registry of Deeds: a comparative study', *Irish Historical Studies*, xviii no. 69 (1972), 61-73.

OUR FRAMEWORK

1. **Introduction:** the special character of this townland in the context of Ulster townlands.

2. **Location** in present day terms with description of characteristic physical features.

3. **History and tradition before the Plantation:** What evidence can we find from tradition, documents, place names, archaeological remains, family names, etc.? Such studies would help us to appreciate also the nature of the revolution in landholding that was introduced by the Plantation.

4. **Estates and the creation of farms:** It is important to grasp the concept of the estate (and the manor) and how the estate was leased by townlands, or by fractions of them, to tenants as compact farms. Within leases, especially on the poorer land, occupiers made an infinite variety of arrangements among themselves: this was known as rundale. In time population increase and subdivision split the early holdings into family farms. Poorer men who could not afford to take leases were relegated to the status of cottiers. After the Famine farms began to be consolidated and cottiers migrated. While the Tenement Valuation records and maps identify the individual farms and their holdings and date the changes, only local knowledge can suggest the reasons.

5. **Population growth and decline:** Census figures after 1841 indicate the rate of loss of both males and females at townland level. The disappearance of inhabited houses reflects the loss of families. Both the Valuation Revision Lists and the 1901 and 1911 census returns suggest what was happening. Church and school registers provide useful supplementary evidence.

6. **Housing changes** reflect other important changes in the community. Examine all the house sites in your townland, checking them off against the Tenement Valuation records and the census material. What class of people occupied each of them? It is important to distinguish between the traditional cottage, the 'riz and slated', the two-storey house, the new labourers' cottages, and modern architect-designed houses. Note especially the dates of rebuilding. Check through family photographs for pictures of houses before modernisation. [The Tenement Valuation books and the Valuation Revision Lists can date these changes. After 1894 the Valuers' Notebooks provide even better information about building changes. The B1 form of the 1901 census is especially valuable for this work.]

7. **Changing farming practices:** What crops were grown, what livestock kept? The acreage of each crop grown in an Electoral Division was returned by the constabulary and published between 1847 and 1850 as *Agricultural Returns* by the government. Afterwards these figures, as well as returns for livestock, were published by Unions. Where these are not easily available, county figures can be found in *Thom's Directory* throughout the second half of the 19th century: they are most useful for showing local trends. How did the decline in crop acreages (after 1859) and the introduction of horse-implements affect the cottiers? How were the farms managed in the first half of this century? What changes have the last fifty years seen?

8. **Development of communications and markets:** The first Ordnance Survey maps c1830 show that by then Ulster had a very extensive road network. What access did your townland have to it? Where did the inhabitants go to market their crops and livestock and to buy goods and services? Did the railways help to open up your district? And motor transport?

9. **The community and its traditions:** Did neighbouring townlands think of this townland as an entity or was it considered part of a larger district? Did the locals think of themselves as a community or did they look elsewhere for leadership? Were they knit together by a church, a local school, a local industry or something else? How did they display their community spirit? Has that feeling changed over time? Has it disappeared? If so, what reasons would you give? How does it view its future?

CREATING THE FRAMEWORK

W. H. CRAWFORD

This publication grew out of a conviction that many people would enjoy the exercise of studying the history of their own townlands and the communities who lived there. Among them are those who have been introduced to the practice of genealogy and have become familiar with valuation records and census returns. Many have acquired a wealth of traditional knowledge from their families and friends and realise that they are well equipped to benefit from an introduction to other sources of evidence prepared for the government or deposited in archives by private individuals. The marriage of such information to local traditions will often stimulate a sequence of new questions that enrich the whole story. Indeed, the real quality of local history lies in its very diversity and the multitude of approaches that can be used to uncover valuable information for weaving into the story.

This chapter amplifies and explains the 'framework' set out in the introduction to this book. In essence it proposes a methodology for anyone setting out on such a study. At the same time it sketches in very broad terms how Ulster rural society evolved over the past four centuries, explains and illustrates some of the factors that have shaped its character, and introduces the relevant sources at each stage of the discussion. Although some of the concepts may seem difficult at first sight, they will be easier to understand when applied to the study of your own townland.

My experience of working with this material over many years leads me to stress the fundamental importance of the landed estates that were created during the Plantation period and the patterns of landholding that they generated through various kinds of leases. These estates survived for more than three centuries, although it has to be admitted that even before their sale to the tenants, many townlands had become in effect the property of minor landowners: they are most easily identified in the printed pages of Griffith's tenement valuation. Since its Plantation origins landed property throughout Ulster had been granted by landlords to tenants by written (later printed) leases whose terms were scrutinised and interpreted by royal judges, over the years, often in favour of the tenants. In contrast, too much emphasis has been laid on the concept of 'rundale' in the Ulster countryside, but it is a blanket term that covers a wide range of arrangements made between tenants, undertenants, and cottiers. Every case of it needs to be examined within the terms of the lease that created it. In the long run, however, landlords and tenants were jointly responsible for the remodelling of these outdated agreements and for creating the 'family farms' that we remember as the most typical characteristic of Ulster rural traditional life in our time.

Just as important in Ulster local history was the role of the landlords and their agents in promoting not only 'estate towns' but also the boroughs that had been placed under their patronage in the early years of the Plantation. Even a glance at a map of Ireland will reveal the great density of towns in Ulster, many of which were once noted for their linen markets or their livestock fairs. This urban network was closely related to the growth of an extensive road network, complete with bridges, promoted and administered through the county grand juries by the landlords and their agents, especially after the Road Act of 1765.

The estates of many landlords benefited by the construction of new roads through the Sperrins and the Donegal mountains, for example, because they encouraged families to carve out new farms in the hill country of the province, using the potato to bring marginal land under cultivation. It is important to realise that over the past four centuries the face of the Ulster countryside has been completely altered by the folk who have inhabited it. Especially in the century before the Great Famine many thousands of acres of bogland and scrub were brought under arable or pasture.

THE IMPORTANCE OF MAPS

In this investigation our starting date should be the present and we should begin with a close and thorough examination of the district using first the latest edition of the Ordnance Survey map and then the Revised Edition of the Ordnance Survey map made about 1860. Because not all field boundaries were inserted in the first edition of the Ordnance Survey maps for Ulster made in the 1830s, it is wiser to use instead this Revised Edition, a superb example of the mapmaker's art. If working copies are prepared from the 1860 edition (as in this book), they can then be annotated and coloured to present the research findings. **Remember to keep an unmarked copy of it for the production of copies.** We can use these working copies, for example, to record significant changes between the successive editions of the 6 inch to the mile Ordnance Survey maps (held in PRONI). On to the first of the xerox copies should be transcribed from the VAL/12D maps the boundaries of farm-holdings and locations of buildings about 1860, because these maps contain the first ever comprehensive coverage of such information for the whole island of Ireland. When this has been completed for the townland it is worthwhile to transcribe the information given on the same sheet number of VAL/1A for the Townland Valuation

J.H. ANDREWS, *History in the Ordnance Map: an introduction for Irish readers* (Dublin, 1974) was designed for local historians and contains the most complete guide to the information available from the great series of maps published by the Ordnance Survey of the United Kingdom for Ireland between 1824 and 1922. It illustrates eighteen maps reproduced at original scale and seven national maps to index all town plans and one-inch maps. A revised 1993 edition can be obtained from David Archer, The Pentre, Kerry, Newtown, Montgomeryshire, Wales, SY16 4PD. £7.90 stg. incl. P&P.

done in the 1830s. On this Valuation map, however, remember that the townland was divided not into farm holdings but into convenient areas to be assessed for valuation.

Various questions arise from the initial study of the map. The most obvious relate to the boundary of each townland in terms of its neighbours. From the patents granted to landlords by the Crown and from the Bodley maps (see page

Townlands in Shankill Parish [Lurgan, Co. Armagh] as marked on the Bodley map (PRONI)

12) for six of the nine counties, we should be able to find out whether or not the townland existed as an independent entity at the time of the Plantation. If it did not, then we need to search for the first mention of it, at first in estate documents such as title deeds and leases, and then in the Down Survey of the mid 1650s, the 'census' of 1659, and the hearth-money and poll tax returns of the 1660s. We are more likely to find townlands with names that we recognise in those districts colonised by British settlers in the early years of the Plantation than in the more extensive and remote districts of marginal land used for the summer grazing of cattle. We need to consider the relationship that any new townland might have had to its predecessor. The history of townlands and their creation may be more complex than we have reckoned and it may differ from region to region.

NUMBER OF TOWNLANDS IN COUNTY ARMAGH ACCORDING TO 17TH CENTURY SURVEYS

784...Bodley's Plantation Maps of 1609
854...Cromwell's Inquisition of 1657
566...Poll Tax of 1660
665...Hearth Money rolls 1664-5
923...Books of Survey & Distribution late seventeenth century
963...Ordnance Survey 1830s

When T.G.F.Paterson was preparing this list of 'County Armagh householders 1664-5' from the Hearth Money rolls for *Seanchas Ardmhacha* in 1981, he found these discrepancies in the number of townlands in County Armagh. He suggested that the figures of the 1660s might reflect the number of uninhabited townlands due to the previous two decades of unrest. The differences between the other figures, however, emphasize how important it is to investigate the history of individual townlands.

VALUATION RECORDS

A major reason for introducing the Ordnance Survey to Ireland in 1824 was reform of the archaic taxation system. To introduce a more equitable method it was necessary to map the country, measure vast tracts of land, and calculate their value. The Valuation Act of 1826 specified that the basic unit of land measurement should be the townland and so this scheme was referred to as the **Townland Valuation**. The valuators were instructed 'to observe the slope and altitude of the land, to dig up soil samples, and to divide each townland into lots of more or less uniform physical character, each of which would then be assigned a certain value in shillings per acre.' This **Townland Valuation**, therefore, provides a very accurate survey of the natural environment of each and every townland in Ireland before the Famine following a century of land reclamation. We suggest that you should try to retrace the steps of the valuators, surveying the townland and identifying all its features, landmarks, and buildings as they would have seen it nearly two centuries ago. In PRONI the **Townland Valuation** is listed as VAL/1A (annotated maps) and VAL/1B (manuscript field books). Town plans are in VAL/1D. [See also *1830s Townland Valuation: valuation of Property*]

Although the **Townland Valuation** did make the imposition of taxation more equitable, it did not assess individuals. Therefore the Irish Poor Relief Act of 1838 (6&7 Wm IV, c.84) which introduced the workhouse system with its poor law unions to Ireland, required the Poor Law Guardians in each union to make a special Poor Law Valuation in order to levy poor rates. It was replaced in turn as the basis of all local taxation by the **Tenement Valuation** under an act of 1852 (15&16 Vict., c.63) although the new valuation was not completed until 1865. The valuators had to map and calculate the value of *not only townlands but also tenements, or 'holdings'*, so that the poor rates could be levied on every holder of property in every union. It even became the basis of assessment when income tax was introduced to Ireland in 1853. In PRONI the **Tenement Valuation** is listed as VAL/2A (annotated maps) and VAL/2B (manuscript field books). Town Plans are in VAL/2D.

These VAL/2B field books were edited and published from 1858 to 1864 under the supervision of the Commissioner of Valuation, Richard Griffith, and so they are often referred to as **Griffith's Valuation**. The printed books and annotated maps present a comprehensive picture of the tenurial geography of mid-nineteenth century Ireland.

Since 1865 both the maps and the field books of the **Tenement Valuation** have been regularly updated and annotated with coloured inks that aid identification of individual changes. They illustrate such historical processes as the sale of estates, the consolidation of holdings into larger farms, and the disappearance of cottier houses. These volumes of **Valuation Revision Lists** for the period 1865 to 1935 are catalogued in PRONI under VAL/12B and /12F with their related maps (known as the Star & Union maps) under VAL/12D. After 1894 **Revising Valuer's Office Notebooks** [VAL/12A] provide more detail about the revaluation of altered buildings. Town plans are in VAL/12E.

The records of the First Northern Ireland General Revaluation (1935-54) are held in PRONI under VAL/3, those of the Second (1956-72) under VAL/4, and those of the Third (1976>) under VAL/14.

The various editions of *Instructions to Valuers* are listed in VAL 13

For the creation and the significance of the Tenement Valuation see the chapter by W.E Vaughan on 'Richard Griffith and the Tenement Valuation' in G. L. Herries Davies & R. C. Mollan (eds), *Richard Griffith 1784 – 1878* (Dublin, 1980).

If you wish to consult the Valuation records in PRONI you should first become familiar with the detailed summary by T. Parkhill entitled 'Valuation Records in the Public Record Office of Northern Ireland' in *Ulster Local Studies*, 16, no 2 (winter 1994).

Once we have established the date of the original townland boundary, we need to trace it out on the ground to find out how it was defined. Very often the boundary followed the line of a stream but elsewhere it usually had to be constructed or defined. Seventeenth century leases often required tenants to 'mear and ditch the outbounds and plant them with whitethorn quicksets'. Timber trees such as sycamore, ash, holly, or crab-apple, were planted on these ditches. Where stones had to be cleared from the land the obvious solution was to build stone walls. In boggy or marshy ground an early practice was to define the boundary with 'mearing stones'. There are many references in estate papers to the settlement of boundary disputes by consulting the oldest inhabitants.

BOUNDARY PROBLEMS ON THE ESTATE OF THE ARCHBISHOP OF ARMAGH 1703
[PRONI T/848 *Ash's View of the Archbishopric of Armagh, 1703*]

Lord Primate has three townlands which lie within the above parishes. Their names or denominations are mentioned in the lease. When I was upon the place I made diligent enquiry after them but could not be informed of them. They are in the lease I suppose called by the old names and are now not known by them, so I cannot at present give any particular account of them. Since my return to Dublin I searched in the Surveyor's Office expecting there to be informed, but found nothing of them. I then waited on the Earl of Mount Alexander, one of the lessees, and desired that his Lordship would be pleased to order his agent (pursuant to the covenants in his lease) to trace the mears and bounds of those townlands and give an account thereof, also of the names they are known by to his Grace the Lord Primate. And for answer his Lordship was pleased to say that he would give directions according, but (further adding) 'Truly I don't know whether my agent will be able to do it or not for they be intermixed with my own estate and are hardly distinguishable.' [p.31]

Ballelackan which is now called Outlackan Mr John Ball has taken about twenty acres of land and added it to Tullevan his own estate. This as I was informed upon the place upon enquiry. I find that he who was to make this appear is long since dead and I cannot yet meet with anybody that knows the meers so well betwixt the two townlands as to make out Lord Primate's rights to these twenty acres. It is owned the Church has been out of possession many years and indeed I don't yet meet with anybody that can prove the Church ever in possession. I gave orders to enquire further after it. [p.41]

There is a dispute between Mr Stewart's tenants to Aghakniduffe about mears and boundaries. Lord Primate's undertenants have been in possession, as I am informed, time out of mind of the acres in question. The dispute about a Farren-Saggart or a small parcel of land which [runs] from the ditch of the said Farren-Saggart (which is ley land and enclosed) up the hill northwards by a small ridge which seems to have been a fence or enclosure, and then turns eastward etc. The two townlands are bounded with Lord Charlemont's land North, West, and South, Mr White and Mr Stewart's land South and East.' [p.9]

After settling the mearings we can investigate how the original townland was sub-divided into compact farms, each with its own farmhouse. Often these early farms corresponded with natural sub-divisions of the townland. Leases refer sometimes to 'quarters' and occasionally to 'islands' of arable land in the bogs. These sub-denominations are more likely to be discovered on surviving estate maps than on Ordnance Survey maps. Nevertheless, because most of these farms, in their turn, became sub-divided into even smaller holdings, it is often possible to determine the original boundaries. There is no substitute for examining the mears and fences on the ground!

Sub-division created other problems. One of the most important for any farmer was access from his farm to a main road, referred to in law as 'a right of way'. The range of solutions devised to solve this problem has left its mark on the landscape ranging from the maze of narrow lanes picking up cottage after cottage in the densely populated fine-linen weaving countryside of North Armagh, to the spur lanes running off main roads to the several farmsteads along their routes in County Antrim, or the long loanings climbing up to the last cottage in the marginal lands of the Sperrins. And, of course, the construction of a new road could mean the re-orientation of the rights-of-way. In short, it can be well worthwhile to take a second look at the roads and lanes in each townland.

> G. HAYES-McCOY, *Ulster and other Irish Maps c1600* (Dublin, 1964)
>
> V. HALL, 'The vegetational landscape of mid Co Down over the last half millenium: the documentary evidence', *Ulster Folklife*, 35 (1989) and 'The woodlands of the Lower Bann Valley in the seventeenth century: the documentary evidence'. *Ulster Folklife*, 38 (1992)
>
> N. CANNY, 'Hugh O'Neill, earl of Tyrone, and the changing face of Gaelic Ulster', *Studia Hibernica*, x (1970)
>
> H. MORGAN, *Tyrone's Rebellion, the outbreak of the Nine Years' War in Tudor Ireland* (London, 1993)
>
> P. J. DUFFY, 'The territorial organisation of Gaelic landownership and its transformation in County Monaghan, 1591-1640', *Irish Geography*, xiv (1981), pp 1-26
>
> M. O'DOWD, 'Gaelic economy and society' in C. Brady & R. Gillespie, eds, *Natives and Newcomers* (Dublin, 1986)

The location of ancient churches, monasteries, castles, and other older monuments on the map should remind us that every townland had a history before the Plantation. It could prove very valuable, therefore, to visit the reading-room at the Monuments & Buildings Record at 5-33 Hill Street (just off High Street), Belfast BT1 2LA (telephone 01232-235000; fax 01232-543111) and mark up on your xeroxed map the location of the field monuments in the townland. Information will be available about some of the sites and, if you know of others, you can add to the official record and contribute to future research. Sometimes old estate maps note ancient sites. Although such source materials may be scarce, we have to use them in conjunction with geography and archaeology in order to gain some concept of the heritage of the district. Look through J.Mallory & T. McNeill, *The Archaeology of Ulster* (Belfast,1991) and the published volumes of the Place-Name Survey for potential approaches. Very valuable, too, in understanding the changing structure of Ulster society at that time is K. Simms, *From Kings to Warlords* (Woodbridge, 1987).

ESTATES AND THE CREATION OF FARMS

Townlands cannot be studied in isolation especially after they became components of the new estates that were created throughout Ulster during the reign of King James I. Before the Plantation scheme was prepared by the Crown, several adventurers managed to get large estates for themselves in the counties of Antrim and Down. In 'The making of an Ulster great estate: the Chichesters, Barons of Belfast and Viscounts of Carrickfergus, 1599-1648'(*Proceedings of the Royal Irish Academy*, vol.79, C, number 1) Peter Roebuck has demonstrated the problems of managing such large estates. County Monaghan had been reorganised already among its Irish owners. The remaining six counties in Ulster were confiscated by the Crown after the Flight of the Earls in 1607 and reallocated to new owners, the majority of whom came across the sea from Britain.

Because there had never been any adequate surveys of these six confiscated counties, the Crown was forced to adapt the existing Irish measurements of townlands. Their relative location was then sketched roughly on the basis of evidence provided by native juries: these maps have survived and are known to students as the Bodley maps. Their history is explained by J.H. Andrews in 'The maps of the escheated counties of Ulster 1609-10', *Proceedings of the Royal Irish Academy*, vol 74, section C, no. 4 (1974). The new estates were based on these maps. The Government's plans ensured that the estates would be much less extensive than those granted in Antrim and Down but, like them, they were compact and many of them were large enough to sustain an embryo market town.

In historical studies of the Plantation project it has been overlooked often that the Crown insisted that every landowner had to lease the bulk of his estate to tenants who would hold their lands according to any of the forms of tenure then current in England. The landowner was therefore not given liberty to treat his estate as a ranch but was required to attract tenants to inhabit it. If he wished to profit from his lands, the landowner had to negotiate the terms of leases with potential tenants and then help them to make a success of their holdings so that they could pay money rents. The government enforced this provision by sending commissioners on several occasions between 1610 and 1622 to inquire about the progress of the settlements and especially about the nature of the tenancies that had been granted.

COMMISSIONERS' REPORTS ON THE BROWNLOW ESTATE AT LURGAN, COUNTY ARMAGH

1611: John Brownlow, 1500 acres, and his son William Brownlow, 1000 acres; both resident and dwelling together in an Irish house; have brought over 6 carpenters, 1 mason, a tailor, and six workmen; 1 freeholder and six tenants upon their land; preparations to build 2 bawns; some muskets and other arms in readiness. (*Calendar Carew MSS*, vol. iv, 225)

1613: John Brownlow, the father, with his wife and family, together with his son William Brownlow, are resident on their proportions, having fitted themselves for the time being in a house of stone and clay, on the ruins of an old chapel, being in a place of good safety on that side of Lough Chichester. Their stock of cattle they have on the ground, but as yet very few tenants; those which John Brownlow brought over, which were 40 or 50, by reason of the hardness of the country having all forsaken him. Howbeit by that time he has perfected his building, which he hath now in hand, both of a bawn and house, for which the most part of his materials are in place in a well-chosen seat for that purpose, he doubteth not but to people his country sufficiently; to which end he is building of certain tenements, whereof two are already finished, and other frames set up, where his town shall be, and hath a windmill ready framed and presently to be reared. (*Historical MSS. Commission, Hastings MSS*, vol. iv, 174)

> DETAILS ABOUT THESE GRANTS OF NEW ESTATES MAY BE FOUND IN
>
> George Hill, *An Historical Account of the Plantation of Ulster,* (Belfast, 1877)
>
> *Irish patent rolls of James I: facsimile of the Irish record commissioners' calendar prepared prior to 1830* (Irish Manuscripts Commission, 1966)
>
> *Calendar of patent and close rolls of chancery in Ireland, Charles I, years 1 to 8,* ed. James Morrin (Dublin, 1864)
>
> *The Civil Survey, A.D. 1654-56*, ed. R. C. Symington (10 vols, Irish Manuscripts Commission, Dublin, 1931-61)

1619: William Brownlow, Esq., hath two proportions, viz Dowcoran, being 1,500 acres, and Ballymoney, 1,000 acres. Upon the proportion of Ballynamoney there is a strong stone house within a good island; and at Dowcoran there is a very fair house of stone and brick, with good lime, and hath a strong bawn of timber and earth with a palisade about it. There is now laid in readiness both lime and stone to make a bawn thereof, which is promised to be done this summer. He hath made a very fair town, consisting of 42 houses, all of which are inhabited with English families, and the streets all paved clean through; also two water mills, and a wind mill, all for corn; and he hath store of arms in his house. I find planted and estated on this land, of British families,

Lessees for years, 52, viz 1 having 420 acres; 1 having 300 acres; 1 having 240 acres; 3 having 200 acres apiece; 1 having 120 acres; 13 having 60 acres apiece; 8 having 50 acres apiece; 6 having 40 acres apiece; 6 having 30 acres apiece; 9 having 26 acres; 1 having (10(0?) acres; 1 having 11 acres; 1 having 5 acres.

Freeholders: 5 viz - 5 having 120 acres apiece.

Total, 57 families who have divers under them; and all these have taken the Oath of Supremacy, and are able to make a hundred men with arms. There is also good store of tillage, and not one Irish family upon the land. (George Hill, *An Historical Account of the Plantation of Ulster*, Belfast, 1877)

1622: William Brownlow Esq hath two proportions, viz Dewcorran containing 1500 acres, upon which is built a good house or castle of stone and brick, laid with lime, 3 stories high, wherein himself, his wife, and family, now inhabit. This house is compassed with a strong bawn of lime and stone; and he is purposed to make another opposite. He hath made near adjoining a good village, consisting of 40 houses, inhabited with English tenants, on both sides the streets, in which a good windmill stands.

He hath also on another proportion, called Ballynemoney, where he hath built a house of lime and stone, standing within an island, in which one Wilfred Trueman dwelleth, and holds the house and 60 acres of land in fee simple.

Upon both proportions:-

Freeholders; 3 having 100 acres apiece, 5 having 60 acres apiece.

Leaseholders and Cottagers: 1 having 240 acres, 1 having 140 acres, 2 having 120 acres apiece, 2 having 100 apiece, 2 having 60 acres apiece, 4 having 50 acres apiece. The rest (59 of them), some have 40 acres, some 30, some 20, some 11, and some less, but all have some land to their houses for 21 years, and some for longer terms. They are able to bring 160 men into the field, armed with pikes, callivers, or other weapons, and he hath in his castle, shot and pikes for fifty men. But there are on these proportions (as we are credibly informed) 24 Irish families. (PRONI T/1576)

Although the new landlords might have preferred to make minimum concessions, they were forced by a shortage of potential tenants to offer good terms and even to make leases to Irishmen. After legislation in 1628 (see *Calendar State Papers Ireland, 1625-32*, pp. 349-52) many of the landlords were prepared to take out new patents and pay an increased rent to the Crown for permission to lease up to a quarter of their individual estates to Irishmen. As a result, the practice of granting leases was widely established in Ulster from Plantation times. Every landlord wanted tenants who could afford to pay rents regularly (even if they had to be extracted from them in the courts as debts), to develop their holdings by fencing the outbounds and erecting a dwelling-house, and to carry out the covenants in the leases. Would-be tenants appreciated the value of a lease in terms of security of tenure as well as security for loans and mortgages; at the same time, however, they were well aware of the obligations that they would be incurring. In the event those who failed usually ran away.

CONTENTS OF LEASES

(a) Description of the premises; (b) Rights and royalties reserved to the landlord; (c) Term or length of the lease; (d) Rent; (e) Payment of duties; (f) Penalty for non-payment of rent; (g) Penalty for alienation; (h) Reserving the right to make roads through the premises; (i) Covenant by tenant to build a house; (j) Tenant to make enclosures; (k) Suit to mills: Tenant bound to grind at the landlord's mill; (l) Suit to court: Tenant bound to attend lord's court; (m) Tenant to plant orchard; (n) Tenant to keep premises in repair; (o) Landlord promises his tenant peaceful enjoyment of the holding; (p) Tenant to maintain the mill race and water courses.

In these leases the basic unit of measurement was the townland although contemporaries recognised that the majority of townlands contained subdivisions with names of their own: sometimes these subdivisions became townlands in their own right. In the more remote districts a substantial tenant might obtain several townlands but near the towns he would be fortunate to get as much as a single townland. Especially in the early years of the Plantation, landlords valued such substantial tenants highly because they were potential allies or at least assistants in organising or administering their estates. The 'freeholds' that landlords granted to them, remained a rare but important feature of the countryside.

MEASURES OF LAND USED IN ULSTER IN THE PAST

	Irish	English or statute	Cunningham or Scotch	Woodland or Burleigh
1 Irish acre =		1.62	1.254	1.361
1 English acre =	0.617		0.774	0.84
1 Cunningham acre =	0.797	1.29		1.085
1 Woodland acre =	0.735	1.19	0.92	

CREATING THE FRAMEWORK

> In all the measures there were 40 square perches to the rood and 4 roods to the acre. The distinction between the several measures, therefore, relates to the length of the perch: Irish perch = 7 yards; Cunningham perch = 6.25 yards; Woodland perch = 6 yards; Statute perch = 5.5 yards. This gives the Irish acre 7840 square yards, the Cunningham acre 6250 square yards, the Woodland acre 5760 square yards, and the Statute acre 4840 square yards
> On the history of land-surveying in Ireland, see J.H.Andrews, *Plantation Acres: an historical study of the Irish land surveyor and his maps* (Belfast, 1985).

Elsewhere, over succeeding generations, townlands fractured into smaller but still compact farms. The timing, extent, and nature of this process depended to a great extent on the leasing policies of landlords, although their decisions were often responses to changes in the wider community. The primary instinct of a tenant was to preserve his farm intact for the next generation but in most families children would insist on sub-dividing it after his death. If the father was intent on preserving the home farm by leaving it intact to his eldest son, he could satisfy the other children only by endowing them with money, purchasing other farms, or setting them up in trade, commerce, or a profession. Even in the seventeenth century there was a busy land market which landlords tried to control by insisting that they had to approve the transactions.

> DETAILS OF THE LEASING IN THE EIGHTEENTH CENTURY OF THE TOWNLAND OF Ballyhenry [East] in the parish of Aghanloo on the Connolly estate near Limavady, County Londonderry, as transcribed in the leasebook (PRONI D/2094/45)
>
> Ballyhenry: 148a.2r.23p. Scotch = 191a.3r.31p. English: all arable ground
>
> 1713 Let for £19.14s.6d. (about 2s.8d. per acre)
> 1745 Let to Fred Smith for £39 (about 5s.3d): advance in 32 years 2s.7d per acre
> 1766 Let to John Smith for £47.6s. (about 6s.4.5d): advance in 21 years 1s.1.5d
>
> Ballyhenry divided by Smith into Upper, Middle, and Lower Thirds.
>
> 1750 When the kingdom had not recovered [from] the effects of the Rebellion which immediately preceded it, the Upper Third was let for 21 years to John McConnell and partners. Connell paid 10s. per acre: his son John Connell proves this, and believes and always understood that the other partners paid the same rent: he is the only witness that lived on the lands at that time, the others being either dead or abroad.
>
> 1750 The Middle and Lower Thirds let for 21 years to tenants all of which are dead. The widow of one of them, James Dinning, is living and continues to hold a few acres of the Middle Third – the aforesaid John Connell believes and always understood that these tenants paid 10s. per acre.
>
> In the year 1766 when John Smith obtained leases from Lord Conyngham, the tenants above mentioned would have surrendered their leases (of which 5 years remained) and paid 13s. per acre on condition of getting new leases of the same term he had from Lord Conyngham.

Another instinct of a tenant was to take on undertenants who would pay their rents to him in cash, work, or kind. Whenever land was in great demand the tenant often decided that subletting parts of his farm, especially the outskirts, was more profitable than farming it. He had to be careful, however, not to provide the sub-tenant with a permanent claim to the holding. If he did, the landlord could argue that the tenant was giving up to the sub-tenant his *tenant-right* of the piece of land he had sublet. When the lease came up for renewal, the landlord could decide to let the holding directly to the prosperous sub-tenant, thus converting him into a leaseholder. As a result many farms were split into much smaller farms. By 1800, for example, it was reckoned that the average size of farms in the linen county of Armagh was less than ten acres. Elsewhere in Ulster it would appear that farmers managed to prevent this from happening and so retained their original holdings. In such circumstances subtenants became merely cottiers who held their smallholdings or 'cottakes' at the whim of the farmer.

The Tenement Valuation (VAL/2B) provides the earliest comprehensive picture about the numbers, location and distribution of cottier households throughout the province. The term *cottier* was applied to anyone who did not hold his land by a written lease from the landlord. Cottiers worked for farmers to pay for accommodation and some land to cultivate (the *dry-cottake* as opposed to the *wet-cottake* which included grazing for a cow). In the eighteenth century landlords had been quite prepared to concede that farmers should keep cottiers to help them work their farms or mills but they had always objected strongly to farmers packing their farms for profit with cottiers for whose conduct and welfare they took no responsibility. As the tenant-farmer, for his part, had every reason to fear that at the termination of lease his landlord would recognise the cottier's claim to a lease of the cottake, he was not prepared to concede any such claim. Cottiers were most numerous on marginal lands where they could plant their potato crops and obtain a ready supply of turf free for the cutting and they were blamed too for stealing timber from woods and hedgerows planted on the estates. By the time of the Tenement Valuation, however, the cottier class was still reeling from the devastation it had suffered in the Great Famine, and still migrating to the cities or even further afield. In various parts of the province cottier families were sustained still by firms 'putting out' textile work throughout their districts: handloom-weaving around north Armagh, whitework and other embroidery from north Down to south Donegal, and shirt-making around Londonderry.

Travellers through the lowlands of Ulster in the mid-nineteenth century saw a landscape of dispersed farms with attendant cottier houses and small-holdings, all heavily cultivated. The patterns of fields on the lowland farms with their hawthorn (whitethorn) hedgerows contrasted markedly with the extensive townlands of the uplands where houses tended to cluster on patches of good land and fences were walls of stone cleared from the fields. There men of some substance, who had secured leases from their landlords for one or more townlands, had acted as middlemen by setting farms to poorer men. Many of these middlemen avoided granting leases to these poorer men because that would have given them some security of tenure: here, too, the middlemen feared that the landlord might seize a suitable opportunity such as the renewal of the 'head' (or main) lease to let such farms directly to the occupiers. In time, however, this class of middlemen was forced out by a combination of the farmers who had reclaimed these lands and the landlords.

On some estates landlords leased farms to groups of partners, making each of the partners jointly responsible for payment of the rent: if one of the farmers could not pay his rent, the other partners were still liable for the whole rent. Within the framework of such a lease families and their relatives and other partners organised the collection of rent and allocated land. This practice was known as *rundale* and it displayed infinite variations because, in the absence of legal adjudicators, participants made arrangements to suit circumstances. Its major asset was flexibility that often suited short-term situations, such as the aftermath of a death in a family. In the longer term, however, it was likely to lead to bad blood between the parties. For this reason it was viewed as a major obstacle in the long term to the introduction of improved farming practices that were necessary to exploit the commercial markets expanding throughout the province. It often proved difficult for partners to make permanent divisions of land that had been held in partnership, unless the owner of an estate or his agent was prepared to intervene to supervise and underwrite the transaction. Even after permanent field boundaries were defined, the practice of holding the mountain grazing in common continued so that today every farmer knows how many *soums* (units of grazing) he can claim there: the actual valuation of these soums can be found in the manuscript books of the Tenement Valuation about 1860 (VAL/2B).

> It is worthwhile to examine the names of the farmers in your townland listed in the **Tithe Composition Applotment Books** (FIN/5) that were compiled for almost every parish in Ireland in the years 1823 to 1837. In some parishes tithes were not paid for historical reasons. Under the Tithe Applotment Act of 1823 two commissioners (one representing the ratepayers and the other the Church of Ireland) valued every holding in each parish, assessing the sum that each ratepayer should pay. We need to match this evidence with estate rentals to identify which of these ratepayers held their land directly from their landlord and which from farmers. The census returns that have survived for some parishes in County Londonderry in 1831, should help us to distinguish farmers from cottiers.

By the early nineteenth century Ulster was fast becoming the province of the small tenant farmer. This trend was further accentuated by the decline of the hand-spinning of linen yarn and later in the century by the collapse of handloom-weaving in many parts of the province. As fewer farmers were able to supplement their farm incomes by domestic industry, they had to farm more intensively on farms that were among the smallest in Western Europe. In contrast with the easing of landlord-tenant relations during the growing prosperity of the eighteenth century, the nineteenth century witnessed increasing tension between landlord and tenant that became known as the 'land problem' or the 'land question'. In the thirty years that succeeded the Great Famine the landlords were successful in their struggle to maintain their legal rights but the Land Acts of 1870 and 1881 and the beginning of a long recession in agriculture undermined their determination.

> 'By 1914 three-quarters of occupiers were buying out their landlords, mostly under the great acts of 1903 and 1904, which directly initiated the decisive decline of tenancy and led to the transfer in ownership of about nine million acres to the occupiers. In the 1920s, in both parts of Ireland, land purchase was made compulsory and the remaining tenanted land was taken from the landlords. The most striking sign of the decline of landlordism, the disappearance of the gentry from the countryside, was only evident from that decade: by the 1970s hardly one quarter of the mansion houses of the 1870s were lived in by descendants of nineteenth-century landed families.' (W. E. Vaughan, *Landlords and Tenants in Ireland 1848-1904*, Dundalk, 1984, p.39)

To discover when and how this major change in landownership was implemented in your district, consult the Valuation Revision Lists (VAL/12B). This can be checked with the archives of the Irish Land Commission and the Land Registry, which is especially useful for the many tiny estates that had been created by families over the previous two and a half centuries. Less typical but of more value are the surviving records of the great estates because they were administered by professional staff. Some of them contain illuminating correspondence about the sales.

When the ownership of land passed from landlords to farmers under the Land Acts, an old device known as 'conacre' reappeared in a new guise. Whereas the estate office had been responsible for confirming a tenant's title to his land, the new owners had to protect their own rights with the paid help of solicitors. How could they lease any of their newly-acquired land to another farmer without themselves running the risk of losing their title to it? To solve this problem the concept of conacre was resurrected. Before the Famine conacre was applied mainly to agreements made between farmers and cottiers: in return for the permission of the farmer to let him plant and harvest a crop of potatoes or keep a cow on the farmer's land, the cottier agreed to provide so many days of work on the farm. Although the cottier class was all but destroyed by the Famine, the concept of conacre survived but it was applied instead to arrangements between farmers on the grounds that a conacre agreement did not interfere with the owner's rights. Farmers who owned some land that they were not in a position to cultivate that year, arranged with local auctioneers to let the grazing for the year. Although the term has been explained as an 'eleven month tenancy', it has no standing in law in Northern Ireland and is purely an arrangement. It is a useful device for those farmers wanting to supplement grazing or to use modern machinery more economically in taking a cash crop. It is essential, too, for those farmers who find they can no longer work their land but are not in a position to sell it. Conacre land is the only land available for letting and high rents have become customary because its price responds to general economic trends as well as changes in the circumstances of individual families. It is not too much to claim that conacre lubricates the operation of the land system throughout Ireland. Any information you can elicit about its operation in your townland over the past century should reveal much about the changes that have occurred in the management of land over the last century or so.

CONACRE: opinions recorded by J. C. W. Wylie in *Irish Land Law*, London, 1975, pp.816-7.

20.26..The dealing called con-acre in this country is a very peculiar one. The person who takes the con-acre has no absolute right to the crop. He has not a right to take the crop, with merely an obligation to pay for it as a debt. But the person who allows the land to be tilled retains the dominium over the crop, of holding it until the stipulated amount shall have been paid. He can prevent the con-acre holder from removing the crop from the ground before payment. Can he have the power of thus preventing the removal of the crop, if he has not possession of the ground? Does not the right to obstruct and prevent the removal of the crop involve the right to the possession of the soil on which the crop rests. It seems to me that it does.

20.27..Because he may not hold the land after the end of the season, the conacre tenant will take everything he can out of the land and put nothing in. Any manure he applies is of short term effect such as nitrogen to boost a grass crop. He will not spend any money on repairs to fences and gates because he feels that he may lose the benefit at the end of the season. In the result, the state of the land let over a number of years deteriorates quite steadily and the yield falls off. One device to overcome the possibility of an unintended tenant right is the conacre agreement for one season with covenant to renew for a specified number of successive seasons. This is not widely used as its drafting is beyond the capacity of the average country auctioneer who usually arranges these conacre lettings. (quoting evidence of an experienced solicitor from *Survey of the Land Law of Northern Ireland*, 1971, para.287, wherein it was also reported that about 17 per cent of agricultural land in Northern Ireland was then so farmed.)

All these factors, however, tended to confirm the strength of the relationship between farms and families. A survey of farming in the province as late as 1952 concluded: 'In Ulster the farm is usually a family concern and not only a livelihood but a way of life. Although the days of subsistence farming are gone, only the large farms are thought of as commercial enterprises.' (D. A. Hill in *Belfast in its Regional Setting*, Belfast,1952, p.166) We can appreciate now that that great revolution has taken place in our lifetime. Recording the experiences of individual families and the histories of the individuals who comprised them, is an essential step in helping future generations to understand this important phase in the history of rural Ulster, a phase that has left indelible marks on our culture and heritage. Family trees, scrap-books, correspondence, marriage and testamentary records, gravestone inscriptions and photograph albums are the source materials that ought to be preserved. Such material has been well used in *Families of Ballyrashane*, (Belfast, 1969) and other volumes by the Rev Dr T. Hugh Mullin and his wife, Mrs Julia E. Mullin.

These great changes in landownership, however, need to be viewed against the background of the great population changes that have swept over Ireland in the past three or four centuries. The colonisation of both the hill country and the wastes of bogland was linked to the rapid increase in population. The consolidation of the family farm system has also to be viewed against a long period of population decline that can best be appreciated by studying the census returns collected and analysed by the government.

THE DECLINE OF POPULATION

The peak of the population explosion may have been reached about the time of the 1841 census which was, by coincidence, the first census to provide population statistics by individual townlands rather than parishes. The territorial divisions used in the censuses of 1841 and 1851 were County, Barony, Parish, Town, and Townland. From 1861 the Parish was replaced by the Poor Law Union and Electoral Divisions. Nevertheless, the Townland remained the basic unit until 1911 and was used also for the 1926 census in Northern Ireland. To obtain townland figures for the later censuses of 1937, 1951, 1961, 1971, 1981, and 1991, contact the Census Office, Arches Centre, 11-13 Bloomfield Avenue, Belfast BT5 5HD. The figures are set out under these headings:

Townland	Persons			Houses			
	Males	Females	Total	Inhabited	Uninhabited	Building	Total
Ballymore	38 +	40 =	78	15 +	3 +	2 =	20

A table of these figures drawn from the censuses from 1841 to 1991 enables us to draw some conclusions about the rate of decline and its character. It is important to concentrate on the number of inhabited houses at each census rather than the total number which includes both uninhabited houses and houses under construction. Any fall in the number of inhabited houses implies the departure of whole families, no matter the size. When the number of persons falls without a corresponding drop in the number of houses, we may infer that individuals were leaving home. As the census abstracts give the numbers of both men and women, we can consider why one sex rather than the other was leaving at any time: the men might be going off to seasonal work elsewhere or the women might be going off to look for employment after the local collapse of textile crafts.

The Tenement Valuation and the Annual Revision Lists identify the names of the families that were leaving these houses so that we are given an opportunity to find out something more about them. Their names may appear in the records of local churches. Their children's names may be found in the National School Registers held in PRONI (SCH) which often identify the previous school attended by newcomers, record the children's academic attainments, and sometimes note the circumstances of their departure. We are fortunate that the actual census returns made by each household in Ireland are available for the 1901 and 1911 censuses. They provide much useful information about religious affiliation, occupations, basic educational standards, counties of origin, and relationships within the families. Indeed, the older generation may be stimulated by a sight of the census returns to recall valuable information about some of the individuals mentioned.

Although everyone is aware of the sickness and deaths caused by the Great Famine, we often forget about the local impact of epidemics or endemic diseases on the rural population. There are stories about whole families being wiped out in epidemics and there was always a high incidence of tuberculosis in communities. The most likely source for corroborating such information is the records of the local dispensaries which predated the workhouse system but were taken over by the Boards of Guardians as a result of legislation to cope with the Famine.

HOUSING

By investigating the changes that have occurred in the construction of local houses townland historians can contribute to the study of rural housing in their district. Here they are dealing with the remains of structures that can tell us much about the lives of our forefathers. They need to assess the buildings in their own townlands on one hand against the environment and the availability of raw materials, and on the other against the policies of the estate and social changes in the world beyond. All these matters have been well presented, documented, and illustrated by Alan Gailey in *Rural Houses of the North of Ireland* (Edinburgh, 1984) where he has called for locally based studies. He has added that it is important to examine how the inhabitants used the insides of their houses.

The starting point for local historians is, once again, the Tenement Valuation (VAL/2) carried out about 1860, because its notebooks and maps identify and value all the houses in each townland. The Annual Revision Lists and their maps (VAL/12) enable us to keep track of each of these properties and to date changes in ownership, renovation and reconstruction as well as destruction. For the years 1901 and 1911 we can compare the information from the Annual Revision Lists with more detailed information contained in the census returns. This census information was first collected for the census of 1841 but none of this material has survived for any date before 1901. In the report of the 1841 census the government explained its method for classifying houses:

> The value or condition of a house, as to the accomodation it affords, may be considered to depend mainly on – 1st, its extent, as shown by the number of rooms; 2nd, its quality, as shown by the number of its windows; and 3rd, its solidity or

durability, as shown by the materials of its walls and roof. If numbers be adopted to express the position of every house in a scale of each of these elements, and if the numbers thus obtained for every house be added together, we shall have a new series of numbers, giving the position of the house in a scale compounded of all the elements, i.e. their actual state. We adopted four classes, and the result was, that in the lowest, or fourth class, were comprised all mud cabins having only one room; in the third, a better description of cottage, still built of mud, but varying from two to four rooms and windows; in the second, a good farmhouse, or in towns, a house in a small street, having from five to nine rooms and windows; and, in the first, all houses of a better description than the preceding classes.

This programme appears to have continued without significant alteration. According to the actual census forms of the 1901 census each enumerating constable was instructed to fill in the columns numbered 6 to 11 on the census form B1; House and Building Return as follows:

(column 6) WALLS: If walls are of stone, brick or concrete, enter the figure 1 in this column; if they are of mud, wood, or other perishable material, enter the figure 0.
(column 7) ROOF: If roof is of slate, iron, or tiles, enter the figure 1 in this column; if it is of thatch, wood, or other perishable material, enter the figure 0.
(column 8) ROOMS: Enter in this column:-
for each house with one room only the figure   1
for houses with 2, 3, or 4   rooms   2
"   5 or 6   "   3
"   7, 8 or 9   "   4
"   10, 11, or 12   "   5
"   13 or more   "   6
(column 9) WINDOWS IN FRONT: State in this column the exact number of windows in front of house.
(column 10) TOT the figure you have entered in columns 6, 7, 8 and 9, and enter the total for each house in this column.
(column 11) CLASS OF HOUSE: When total in column 10 is
1 or 2   enter   '4th'
3, 4, or 5   "   '3rd'
6, 7, 8, 9, 10 or 11   "   '2nd'
12 or over   "   '1st'

Unfortunately such a classification system conceals the major factor of the durability of houses according to the materials used in their construction. We should classify them instead according to the information in columns 6 and 7:

(i) mud and thatch; (ii) mud and permanent roof [slate, iron, or tiles]; (iii) brick or stone [or concrete] and thatch; (iv) brick or stone [or concrete] and permanent roof. Relating this information to the Tenement Valuation and the Annual Revision Lists would enable the townland historian to identify and examine some elements of modernisation in the housing stock. [For a worked example see W. H. Crawford, 'A Handloom Weaving Community in County Down', *Ulster Folklife*, 39 (1993), 1-14]

CREATING THE FRAMEWORK

Recently Sir Charles Brett in the introduction to his study of *Buildings of County Antrim* (Belfast,1996) drew attention to the value of the manuscript books and maps of the Townland Valuation (VAL/1A&B) for the study of rural housing in the 1830s. Because this pioneer survey was such a vast undertaking, the Valuation Office had to confine its original survey to buildings worth more than £3 a year to rent. As a result, the majority of townlands visited by the valuators bear the epitaph: 'There are no houses in this townland worth £3.' Nevertheless there was still so much work to do that the government in 1838 raised the level to £5. Most of the surviving VAL/1B notebooks contain a separate section with calculations for buildings valued at less than £5 and even £3. The valuation was calculated on the dimensions of each property as well as the age and quality of the buildings: such information should not be overlooked.

IN THE TOWNLAND VALUATION EVERY PROPERTY EXAMINED
BY THE VALUATORS WAS RANKED ACCORDING TO THE TABLES
PUBLISHED IN INSTRUCTIONS TO THE VALUATORS
(1839), PARAS. 131 AND 135 .

NEW, OR NEARLY NEW
A+ Built, or ornamented with cut stone, and of superior solidity, and finish.
A   Very substantial building, and finish, without cut stone ornament.
A- Ordinary building and finish or either of the above when built 20 or 25 years.

MEDIUM
B+ Medium (not new,) but in sound order, and good repair.
B   Medium, slightly decayed, but in good repair.
B- Medium, deteriorated by age, and not in perfect repair.

OLD
C+ Old, but in repair.
C   Old and out of repair.
C- Old, and dilapidated, scarcely habitable.

Table for Dwelling Houses
1   Includes all slated dwelling-houses, built with stone, or brick, and lime mortar.
2   Thatched houses, built with stone, or brick, and lime mortar.
3   Thatched houses, having stone walls, with mud, or puddle mortar; dry stone walls pointed, or mud walls of the best kind.
4   Basement stories of slated houses, used as dwellings.

Table for Offices
1   Includes all slated offices, built with stone, or brick walls, with good lime mortar.
2   Thatched offices, built with stone, or brick walls, and lime mortar.
3   Thatched offices, having stone walls, with mud or puddle mortar, dry stone walls pointed, or good mud walls.
4   Thatched offices, built with dry stone walls.
5   Basement stories, or cellars used as stores.

In this study of housing it is important not to overlook the provision of 'labourers' cottages' early this century. Labourers' cottages were built by the new Rural District Councils (created by the Local Government Act of 1898) to carry out the terms of the Labourers (Ireland) Acts of 1883 and 1906. Between 1919 and 1939 4,300 were built throughout the province but their distribution is very uneven. Information about local initiatives and how the new rural councils reached decisions about the location of labourers' cottages in their districts can be found in the records of the rural district councils, held in PRONI as Local Authority (LA) records. So too can the contracts. These cottages were built by local contractors using the same kinds of materials and techniques that they used in the new two-storey houses for the wealthier farmers. These substantial farmhouses attracted special attention in the Revising Valuer's Office Notebooks (VAL/12E).

If we are preparing a record for posterity we should try to include information also about the skilled craftsmen and tradesmen who created and maintained these buildings: the masons, the thatchers and roofers, the carpenters, the painters and glaziers, the blacksmiths, the plumbers and, later, the electricians. Photographs illustrating their craftmanship would perpetuate their memory and record their achievements: the value of family photographs is often overlooked in this context.

CHANGES IN FARMING

It has to be remembered that little of the land in Ulster is naturally fertile and that most of the good land is to be found in river valleys. Much of the remainder of the province is occupied by mountains overlaid with blanket bog. At the time of the Plantation bog and scrubby timber covered many square miles of the lowlands. Immigrants from Britain set about hedging and ditching compact farms and clearing land for tillage. In the barony of Oneilland in county Armagh, for example, the Civil Survey of the mid-1650s recorded: 'The soil of this barony is generally good for tillage and pasture and the finest plantation of Ulster by reason of the English nation that first planted it, most of the same being naturally subject to wet but by their industry drained and made dry.' They were not successful everywhere: attempts to improve poor soils by adding natural fertilisers such as lime and sand often failed because the annual rainfall was considerable enough to leach the soils, especially in the north and west of the province. Nevertheless, it is important to identify the locations of corn-mills and scutch-mills: see H. D. Gribbon, *The History of Water-Power in Ulster,* Newton Abbot, 1969, and W. A. McCutcheon, *The Industrial Archaeology of Northern Ireland*, Belfast, 1980. Although water-powered corn-mills were known in Ulster before the Plantation, many of the new landlords invested in their construction and then required all their tenants in the townlands of the district bound to the mill (known as the *succan*) to bring all their grain to be ground at these manor-mills and pay a proportion of the crop (the *mulcture*, pronounced *mouter*, usually equal to one sixteenth) or pay a fine in default. It would be valuable to learn where and in what circumstances this right of each landlord was surrendered.

Although immigrants from Britain probably doubled the rural population of Ulster before 1710, the morale of farmers was not improved by poor prospects. The labour they had invested in hedging, ditching and enclosing their farms was not compensated by livestock prices until the British government in 1758 lifted its embargo on the shipment of live cattle to Britain. Harvests were generally poor between 1728 and 1746 and there was widespread sickness among men and beasts. Much corn was imported into Ulster from the other provinces and was paid for by the expanding linen industry which gave people cause to hope.

The second half of the eighteenth century witnessed an increasing optimism about the efficacy of new techniques in the improvement of marginal land. When bog was drained and well trenched with the spade, it dried out and could then be planted with potatoes that in turn cleared the ground from weeds and made it fit to bear crops of oats. On such land a long, heavy, spade, termed in Irish the *loy*, was used to undercut sods and then lever them over to form lazy-beds which were preferred to drills for cultivation by the small farmers. Although the extent of cultivation was always limited by the amount of manure that a farm could produce, farmers became very skilful at eking it out by composting it with loam or ashes. In order to save the grain in the head corn crops were harvested with the sickle while grass was mowed with the scythe. It was not until after the Famine that corn began to be cut with the scythe and soon afterwards the horse-drawn reaper was introduced. [See Jonathan Bell & Mervyn Watson, *Irish Farming 1750-1900*, Edinburgh,1986]

The first two years of the Famine forced the government to recognise the need for an accurate estimate of agricultural output throughout Ireland. From 1847, therefore, figures for both crop acreage and domestic animals were collected by the constabulary and published as *Agricultural Statistics* blue-books. The whole project was based on the unit of the townland and twenty-four questions had to be answered about each of some 60,760 townlands throughout Ireland. These townlands were grouped into Electoral Divisions and these in turn into Poor Law Unions. For the first few years only, ending in 1851, figures for crop acreage were provided for each of the Electoral Divisions. As a result it is possible to obtain a valuable snapshot of agriculture in your district by examining the acreage of the various crops grown in the Electoral District that contains your townland. After 1851 a Poor Law Boundary Commission redrew the Electoral Districts while the agricultural statistics were published for Unions only. The names of all the townlands in your local Electoral District are listed at the front of the printed volume of your Union in the *Griffith's Valuation*.

Although the compilers relied on the constabulary to provide them with 'the extent of land under crops', they also employed local people with farming experience to estimate 'the quantity of produce' for each district and to report on the quality of the crops harvested. Because the bulk of the crop was used to feed animals, they decided also to count livestock with figures totalled by counties subdivided into baronies. Their concern to relate changes in the number of livestock to the 'class of persons' that kept the animals, led them to introduce a scale of 'sizes of holdings': (a) less than one acre, (b) 1–5 acres, (c) 5–15 acres, (d) 15–30 acres, and (e) over 30 acres. This idea was extended to the acreage under crops. As a result the tables became too specialised to shed light on the changes at townland or even electoral division level and so the poor law union became the unit. After 1874 even the farm-size breakdown was abandoned.

AGRICULTURAL CENSUS 1861-1921:
CROPS IN ULSTER
in thousands of acres: all Ireland figures in italics

	1861	1881	1901	1920
Total tillage	1953	1779	1588	1754
	5890	*5191*	*4631*	*5251*
wheat	81	41	12	9
	401	*154*	*43*	*50*
barley	17	11	7	6
	211	*219*	*173*	*212*
oats	838	643	529	591
	1999	*1392*	*1099*	*1332*
flax	143	144	55	119
	148	*147*	*56*	*127*
potatoes	388	316	258	244
	1134	*854*	*635*	*584*
turnips	82	90	98	75
	334	*294*	*290*	*277*

Source: *Thom's Directory* (Dublin, annually)

Nevertheless much can be learned from studying the trends. The figures show that the overall crop area continued to increase up to 1860, which was the peak year in the late nineteenth century. Oats then occupied almost half the total cropland but after 1860 their share declined to about one quarter by 1900 with the spread of grassland: wheat and barley acreages soon became insignificant. The potato crop recovered quickly after 1848 to produce excellent crops throughout the 1850s. After 1860, however, the acreage under potatoes gradually fell in proportion to the decline in population; most of the crop was consumed on the farms by humans and animals. As blight remained a problem some farmers preferred to cultivate swede turnips which were reckoned to yield as much milk and manure from cattle as the same quantity of potatoes. Not until the late 1890s did the practice of spraying the tops of the potato plants each summer with Bordeaux mixture become widespread.

The major cash crop in Ulster was flax to supply the linen industry but after the great expansion of that industry first in the boom of the early 1850s and then to take advantage of the cotton famine occasioned by the American Civil War in the early 1860s, the acreage under flax declined steadily. Its yields and prices could not compete with pastoral farming nor, especially after 1890, with the grass seed trade which fitted better into the new crop rotations, stimulated as they were by the use of artificial fertilisers such as superphosphate and sulphate of ammonia.

The introduction and spread of the use of artificial fertilisers along with the rapid growth of the agricultural engineering industry has given the term 'the second agricultural revolution' to the period 1820-80 throughout the British Isles. We should consider the impact of these changes on our townland. The introduction of mineral fertilisers and of specific kinds of machinery can tell us something about the prosperity of individual farms or groups of farmers. Details about those who participated in agricultural shows can be found in local newspapers. Farmers required both capital and knowledge to make such investments. They needed security in their own holdings as well as the opportunity to acquire more land. Where they had such support, a class of strong farmers emerged, bought out their smaller neighbours, and engaged in commercial farming. However, in those regions divided into tiny farms, such as South Ulster, this process of consolidation took much longer. The family farm had labour to spare and the traditional hand implements could cope with all the jobs around the farm. Hired help was cheap and readily available. It was only the more ambitious and well-doing farmers who purchased reapers, barn threshers and churns.

AGRICULTURAL MACHINES IN IRELAND 1865-95

	1865	1875	1881	1886	1890	1895
Churning machines	848	2953	2856	2653	2796	3241
Grubbers	812	741	565	225	302	465
Hay, Chaff & Straw Cutters	1208	1425	2124	254	305	376
Hay Rakes	2478	5618	4420	3525	4121	7184
Manure Distributors		17	9	6	13	15
Mowing & Reaping Machines	1085	10016	11708	9014	11505	14704
Potato Diggers	10	15	38	175	228	477
Threshing Machines	9180	12410	13295	7043	7894	8546
Turnip Slicers	792	1621	1491	593	570	819

Source: *Agricultural Statistics 1895*, p.80

The revolution in farming as it worked out on the ground is well summed up in this undated and unsigned memorandum found loose in an 1878 rental in Lord Lurgan's estate office in north Armagh:

> 'It is not by selling crops in the market that many of the farmers live. It is by rearing and feeding cattle, horse, pigs on the farm produce. Calves of a year and a quarter old are frequently sold at £10; forty years ago, the best cow brought into market would not have given much more. Pork at the above date frequently sold at £1.6s. per cwt., now it is sold at £2.16s. per cwt. Grass seed till of late years was thrown into the dunghill, it is now sold at £1 per cwt. and many take off as much grass seed as pays their rents. Beef at the above date, nearly best in market was bought at 4d. per lb., now from 10d. to 1s. per lb. Butter at above date, best in market sold from 6d. to 8d.per lb., now from 1s. to 1s.6d. per lb. Eggs formerly sold at 4d. per dozen, now from 1s. to 1s.4d. Rents with many were as high then as now. Labouring men's pay as a rule in country places is not more than 2d to 4d per day of a rise. Some of your tenants on Richmount estate notwithstanding having paid hundreds of pounds of bail money for their friends, were able to buy farm after farm all taken off the land they now say is ruining them.' (quoted in F. X. McCorry, *Lurgan: an Irish provincial town, 1610-1970*, Lurgan, 1993, p.93)

Irish farmers were able to benefit from the growing demands of the British market for livestock. This table of 'livestock in Ireland' shows that Ulster's output barely matched the rest of the country. The number of cattle in Ulster increased at only half the Irish rate between 1861 and 1901 and fell slightly over the following two decades. Sheep figures did rise more quickly in Ulster but from a lower base: although the number of sheep increased by almost 55% between 1861 and 1920 Ulster had still only one-sixth of the Irish flock. The Ulster county with the largest flock was Donegal and its woollen tweed industry was enjoying prosperity. Eggs and poultry did bring cash into the kitchens while pigs remained a standby.

AGRICULTURAL CENSUS 1861-1920: LIVESTOCK IN ULSTER
in thousands: all Ireland in italics

	1861	1881	1901	1920
horses	190	173	178	186
	634	*574*	*594*	*582*
cattle	1022	1028	1209	1192
	3472	*3954*	*4673*	*5197*
sheep	387	379	643	600
	3556	*3259*	*4378*	*3708*
pigs	243	249	315	175
	1102	*1088*	*1219*	*977*
goats	na	74	81	85
	190	*267*	*312*	*261*
poultry	na	4583	7033	na
	10371	*13966*	*18811*	*na*

Source: *Thom's Directory*

Although the basic character of agriculture in the province changed little, the new government of Northern Ireland did tackle the problem of 'the marketing of Northern Ireland agricultural produce.' A substantial report with that title published in 1932 describes in great detail the marketing of cattle, pigs, fat and store lambs, poultry, and turkeys as well as the people involved in the trade. The opinions expressed there were reflected in the introduction by the government of marketing schemes such as those for pigs (1932), potatoes (1935) and eggs (1924-36).

The Second World War saw a great but brief intensification of tillage to grow oats and flax. More than 800,000 acres came under the plough, recalling the landscape of a century before. In 1945 there were 448 thousand acres of oats, 190 thousand of potatoes, 21 thousand of turnips, and 80 thousand of flax. After the war those figures tumbled quickly although in the 1960s barley was popular for a decade and displaced oats. Tillage gave way to grass as the number of cattle increased by almost one third in a decade. This was accelerated by entry into the Common Market. In 1975 cattle numbers reached an all-time peak of 1,626 million and the number of sheep has doubled to more than 2.6 million in the 1990s. The pig population reached 1.25 million in 1965 but like poultry fell back in the mid 1970s due to world shortages of grain and high cereal prices. There are now fewer pig herds and poultry flocks, concentrated on fewer farms.

NORTHERN IRELAND AGRICULTURAL CENSUS 1942-92

LIVESTOCK in thousands

	1942	1952	1962	1972	1982	1992
cattle	827	941	1100	1444	1450	1576
sheep	742	795	1209	1004	1242	2657
horses	80	35	9	1	-	-
pigs	271	676	1182	1047	642	588
poultry (x 1000)	14.6	16.5	9.6	14.9	11	12.3

CROPS in thousands of hectares (1 hectare = 2.471 acres)

	1942	1952	1962	1972	1982	1992
total tillage	335	205	159	89	78	68
barley	6	2	52	51	48	37
oats	192	122	66	12	3	3
flax	30	9	-	-	-	-
potatoes	76	55	31	15	14	12

Source: *Agriculture in Northern Ireland*, January 1993

COMMUNICATIONS AND MARKETS

Ulster has been well served by numerous market towns and the density of its road network which in some places is among the greatest in Western Europe. That character has owed much to the compact estates granted by the Crown to the new landlords for it was they who encouraged the creation of numerous market towns and organised road-making through their estates. Under an act of 1615 responsibility for the construction and maintenance of roads had been imposed on each parish by requiring its inhabitants to provide six days free labour on the roads each year. The onus of building and maintaining bridges was given to the justices of the peace for each county and they were enabled to levy a county tax or cess with the assent of the grand jury. In these circumstances the quality of local roads depended on the initiative of the landlord or his agent.

By the early eighteenth century the parish system could not cope with the increase of road traffic generated by the growing linen industry. The first government solution was the introduction of turnpike roads in the 1730s in the east of the province but they were not extensive enough to cope with the demand. In 1758 Parliament decided to exempt day labourers from the statutory six days' labour because compulsory unpaid work was recognised as 'burthensome to the poor', a move that threw the burden of statutory labour back on to the small farmers, cottiers, and weavers. As a result of the Oakboy disturbances that followed, Parliament passed the 1765 Road Act to abolish the six days' labour and to authorise the grand jury of each county to raise a county tax, or cess, to build and maintain roads and bridges.

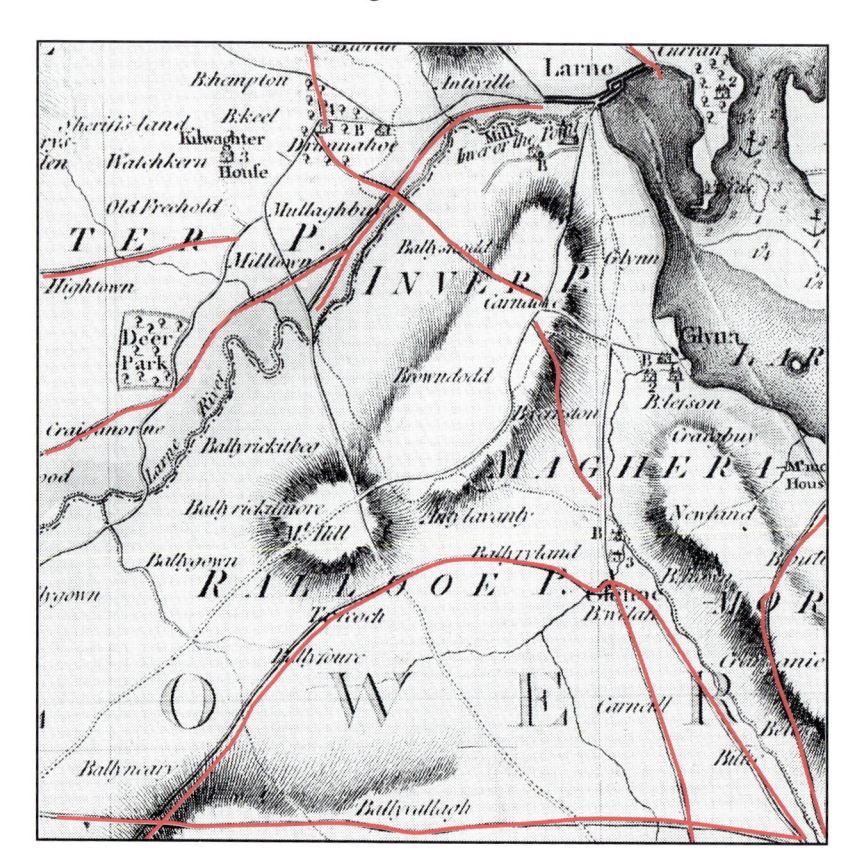

Extract of Lendrick's map of County Antrim 1808 version marking new roads, seen here in red (PRONI)

This act changed the national attitude to road-building. More and more money became available for the renewal and expansion of the road network and it was seen as an ideal way to employ the labourers. Within the following century thousands of miles were constructed or remodelled throughout Ireland and they opened up many square miles of marginal land to colonisation and cultivation. This revolution can best be traced on the large wall maps of individual counties prepared for their respective grand juries and hung in the courthouses for regular consultation. Most valuable in this context is John Lendrick's map of County Antrim of 1780 because it was updated in 1808 to incorporate the revised network of roads: comparison of the two maps reveals the vast increase not only in the mileage of roads but in the great stretches of countryside that were made accessible. John McEvoy in his *Statistical Survey of the County of Tyrone* (1802) confirmed these observations for his own county when he recommended the updating of the county map made for the grand jury by the McCrea brothers of Strabane between 1774 and 1776.

COPIES OF ULSTER COUNTY MAPS COMMISSIONED
BY GRAND JURIES, HELD IN PRONI

Antrim by James Lendrick 1780 (D/1062/22/4), revised by James Williamson in 1808 (T/1971/1)
Armagh by John Rocque 1760 (D/602/1)
Donegal by William McCrea in 1801 (D/1213/13)
Down by Oliver Sloane in 1739 (T/1763/2); by Kennedy in 1755 (D/695/M/2); by James Williamson in 1810 (D/616/1)
Fermanagh by Gabriel Montgomery was never finished but a chart of Lough Erne and Donegal bay including adjacent country by G. Montgomery and son appeared in 1818 (D/2297/1)
Londonderry by George Vaughan Sampson in 1813 (D/174/1)
Monaghan by William McCrea in 1793 (T/2463/1)
Tyrone by William McCrea and George Knox in 1813 (D/173/1)

Landlords were not slow to take advantage of this unique opportunity to improve their own prospects. Many of them promoted or revived market towns on their estates because the law stipulated that main roads could be laid out only between market-towns or (after 1765) between market-towns and the sea-coast. The landlords often indicated their intention by purchasing from the Crown patents permitting them to hold weekly markets in their towns. They were then in a position to apply to the grand jury to link each new market-town with its neighbours. They also managed the maintenance of the minor roads on their estates. These processes extended the network of roads throughout the countryside. In the long run many of the new market-towns failed to develop or sustain a weekly market but the new roads continued to be maintained and improved at the charge of the county.

These new roads also opened up the country for settlement and facilitated the transport of turf, timber, lime, and manure as well as provisions and animals to market. Soon there was a great increase in the number of wheel-cars kept by farmers and after 1800 the Scotch cart drawn by heavy horses became a more familiar sight throughout the province. Alongside the new roads in the hill country landlords marked out farms and often provided timber and lime for the new tenants to build houses. By charging low rents the landlords were able to attract many families who could no longer compete in the well-populated lowlands. It was the newcomers who created farms for succeeding generations of their families. The colonisation of the uplands, bogs and other waste lands during the century before the Famine is one of the most underrated factors in the making of the Ulster landscape. The farmers were serviced by the small market-towns with their hardware stores, local craftsmen, and monthly fair-days, so that government valuers were required to take into account the distance of each farm from the neighbouring towns.

It is important, therefore, to examine first the Ordnance Survey maps and then the county maps as well as estate maps to determine what impact the construction of new roads had on your townland. The Townland Valuation may be especially useful. Did any of these roads cut through or modify older field boundaries, as the railway was often to do in the 1840s? Did they lead to the dispersal of farmhouses throughout the townland, the construction of new houses (often along the

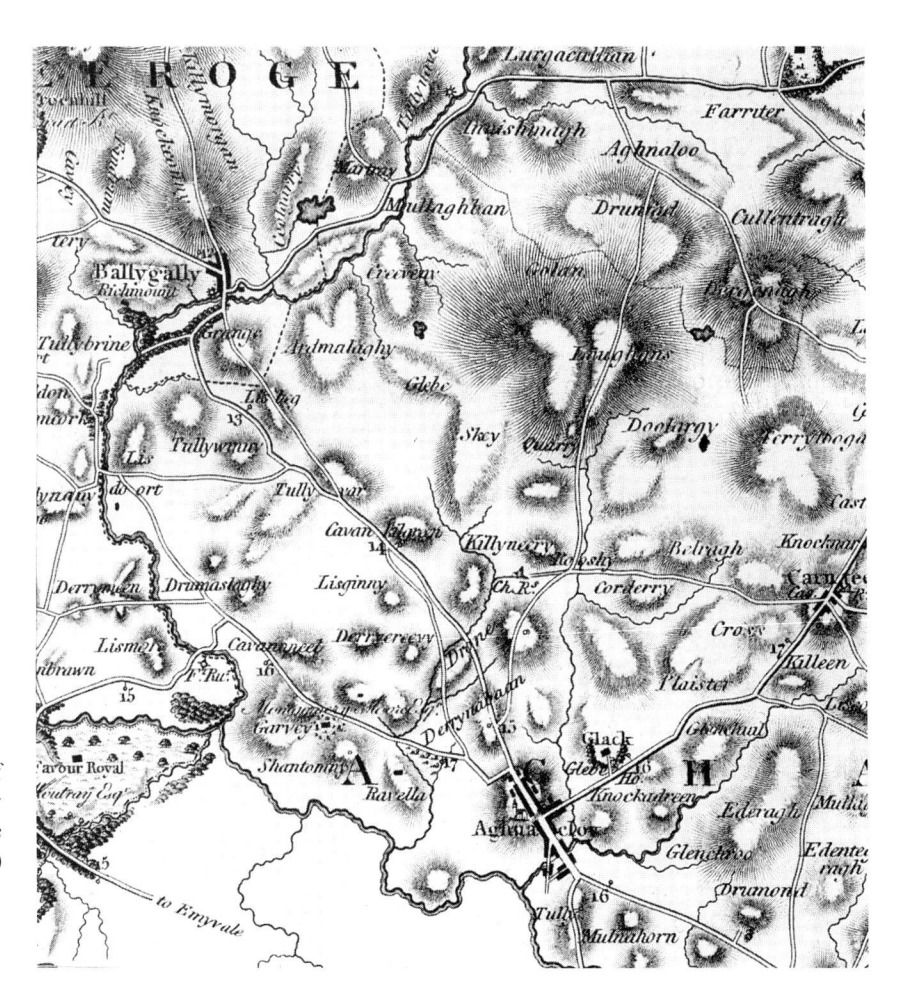

Extract from the county map of Tyrone published in 1813 by William McCrea and George Knox (PRONI D/173/1)

new road), or the reorientation of existing houses with their rights-of-way? Did they open up access to new quarries, limepits, and turf-banks? Did they affect the way that rural folk viewed neighbouring towns and townlands?

The great importance of the road network in Ulster was eclipsed in men's minds for nearly a century by the advent of the railways in the 1830s. Most of the carriage of goods and passengers was transferred from the cart and the stagecoach on the roads to the new lines of railway track that searched out the easiest gradients from one river valley to the next. The local railway station became an institution and a focus for both economic and social activity as train speeds rose and charges fell. Towns without convenient stations were bypassed and lost their fairs and markets to better-placed rivals. By the 1930s, however, with the development of the petrol engine, road transport was coming back. It provided dealers with their own transport, enabling them to visit the farms and purchase on the doorstep, especially eggs and potatoes. Delivery men too graduated from horse-transport to motor-transport. The second half of the twentieth century has witnessed a revolution in road-transport with container-lorries penetrating into every farmyard.

Throughout all these years the frequency and the character of markets and fairs evolved. The function of a weekly market was to supply provisions to the townspeople who, in their turn, provided essentials and services for the farmers. When the original patents for weekly markets and fairs had been taken out by the first settlers, they usually named two fairs in the spring and summer of each year. Many of these earliest fairs had lasted for three days and were designed to attract dealers from distant parts to come and purchase the surplus produce of the district. By 1700 many market towns held four seasonal fairs to promote the cattle economy: they were listed in the almanacs. By 1800 the growing prosperity of Ulster and its cattle trade was reflected by monthly fair days that were likely to coincide with the fixed weekdays of the markets. Many of the smaller towns that could not sustain a weekly market, did manage to retain these monthly fair-days into this century. [See W. H. Crawford, 'The Evolution of the Urban Network' in W. Nolan, L. Ronayne, and M. Dunlevy, *Donegal: History & Society*, Dublin, 1995]

The organisation and administration of fairs and markets was the task of the owner of the market patent who was usually the owner of the estate and its town. The Crown required him to maintain law and order in the fairs and markets, to check the weights and measures used in them, and to provide ready justice in his manor courts. In return he or his agent could collect tolls and customs. An act of 1819, however, which ordered the owners of market rights to display toll-boards with their charges and their signatures, caused problems for those owners who could not prove their title. This provided a pretext for others who were determined to evade tolls and customs and after a protracted campaign most markets and fairs in Ulster – but by no means all – had been rendered toll-free by about 1840. Those towns whose town commissioners did exert themselves to provide facilities for the farmers such as market-yards, public weighbridges, and enclosed fair-hills, did succeed in attracting custom from their smaller neighbours. In its essentials this character of marketing agricultural produce changed little before the 1930s.

THE COMMUNITY

In the final instance it has to be reiterated that at the heart of all this research lies the history of a community. We should consider first the origins of this community in the period under review. Was this townland occupied by British settlers or did it remain in the possession of native families? The history of several townlands suggests that throughout the seventeenth century British immigrants continued to secure leases at the expense of native families but that quite early in the eighteenth century some kind of balance came about in spite of the Penal Laws. After that time the character of a townland was less likely to change its ethnic complexion. Even if the lease of the townland was in the hands of a Protestant middleman the Catholic undertenants would often be left to organise the pattern of landholding among themselves: in time many of these families would gain recognition as tenants of their farms. It is important to identify dominant families within each townland, especially when they were prepared to assume leadership roles. They often played vital roles in the congregations of local churches and in the management of national schools and in return they looked to the clergy and the schoolmaster for active support.

Another major factor in the everyday life of the community was the presence or absence of a landlord or his resident agent. The community benefited when there was someone resident to manage the estate, provide leadership and employment, and sort out problems and quarrels. Without him, problems would undermine community spirit and bad blood run from generation to generation. A well-managed estate attracted tenants and most of the serious problems were created by tenants rather than by their landlord. By the mid-nineteenth century, however, relations between landlords and tenants were deteriorating due to changing circumstances and culminated by the end of the century in the sale of many estates to the tenants. Although tenant-ownership gave the farmer security before the law it did not bring prosperity in the long agricultural slump that lasted from the 1880s to the 1930s. The newly-independent farmers could no longer turn to the estate for help in emergencies and so they had to turn instead to solicitors and lawyers, bankers and shopkeepers, and finally to the government.

In the hope that competition among buyers would mean better prices for their crops and stock, farmers attended weekly markets and the seasonal or monthly fair-days in all the neighbouring towns. Although the townspeople resented the mess and inconvenience caused on these occasions, they needed the custom of the farmers. While they were there they frequented pubs, shops, forges (and later, garages), tradesmen, and solicitors, and were likely to run up significant debts. In turn their farms were visited by pedlars, cattle dealers, egg and poultry men, bread and grocery salesmen, and an increasing number of government officials.

That heyday has gone. Over the past century and a half the population of many townlands has been decimated and rural communities continue to decline with the advance of commercial agriculture. Soon it may be too late to research their history.

FORTTOWN

FORTTOWN

W. MACAFEE

As I was born in Forttown nearly sixty years ago but have not lived there for almost forty of them, I have written this paper from both the 'insider' and 'outsider' points of view. Forttown is a townland situated in an area of relatively fertile soils and hence a good farming area. Even in the nineteenth century the farms were quite substantial and there has been a reasonable degree of continuity of settlement in that of the five farms which existed in 1859, three still remain and two of these are inhabited by descendants of the 1859 families. Nevertheless it has changed dramatically, particularly in the last fifty years.

LOCATION, PHYSICAL FEATURES, PLACENAMES AND HISTORY BEFORE THE PLANTATION

Forttown is located on a ridge of higher ground which lies approximately three miles north, north-west of the town of Ballymoney in the County of Antrim. This district is in fact known as the Seacon moraine,[1] a ridge-like feature deposited at the southern extremities of the Scottish ice sheet which occupied the North Antrim area some 10,000 years ago. This ice sheet was responsible for not only the Seacon moraine but also the better-known Armoy moraine which extends along the Bush valley from Armoy to Ballymoney. Both of these can be seen on the accompanying map, figure 1, which shows areas over fifty metres in height.

The placename Forttown is fairly explicit. It means 'the townland of the fort' or, more accurately, 'the rath'. The Ordnance Survey Memoir for the Parish of Ballymoney (1832) makes particular reference to this fort. It states:

> In Fort Town there is a remarkable mound, once surrounded by a ditch now destroyed. The top is flat and circular and one chain in diameter. It is fifteen feet high from the level of the adjoining field.[2]

Reference is also made in the same page to the presence of a cave in the next field to the rath (most probably the remains of a souterrain) and to the discovery of Bronze Age artefacts. Clearly this was a long settled area and the fact that later settlements are clustered around the rath suggests that this part of the townland was regarded as the best site by countless generations and by different cultures.

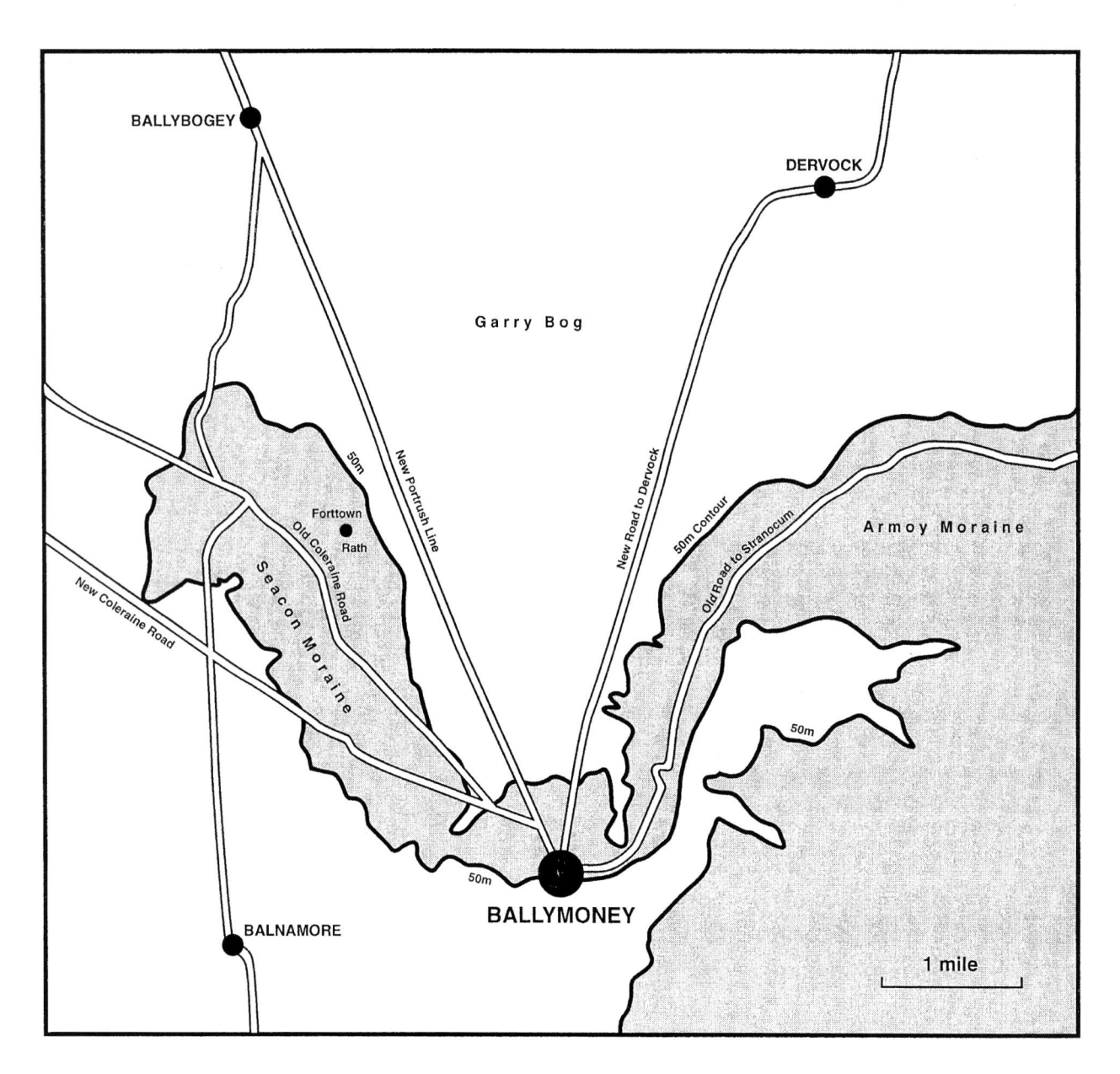

FIGURE 1
The geography of Forttown and the surrounding area

It would appear, however, that the name Forttown was not used in any 'official' sense before Archibald Stewart's survey of the Earl of Antrim's estate in 1734.[3] During the medieval period the area which included Forttown appears to have been called Tullaghgore, which means 'the hilly place of an assembly'. Figure 2 shows the location and areal extent of Forttown, Tullaghgore and the surrounding townlands which make up not only medieval Tullaghgore but the wider Seacon district.[4]

The Ecclesiastical Taxation of the Dioceses of Down, Connor and Dromore, 1307[5] makes specific reference to the parish and church of Talacorre. The following reference to a church in Tullaghgore is made in the Ordnance Survey Memoirs:

> There is a tradition that in the townland of Tullaghgore there formerly stood an old church. There is no memory of where its site was, or any particulars connected

with its history, i.e. its erection, destruction, etc.....It is traditionally received by the parishioners in that district that the townlands of Tullaghgore, Bootown, Forttown, New Buildings, Kirkmoyle or Kilmoyle Upper and Kilmoyle Lower once formed a parochial district of themselves. There is nothing remembered of its history.

At the same time the Ordnance Survey Memoir also makes reference to a church in Kirkmoyle:

In the townland of Kirkmoyle is the site of the parish church.....it appears to have been deserted on account of its small size, probably combined with the increasing numbers of the congregation. In drawing[s] there is a ground plan of the foundations and the small graveyard which still surrounds it. It is forty nine feet in length from out to out by sixteen feet breadth. The foundations are at an average three feet thick....very few stones appear, the whole being overgrown by the green sod. There are no tombstones in the yard but burials of the poorer sort still occasionally take place in it. Its boundaries are not the original ones. It formerly extended over the whole field in which it is situated, but by permission of the landlord the tenants have lately circumscribed and considerably diminished its area.[6]

FIGURE 2
The location and extent of Forttown and surrounding townlands

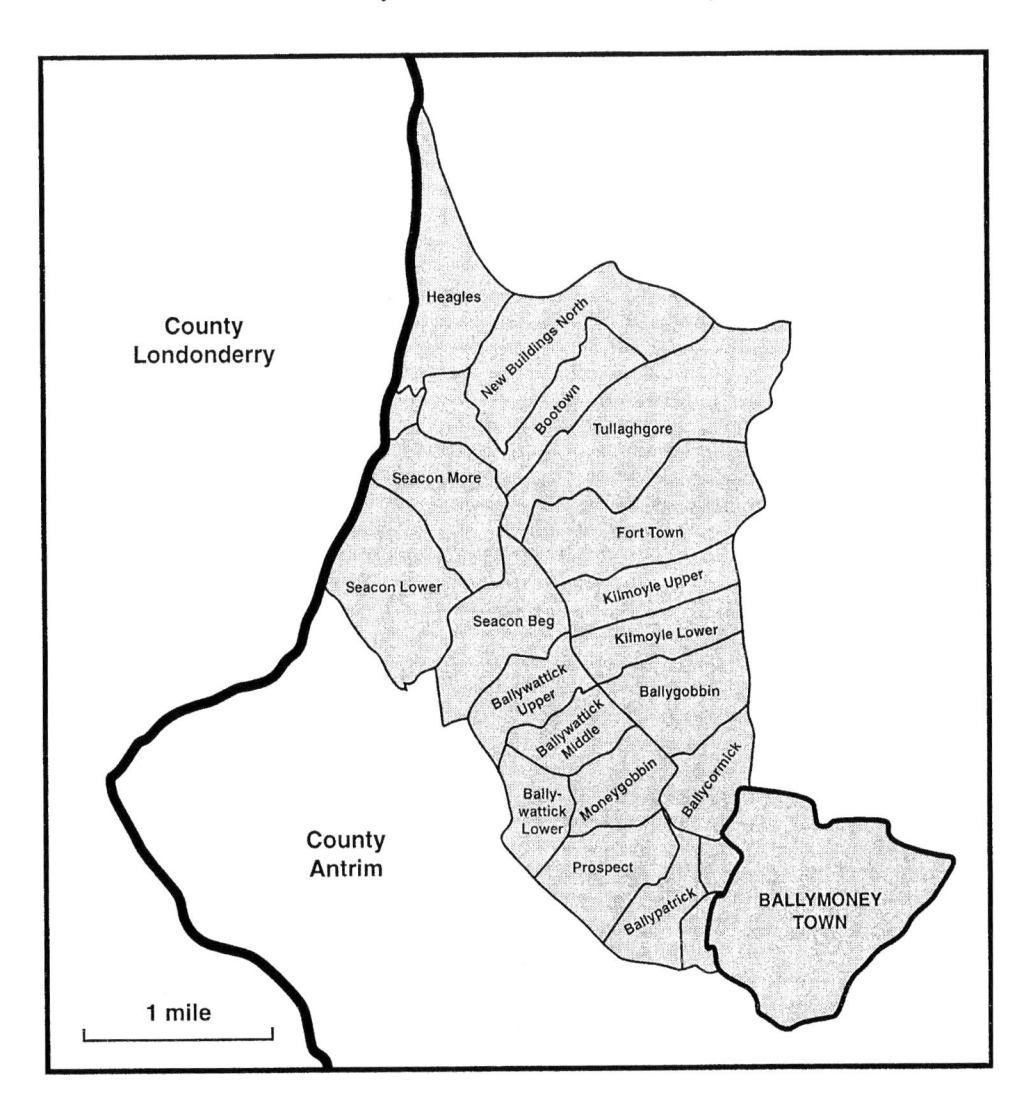

The graveyard of this church is still visible in the townland today and some of the older members of the community can still recall the graveyard being used for the burial of still-born children.

The weight of evidence points to Kilmoyle being the site of the church of Tullaghgore. This church was clearly an Anglo-Norman foundation but very probably could have been on, or near, the site of an earlier Christian and, not unreasonably, a pagan foundation. The nearby townlands of Ballygobbin and Moneygobbin mean 'St. Cuthbert's townland' and 'St. Cuthbert's shrubbery' respectively, suggesting that the general area had an association with religious foundations.

By the seventeenth century the townlands of Tullaghgore and Kilmoyle, within the parish of Ballymoney, were being referred to in documents and maps. However, the townlands of Forttown, Bootown, Newbuildings North and Heagles were still absent from these maps and documents, so it must be concluded that they were taken as part of Tullaghgore.[7] Even as late as 1851 Tullaghore was listed as a separate parish in the official Census Returns. However the parish at that time was contiguous with the modern townland of Tullaghgore. The former townlands of the old parish, including Forttown, had become part of the parish of Ballymoney which was in the Barony of Upper Dunluce. It would appear, therefore, that the townlands of Forttown, Bootown, Newbuildings North and Heagles were, officially, post-Plantation creations. That is not to say that local people would not have used these names to identify places within the larger Tullaghgore area long before they were given official status.

With the advent of the Workhouse in the nineteenth century, Forttown became part of the Ballymoney Poor Law Union – Seacon Electoral Division. In 1898 the Poor Law Unions were replaced by Urban and Rural District Councils and Forttown became part of Ballymoney Rural District and was allocated to the Kirkmoyle Electoral Division. Today it lies within the Ballymoney District and persons living in the townland have been given urban addresses such as 148 Seacon Road, Ballymoney, BT53 6PZ.

COLONISATION OF THE AREA DURING THE SEVENTEENTH CENTURY

Throughout the seventeenth century the North Antrim area as a whole saw a significant influx of colonists. Whilst some of these immigrants would have been English soldiers, the majority were lowland Scots who would have been farmers, craftsmen and labourers. There had also been a substantial movement of Highland Scots into North Antrim during the sixteenth century following in the wake of the MacDonnells who had acquired the Glynns and the Route.

Pender's Census of 1659[8] (more accurately a Poll Tax Return) provides us with an estimate of the numbers of people in Tullaghgore and Kilmoyle by the middle years of the seventeenth century. Again it is assumed that Tullaghgore includes the townlands listed above.

TOWNLAND	ENGLISH	IRISH	TOTAL
Tallaghgore (Tullaghgore)	22	13	35
Kilmoyle	7	2	9
Total	29	15	44

It seems strange that the compiler of this 'census' divided the population into English and Irish only. In most other counties within Ulster the usual division was English, Scots and Irish. In this area of North Antrim there would have been four different groups of people at that time viz. English, Lowland Scots, Highland Scots and Native Irish. Crown officials had a tendency to group Highland Scots with Irish but the presence of a substantial number of Lowland Scots would probably have led to further confusion. Because of this, the division into English and Irish is not helpful and probably inaccurate. However the total figure for the townlands might give some estimate of the numbers of persons present in the area by the middle of the seventeenth century. The figure of 44 which probably represented the number of adults aged 15 or more, would suggest a total population of some 110 persons living in the Tullaghgore/Kilmoyle area by the middle of the seventeenth century. This compares with a total of 491 persons for the same area in 1841. Interestingly, the present day population of this same area has returned to a figure much closer to that of the mid-seventeenth century.

A further source, the 1666 and 1669 Hearth Returns[9] for the Parish of Ballymoney, listed the following owners of hearths in the area. Again Tullaghgore refers to a much larger area than the present day townland.

> TULLAGHGORR (TULLAGHGORE)
>
> James Cromey (3), Roris Sonne, Pat Glenn, John Neilsone, Thomas Boyd, Widd Clerke, Robert Donaldsone, Geo Watsone, Thomas Jamesone, William Dickey, Hugh Nocke, Patrick Glenn, Robert More (2), John Moriall, John Logan, Widd Moriall, Robert Kiningham, Pat Glenn.
>
> 1 Quarter of Kilmoyle
>
> William Hendersone, Widow Moore, Robert Clerke.

Assuming that each hearth represented one household and each household consisted of approximately 4.7 persons, this would suggest a population of around 100 persons. It is generally agreed that both the Poll Tax Returns and the Hearth Returns are both defective due to tax evasion and exemption coupled with corruption and laziness on the part of many collectors.[10] It must be stressed, therefore, that the numbers and names which are listed above are simply a partially-open window on the population and families which inhabited the area during the middle part of the seventeenth century.

It is noticeable that the bulk of names listed in these Hearth Returns are of Lowland Scot or English extraction and result from the efforts of Sir Randal MacDonnell and his son, the second Earl of Antrim, to colonise the region with improving tenants from the Scottish lowlands after 1603 and the settling of English soldiers particularly after 1650.

My own family name McDuffy (now McAfee or Macafee) appeared in the adjacent townland of Seacon Lower or Seacon Irish where two John McDuffys were listed. The McDuffys formed part of the general movement of the Scottish MacDonnells into the Glens of Antrim and the Route. The MacDonnells first acquired a foothold in the Glens through the marriage of John Mor MacDonnell to Margery Bissett in 1399. Families such as the MacDuffies had been moving over from Colonsay and Islay from as early as 1494. However, as mentioned above, many of these Highland Scots families were looked upon in the same light as the Native Irish by the English Crown and its officials. The fact that the McDuffys were located in a townland with the suffix 'Irish' would tend to confirm such a view.

Interestingly there is no great continuity of names through to the nineteenth century and the present day. A comparison of surnames in 1669 with those in Griffith's Printed Valuation of 1859 reveals that there were only three surnames holding land in the district in 1860 similar to those of 1669 – Boyd in Forttown, McAfee (McDuffy) in Bootown and Thompson in Bootown. Clearly, without parish register evidence, it is difficult to be certain that these were in fact descendants of the 1669 households. Today only the name Boyd is present in the general area. Even allowing for the fact that the Hearth Returns did not list the names of all householders present in the area by the middle of the seventeenth century and the fact that a name can disappear through lack of male heirs, there appears to have been a considerable influx of new names into the area after 1669. Perusal of the 1666 and 1669 Hearth Returns for the general district would suggest that some of these names were present in adjacent townlands. Nevertheless, it does appear that the vast majority of the newcomers came from much further afield, probably due to the migrations of Scots in the latter part of the century and subsequent internal migration within the province.[11] Indeed within Forttown tradition has it that the Boyd family came from outside Limavady and there is documentary evidence that the Forsythe family also came from outside Limavady.

ESTATES AND THE CREATION OF FARMS
(TENANTS AND COTTIERS)

Forttown lay within the area of North Antrim which had been occupied by the MacDonnells during the sixteenth century. On 28 May 1603 King James I granted this area known as 'the Route and the Glynns' to Sir Randal MacDonnell, the first Earl Of Antrim. In order to encourage settlement and raise revenue the family sold or leased in perpetuity considerable tracts of land within North Antrim which became estates in their own right e.g the Macnaughtens at Dundarave, Bushmills; the Leslies at Leslie Hill, Ballymoney; and the Montgomerys at Benvarden. Forttown became part of the Cromie estate. The name James Cromey was listed as having three hearths in Tullaghgore in 1669 which suggests a reasonably substantial dwelling. However it is impossible to say where exactly this house was located or whether Cromey himself lived in it. I suspect the house was probably located close to the 'fort' in Forttown. The survey by Archibald Stewart of 1734 shows quite clearly that a Mr Cromie was holding the townlands of Forttown, Tullaghgore, Bowtown, Newbuildings and the Heagles. On 22 April 1738 Michael Cromie, a merchant living in Dublin, acquired from the Earl of Antrim, the seven quarterlands of Tullaghgore for ever for a consideration of £240 and a rent of £30.[12] The Cromie family eventually resided at Cromore House near Portstewart and continued to be landlords of Forttown and the surrounding area until Wyndham's buying-out act of 1903. In the latter years of the nineteenth century, because of no male heirs and the marriage of a daughter, it became known as the Montague estate.

Unfortunately we do not have precise enough records for the Cromie estate, particularly during the eighteenth century, to examine in detail the leasing of the land and the creation of farms. Alexander Burnside, from Seacon, who gave evidence to the Devon Commission in 1845 stated that the tenure at that time was generally from and under the original proprieter (John Cromie) – some holding as tenants-at-will, others during one life or twenty one years, whichever was the longer.[13]

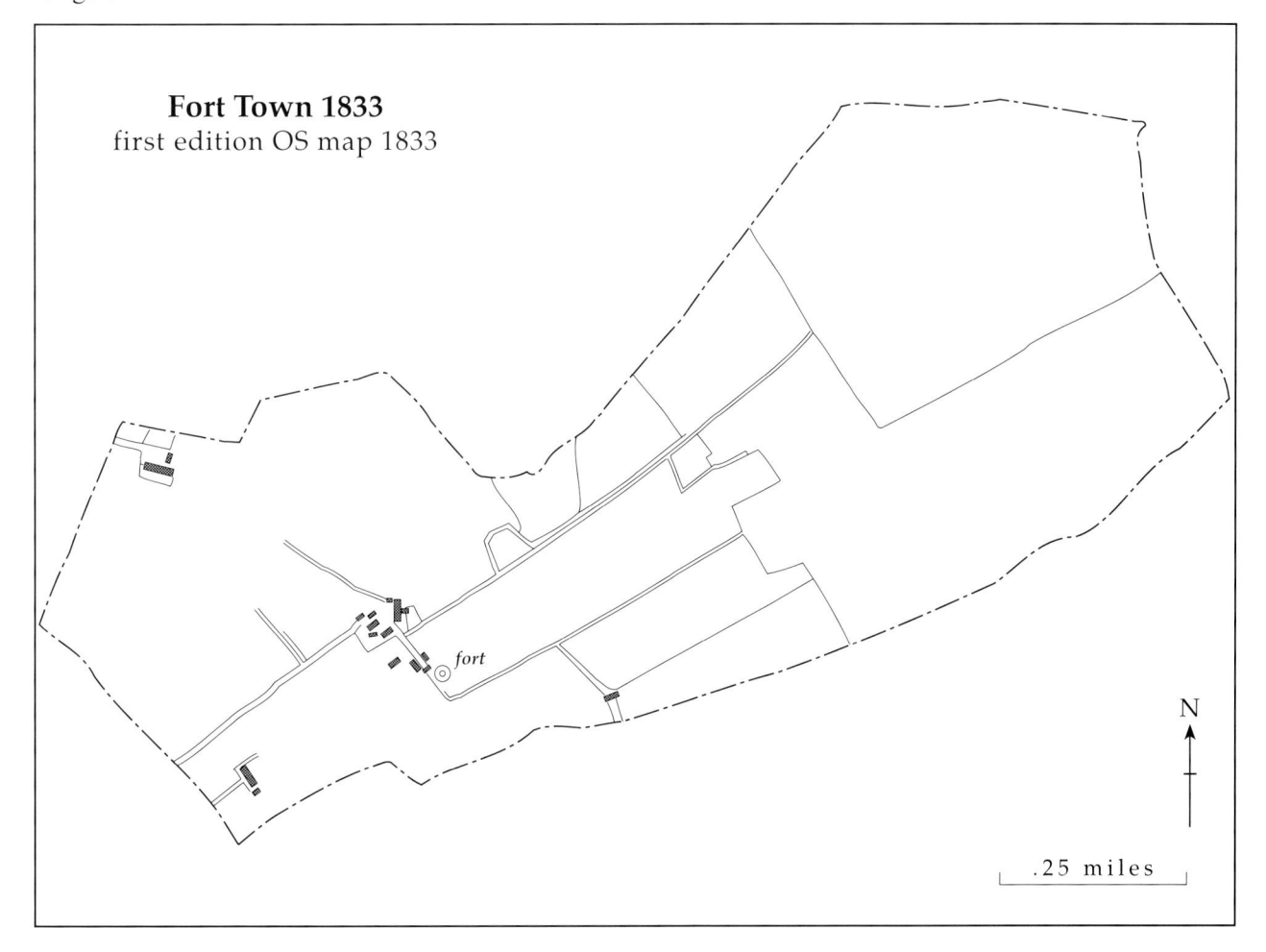

Fort Town 1833
first edition OS map 1833

TOWNLAND VALUATION (1833)

Forttown lies on the eastern slope of the Seacon moraine about two miles north of Ballymoney. A cluster of houses contained four of the five farmsteads. The quarter of the townland at the crown of the slope is described by the valuators as very good arable land while the neighbouring quarter was mossy arable and pasture. Although the remaining lower half of the townland was still valued as almost worthless bog, the OS map indicates a mearing drain along the boundaries with the neighbouring townlands of Tullaghgore, Garry Lower, Drunkendult and Kilmoyle as well as several lanes that link the bog with the houses – WHC.

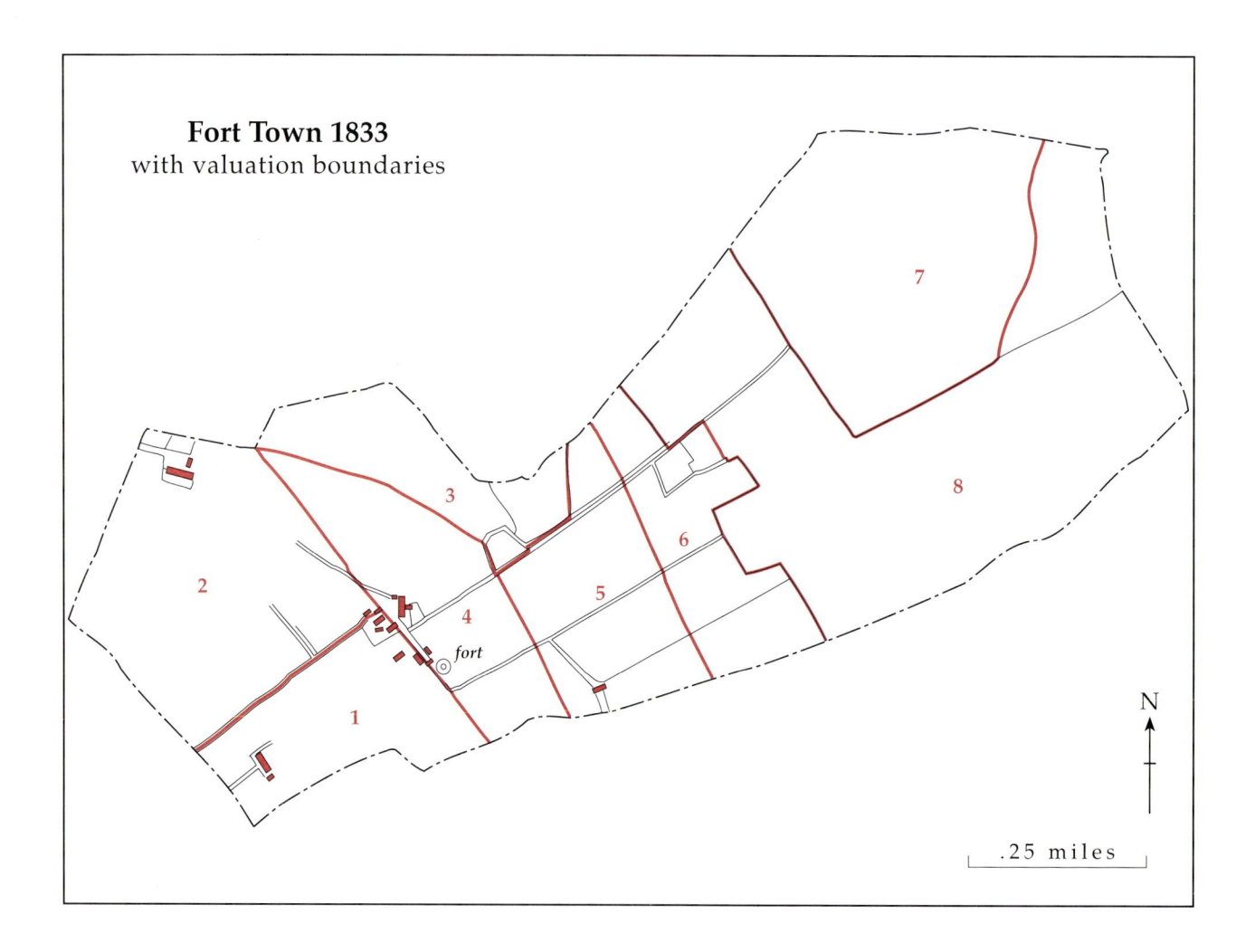

Fort Town 1833
with valuation boundaries

FORT TOWN, PARISH OF BALLYMONEY   VAL/1B/142B

		QUANTITY	RATE PER STATUTE ACRE	AMOUNT
1	Very good clayey and gravelly arable	22a 0r 28p	19s	£21 1s 3d
	also Meadow and light arable	1a	13s 6d	13s 6d
	also waste at house	1r		
2	Good clayey and gravelly arable	41a 0r 4p	16s	32 16s 4d
	also Cold and mossy arable	5a 3r	11s	3 3s 3d
3	Clayey and mossy arable and meadow	14a 1r 26p	13s	9 7s 4d
	also Clayey and gravelly arable	5a		
4	Very good arable clayey and gravelly	24a 1r 31p	19s	23 4s 5d
	also Fort	1r	8s	2s
	also waste at houses	1r		
5	Cold clayey pasture, portion of mossy	17a 2r 18p	11s 6d	10 2s 6d
	meadow also good gravelly arable	6a 1r	18s 6d	5 15s 7d
6	Mossy arable	23a 3r 34p	8s 6d	9 17s 3d
7	Red bog	54a 1r	3d	13s 6d
8	Green and heathy boggy pasture	88a 3r 23p	1s 4d	5 18s 6d
		304a 3r 4p		£126 15s 3d

Samuel Nicholson, Baronial Valuator, 21 Jan 1833
Charles Pollock, Assistant Valuator
James McElrevy, Assistant Valuator

FIN 5A/40 TITHE APPLOTMENT OF FORTTOWN (Fourthtown), parish of Ballymoney, 132 acres, taken by Stewart Moore & James Thomson, commissioners, 29 October 1825. Head landlord, John Cromie, Esq

James Boyd	6s 8d	Samuel Simpson	£1 5s 8.5d	John Elder	£1 3s 9d
Samuel Pinkerton jun	19s 2d	Samuel Pinkerton sen	19s	Samuel Pinkerton sen	11s 3d
John Anderson	12s	Samuel Houston	£1 8s 3d	John Taggart sen	13s 3.5d
John Taggart jun	6s 2d	Richard Taggart	6s 2d	James Cooper	2s 6d
James Small	1s 3d	Robert Small	1s 3d	Martha Small	2s 6d

TOTAL : £12 8 11 out   of £1,100

TITHE APPLOTMENT BOOK (1833)

In his evidence to the Devon Commission in 1845 Alexander Burnside had said that it was then common to put two or three small farms into one. This Tithe Applotment of 1833 values 15 separate holdings ranging from Boyd's holding (which is assessed at slightly more than one quarter of the whole townland) to the small holdings of the three members of the Small family totalling just over 5%. The 1859 Tenement Valuation indicates only five farms although there were still 15 occupied houses. Estate records should indicate how and when these changes occurred – WHC

PARISH OF BALLYMONEY.

No. and Letters of Reference to Map.		Names.		Description of Tenement.	Area.			Rateable Annual Valuation.						Total Annual Valuation of Rateable Property.		
		Townlands and Occupiers.	Immediate Lessors.					Land.			Buildings.					
		FORT-TOWN. (Ord. S. 11 & 12.)			A.	R.	P.	£	s.	d.	£	s.	d.	£	s.	d.
1	a	James Boyd,	John Cromie,	House, offices, and land,	75	1	0	56	10	0	3	10	0	60	0	0
–	b	James Fullerton,	James Boyd,	House,					—		1	0	0	1	0	0
–	c	Andrew M'Loughlin,	Same,	House,					—		0	10	0	0	10	0
–	d	James M'Neese,	Same,	House,					—		0	15	0	0	15	0
–	e	Unoccupied,	Same,	House,					—		0	10	0	0	10	0
–	f	Marian M'Bride,	Same,	House,					—		0	10	0	0	10	0
2 A					4	0	32	3	15	0		—				
– B	a	Samuel Elder,	John Cromie,	House, offices, & land,	6	1	2	5	15	0		—		14	0	0
– C					1	0	35	0	15	0	1	10	0			
– D					7	2	25	2	5	0		—				
–	b	Margaret Elder,	Samuel Elder,	House & small garden,		—			—		0	15	0	0	15	0
3 A					2	2	20	2	0	0		—				
– B					9	0	0	9	0	0		—				
– C		Robert White,	John Cromie,	House, offices, & land,	9	2	0	2	5	0		—		18	0	0
– D					19	1	30	2	5	0		—				
2 c c					0	1	20	0	5	0	2	5	0			
4	a	Robert Forsythe,	John Cromie,	House, offices, and land,	60	0	0	31	10	0	2	10	0	34	0	0
–	b	Robert Fullerton,	Robert Forsythe,	House,					—		0	15	0	0	15	0
–	c	Samuel Moore,	Same,	House,					—		0	15	0	0	15	0
–	d	Patrick Kelly,	Same,	House,					—		0	10	0	0	10	0
5	a	Samuel Pinkerton,	John Cromie,	House, offices, and land,	65	3	30	41	15	0	3	5	0	45	0	0
–	b	William M'Neill,	Samuel Pinkerton,	House,					—		1	0	0	1	0	0
–	c	Thomas M'Cready,	Same,	House,					—		0	10	0	0	10	0
6		John Cromie,	In fee,	Bog,	43	1	10	0	5	0		—		0	5	0
				Turbary,										2	10	0
				Total,	304	3	4	158	5	0	20	10	0	181	5	0

TENEMENT VALUATION (1859)

The most significant change in this map is the new line of road linking Ballymoney and Portrush. The road ran through the mossy arable land along the foot of the hill (6 in the Townland Valuation). More of the cut-out bog had been divided between the five farmers and they had made many small fields for grazing. The Annual Valuation Revision shows that the valuation of all of these farms was reduced a little in 1866, but there were no other significant changes until Forsythes bought the White farm in 1886 and Troland bought the Elder farm in 1888. James Boyd built a new two-storey slated house in 1891 and turned the old house into offices – WHC

Fort Town 1859
revised edition OS map 1859

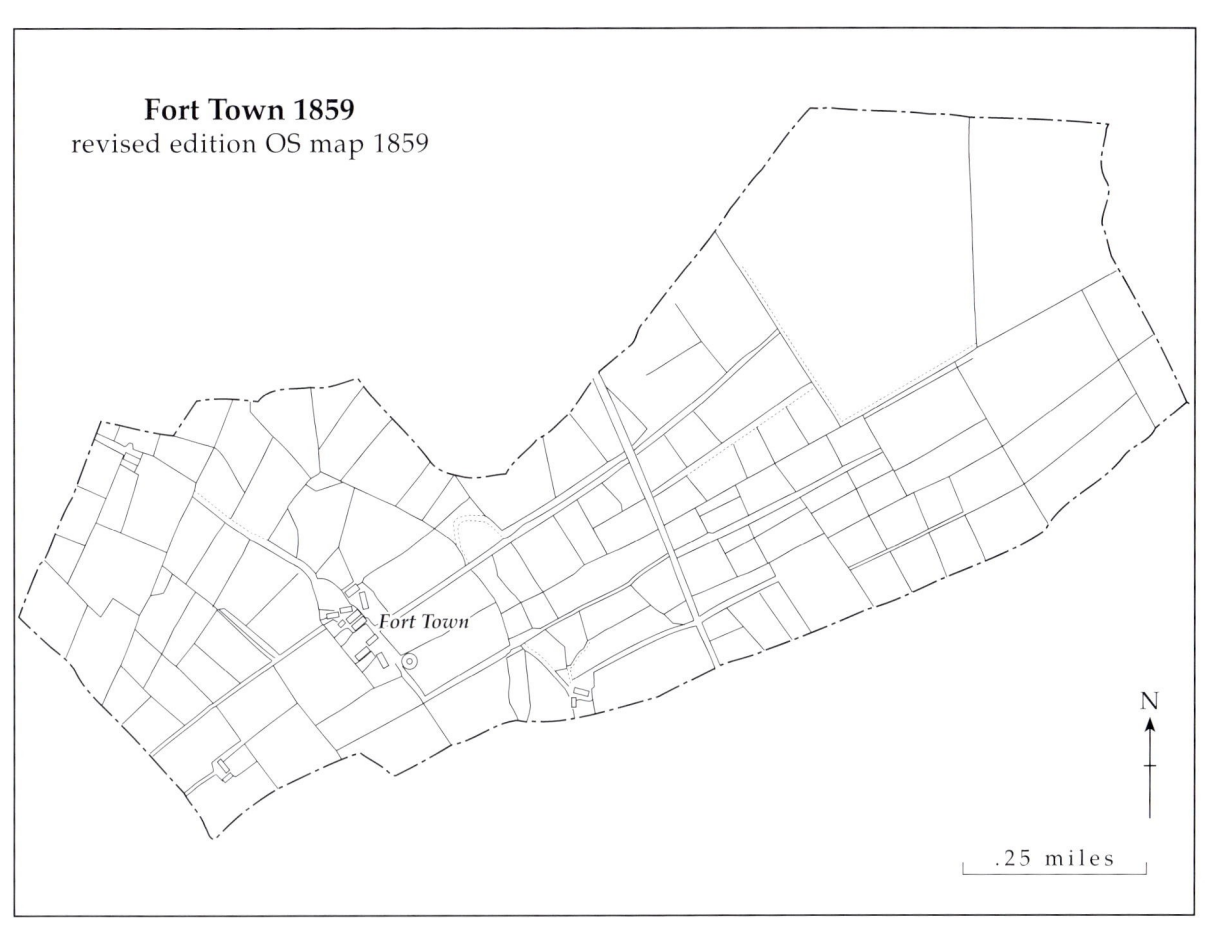

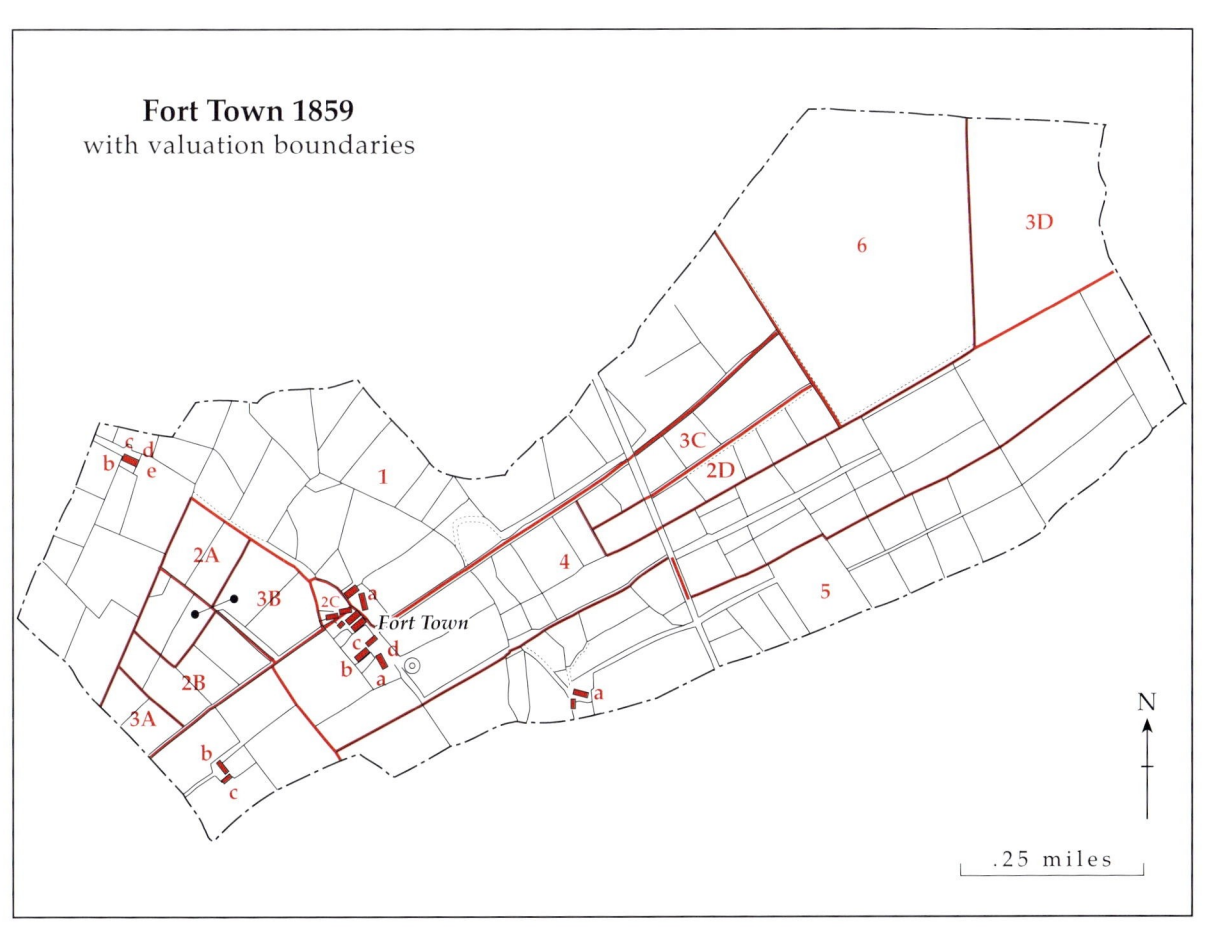

Fort Town 1859
with valuation boundaries

The Griffith's Valuation of 1859 is the first document which provides us with precise details of holdings in Forttown. Accompanying the valuation is a map which shows the location of houses and holdings within the townland. At that time there were five holdings or farms. Three of these holdings – Boyd, Forsyth and Pinkerton – were 75, 60 and 65 acres respectively. The other two holdings of Elder and White were approximately 20 acres and 40 acres respectively but each was subdivided into four smaller plots. On closer inspection of the smaller holdings it is clear that there was only some 11 acres of arable land in each, the remainder being bogland or rough pasture. Some of this land had been reclaimed but a relatively large block of 19 acres was clearly still rough grazing and bogland. The presence of bog and grazing land in the lower end of the townland helps to account for the relatively large size of the other three holdings in the townland. At the same time each of the larger holdings had reasonable quantities of good arable land surrounding the settlements. The quality of land within the townland during the nineteenth century can be seen in the Townland Valuation map of 1833.

The dwelling house and out-buildings of the Forsythe holding were located directly beside the site of the rath which gave the townland its name. The dwelling houses and out-buildings of the Boyd, White and Elder holdings were contiguous with that of Forsythe's but the dwelling house and out-buildings of the Pinkerton holding were sited on their own further down the slope. This pattern of the dwelling houses and out-buildings of farms/holdings being clustered in twos and threes, but each with their own farmyard, was fairly common throughout the surrounding townlands. These clusters tended to occupy the higher, better-drained ground within a townland. Single farms tended to be found on the lower slopes of a townland.

The other ten houses in the townland in 1859 were cottier houses: five of these houses (one unoccupied) were situated on the Boyd farm, three on Forsythe's farm and two on Pinkerton's farm. Cottiers were persons who rented their houses from the farmers with no land attached. They had no security of tenure and could be thrown out of their cottage at short notice. Most cottiers were tied to the farmers for employment and were usually given a certain number of potato drills in a field and and permission to cut peats in the bog. Whilst some could supplement their income through other trades such as carpentry, stonemason, linen weaving, etc. most were totally dependent on the farmer for employment. Unfortunately such employment was both seasonal and casual.

This pattern in Forttown revealed by Griffith's Valuation of 1859, of relatively substantial farms and cottier houses interspersed with some smallholders suggesting earlier subdivision of farms, was fairly typical of the wider Seacon district. This is consistent with Burnside's evidence to the Devon Commission in 1845. He stated that farms ranged in size from twenty to eighty acres, and that although rundale had been common about fifty years ago, no rundale was allowed now.[14] Burnside stated that it was now common to put two or three small farms together, or into one. When pressed on this point he replied – 'it has been done a good deal, but not until lately'.

Within Forttown the process of consolidation continued throughout the nineteenth century. In 1886 Robert Forsythe bought White's holding for £250, the sum not being fully paid until 1888. It must be remembered that Forsythe was purchasing only the interest or tenant right of the farm: he would still be required to pay a rent to the landlord at that time. White reserved for his natural life 'the house on the said premises now used as a potato house to be converted by Robert White into a dwelling house together with the garden'.[15] The Elder holding was taken over by James Troland in 1888 and during the twentieth century this holding passed, firstly, into the hands of David Hanna and then Boyd Campbell. Eventually it became part of the Forsythe holding. The entire Forsythe holding is still in the hands of the Forsythe family.

The Boyd holding expanded by incorporating farms in the adjacent townland of Tullaghgore. Although the Boyd farm is now in the hands of the Cameron family from Ballymena, descendants of the Boyd family now live in the adjoining townlands of Tullaghgore and Seacon Beg.

The Pinkerton holding is presently in the hands of Samuel McLean whose father, also Samuel, had married the daughter of Sheriff Pinkerton around 1907. Interestingly Samuel McLean's grandfather, William John, had been to Australia with his brother, Samuel, where they had been involved in the lumbering business. They had returned home during the 1880s and had bought the interest in two farms in the nearby townland of Ballywattick Middle.

This process of incorporating smallholdings into some of the larger farms took place throughout the entire Seacon district. In fact between 1859 and 1901 the number of farmers within the Seacon district decreased by almost a third. Smallholdings were usually vacated because the tenants were finding it hard to survive; the sale of their interest or tenant right of the farm could provide them with sufficient cash to emigrate. Few smallholders would have had sufficient capital to move to a larger farm. Of course some farms will appear to have changed hands because of a name change but this is simply due to the absence of male heirs and the marriage of one of the daughters. Whilst there is one example of this in Forttown, this does not appear to have happened on an extensive scale throughout the wider area – only two such marriages took place between 1859 and 1950 – Parkhill in Tullaghgore and Getty in Kilmoyle Lower. Because of this and because of the predominance of slightly larger farms over small holdings even in 1859, there is a continuity of names amongst the farming families from the nineteenth century through to the 1950s. Certainly I had no difficulty in recognising most of the names of the farmers listed in Griffith's Valuation of 1859.

On the other hand the names of the cottier population were not so familiar to me. I was not able to identify any of the names of the cottier population listed in Forttown in 1859. Only a very few were familar to me throughout the wider

Seacon district at that time. I recognised only two of the five listed in the 1901 Enumerators' Returns for Forttown. However, I was able to identify about a third of the names of cottiers in the wider district. In many ways this was not surprising. Vaughan has described this section of the population after the Famine as a transient group *en route* to emigration or to inheriting a farm elsewhere, the former being the more likely option.[16] Such a view is borne out by the fact that only the names of five of the cottier households listed in Griffith's Valuation of 1859 were recognisable in the 1901 Enumerators' Returns.

Throughout the wider Seacon district the number of cottier houses fell by a quarter between 1859 and 1901. In 1901 there were still thirty-seven cottier houses in the Seacon district – twenty-one of the heads of household described themselves as labourers or agricultural labourers, six were domestic servants, two were surfacemen maintaining roads, five were linen weavers, two were carpenters and one was a shoemaker.

Within Forttown there were still two occupied cottier houses on Pinkerton's farm. On the Forsythe farm only one was now occupied: the rest were either unoccupied or had been 'tumbled'. Again on Boyd's farm only one cottier house in Forttown was occupied, the rest were down or unoccupied. However, there were six occupied cottier houses on Boyd's entire farm in 1901, an increase of one on 1859. This had resulted from the Boyd family's takeover of several smallholdings in the neighbouring townland of Tullaghgore and the transfer of some of their cottiers from Forttown to the vacant farm houses in Tullaghgore.

Despite the turnover in the cottier population between 1859 and 1901 the interesting point to note here is that it did not decline as much as one might have expected. Although the more substantial farms were swallowing up the smaller holdings they still needed labour throughout the year. There is also evidence that some of the displaced smallholders joined the ranks of the cottier population.

CHANGES IN POPULATION

Table 1 gives details for Forttown of population and house figures on a decennial basis for the period 1841 to 1991. The figures clearly show that the Famine had little effect here; in fact the population of the townland increased during the Famine decade. This was due to the fact that the townland was inhabited by relatively substantial farmers and not dominated by smallholders. The real changes began to occur after 1851 when the population dropped decade by decade until it was only 51 in 1901 (a reduction of 45% since its highest in 1851). The population of the townland remained around 50 until the time of the Second World War. In the postwar period the population was halved again and today appears to have stabilised at around twenty.

Clearly within the boundaries of Forttown, the major reason for the decrease in population during the latter half of the nineteenth century was the removal of cottier houses. Occupied cottier houses in Forttown fell by just over a half between

CENSUS RETURNS FOR FORTTOWN

parish of Ballymoney, DED of Seacon (later of Kirkmoyle), union of Ballymoney

	INHABITANTS			HOUSES			
	MALES	FEMALES	TOTAL	INHAB	UNINHAB	BUILDING	TOTAL
1841	42 +	45 =	87	17 + 1 + 0 =			18
1851	45 +	48 =	93	15 + 0 + 0 =			15
1861	43 +	43 =	86	17 + 0 + 0 =			17
1871	38 +	35 =	73	16 + 0 + 0 =			16
1881	30 +	30 =	60	12 + 0 + 0 =			12
1891	33 +	30 =	63	12 + 1 + 0 =			13
1901	26 +	25 =	51	9 + 3 + 0 =			12
1911	25 +	18 =	43	8 + 3 + 0 =			11
1926	23 +	24 =	47	7 + 2 + 0 =			9
1937	25 +	27 =	52	8 + 0 + 0 =			8
1951	na		29	7 + 0 + 0 =			7
1961	12 +	9 =	21	6 + 0 + 0 =			6
1971	15 +	11 =	26	6 + 0 + 0 =			6
1981	13 +	11 =	24	5 + 1 + 0 =			6
1991	13 +	9 =	22	6 + 0 + 0 =			6

1859 and 1901.[17] However, the removal of cottier houses, whilst a contributory factor, was not the key reason for the decline in population throughout the Seacon district as a whole. Here cottier households declined only by a quarter.

The key factor in reducing population numbers in the general area during the period 1859-1901 was the swallowing up of the smaller holdings by the larger holdings. This process led directly to many individuals and families moving away from the area. Some went to the local towns or further afield to Belfast, Britain, America or Australia. Those smallholders not in debt were able to sell the interest or tenant right of their farm thus providing them with sufficient cash to emigrate. Some were forced to become cottiers.

The process of consolidation of farms also meant that there was little opportunity for the sons of substantial farmers to stay on the land. If the brother who inherited the farm did not marry then his other brothers might be able to stay on the farm if they so wished. If the family could afford it and the son was willing, there was the possibility of education and a profession such as law, medicine or the church. Another possibility was an apprenticeship in the town to the grocery trade, the drapery trade, etc. with the more long term view of setting up a business. Finally there was emigration to America or Australia.

Celibacy is often cited as a major reason for population decline in Ireland during the latter years of the nineteenth century but there is little evidence that it played a major role in reducing the population of either Forttown or the wider

FAMILIES AND POPULATION IN THE TOWNLAND OF FORTTOWN FROM THE CENSUS OF 1901

HOUSE NO	NO OF PERSONS	FORENAME	SURNAME	RELATIONSHIP	RELIGION
1	1	Mary Ann	Given	Head of Family	Presbyterian
2	7	William	Macafee	Head of Family	Presbyterian
2		Eliza	Macafee	Wife	Presbyterian
2		Rose Ann	Macafee	Daughter	Presbyterian
2		Maggie	Macafee	Daughter	Presbyterian
2		Robert	Macafee	Son	Presbyterian
2		William	Macafee	Son	Presbyterian
2		Jannie	Macafee	Daughter	Presbyterian
3	5	Sheriff	Pinkerton	Head of Family	Presbyterian
3		Jeanie	Pinkerton	Daughter	Presbyterian
3		John	Pinkerton	Brother	Presbyterian
3		Robert	Hart	Nephew	Presbyterian
4	10	William Browne	Forsythe	Head of Family	Presbyterian
4		Elizabeth Wallace	Forsythe	Wife	Presbyterian
4		Robert	Forsythe	Son	Presbyterian
4		James Wallace	Forsythe	Son	Presbyterian
4		Ellen Moore	Forsythe	Daughter	Presbyterian
4		Samuel Hunter	Forsythe	Son	Presbyterian
4		William Browne	Forsythe	Son	Presbyterian
4		John Curry	Forsythe	Son	Presbyterian
4		Margaret Moore	Forsythe	Daughter	Presbyterian
4		Elizabeth Wallace	Forsythe	Daughter	Presbyterian
5	4	James	Parkhill	Head of Family	Presbyterian
5		Mary Jane	Parkhill	Wife	Presbyterian
5		Bessie	Parkhill	Daughter	Presbyterian
5		Kate	Taylor	Visitor	Presbyterian
6	8	James	Boyd	Head of Family	Presbyterian
6		Martha	Boyd	Wife	Presbyterian
6		John	Boyd	Son	Presbyterian
6		Mary Brown	Boyd	Daughter	Presbyterian
6		Matilda	Boyd	Daughter	Presbyterian
6		Eliza Curry	Boyd	Daughter	Presbyterian
6		Leslie	Tosh	Servant	Presbyterian
6		Francie	Morgan	Servant	C of Ireland
7	Unoccupied				
8	Unoccupied				
9	Unoccupied				
10	9	James	Trolland	Head of Family	Presbyterian
10		Anne?	Trolland	Wife	Presbyterian
10		Samuel	Trolland	Son	Presbyterian
10		Elisa Jane	Trolland	Daughter	Presbyterian
10		David	Trolland	Son	Presbyterian
10		Mary	Trolland	Daughter	Presbyterian
10		James	Trolland	Son	Presbyterian
10		Isabella	Trolland	Daughter	Presbyterian
10		William	Trolland	Son	Presbyterian
11	6	Robert	Mooney	Head of Family	Presbyterian
11		Eliza	Mooney	Daughter	Presbyterian
11		Mary	Mooney	Daughter	Presbyterian
11		Henery	Mooney	Son	Presbyterian
11		Robert	Mooney	Son	Presbyterian
11		Thomas	Mooney	Son	Presbyterian
12	2	Ruth	Howard	Head of Family	Details not given
12		Details not available			

FORTTOWN

EDUCATION	AGE	SEX	PROFESSION	MARRIAGE	WHERE BORN	LANDOWNER
Cannot read	50	F	Servant Farm	Not married	England	Pinkerton Sheriff
Read & write	55	M	Carpenter	Married	Co. Antrim	Pinkerton Sheriff
Read & write	38	F	Married		Co. Antrim	
Read & write	14	F	Scholar	Not married	Co. Antrim	
Read & write	12	F	Scholar	Not married	Co. Antrim	
Read & write	10	M	Scholar	Not married	Co. Antrim	
Read & write	7	M	Scholar	Not married	Co. Antrim	
Cannot read	3	F		Not married	Co. Antrim	
Read & write	60	M	Farmer	Widower	Co. Antrim	Pinkerton Sheriff
Read & write	23	F	Farmer's daughter	Not married	Co. Antrim	
Read	72	M	Farmer's brother	Not married	Co. Antrim	
Read & write	43	M	Servant Farm	Not married	Co. Antrim	
Read & write	53	M	Farmer	Married	Co. Antrim	Forsythe Wm Browne
Read & write	53	F	Married		Co. Antrim	
Read & write	25	M	Farmer's son	Not married	Co. Antrim	
Read & write	24	M	Farmer's son	Not married	Co. Antrim	
Read & write	23	F	Farmer's daughter	Not married	Co. Antrim	
Read & write	19	M	Solicitor's Gen. Clk	Not married	Co. Antrim	
Read & write	18	M	Farmer's son	Not married	Co. Antrim	
Read & write	16	M	Draper's Apprentice	Not married	Co. Antrim	
Read & write	13	F	Scholar	Not married	Co. Antrim	
Read & write	11	F	Scholar	Not married	Co. Antrim	
Read	70	M	Labourer Agric.	Married	Co. Derry	Forsythe Wm Browne
Read	68	F	Married		Co. Antrim	
Read & write	40	F	Not married		Co. Antrim	
Cannot read	66	F	Ser. Dom. (unemplyd)	Not married	Co. Antrim	
Read & write	65	M	Farmer	Married	Co. Antrim	Boyd James
Read & write	63	F	Married		Co. Antrim	
Read & write	38	M	Farmer's son	Not married	Co. Antrim	
Read & write	27	F	Farmer's daughter	Not married	Co.Antrim	
Read & write	23	F	Farmer's daughter	Not married	Co. Antrim	
Read & write	17	F	Nat. Sch. Monitor	Not married	Co. Antrim	
Read & write	17	M	Servant Farm	Not married	Co. Derry	
Read & write	15	M	Servant Farm	Not married	Co. Antrim	
						Boyd James
						Forsythe Wm Browne
						Forsythe Wm Browne
Read & write	50	M	Farmer	Married	Co Antrim	Trolland James
Read & write	40	F		Married	Co. Antrim	
Read & write	19	M	Clerk in store	Not married	Co. Antrim	
Read & write	17	F	Draper's Apprentice	Not married	Co. Antrim	
Read & write	15	M	Scholar	Not married	Co. Antrim	
Read & write	13	F	Scholar	Not married	Co. Antrim	
Read & write	12	M	Scholar	Not married	Co. Antrim	
Read & write	10	F	Scholar	Not married	Co. Antrim	
Read & write	8	M	Scholar	Not married	Co. Antrim	
Read & write	45	M	Shoemaker	Widower	Co. Antrim	Boyd James
Read & write	12	F	Scholar	Not married	Co. Antrim	
Read & write	11	F	Scholar	Not married	Co. Antrim	
Read & write	10	M	Scholar	Not married	Co. Antrim	
Read & write	8	M	Scholar	Not married	Co. Antrim	
Read	5	M	Scholar	Not married	Co. Antrim	
						Boyd James

district at that time. Indeed throughout the whole Seacon district I could only find two examples in 1901 of a celibate head of household who was also a farmer. One was a classic example: a family of Thompsons in Kilmoyle Lower which consisted of five unmarried brothers ranging in age from 64 to 47 with an unmarried sister of 44.

Throughout the district generally, heads of farm holdings in 1901 were usually married or widowed and, furthermore, they all tended to have large families. Table 2 gives details of the families living in the townland in 1901. As table 2 shows, most of the households consisted of a father and mother and their children while the substantial farms kept some live-in servants. Both in Forttown and in the wider area there is some evidence of older, unmarried brothers and sisters living with a married brother but such a practice was certainly not widespread. In fact nuclear families with some live-in servants were more common than extended families.

Furthermore with regard to age at marriage the pattern is similar to that probably established before the Famine. Since this was an area of relatively substantial farms the age at which a farmer's son married, depended on when he had access to a farm. This was often controlled by the timing of the death of his parents, particularly his mother. The result was that few farmers' sons were married before their late twenties or early thirties. Recent research has shown that this pattern of marriage had been well established amongst farming families long before the Famine.[18] Changes in marriage habits were not key factors in causing population decline between 1851 and 1901.

In many ways the family history of the Boyds, Forsythes and Pinkertons illustrate what happened to many farming families during the latter half of the nineteenth century and the first part of the twentieth century.

The Boyd family was probably the longest-established family in the townland. Charlie Boyd, now in his eighties, told me that within the family there is a tradition that the Boyds came originally from the Limavady district. A James Boyd was listed in the 1825 Tithe Applotment Book paying a quarter of the tithe for the townland. A James Boyd was listed as the tenant of a farm of just over seventy five acres in Griffith's Valuation of 1859 and a James Boyd, aged 65, was listed as head of the household in the 1901 Enumerators' Returns. Clearly these are not all the same person. The original James of 1825 had a son, John who died in 1851. The James of 1859 was his son. John had three other sons and in his will he left the farm in Forttown 'to be equally divided share and share alike betwixt my four sons namely James Boyd, John Boyd, Joseph Douglas Boyd and Matthew Boyd as tenants in common and not as joint tenants'.[19] James the eldest appears to have bought out the interests of the others since, by 1859, he was listed in Griffith's Valuation as the occupier of the farm. Matthew had died in 1851, two months after his father. John went to Ballymoney where he eventually founded a drapery business. Joseph Douglas became a solicitor.

James died in 1909. He had three sons: John, James and Robert Forsythe.

James had married his neighbour Martha Forsythe around 1862 which accounts for the christian name Forsythe included in the name of one of the sons. John inherited the farm in 1909 and worked it until his death in 1955. The lives of his two brothers illustrate clearly what often happened to younger brothers on a substantial farm in late nineteenth-century Ireland. The youngest brother, James, emigrated to America and eventually settled in California. Robert Forsythe Boyd became a doctor and was a ship's surgeon sailing to America, West Africa and the Congo. He eventually practised medicine in Portadown and finally in Belfast.

A similar pattern can be seen in the Forsythe family[20] who lived next door to the Boyds. Again Forsythes appear to have originated from the Limavady district. The original tenant of the Forsythe holding was a Samuel Hunter who was a substantial linen merchant with property also in the town of Ballymoney. Hunter married Martha Forsythe of Ballyleighery outside Limavady. They had no children. A nephew of Martha, Robert Forsythe, went to live at Forttown and eventually inherited the farm. This Robert is shown as the occupier of the farm in Griffith's Valuation of 1859. He had married about 1837 after his aunt and her husband had died. He had two sons and four daughters. The elder son, Samuel Hunter did not inherit the farm because he emigrated to America. Instead the farm went to his younger brother, William Brown. William Brown Forsythe had ten of a family – six sons and four daughters. The eldest son, Robert, inherited the farm. One of the sons, a twin, died before he was two years of age. Two sons emigrated to the USA, one emigrated to Canada and one became a solicitor, practising in Limavady. Two of the daughters were teachers and never married.

Clearly both of these farming families had sufficient means to provide education for sons, and indeed daughters, who wished to avail themselves of it and as a result were able to enter professions. However, most of them were forced to practise their professions elsewhere and certainly away from the land.

The third relatively large farm in the townland belonged to the Pinkerton family. Again, like the Boyds and the Forsythes they were listed in the Tithe Applotment Records of 1824 and Griffith's Valuation of 1859. In 1901 Sheriff Pinkerton, a widower aged 60, lived with his daughter Jeanie, aged 23, his unmarried brother John, aged 72, and a nephew Robert Hart, (probably from the adjacent townland of Seacon) on the farm. I have no knowledge of his wife or the original size of his family. We know that this farm passed into the hands of Samuel McLean in 1907 after he married Jeanie Pinkerton. The McLean family came originally from near Bushmills. Two brothers, Samuel and William John, had emigrated to Australia (date not known) and had returned in the 1880s with sufficient capital to purchase a farm each in the nearby townland of Ballywattick Middle. The Samuel McLean who married Jeanie Pinkerton was the son of William John McLean.

It is more difficult to find out what happened to those families in Forttown who were not landholders. As mentioned above this group was much more mobile. There was no continuity of names whatsoever between 1859 and 1901. One can only assume that they emigrated to the town or city or emigrated to America or Australia, or simply died out.

In 1901 William Macafee, my great-grandfather, lived in one of the cottier houses on the farm of Sheriff Pinkerton. He had been born in the townland of Ballywattick Upper in a house which was about a quarter of a mile down the road. His father Robert was a carpenter and apparently was the carpenter for the estate which meant that tenants would bring work to him for repair and he would have been charged with making coffins, etc. According to Charlie Boyd, he, like the blacksmith, would have been given a 'freehold' by the landlord. This explains why he was shown in Griffith's Valuation of 1859 as renting his house and small plot of land (a mere 35 perches) directly from the landlord John Cromie. This also explains why this house is still owned by the family, having been acquired under the buying-out acts. Robert had three sons and five daughters. One of the sons, Robert, and possibly three of the daughters, Eliza, Jane and Anna, emigrated to America, or certainly left the district. The other two sons William and Thomas resided in the house in Ballywattick with their sisters Mary and Nancy. Thomas, Mary and Nancy never married. William married around 1886 when he was forty years of age. His wife, Eliza Thompson was twenty-four. Oral evidence from within the family would suggest that William's wife was not welcome in the house in Ballywattick so William had to move to another house. He moved to Forttown where he was able to carry on his carpentry trade. However, because of his position as the eldest in the family, he had to help support the household in Ballywattick after the death of his father in 1890. Indeed after the death of Thomas and Nancy, Mary came to live in the house in Forttown and the house in Ballywattick was rented to another family.

William had a family of six, two sons and four daughters. The family, except one who was born after 1901, appears in the 1901 Enumerators' Returns. Robert, the elder boy, went into the meal, provisions and grocery trade in Ballymoney and became owner of the Route Cafe in Ballymoney. He married and had two sons and two daughters. He went into local politics and became Chairman of Ballymoney Council. Two of the girls, Rose and Annie, moved to Belfast where they married and the other two girls moved to Ballymoney where Maggie married and Jeanie helped Robert to manage the Route Cafe after his wife died. William, my grandfather, stayed on in the house. He married Elizabeth Wilson in 1919 and had two sons and two daughters. He died in 1925.

Thus for farmer and cottier alike a house and a holding or a reasonable, alternative source of income were the prerequisites for staying on in the townland. The alternatives were emigration, apprenticeship in the town, or education and a profession; the latter was available only to the better off. These forces continued to operate during the first half of the twentieth century. In particular the cottier population continued to decline. Some further consolidation took place but not on the same scale. Marriage habits did begin to change. Not only did farmers marry later but increasingly many of them never married at all. I can remember by the 1950s six or seven farms near my home where the owner was unmarried or the farm was owned by two unmarried sisters. These farms have since been bought mostly by persons coming from outside the area.

The divide between town and country widened and certainly by the 1950s the allure of the city and the prospects for advancement there were very appealing. In the end the dominance of the town over country in terms of employment opportunities, new housing estates, the spread of universal free education, the images of a better life portrayed in cinema, heard on the wireless and eventually seen on the television, plus the fundamental changes in farming, caused the massive withdrawal of people from the countryside. The fact that this area is relatively close to the town of Ballymoney has meant that, in more recent times, some townspeople have moved into the area building large houses set in expansive grounds and these sit side by side with the 'agribusiness' which has now replaced the family farm of yesteryear. Few of the old wallsteads from the nineteenth century are now visible having been bulldozed away with their hedge boundaries to make way for modern farming techniques and new bungalows.

HOUSING

Housing in the townland, and throughout the area in general, usually reflected the wealth and status of the tenant. The Griffith's Valuation of 1859 provides evidence of the value of each house and the adjoining buildings on a holding. It is difficult to be sure about the exact value of a dwelling house at that time since a high valuation could be mainly due to a large number of outbuildings. Nor does it give us any evidence as to whether houses were slated. However the periodic revisions to the Valuation provide evidence of the rebuilding and slating of houses and the House and Buildings Returns of the 1901 Enumerators' Returns provide us with a snapshot of housing and outbuildings at the turn of the century. Table 3 gives details of housing for Forttown in 1901 and table 4 gives details of outbuildings.

As these figures show, Forttown had one Class 1 house (that of James Boyd), four Class 2 houses and four Class 3 houses. All of these houses were built of stone, as was the case in the surrounding townlands. However, only the Class 1 house of James Boyd was slated. The Valuation Revisions of 1885-96 show that this house was built around 1891 and that the old house was being used as offices. This new, 1891 house is still standing today. The 1901 Returns show that this house had twelve rooms with nine windows to the front. Although not slated in 1901, the Forsythe house was a substantial house of probably a storey and a half. This house had been built much earlier in the nineteenth century by Samuel Hunter and would have been still regarded as more than adequate in the second half of the nineteenth century – thus it remained intact until the early twentieth century when it was slated. The other farmhouses appear to have been of the traditional design, single storied and thatched. I remember the McLeans building

TABLE 3

HOUSES IN THE TOWNLAND OF FORTTOWN 1901

NO.	FORENAME	SURNAME	NO. OF PERSONS	FARM HOUSE	COTTIER HOUSE	CLASS 1 HOUSE	CLASS 2 HOUSE	CLASS 3 HOUSE	ROOF SLATED	WIN- DOWS	ROOMS
1	Mary Ann	Given	1		1			1		1	1
2	William	Macafee	7		1		1			4	2
3	Sheriff	Pinkerton	5	1			1			2	4
4	Wm Browne	Forsythe	10	1			1			4	6
5	James	Parkhill	4		1			1		2	2
6	James	Boyd	8	1		1			1	9	12
7		Unoccupd									
8		Unoccupd									
9		Unoccupd									
10	James	Trolland	9	1			1			3	2
11	Robert	Mooney	6		1			1		2	2
12	Ruth	Howard	2		1			1		1	2

SOURCE: 1901 CENSUS ENUMERATORS' RETURNS - HOUSES AND BUILDINGS

their present two-storey house in the early 1950s. This was a time when many new farmhouses were built with the original houses becoming offices.

The houses of cottiers and smallholders would also have been of the traditional design with usually two rooms – a very few had only one room. The Valuation Revisions for 1896-1911 show that most of the cottier houses in Forttown had been vacated by 1910 and were in ruins. Three new labourers' cottages had replaced the cottier houses and these were in the hands of Ballymoney Rural District Council.

Again the number of outbuildings reflected the size and wealth of the farm: coach houses were restricted to the Boyd and Forsythe families. The fact that all farms had a stable is evidence that farms were usually large enough to support at least one horse and usually a team of horses. The presence of the byre, the dairy, the piggery, potato house, etc. reflect the mixed nature of farming at that time.

TABLE 4

OUTBUILDINGS IN THE TOWNLAND OF FORTTOWN 1901

NO.	FORENAME	SURNAME	STABLE	COACH HOUSE	COW HOUSE	CALF HOUSE	DAIRY	PIGGERY	FOWL HOUSE	BOILING HOUSE	BARN	TURF HOUSE	POTATO HOUSE	SHED	TOTAL	LANDOWNER
1	Mary Ann	Given													0	Pinkerton
2	William	Macafee												1	1	Pinkerton
3	Sheriff	Pinkerton	1		2	1	1	2			1			1	9	Pinkerton
4	William Browne	Forsythe	1	1	1	1	1	3		1	1	1	1	1	12	Forsythe
5	James	Parkhill						1							1	Forsythe
6	James	Boyd	1	1	1	1	1	2	1		1		1	1	11	Boyd
7		Unoccupied													0	Boyd
8		Unoccupied													0	Forsythe
9		Unoccupied													0	Forsythe
10	James	Trolland	1		1	1		1		1	1	1			7	Trolland
11	Robert	Mooney													0	Boyd
12	Ruth	Howard						1							1	Boyd

SOURCE: 1901 CENSUS ENUMERATORS' RETURNS - HOUSES AND BUILDINGS

FARMING

Agriculture in Ulster, until relatively recently, has always been portrayed as the family farm practising mixed farming. The description by Alexander Burnside in 1845, when giving evidence to the Devon Commission, would suggest that this area was well on its way to adopting that pattern by the middle of the nineteenth century. According to him, 'the culture is as follows – namely, a five-course rotation: first, potatoes and turnips; second, oats, wheat or barley, sown down with clover and rye grass; third, hay and cut clover for house feeding of dairy stock; fourth, grazing; fifth, oats.'[21] However he added a note of caution that 'not more than one-half of the district adopts this rotation; too many follow no regular plan.' He also stated that few sheep were kept, the stock being principally dairy cattle. He also mentioned improvements to agriculture through manuring with animal manure, by liming, by applying sea shells and by draining. He saw farming societies as having done much good by introducing a superior breed of dairy stock and by giving premiums to the best or most skilful ploughmen.

The Agricultural Statistics for 1850 confirm Burnside's descriptions. It is not possible to give precise details for Forttown as the data are given at District Electoral Division level. At that time Seacon DED contained 5,238 acres covering 172 farms with 2,304 inhabitants. Within this area, Forttown contained 305 acres on 5 farms with 93 inhabitants. Of the 5,283 acres in Seacon DED 2,250, or nearly a half, were under cultivation. This represents a high percentage, especially when the extent of bogland is taken into consideration. Although the major crop was oats with 981 acres, there were also 57 acres of wheat, 33 of barley and 29 of beans and peas. Of the 773 acres of root crops there were 381 of potatoes and 237 of turnips with 223 of flax and 413 of meadow and clover. Forttown, therefore, might have had at least 50 acres of oats as well as 20 acres of potatoes and perhaps 12 to 15 acres of both turnips and flax.

The above descriptions could well apply to Forttown in the late 1940s and early 1950s when I was growing up there. I spent a considerable amount of time on McLean's farm and as I grew older I gathered potatoes, stooked oats, became involved in their thrashing and baling, turned hay and pulled flax or 'lint', as we called it then. The only crops that were not present at that time were wheat and barley, although the latter made a comeback in the 1960s.

I also remember ploughing with a team of horses in the early 1950s. 'Young' Sammy McLean, as he was known then, was a champion ploughman with horses and occasionally he would let me plough, aided by his steady hand, for a few furrows. Sammy McLean was probably one of the last farmers in the area to plough with horses on a daily basis. By that time farmers were using tractors. Charlie Boyd told me that, just about the time of the Second World War, he had great difficulty in convincing his father John Boyd to buy a tractor instead of a new team of horses to replace their ageing team. At first the decision to switch from horse to tractor could hinge on the condition and age of a team of horses on a particular farm. However by the 1950s the question of whether horse or tractor would be paramount had been answered and the latter had won. At first much of the machinery which had been designed for horses was modified to suit the tractors. The local blacksmith, Willie Clarke, who lived in the Bootown, was kept busy for a time modifying and repairing this machinery. This helped to offset the decline in work related to the decreasing number of horses. However, as hydraulic systems became an integral part of the tractor and its associated machinery, the days of the blacksmith became numbered.

Certainly by the 1960s it was obvious that farming was undergoing some fundamental changes. The postwar period saw subsidies and grants to farmers which led to the building of new haysheds, new silos and the enlargement of fields by the removal of hedges. Mixed farming gave way gradually to specialised farming. Oats began to disappear as the horse population declined. Barley became the new cereal, grown to help feed pigs. This new cereal farming brought with it the combine harvester, the pickup baler and the corn dryer. Dairy farming based on silage was probably the most popular of the new specialised types of farming. Farmers were now being urged to see grass as a crop rather than as a fallow field in a crop rotation. Even poultry which had been seen as 'pin money' for the farmers' wives, was now overtaken by new methods: large deep-litter houses began to appear in the rural landscape.

These changes have gone on apace since the 1960s, indeed to such an extent that people are beginning to refer to farming now as agribusiness – i.e. a large scale business using automated methods supplying a market far removed from the local area. It is interesting to note that within Forttown there are now only two operating farms. A third farm is worked by one of the adjoining farms. Throughout the wider area where there were some 55 working farms in 1859, there are now no more than ten. This is because only large farmers have the capital to work the land now and it is often easier for the smaller farmers to let their land to adjoining farmers or indeed to farmers from outside the immediate district.

It is increasingly difficult to find actual remains of the buildings, fields and laneways which were part of the farming landscape of the area when I was a boy. Certainly up until about 1950 there were still many examples of Victorian life and material culture abounding in the general area. Walking through Forttown and the surrounding townlands recently I saw a landscape very different from the landscape I remember forty years ago. Perhaps the most striking difference is that the hedges are so much lower in height and the fields larger in size. Reconstructing that landscape in my mind's eye enables me to 'see' where, for example, flax dams were once located and laneways used to run. The laneways and the flax dams have been swallowed up in the present day fields so well that there is no physical trace of them in today's landscape.

DEVELOPMENT OF THE ROAD NETWORK AND ITS SIGNIFICANCE

When one looks at the location of farms in Forttown and the wider area generally, it is clear that the original farm houses and buildings were sited with regard to the better land. In earlier times there were only two main roads throughout the area. The first, often referred to as the 'old Coleraine' road or the Seacon Road ran along the top of the Seacon moraine and was the main road between Ballymoney and Coleraine. This road was crossed at Seacon by a road coming from Balnamore which went to Ballybogey towards Portrush. All farms required access to one or other of these roads. Most farmers would have seen Ballymoney as their nearest market town.

During the early years of the nineteenth century two new roads were built from Ballymoney, one to the west of the Seacon Road and one to the east. The western road was the new road to Coleraine which was a toll road. The other road was the new road to Ballybogey and eventually to Portrush. Locally the roads are referred to as 'the Coleraine line' and 'the Portrush line' respectively, reflecting the relative straightness of these newer roads, particularly the Portrush one which skirted the edge of the Garry bog. As a result new laneways had to be created from the farms to the new roads. This means that today most farms have now two lanes leading to the old and new roads. This pattern is repeated in many parts of Ulster, reflecting the fact that older roads and original farm settlements tended to hug the relatively higher, drier grounds, whereas better technology allowed the newer roads to forge their way through more low-lying, wetter, often boggy ground. Indeed some of these newer roads now sit well above the fields suggesting that when the roads were laid out originally, the surrounding peat land had not been exploited.

The main settlements on these newer roads tend to be the labourers' cottages which were built at the turn of the century, reflecting the relative scarcity of settlement in the areas through which these new roads were laid out. Many of the original cottier houses had been located in relation to the farms they served rather than the major roads. Thus they were often along laneways which led from the farms to the major roads. However, when the sites for the new labourers' cottages were chosen they were directly on the roadside. Again this pattern is fairly common throughout the province as a whole.

Since roads are lines of communication it is not surprising that crossroads were often seen as meeting places and in the next section on the community we look more closely at this phenomenon.

THE COMMUNITY

Nineteenth-century rural Ireland tended to have a much more dispersed pattern of settlement than rural England. Nevertheless there was a strong sense of community in the countryside. Although it lacked the focus of the agricultural village people tended to foregather at certain places or buildings over a wide area. In other words, whilst people always acknowledged that they belonged to a certain townland, in my experience, the sense of community spread beyond the geographical boundaries of one townland.

One of the most important institutions which helped to shape the community was the local school – Seacon Public Elementary School which, when I attended it, was situated beside Hanna's farm and shop at the bottom of Seacon hill. The principal of the school at that time was Mrs Henry and her assistant was Mrs Morrison. In many ways the catchment area of the school could be used as a crude way of delineating the district. Children came to this school not only from Seacon but also from Ballywattick, Kilmoyle, Forttown, Tullaghgore, Bootown and Newbuildings. Friendships were forged at school and as a child you became aware of other families and townlands within the wider district. The day school doubled as a Sunday school and I can remember attending Sunday school there on Sunday afternoons, having been at morning Sunday school and church in St. James's Presbyterian Church, Ballymoney.

Since Forttown and the surrounding townlands lay within three miles of the town of Ballymoney, families attended one of the churches in the town. This meant that there was no single church which could give the district the kind of focus that might be found in other areas such as Ballywatt, Ballyrashane or Kilraghts but it did mean that folk visited the town more regularly. Most of the families in Forttown and the general area were Presbyterians, with a scattering of Reformed Presbyterians, Church of Ireland and Roman Catholic. There was a group of families in Seacon – the McKays, the Harts, and the Burnsides who are listed in 1901 Census as Unitarians. As a boy, I can remember the Unitarian Church in Charles Street in Ballymoney. That building has gone and the site is now occupied by Riada House, the offices of Ballymoney District Council.

I can remember one other building which was used by most of the community. This was the Newbuildings Flute Band Hall, a nissan hut situated in Seacon More. I believe that it was a relic of the Second World War which had been acquired by the band. The original hall was in Newbuildings near the new Portrush road but clearly this relatively new nissan hut was seen as a better alternative. I seem to remember that this band associated itself with the Independent Orange Order and were great rivals of Benvarden Flute Band who were associated with the original Orange Order. The former were referred to as 'The Hairies' and the latter as 'The Froggies'. Why, I don't know. The hall was used for concerts, Sunday school soirees and dances. These events usually took place during the winter months and I can remember walking along relatively dark roads to concerts and soirees. There seemed to have been many people on the move at that time along the roads and on the way we would meet up at junctions and crossroads with families coming from various directions. By contrast today, people would move by car and would probably go to events in the town.

The fact that most people at that time either walked or rode a bicycle meant that people met each other along roads and there were certain places which were regarded as meeting places. Indeed, there were two key meeting places in the area. The first which was known as 'the Sheddings' was on the new Coleraine road at the point where it was crossed by the old Balnamore/Ballybogey road. There was a shop here which was known locally as the 'Lemonade House'. In 1901 it was owned by the McQuigg family and I can vaguely remember descendants of that family running it in the 1940s/1950s. This was a general meeting place but its importance was added to by the fact that there was a bus stop there; later on a petrol-filling station was built there and just up the road a relatively large number of cottages was built carrying on the tradition of labourers' cottages begun at the turn of the century. In many ways this would now be seen as Seacon village whereas the original Seacon village, if there ever was one, would have been up on the higher ground of Seacon More much closer to the old Coleraine road. The second meeting place was in the townland of Tullaghgore where a laneway leading from a myriad of lanes in Newbuildings and the Bootown met the main Tullaghgore road and lanes from within Tullaghore itself.

These meeting places were places where people could simply chat, exchange banter and generally socialise. They were probably more frequented during the long summer evenings when games such as horseshoes were played. Cards were also played but these were much more clandestine activities and had their own secret locations. In addition to these more permanent meeting places there were also houses or groups of houses that attracted people. Sammy McLean recalls how in the late 1920s/early 1930s he and his brothers and other young men would go to a house in Ballywattick on a summer's evening to kick football and generally socialise. Incidentally the football was not always a leather one. I can remember whilst at primary school in the 1940s playing football with a pig's bladder until it burst. The pigs had been killed the night before on a local farm and one of the farmer's sons had brought the bladder to school the next day.

Having been away from the area for almost forty years it is difficult for me to say what sense of community is there today. Many of the people who live there today work elsewhere. I suspect many of their relations and friends live elsewhere. The rural area is now an appendage of the town rather than the town being the servant of the farming community. This process which began probably during the second half of the nineteenth century has created, I think, a very different community from the one that I can remember even in the 1950s. I suspect also that the community of the 1950s had a much closer link to the Victorian community of the nineteenth century. I have vivid memories of folk using tools and furniture that are now part of the heritage industry. At the same time the community had the seeds of change growing within it at that time – the changes in farming, the allure of the big city, the spread of universal, free education, the images of a better life portrayed in cinema, heard on the wireless and eventually seen on the television. These new, twentieth century forces have produced a community and landscape that is different from the one in which I grew up.

At the same time, we must remember that the countryside is as a much a creation of people as it is of nature and over the centuries it has gone through many physical changes that have reflected the various ways in which people living there have either decided or have been forced to make their living. Perhaps the greatest threat that the countryside now faces is the fact that increasingly fewer and fewer of the people who live there actually make their living there.

ACKNOWLEDGEMENTS

I should like to acknowledge the assistance given to me by the following people when trying to reconstruct families and events in the townland:
  Mr Charlie Boyd, Miss Nonagh Boyd, Mr Sammy McLean, the Forsythe and Caldwell families, Mrs J. E. Mullin and members of my own family particularly Miss Margaret Macafee.
  I should also like to thank Sharon Malcolm for producing figures 1 and 2.

NOTES

1 Even today the general district is often referred to as Seacon and for the purposes of this essay any reference to the wider district means reference to the Seacon district. The townlands which comprise this area are shown on the map in figure 2.
2 A. Day & P. McWilliams (eds.), *Ordnance Survey Memoirs of Ireland, vol. 16: Parishes of County Antrim V*, (Belfast, 1992) p. 21.
3 PRONI T/904, p. 28.
4 In figures 1 and 2 Tullaghgore occupies the eastern side of the Seacon moraine and Seacon (More, Beg and Lower) the western side of the moraine. The place name Seacon means the 'Seat of Con'. Clearly both Tullaghgore and Seacon situated together on this prominent area of higher ground surrounded by bog and swamp were, together, of some significance in the general region.
5 W. Reeves, *Ecclestiastical Antiquities of Down, Dromore and Connor*, (1847) (Reprinted by Braid Books and Moyola Books, 1992), p. 81.
6 *Ordnance Survey Memoirs, vol. 16*, pp. 19-20.
7 According to S.T. Carleton, *Heads and Hearths: the Hearth Money Rolls and Poll Tax Returns for County Antrim, 1660-69*, (Belfast, 1991), p. 80, Tullaghgore included the present day townlands of Tullaghgore, Forttown, Bootown, Newbuildings North and Heagles. Carleton (p. 80) also states that in the Downe Survey Barony Map the townland of Heagles was known as Liballimonvard, the townlands of Bootown and Heagles as Cloghan and the townlands of Forttown and Tullaghgore as Tullaghgore.
8 S. Pender, *A Census Of Ireland, circa 1659*, (Dublin, 1939) p. 14.
9 PRONI T/3022/4/1 (1666) & PRONI T/808/14889 (1669). The Hearth Tax was introduced into Ireland in 1662. A sum of two shillings per annum had to be paid on all chimneys, stoves and hearths unless the occupier of the house was exempt from payment. More substantial houses with more than one hearth had to pay more e.g. Cromey in Tullaghgore was deemed to have 3 hearths and More 2 hearths.
10 See S. T. Carleton, *Heads and Hearths*, pp. 175-187 and W. Macafee, 'The Movement of British Settlers into Ulster during the Seventeenth Century' *Familia*, Vol. 2, No. 8, pp. 95-97.

11 W. Macafee, 'The Movement of British Settlers into Ulster', pp. 108-110.
12 PRONI Antrim Estate Papers D/2977/3A/3/2/40/1A&B.
13 *Report from Her Majesty's Commissioners of Inquiry into the State of the Law and Practice in Relation to the Occupation of Land in Ireland*, (*Report of the Devon Commission*), British Parliamentary Papers, 1845, Vol. XIX, p. 626.
14 *Ibid*, pp. 625-626.
15 T. H. Mullin & J. E. Mullin, *Roots in Ulster Soil: A Family History*, (Belfast, 1967), p. 131.
16 W. E. Vaughan, *Landlords and Tenants in Mid-Victorian Ireland*, (Oxford, 1994), p. 10.
17 The main reason for the apparent sharp decline in the cottier population in Forttown between 1851 and 1901 was their rehousing in vacated houses of smallholders taken over by Boyd in the neighbouring townland of Tullaghgore.
18 W. Macafee, 'The Demographic History of Ulster, 1750-1841', Chapter 4 of H. T. Blethen & C. W. Wood Jr., eds., *Ulster and North America: Transatlantic Perspectives on the Scotch Irish*, (The University of Alabama Press, 1997), p. 52.
19 T. H. Mullin & J. E. Mullin, *Roots in Ulster Soil*, p. 128.
20 An account of the Forsythe family appears in T. H. Mullin & J. E. Mullin, *Roots in Ulster Soil*, pp. 119-139.
21 *Report of the Devon Commission*, p. 625.

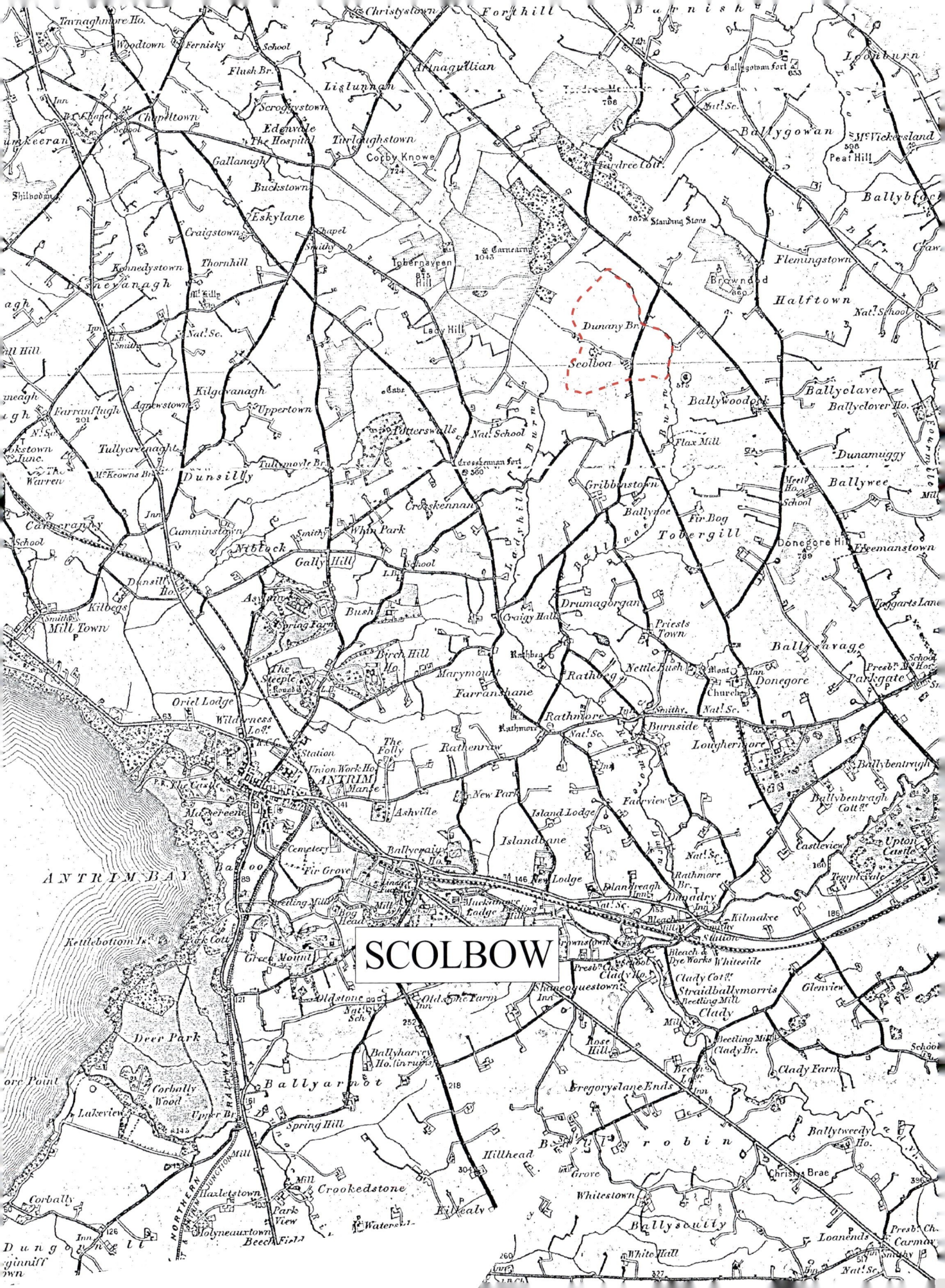

SCOLBOW

Key to townlands

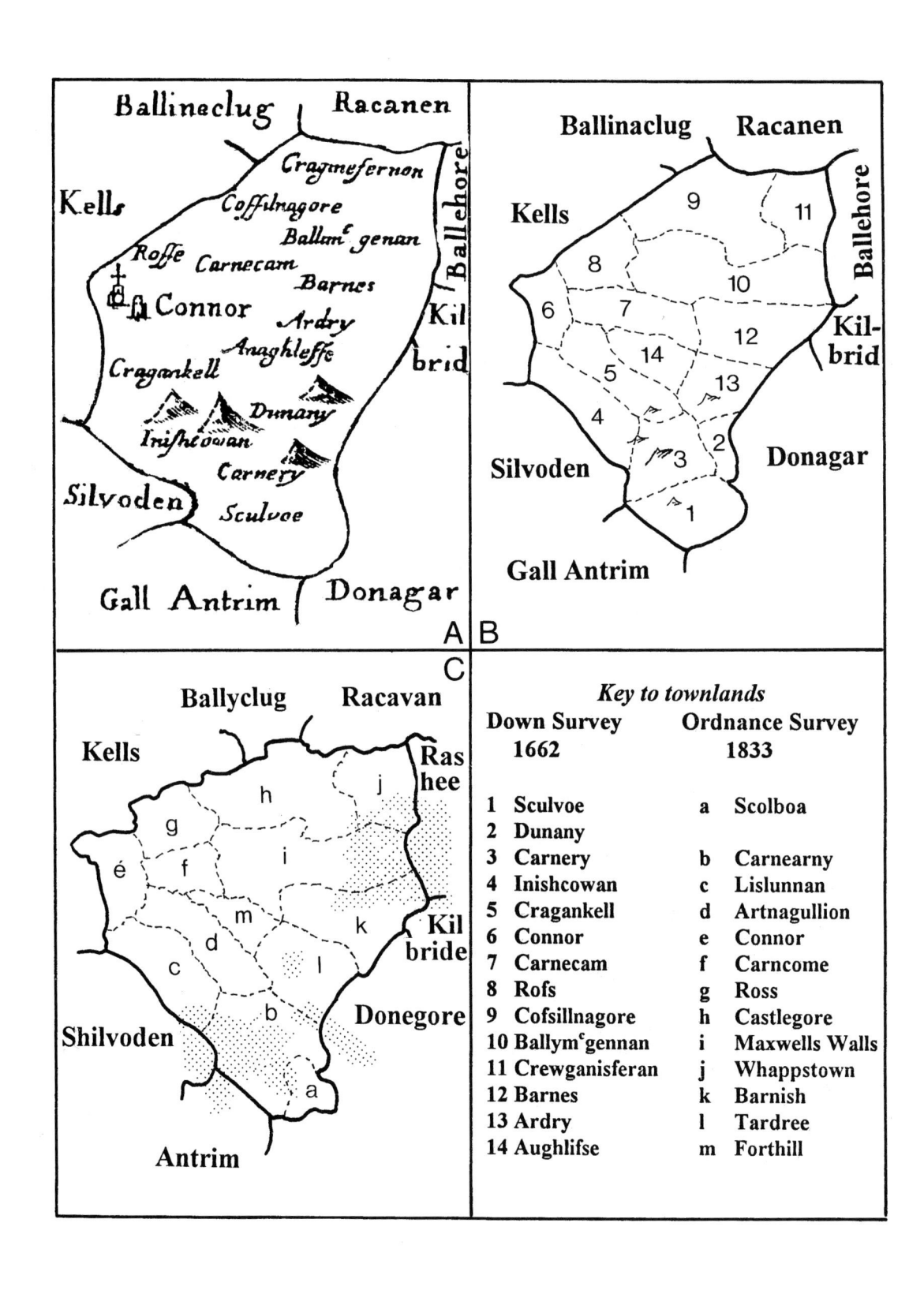

Down Survey 1662		Ordnance Survey 1833	
1	Sculvoe	a	Scolboa
2	Dunany	b	Carnearny
3	Carnery	c	Lislunnan
4	Inishcowan	d	Artnagullion
5	Cragankell	e	Connor
6	Connor	f	Carncome
7	Carnecam	g	Ross
8	Rofs	h	Castlegore
9	Cofsillnagore	i	Maxwells Walls
10	Ballym^{c}gennan	j	Whappstown
11	Crewganisferan	k	Barnish
12	Barnes	l	Tardree
13	Ardry	m	Forthill
14	Aughlifse		

SCOLBOW

R.H. FOY

*And someday, Lower Scolbow, aye, and Upper Scolbow
for all its pride and vaunting superiority over Lower Scolbow,
will be one with Nineveh and Tyre*

BONAR THOMPSON *PACE* RUDYARD KIPLING

Today they are quieted. Rude sounds of life no longer echo around Upper and Lower Scolbow, nor will Big Margaret ever sing again as she feeds her strident geese. For the farming folk who laboured on the raw slopes of an Antrim hill have gone, dust these many years, leaving behind but memories and ruins. The Scolbows can be found by travelling north from the Six Mile Water, close by historic Moylinny, through regal Rathmore and Rathbeg, and going beyond Drumagorgan and Ballynoe. On a spur of Carnearny Mountain, they offer panoramic vistas southwards to Divis and the distant Mountains of Mourne, while the glittering expanse of Lough Neagh almost touches the south-western horizon. Ascending the larger hills and mountains of Ulster, the landscape changes from productive pastures to the wastes of rough grazings and bogs. Scolbow townland, which reaches 750 feet, sees such a change, for some fields, on the steep south facing slopes, are well drained and fertile, but many more are not, being a mixture of wind-swept rushes and coarse grasses. Despite this unpromising resource, Scolbow's 268 acres contrived to support a population of 90 persons in 1841 and, for generations, all human life in the townland reverberated around the two clachan settlements of Upper and Lower Scolbow. Now they are abandoned, redundant to the needs of a modern age.

*The name was spelt differently by different persons according to
their upbringing, rank, educational status, inclination or fancy.*

BONAR THOMPSON

Scolbow is a unique townland name in Ireland but the 'official' spelling of the Ordnance Survey is *Scolboa*; a spelling which is distinguished by being absent

Figure 1

from everyday use and rarely observed in letters, nor evident in everyday speech. The inclusion of an *a* in *Scolboa* may be the result of some hasty transcription error, with the final *w* in Scolbow being replaced with *a*. An early spelling encountered is *Scolvoe* in Petty's Down Survey map of 1666 (Fig. 1A). Perhaps this errant *v* is also the result of another transcription error of an open *b* for *v*. After 1666, this *v* disappears from view except for two documents of the 1830s when *Scolva* is used in a farm map drawn by W.H. Waters in 1831 and in a lengthy legal document of 1838 – both made close to the time of the first Ordnance Survey of the townland in 1833. Elsewhere, the *v* is replaced by *b*.

Two years after the Down Survey, *Ealbagh* was used in the Hearth Money Roll of 1669. Here the initial *Sc* has been replaced by a single *E*, again not an impossible transcription error, given the long-hand script of the day. *Scolbogh* appears in a 1705 rent-roll followed by *Scolbough* in a 1733 rental. *Scolbough* persisted for over a century as it was used in a tithe rent-roll of 1843 and in an 1836 emigrant letter from Pittsburgh. *Scalbo* was used in a list of tithe payments due in 1835 but another emigrant letter sent in 1842 provides the first *Scolbow*. From the mid-nineteenth century Scolbow became almost a vernacular standard, appearing in Ladyhill National School rolls which opened in 1848, emigrant letters and in newspaper reports of court cases; for the people of Scolbow were not always a peaceable race. Occasionally an abbreviated *Scolbo* creeps in, appearing in newspapers and in an 1858 farm map.

In rural country Antrim at the end of the nineteenth century death cards were a popular means of announcing deaths and the times and venues of burials. Indeed, attendance at a funeral almost required the receipt of a card. The twelve cards reproduced here provide an indication of the local orthography between 1885 and 1911 (Fig 2). Nine favoured *Scolbow* with one each for *Scolbo* and *Scalbo*. Each of these eleven cards was issued for long term residents of Scolbow. In contrast, the sole card in favour of the Ordnance Survey spelling of *Scolboa* was printed for a young man whose family was not long resident in the townland. Comparing *Scolbough* or *Scolbogh* with *Scolbow*, the latter may be considered an abbreviated spelling of *Scolbough* for, in the locality, the pronunciation of *bow* resembles *bough* or *bow* as at the front of a ship rather than the *bow* used to shoot arrows.

Placenames prefixed by *Scol* are uncommon in Ireland but Scolbow almost certainly owes its derivation to the Irish name given to the townland. While townland names may now be admired and cherished for their own sake, their origins can often be traced to hard-headed judgements as to the character of the land. The earliest written version is found in a 1621 inquisition defining districts in county Antrim, which gives *Ardneskulbo* as the northern limit of the tuogh of Moylinny where it meets Connor. *Ard* is well known as describing a height and this is consistent with the location of Scolbow and the diminutive *ne* can be recognised as meaning 'belonging to'. What *skulbo* refers to is more open to debate and Dr Pat McKay of the Place-Name Project at Queen's University Belfast

Died,

At her residence, Scolbow, on Monday, the 16th March, 1885,

ANNIE J. M'MEEKIN,

AGED 18 YEARS.

The remains of my dear Niece will be removed for interment in Donegore Burying Ground, on Wednesday, the 18th inst., at Three o'clock p.m.

Yours respectfully,
CHARLES WARWICK.

Died,

On Sabbath, 23rd May, 1886, at his Father's residence, Scolbow,

JAMES WARWICK

AGED 33 YEARS.

The remains of my beloved Son will be removed for interment in the Family Burying Ground, Donegore, on Tuesday, 25th inst., at Three o'clock p.m.

Yours respectfully,
CHARLES WARWICK.

Died,

At her residence, Scalbo, on Friday, 4th February, 1887,

MARY WILSON,

AGED 84 YEARS.

The remains of my dear Mother will be removed for interment in Donegore Burying-Ground, on Monday, 7th inst., at 10 o'clock a.m.

Yours respectfully,
JOHN WILSON.

Died,

AT HIS RESIDENCE, SCOLBOW, ON THURSDAY, 7TH JUNE, 1888,

JOHN WARWICK,

AGED 51 YEARS.

The remains of my beloved husband will be removed for interment in the Family Burying-ground, Donegore, on Saturday, 9th Inst., at Three o'clock, p.m.

Yours Respectfully,
ANNA L. WARWICK.

Died,

AT HIS RESIDENCE, SCOLBOW, ON WEDNESDAY, 16th SEPTEMBER, 1891,

WILLIAM MONTGOMERY,

AGED 79 YEARS.

His remains will be removed for Interment in the Family Burying-ground, Donegore, on Friday, 18th inst., at 2 o'clock, p.m.

Yours Respectfully,
JOHN MONTGOMERY

Died,

At her residence, Scolbow, on Wednesday, 23rd August, 1893,

JANE WARWICK,

Aged 52 Years.

The remains of my beloved wife will be removed for interment in Donegore Burying-Ground, on Saturday, 26th inst., at 12 o'clock, noon.

Yours respectfully,
ARTHUR WARWICK.

Died,

At her residence, Scolbow, on Thursday, 24th May, 1894,

ANNA L. WARWICK,

Aged 51 Years

The remains of my beloved mother will be removed for interment in the family Burying-Ground, Donegore, on Saturday, 26th inst, at 12 o'clock, noon.

Yours respectfully,
JAMES WARWICK.

DIED,

At his residence Scolbow on 16th May 1898 my dear Son Wm Robert

Aged 17 Years.

His remains will be removed for interment in 2nd Donegore Burying-Ground, on Wednesday the 18 instant, at 10 o'clock.

Yours respectfully,
Alex O'Neill

Died,

At his residence SCOLBOW, on Saturday, 12th August, 1899,

CHARLES HAY,

Aged 64 Years.

The remains of my beloved husband will be removed from his late residence for interment in DONEGORE Family Burying-ground, on Monday, 14th August, at Eleven o'clock, a.m.

Yours respectfully,
SARAH HAY.

DIED,

At her Residence SCOLBOW, on SUNDAY, 18th May, 1902,

MARGARET.

The remains of my dear sister will be removed for Interment in the Family Burying-Ground DONEGORE, on Tuesday, 20th Inst., at 12 o'clock, noon.

Yours respectfully,
ARTHUR WARWICK.

DIED,

At his Residence, SCOLBO, on Thursday, 29th August, 1907,

JAMES LATIMORE.

The remains of my beloved husband will be removed from his late residence for Interment in BALLYLINNEY BURYING-GROUND, on SATURDAY, 31st inst., at 12 o'clock, noon,

Yours respectfully,
MARY LATIMORE.

DIED,

At his nephew's residence, SCOLBOA, on Tuesday, 28th February, 1911,

DAVID MOORE.

The remains of my beloved uncle will be removed from the above address for interment in DONEGORE BURYING-GROUND, on THURSDAY, 2nd MARCH, at One o'clock, p.m.

Yours Respectfully,
ROBT. LATIMER.

Figure 2
Death cards

has proposed two alternative derivations. The first traces the name to the word *scolb*, which is a twig or scollop used to make secure the thatch on a roof followed by *ach,* a place or edifice. From this, *Ardneskulbo* refers to 'the height of the place of twigs', perhaps alluding to a district with many shrubs and small trees. This derivation attempts to take into account the local pronunciation which, as has been mentioned above, tends to, but not always consistently, end Scolbow as a short-sounding *bough* rather than an open *bow*. If one tends to think that the ending of the first spelling of *Ardneskulbo* made in 1621 should be pronounced as we would read it, i.e. as an open *bow*, then a quite different derivation can be made. In this Scolbow is anglicised from the Irish *Scumhal Bó* – 'the steep place of the cow'. *Scumhal* is a precipice, steep slope or hill and, although usually anglicised to *skool*, could appear as *Scol*. Part of the townland is indeed precipitous and almost cliff-like and can only be scrambled up with difficulty. Including the Irish *Bó* for cow in the name would refer to the grazing capabilities of the district. As *Ard* refers to a height, we have *the height of the steep place of the cow*. Today, this remains an accurate description of the townland given its elevation, the steep lane running past Upper and Lower Scolbow and the occupation of the land by beef cows.

Remote from public haunt, a place most inaccessible, very nearly impassable and altogether indefensible

BONAR THOMPSON

Scolbow finds no mention in any of the Irish annals and the passage of time has cast a veil over its settlement before the seventeenth century. Although a very fine bivallate rath sits close by in neighbouring Ballywoodock, Scolbow contains no raths or souterrains, suggesting little settlement in the early Christian era. In medieval times it was part of the Cinament of Dough Connor, a tuogh or territory owned by the church. The rents of Connor were payable to the Abbot of Templemoyle Abbey in Kells (County Antrim). With the eclipse of the twin villages of Kells and Connor as ecclesiastical centres, these rents, for what was then the Parish of Connor, were claimed by the amalgamated Bishopric of Down, Connor and Dromore. Thus, although it lies in the Six Mile Water valley and is closer to the town of Antrim, Scolbow was linked by ownership to Connor and the adjacent Kells Water – Glenwherry valley.

As church lands rarely changed ownership, they tend not to be found among the patent-rolls and land leases which provided a legal legitimacy to the transfer of ownership from the dispossessed in seventeenth-century Ulster. For Scolbow and the other townlands in Connor Parish, early references to individual townlands are doubly scarce. Generally the parish was referred to collectively as either the Sixteen Towns of Connor, the Bishop's Lands, or the Territory and Manor of Connor. It was quite common for parishes such as Connor and Antrim to be referred to as containing sixteen towns when they emerged from the medieval period. But today there are only thirteen townlands within the old parish boundaries of Connor. The earliest surviving maps and a description of Scolbow come from William Petty's Down Survey, which was done around 1660 and covered those lands forfeited because of the Rebellion of 1641 as well as church lands. It is available today as county, barony and parish maps and in *Books of Survey and Distribution* which give townland names, areas and owners who lost their property as a result of involvement in the 1641 Rebellion. The Survey shows that, in 1660, the sixteen townlands of the Parish of Connor had been contracted to fourteen, or one more than the present total. Three maps of Connor Parish are reproduced here: two from the Down Survey and the third as surveyed by the Ordnance Survey in 1833 (Fig. 1).

Comparing the two maps produced by Petty around 1660 with the 1833 map, it is clear that the shape and integrity of the Parish of Connor have remained unchanged as have most townland boundaries. In contrast, about half of the townland names have changed, for example *Crewganisfernan* now corresponds to Whappstown. Scolbow, as already described, is readily recognisable as *Scolvoe*. The extra townland recorded in 1666 was *Dunany*. From the townland boundaries surveyed in 1660 and 1830, Scolbow was very much larger in the past than it is today. Indeed it may be suspected that the area of the ancient Dunany townland corresponds more closely to the present Scolbow, but the former's location was to the north of today's Scolbow.

In the Down Survey *Book of Survey and Distribution* for Armagh, Down and Antrim, Scolbow is listed as covering the equivalent of 584 modern acres compared to the present total of 268 acres. It was, in 1660, larger than Carnery/Carnearny, yet today Carnearny is four times the area of Scolbow. Better agreement can be obtained when the combined area of Scolvoe, Carnery and Dunany of 1408 acres is compared to the combined 1360 acres for Scolbow and Carnearny in 1833. To account for this, the western half of Scolbow and the old Dunany townland must have been merged with Carnery to give an enlarged Carnearny. The Down Survey descriptions of Scolvoe and Carnery townlands indicate each contained mountain-top land classed as unprofitable but these mountain tops are now only found in Carnearny. This transfer of the mountain tops may have been done to create land for game for, although the hill-tops are now cloaked with conifers, they were, until the early years of the twentieth century, used for hunting by the Lords Massereene of Antrim Castle who maintained a game-keeper on the mountain. The presence of game and a game-keeper were sources of temptation and aggravation to some of Scolbow's residents. Today the townland name of Dunany survives as Dunany Bog, which forms Scolbow's north-eastern march with Carnearny and Dunany Bridge which marks the boundary of Scolbow with Browndodd.

LANDLORDS AND TENANTS

Successive Bishops of Down and Connor avoided the aggravations and obligations arising from the day to day dealings between landlord and tenant by leasing their church lands in large blocks to local landlords who, in turn, subdivided the land amongst tenant farmers. The farmers of Connor had the same landlord as in the neighbouring parish of Antrim for in 1621 the *Manor and Lands of Connor* were let to Sir Hugh Clotworthy of Antrim for sixty years at a rent of £10. In 1606 the Clotworthy family had obtained the 'Sixteen Towns of Antrim' from Sir Arthur Chichester, so the acquisition of adjacent Connor extended the Clotworthy lands and income. By 1696 the Clotworthy family had merged by marriage into the Skeffingtons and been ennobled as the Lords of Massereene. In that year a twenty-one year lease between Lord Massereene and the Bishop of Down and Connor commenced for the *Territory & Manor of Connor in the County of Antrim containing Sixteen towns* at a rental of £100 per year. Some measure of the profitability of this lease comes from a 1701 account indicating the annual rent from Connor Parish due to his Lordship was £199.50. By 1838 the Connor lease was costing Massereene £493 per year against an annual income of over £3200.

Although Scolbow was part of the Massereene estates from around 1620, it and the other Connor townlands do not appear in the earliest surviving Massereene rent-rolls held in the Public Record Office for Northern Ireland. The first intimation as to who were the residents of Scolbow comes from the Hearth Money Rolls of 1669 which record only six names. As these six were spread over some 1400 acres, covering Carnearny and Dunany, the landscape could only have been sparsely populated. Three were of native Irish stock, Ogan O'Close, Owin O'Murgan and Pat McCluney, and remaining were Robert Meltheram, William

---

TABLE 1

FAMILY NAMES FROM SCOLBOW
Fraction denotes portion of townland farmed

YEAR: 1669 HEARTH MONEY ROLL (INCLUDES CARNEARNEY)	1705 MASSEREENE RENT ROLL	1733 MASSEREENE DUTY BOOK
John Taggart	Jno Taggart (1/3)	John Taggart (1/3)
William Hunter	John Wilson (1/3)	Francis Wilson (1/6)
Robt Maltheram	David Warrick (1/3)	Nathaniel Wilson (1/6)
Pat McCluney		Jim Wilson (1/6)
Ogan O'Close		Andrew Warwick (1/6)
Owin O'Murgan		

YEAR: 1838 ESTATE RENTAL	1844 TITHE RENTAL	1860 POOR LAW VALUATION
William Warwick (1/3)	John Warwick (1/3)	James Warwick (1/3)
David Hay (1/12)	David Hay (1/12)	David Hay (1/12)
Sam McAlonan (1/12)	Sam McAlonan (1/12)	William Barber (1/12)
David Warwick (1/12)	David Warwick (1/12)	Cath. & Sam Warwick (1/12)
James Warwick (1/12)	James Warwick (1/12)	Charles Warwick (1/12)
James Warwick (junr) (1/12)	James Warwick (1/12)	John Warwick (1/12)
William Moore (1/12)	William Moore (1/12)	William Moore (1/12)
John Warwick (1/12)	William Montgomery (1/12)	William Montgomery (1/12)
John Wilson (1/16)	John Wilson (1/16)	James Wilson (1/16)
William O'Neil (1/48)	William O'Neil (1/48)	William O'Neil (1/48)

Hunter and John Taggart (Table 1).

The next listing of the inhabitants of Scolbow comes from a 1705 Massereene rent ledger which refers to the tenants of the *Lower Part of Scolbogh,* but it is not clear what area this refers to. Was it only part of the modern townland now known as Lower Scolbow, or the whole of the modern townland? If it was the whole townland, the *Lower Part* referred to could be an acknowledgement of the contraction of the old townland when part of it had been lost to Carnearny. The 1705 rental does not give the areas rented in either Scolbow or in any of the Connor townlands, as land was allocated as fractions of townlands. This contrasts with the Massereene estates along the Six Mile Water where, although rents are also listed by townlands, the area of each tenancy is usually given, albeit in a mixture of Scotch and Plantation acres.

The 1705 rent-rolls list three tenants in Scolbow: John Wilson, David Warrick and Jno Taggart, which was the sole surname to survive from the 1669 Hearth Roll. There is nothing to suggest that these men were anything other than of Presbyterian stock, a townland religious affiliation that never changed over the years. Each tenant farmed on a twenty year lease, dating from 1696, and their combined annual rent was £10. Another listing of tenants comes from the 1733 Duty Book for the Massereene estates which lists tenants' obligations to the landlord. These were duties due in addition to the rent paid, although as an alternative, the payment of a fine or fee could be made. Tenants of Connor's Sixteen Towns were obliged to provide the landlord with days of work. Other Massereene tenants were additionally required to provide poultry (geese, ducks and capons) to his Lordship's table. For Scolbow in 1733 there was a duty of ten days labour or a fine of two old pence per day missed.

No distinction between Upper and Lower Scolbow is made in the Duty Book, which refers only to Scolbough. The five tenants listed in 1733 shared all the surnames found in 1705, a consistency suggesting that the *Lower part of Scolbogh* referred to in the 1705 rental was in fact the modern townland. The basic townland division of 1705 into three portions also remained in 1733, but two of these portions had been further sub-divided between two tenants. Thus John Taggart received a one-third share, Francis and Nathaniel Wilson shared another one-third portion as did Andrew Warwick and John Wilson.

After 1733, Taggart is not encountered in the records of Scolbow, but Wilsons and Warwicks would continue on to the 1940s. In time, Warwick was to dominate the townland, with five Warwick farms in 1838. Although they are now long gone from Scolbow, Warwicks can still be found in neighbouring townlands and they have a tradition that three or four Warwick brothers arrived from Scotland around 1648. Only one brother was to remain and settle in this district while the others went their own ways. At first they found shelter at a place known as the Black Knoughs near Ballywoodock which is close to Scolbow. However adjacent to Scolbow, in Browndodd townland, the Black Knowes was the name of a Warwick farm for many years, a name which owes perhaps more to family tradition than indicating the precise site of the original Warwick 'home farm' in the district. In the 1666 and 1669 Hearth Money Rolls, Warwicks were not listed as resident in Browndodd and were found only in Ballynoe: John Warrick in 1666 and Adam and John Warrick in 1669.

Lists of Scolbow tenants are absent from 1733 up to 1837, when the Tithe Applotment Book appeared with tenants' names, farm size and tithe payments – hardly a welcome tax to the Presbyterians of Scolbow. After church tithes were abolished, the payment of the new Poor Law rates, which supported the workhouse in Antrim town, cannot have been welcomed with any enthusiasm either. The Griffith's Valuation Survey for 1862 provides maps, rateable values of land and buildings, farm areas and tenant lists. In addition to these, there survives a list of rents due from each tenant in the year of 1838 and a listing of tithe payments and farm areas for 1843. These listings have been used to indicate the sub-division of farms in Scolbow in Table 2.

TABLE 2

SCOLBOW TENANTS, RENTS AND TYTHES AROUND 1840 AND POOR LAW VALUATIONS IN 1862

	TENANT 1838	1838 FARM AREA ACRES	1838 RENT £	1843 TITHE £	TENANT 1843	POOR LAW VALUATION 1862 TOTAL £	LAND £	BUILD-INGS £	FARM AREA ACRES	TENANT 1862
Upper Scolbow	William Warwick	84.0	29.75	1.53	John Warwick	35.50	33.75	2.25	86.6	James Warwick
	David Hay	21.0	8.00	0.41	David Hay	10.50	9.50	1.00	21.3	David Hea
	Sam McAlonan	19.6	6.50	0.33	Sam McAlonan	10.00	9.00	1.00	20.0	William Barber
	David Warwick	21.6	7.90	0.41	David Warwick	10.50	8.00	2.50	20.9	Cath. & Sam. Warwick
	James Warwick	20.3	7.00	0.37	James Warwick	10.00	8.50	1.50	22.0	Charles Warwick
Lower Scolbow	James Warwick (Jnr)	21.4	7.23	0.37	Wm. Montgomery	12.50	11.00	1.50	21.5	John Warwick
	William Moore	22.9	7.35	0.38	William Moore	13.00	11.75	1.25	23.3	William Moore
	John Warwick	28.9	11.13	0.57	James Warwick	17.00	15.00	2.00	29.1	William Montgomery
	John Wilson	16.5	6.00	0.31	John Wilson	8.00	7.00	1.00	17.9	Andrew Wilson
	William O'Neil	5.8	2.00	0.10	William O'Neil	3.50	3.00	0.50	6.1	William O'Neill
Total Upper Scolbow		166.4	59.15	3.06		76.50	68.25	8.25	170.8	
Total Lower Scolbow		95.6	33.70	1.73		54.00	47.75	6.25	97.9	
Total Scolbow		262.0	92.85	4.79		130.50	116.00	14.50	268.6	

By 1837 Upper and Lower Scolbow each had five farms. Those in Upper Scolbow represented 63 per cent or almost the two-thirds of the townland, with Lower Scolbow having the remaining third. Whether the superior farm size of Upper Scolbow over Lower Scolbow formed a factual basis of Bonar Thompson's reference at the start of this chapter to the 'vaunting superiority' of Upper Scolbow over Lower Scolbow remains open to speculation. In Upper Scolbow, the four smaller farms were almost identical in area, at around 20 acres each. Taken

SCOLBOW

together, their area therefore equals in size and value the remaining farm in Upper Scolbow of some 86 acres. This farm represents in turn about a third of the townland. Thus, we have the basic division of the townland into three parts found in the 1705 rent ledger persisting in 1837. However in the intervening period considerable sub-division of land had taken place. Only one farm, listed in 1733 for John Taggart as occupying a full one-third portion, and farmed in 1837 by John Warwick of Upper Scolbow, appears to have survived intact. The remaining two-thirds of the townland had been subdivided into eight farms each with about one-twelfth of the townland.

There was one exception to this neat sub-division for, sometime between 1831 and 1837, six acres of land from William Wilson's one-twelfth portion in Lower Scolbow was used to create the small holding of William O'Neill. The holdings of Wilson and O'Neill listed in 1837 together make 23 acres, the same total as

Figure 3

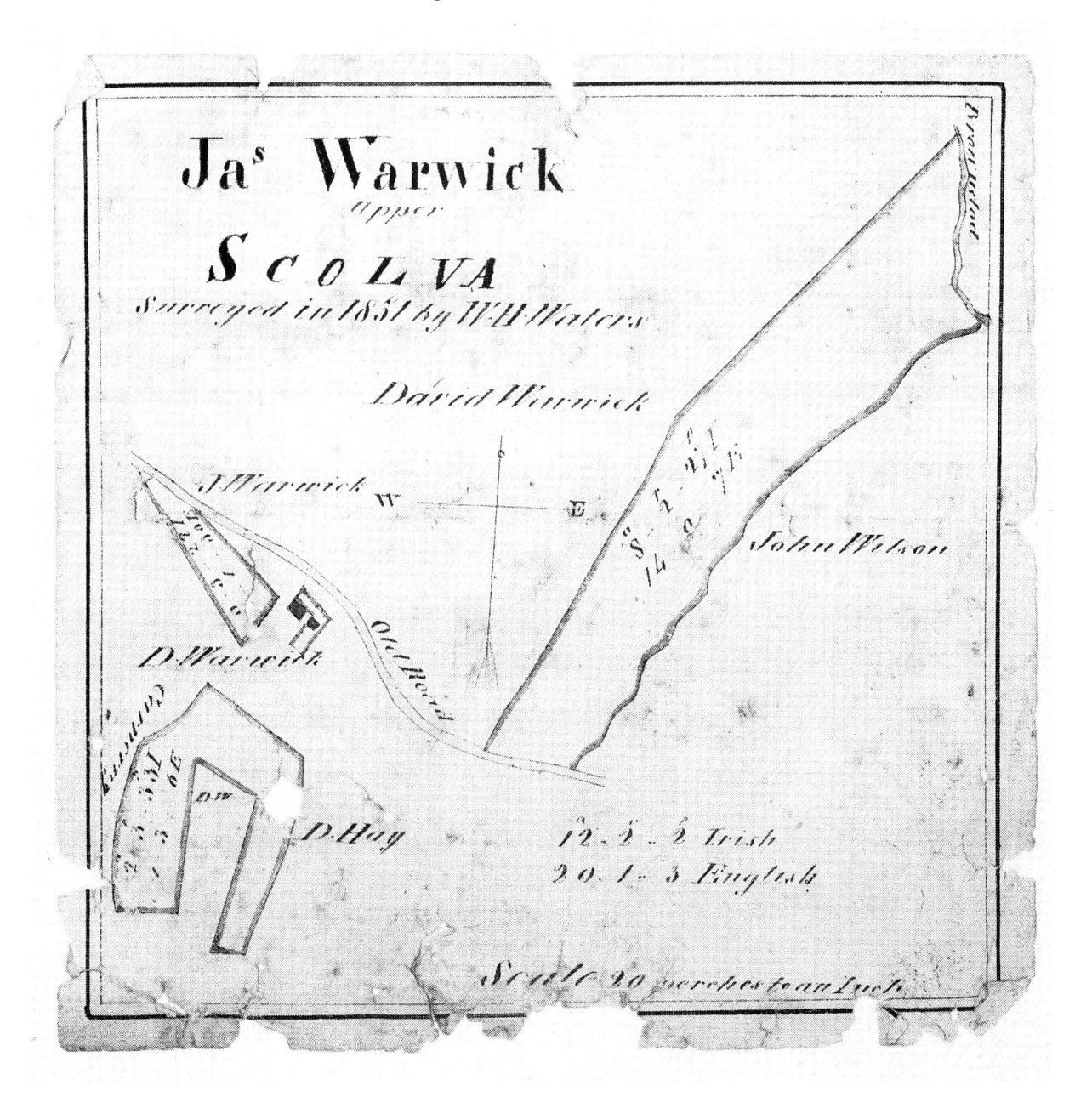

for two other farms in Lower Scolbow. However, if the division of Lower Scolbow, as a third of the townland, had been into four equal holdings, it would be expected that the remaining farm, tenanted by John Warwick in 1837 and William Montgomery in 1862, should also be around 23 acres. Why it is somewhat larger, at 28 acres, suggests at least one uneven partition of land.

William O'Neill's is the only instance of land sub-division which can be identified after 1811 and it can be said with certainty that none took place after 1837. When O'Neill's farm was created can be inferred from successive maps of a Warwick farm in Upper Scolbow drawn in 1811, 1831 and 1858. Each map gives the names of neighbouring farms and in the 1858 map O'Neill is shown as a neighbouring farmer but not on either of the 1811 or 1831 maps when the number of neighbouring tenants was one less than in 1858. These differences mean that no sub-division had taken place in 1831 but, by the time of the Tithe Applotment Book in 1837, the farm of William O'Neill had appeared. With this admittedly scanty evidence for the consistency of neighbouring farms shown on the 1811 and 1831 maps, it appears that the townland sub-division had largely been completed by 1811.

Scolbow land is of uneven quality and some ingenuity was required to ensure that each tenant got a fair share of good and poor land. This resulted in a complex distribution of land as shown in the division and quality of land in 1860 (Fig. 4). The quality of land can be judged from its rateable value and the poorest, valued at an annual rent of around 30p per acre, is to the north and east. The best quality land on the south facing slope between the two clachans was worth up to 89p per acre. In Upper Scolbow, where the contrast in land quality was greatest, each farm possessed one portion of poor quality land which, in the farm of James Warwick, was a narrow strip of land (Fig. 3).

The simplest layout was for the largest farm, John Warwick's in Upper Scolbow, which had escaped sub-division. It consisted of two regularly shaped pieces of land, whereas the much smaller farm of James Warwick in Upper Scolbow had two parcels of good land plus one of poor land. In three other farms, the arable land was subdivided into two (Fig. 4). This suggests that, when a farm was sub-divided, the arable land was allocated with some care, so that each of the new holdings shared in the very best of it as well as some of not-quite-so-good quality. This pattern of division has elements of the Irish rundale or Scottish runrig system of farming and was associated with clachan settlements typified by Upper and Lower Scolbow.

Early records of social conditions specifically relating to Scolbow are more or less absent. The note-book accompanying the first poor law valuation of 1833 noted that the townland had no peat bogs for fuel within a distance of three miles, but that the inhabitants cut 'screw turf', the peaty top soil found in the wetter parts of the townland. Passing references to mortality at Scolbow concern the Warwick and Hay families of Scolbow in the 1830s and their minister, Robert Magill of the Mill Row Presbyterian meeting house in Antrim. Magill had a strong interest in medicine and genealogy and his record of family genealogies of

Figure 4
A comparison of land values and farm holdings in Scolbow in 1860. The lighter shades of the upper map denote land of diminishing quality and lower rental valuations. The lower map shows how the land was divided between the 10 tenant farms. The hatched line denotes the boundary between Upper and Lower Scolbow farms. These maps were created from Arcview GIS and are based on the 1859 Poor Law Valuation and OS maps

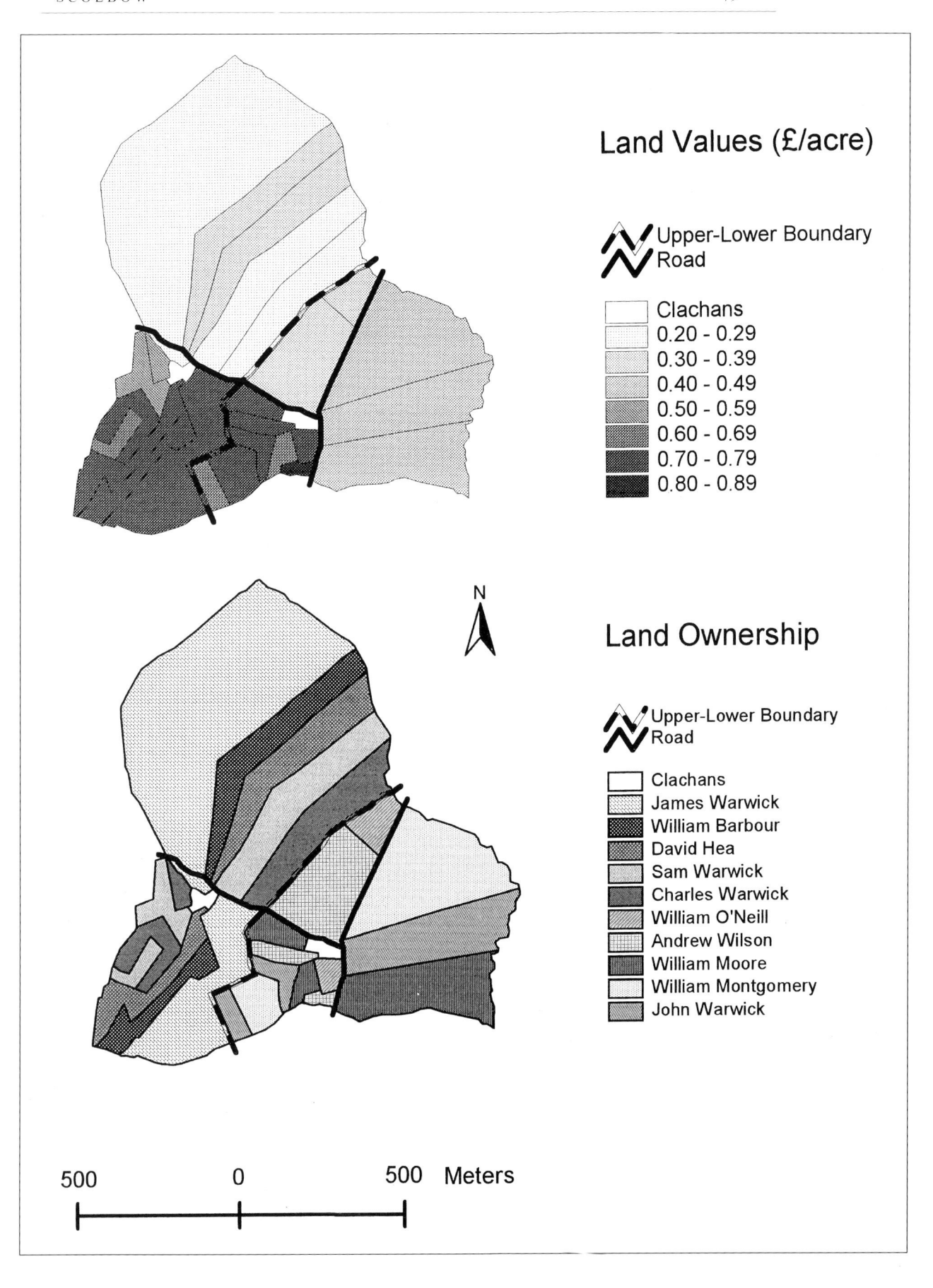

Land Values (£/acre)

Upper-Lower Boundary
Road

- Clachans
- 0.20 - 0.29
- 0.30 - 0.39
- 0.40 - 0.49
- 0.50 - 0.59
- 0.60 - 0.69
- 0.70 - 0.79
- 0.80 - 0.89

Land Ownership

Upper-Lower Boundary
Road

- Clachans
- James Warwick
- William Barbour
- David Hea
- Sam Warwick
- Charles Warwick
- William O'Neill
- Andrew Wilson
- William Moore
- William Montgomery
- John Warwick

500 0 500 Meters

the Mill Row congregation notes that Patrick Warwick, an infant son of Andrew and Eliza Warwick, died of the small pox in 1832. To what degree this highly contagious disease left its mark, either literally or through death, on others in Scolbow is not known. However the Rev. Magill was not a passive bystander in this matter for in the 1820s his diaries show that he was personally carrying out the inoculation of children in Antrim with cow-pox to provide them with immunity against the much more deadly small-pox. Another stealthy killer was operating in Scolbow for Mary-Ann Hay had died of consumption shortly before her tenth birthday. Otherwise infant mortality was little in evidence for both these families. Patrick Warwick was the only one of ten children to die young, while Mary-Ann Hay was the only casualty of nine children. An indication of the affection and esteem a minister could be held is evident from the fact that David and Margaret Hay chose to christen a son Robert Magill Hay and a daughter Ann Jane Magill Hay, her Christian names being the name of Magill's wife, Ann Jane.

Although the Great Famine swept through Ireland between 1845 and 1851, it had no discernible impact on the tenancies of the Scolbow farms, for no farms were merged nor did any tenancies change hands. Alongside the farmers in Scolbow there was a humbler class of tenant: the landless labourers or cottiers who lived in two-roomed cabins or cottages. As under-tenants to farmers for

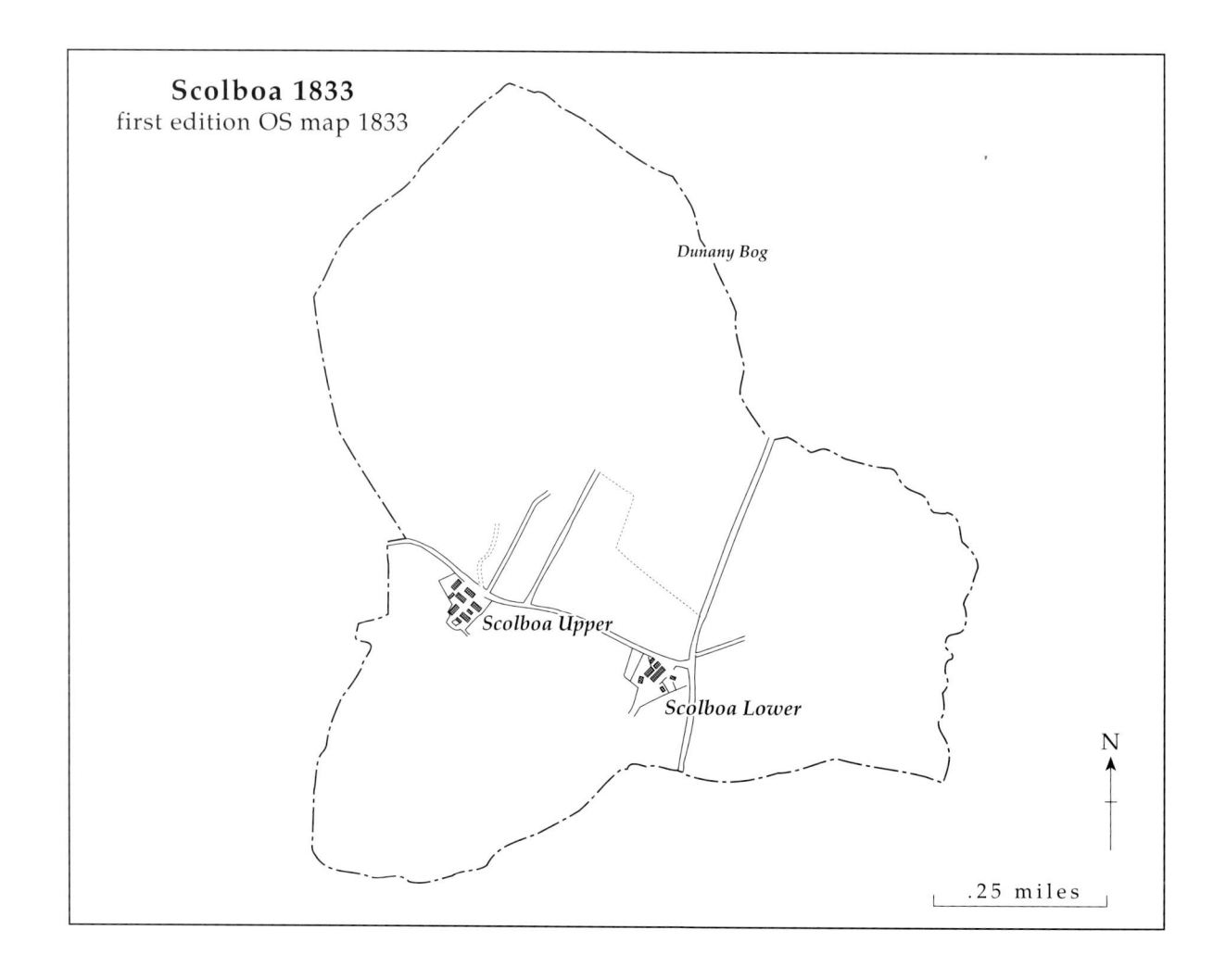

Scolboa 1833
first edition OS map 1833

Dunany Bog

Scolboa Upper

Scolboa Lower

N

.25 miles

whom they worked, they can easily be overlooked for, without land of their own, they did not pay any tithes. However, as a class they never appeared to have been very numerous in Scolbow. The 1841 census lists fifteen houses occupied compared to ten farms, suggesting five labourers' cottages. By the close of the Famine in 1851, the difference between farms and houses in Scolbow was only reduced by one to four. A survey of the entries to the workhouse in Antrim town shows only a handful of admissions from the whole of the parish of Connor during the Famine years. Given the severe means test which paupers seeking admission to the workhouse had to satisfy, the evidence is that the conditions of abject destitution seen in the west of the Antrim Poor Law Union did not touch Scolbow during the Famine.

Nonetheless, the Famine decade saw the largest recorded population decline in Scolbow, with a reduction of sixteen between 1841 and 1851, most likely from emigration. In this respect the Famine decade provides a landmark in the history of the townland, for it was the beginning of the end of Scolbow. From this decade onwards, a period of population decline began which was to continue to 1991. In percentage terms, the 18% population decline between 1841 and 1851 was exceeded in subsequent decades: 23% between 1871 and 1881, 20% between 1881 and 1891, and 26% between 1901 and 1911. Initially only cottier houses were abandoned so that none of these remained in Scolbow by 1891. Only between 1881 and 1891 was the first farmhouse abandoned.

TABLE 3

SCOLBOA, parish of Connor, DED of Connor, union of Antrim, rural district of Antrim, barony of Lower Antrim, county of Antrim

YEAR	INHABITANTS MALES FEMALES TOTAL	HOUSES INHAB UNINHAB BUILDING TOTAL
1841	46 + 44 = 90	15 + 1 + 0 = 16
1851	39 + 35 = 74	14 + 0 + 0 = 14
1861	39 + 33 = 72	12 + 0 + 0 = 12
1871	35 + 27 = 62	13 + 0 + 0 = 13
1881	23 + 23 = 46	11 + 0 + 0 = 11
1891	22 + 14 = 36	8 + 1 + 0 = 9
1901	18 + 13 = 31	8 + 1 + 0 = 9
1911	16 + 7 = 23	6 + 2 + 0 = 8
1926	8 + 11 = 19	5 + 0 + 0 = 5
1937	3 + 9 = 12	4 + 1 + 0 = 5
1951	na = 8	na = 4
1961	4 + 2 = 6	4 + 0 + 0 = 4
1971	4 + 4 = 8	4 + 0 + 0 = 4
1981	1 + 1 = 2	1 + 3 + 0 = 4
1991	1 + 0 = 1	1 + 0 + 0 = 1

The occupants of the small cottages are not only easily overlooked but are also difficult to identify. Who were they, what did they do? Their connections with the particular area were often short-lived as they moved on to better opportunities. A few are recorded in the Poor Law valuation records, while other names of this forgotten part of the community turn up in the rolls of Lady Hill National School. Children from Scolbow resorted to the one-roomed schoolhouse at Ladyhill from 1848 while before that there was a Sunday School at Ballynoe. Amidst the Warwicks and Wilsons in the Ladyhill school rolls, other names appear: Sarah and Jane Scroggy attended between 1874 and 1885. Their father is listed as a labourer from Scolbow, as was the father of Martha English who attended for a year in 1892 when aged eight. Other cottier homes were headed by women. In 1862 Elizabeth Johnston was renting a small cottage from William O'Neill, whose own farm of six acres can hardly have supported a family. Who this Elizabeth was we do not know, a widowed sister perhaps. Eliza Moore at school, aged seven in 1884, was the daughter of a charwoman from Scolbow; often this was the only occupation open to the single female who did not have the trade of dressmaking to rely on.

A glimpse into this largely anonymous world of women comes from the pen of Bonar Thompson who was born in Carnearny, at the end of the lane which winds its way past Upper Scolbow from Lower Scolbow. Thompson's mother, Matilda Bonar, was not married when she gave birth in 1888 at the age of eighteen. She left her child to the care of her Aunt Eliza Thompson and departed to find work in Belfast and Manchester. Bonar Thompson thought Aunt Eliza was always old; not surprisingly as she was forty-nine when she began to look after her infant nephew. The census record of her household in 1901, describes her as a dressmaker but Thompson described her source of income as a few hens, while a goat was kept for milk. Also sharing her two-roomed cottage in 1901 was an elderly sister-in-law and widow, Jane Thompson who was eighty-six years of age, and listed as a linen weaver. It was Aunt Eliza who was to feature strongly in Thompson's autobiographical *Hyde Park Orator,* published in 1933. Although his account was not unkind, his over-emphasis on his former neighbours' weaknesses and eccentricities did not find much favour with them.

Aunt Eliza's damp two-roomed cottage formed part of a clachan. That family relationships in that part of County Antrim were not always straightforward and often too close, may be judged from the fact that Aunt Eliza's neighbour was John Bonar, the former master of Ladyhill School, an uncle of Bonar Thompson's mother. With the Master lived his sister, Mrs Bambridge and her son John Bambridge, who was, in turn, Bonar Thompson's own father and his mother's cousin. Thompson complained that his great misfortune was not to be born out of wedlock but out of pocket. His birth register name of John Bonar credits him with his mother's surname, his Ladyhill school register (1895) records him as John Bambridge, as does the 1901 population census, presumably for the father who disowned him. In a Manchester courtroom of 1906 he was John Bonar

Thompson to be followed by Bonar Thompson who resided in London where he was, as he put it, famous a number of times. The following descriptions of the circumstances of his birth and also of Scolbow in the 1890s are taken from *Speaking for Myself* and a chapter *Dayspring Mishandled*.

> I was conveyed, furtively and surreptitiously and bundled hastily and unceremoniously into the smaller of the two damp, musty, earthen-floored rooms of a dilapidated cottage at the foot of Carnearny mountain.... From the moth-eaten door of Aunt Eliza's injurious cottage, a powerful and skilful stone-thrower might have thrown a stone half way to Upper Scolbow. Upper Scolbow had three farmhouses, built of stone and with roofs roughly thatched, that were occupied by farmers and their families. A difficult, narrow declivity led to Lower Scolbow where farm people lived in four houses of a similar description, except that one was white washed on the outside and was slated. They were quite decent friendly souls; but there were no children in any of these villages and I would have no playmates to associate with of my own size or weight.

A characteristic of Bonar Thompson's descriptions of his boyhood in Scolbow and Carnearny is that none of them is completely accurate. So it is with the above passage, for the census of 1901 records that although there were three occupied houses in Upper Scolbow, plus one unoccupied, there were five not four houses in Lower Scolbow. The census also records that only four houses, one in Upper Scolbow and three in Lower Scolbow were thatched – the remainder were slated! It is in the final and accurate sentence of the above extract, bemoaning the absence of children, which gives warning of the impending demise of Upper and Lower Scolbow.

Decent farming folk
BONAR THOMPSON

'Farmer' was the most common fathers' occupation given for the children at Ladyhill School, but one Warwick family from Lower Scolbow was an exception to this, as it included a tailor for at least two generations. An indenture survives from 1867 binding John Gawn of Carnearny to serve an apprenticeship to be a tailor with Arthur Warwick of Scolbow. Arthur's son George was also carrying on this trade when the 1901 census was taken, while another son, Thomas, was apprenticed to a draper. Of the remaining adults in the 1901 census, most were listed as farmers, farm servants or labourers. Exceptions were Eliza Warwick of Upper Scolbow who had returned to Ladyhill School as a work-mistress. Her cousin Frank Gibb was living at Scolbow while working as a stone mason, probably in one of the nearby Tardree stone quarries.

SCOLBO, parish of Connor   VAL/1B/12

		QUANTITY	RATE PER STATUTE ACRE	AMOUNT
1	Green pasture part with heath + moss	47a 1r 36p	4s 6d	£10 13s 7d
2	Rather shallow arable with some moory spots (elevated)	12a 0r 13p	7s 6d	4 10s 8d
3	Coarse green + rushy moory pasture	30a 2r 9p	5s 3d	8 0s 4d
	also coarse arable	2a	7s 6d	15s
4	Mixed arable (very poor)	18a 0r 14p	6s 6d	5 17s 6d
	Medium arable	2a	9s 6d	19s
	Rushy pasture	1a	3s	3s
5	Dry green pasture	20a 0r 3p	4s 6d	4 10s 1d
6	Good green pasture with a part inferior	63a 3r 3p	6s 3d	21 9s 9d
	also arable	1a	8s	8s
7	Mixed qualities of soft arable highly situated and exposed	41a 0r 5p	10s 6d	21 12s 1d
	also Shallow arable on rock	3r	7s 6d	5s 7d
	also House waste	1a 0r 10p		
	also Good deep soft arable	11a	12s 9d	7 0s 3d
8	Cold arable and meadow	11a 2r 24p	8s 6d	4 19s
		268a 2r 19p		91 3s 10d

There are no houses in this townland worth £5 a year

Alex Woffington, Baronial Valuator, 4 June 1835
Dennis Freeman, Assistant Valuator
R Wynne, Assistant Valuator, replaced by Anthony McCullagh by 19 March 1836

Turf distant 3 miles, lime 8 miles: no turbary in this townland but scraw turf are cut... Scolbo is divided into three divisions - John Warwick holds one third at £30; the second is held by sundry persons having separate leases, paying altogether about £30; the third division pays a little above £30. [on separate page of same volume]

SCOLBOW

TOWNLAND VALUATION (1835)

Scolboa lies on a south-facing spur of Carnearney mountain near the road from Parkgate to Connor. As most of Scolboa lies above the 600 foot contour and contains little fertile land, it is surprising to find it occupied by farmers as early as the mid 17th century. Only the 52 acres in (7), which contains both the house clusters of Upper and Lower Scolboa, were valued at more than 50p per acre.

It is unusual for the Townland Valuation to contain information about the farms: 'Scolbo is divided into three divisions - John Warwick holds one third at £30; the second is held by sundry persons having separate leases, paying altogether about £30; the third division pays a little above £30.'
The 1831 map by W.H. Waters of James Warwick's holding shows the layout of this farm–WHC.

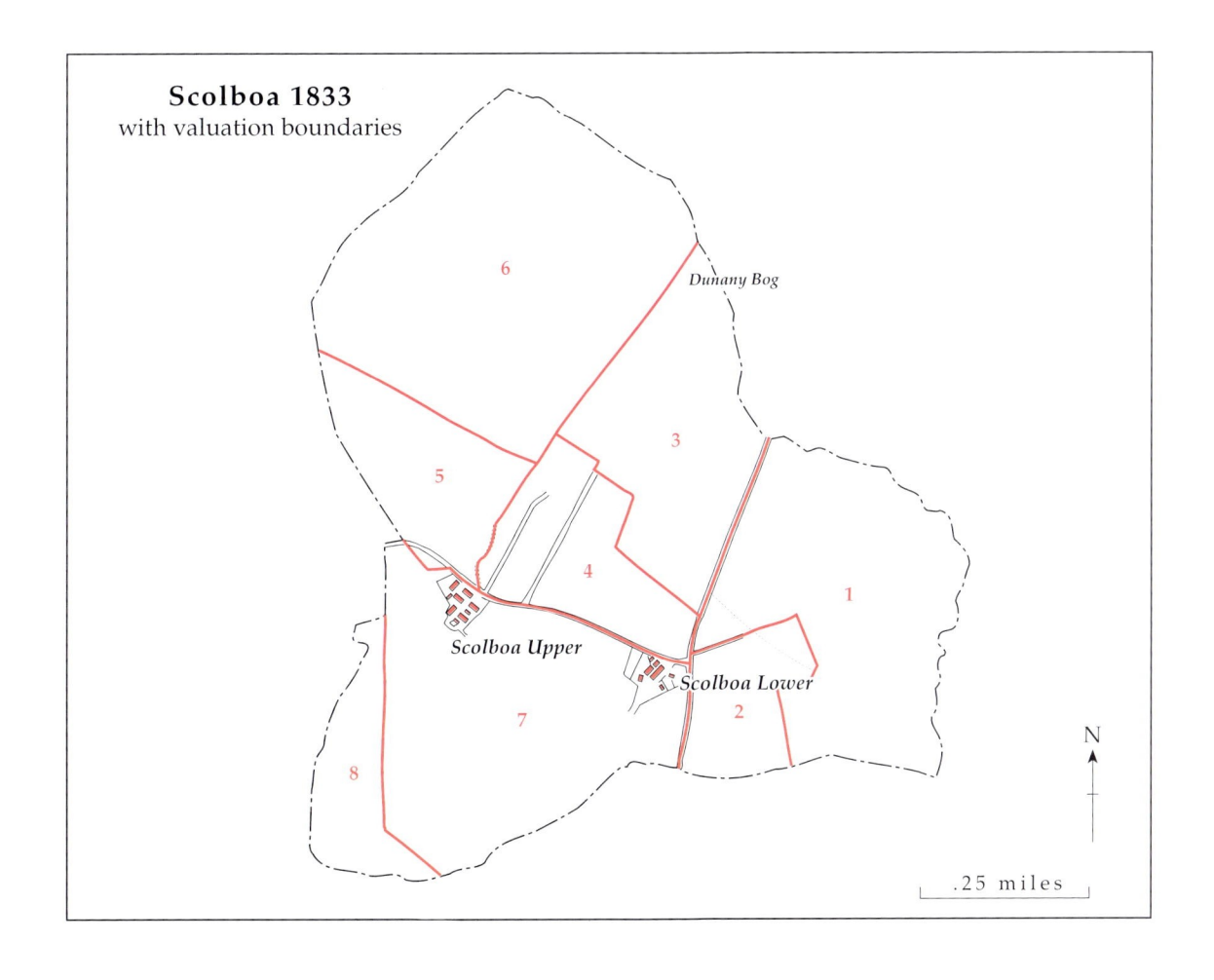

Scolboa 1833 with valuation boundaries

Scolboa
revised edition OS map 1859

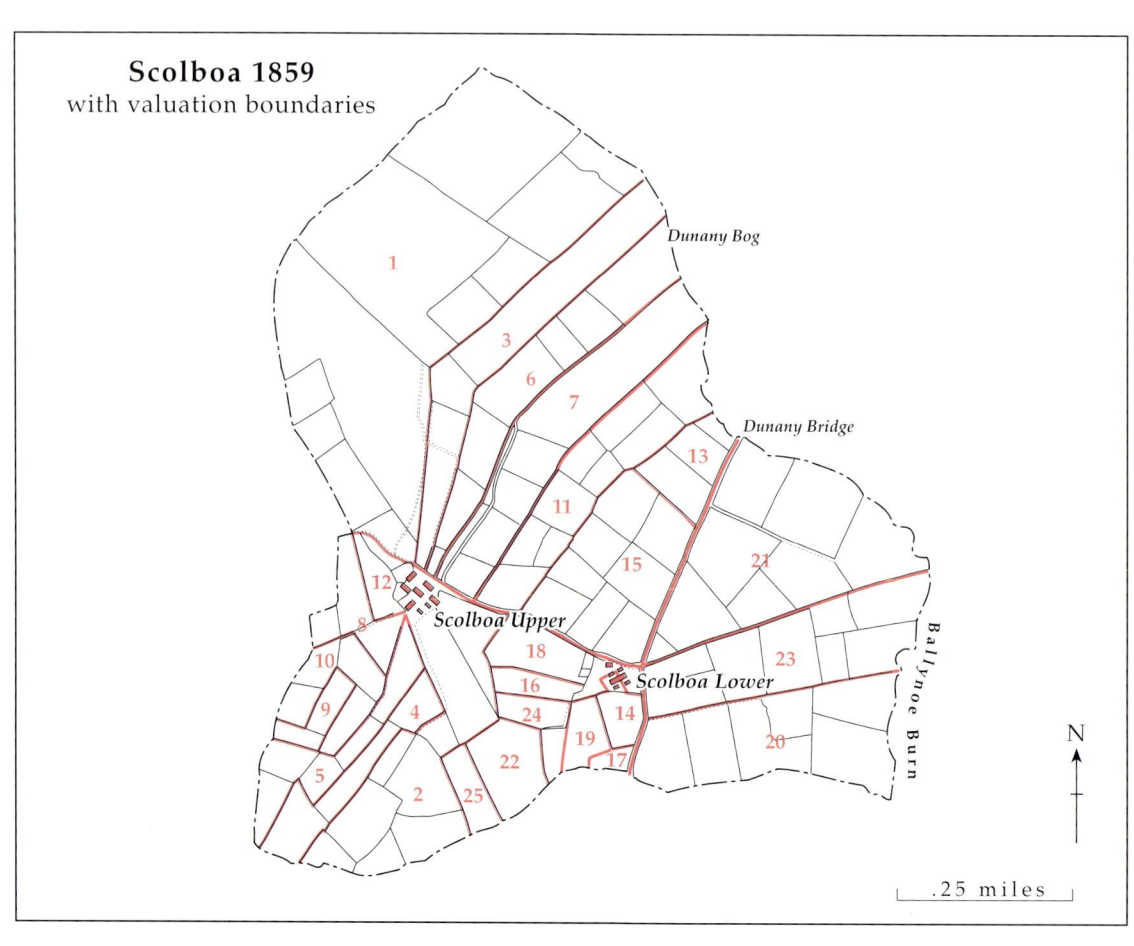

.25 miles

Scolboa 1859
with valuation boundaries

.25 miles

Thompson to be followed by Bonar Thompson who resided in London where he was, as he put it, famous a number of times. The following descriptions of the circumstances of his birth and also of Scolbow in the 1890s are taken from *Speaking for Myself* and a chapter *Dayspring Mishandled*.

> I was conveyed, furtively and surreptitiously and bundled hastily and unceremoniously into the smaller of the two damp, musty, earthen-floored rooms of a dilapidated cottage at the foot of Carnearny mountain.... From the moth-eaten door of Aunt Eliza's injurious cottage, a powerful and skilful stone-thrower might have thrown a stone half way to Upper Scolbow. Upper Scolbow had three farmhouses, built of stone and with roofs roughly thatched, that were occupied by farmers and their families. A difficult, narrow declivity led to Lower Scolbow where farm people lived in four houses of a similar description, except that one was white washed on the outside and was slated. They were quite decent friendly souls; but there were no children in any of these villages and I would have no playmates to associate with of my own size or weight.

A characteristic of Bonar Thompson's descriptions of his boyhood in Scolbow and Carnearny is that none of them is completely accurate. So it is with the above passage, for the census of 1901 records that although there were three occupied houses in Upper Scolbow, plus one unoccupied, there were five not four houses in Lower Scolbow. The census also records that only four houses, one in Upper Scolbow and three in Lower Scolbow were thatched – the remainder were slated! It is in the final and accurate sentence of the above extract, bemoaning the absence of children, which gives warning of the impending demise of Upper and Lower Scolbow.

Decent farming folk

BONAR THOMPSON

'Farmer' was the most common fathers' occupation given for the children at Ladyhill School, but one Warwick family from Lower Scolbow was an exception to this, as it included a tailor for at least two generations. An indenture survives from 1867 binding John Gawn of Carnearny to serve an apprenticeship to be a tailor with Arthur Warwick of Scolbow. Arthur's son George was also carrying on this trade when the 1901 census was taken, while another son, Thomas, was apprenticed to a draper. Of the remaining adults in the 1901 census, most were listed as farmers, farm servants or labourers. Exceptions were Eliza Warwick of Upper Scolbow who had returned to Ladyhill School as a work-mistress. Her cousin Frank Gibb was living at Scolbow while working as a stone mason, probably in one of the nearby Tardree stone quarries.

For long periods during the summer I was away from school, working in the fields. My aunt loaned me out to the neighbouring farmers

BONAR THOMPSON

Frequent absences ensured that many a child in the nineteenth century attending Ladyhill National School received a fragmented, if extended, schooling. For the very youngest, poor attendances in the winter were accompanied by entries in the school roll-book such as 'too cold' or 'kept at home'. As the children got older, winter attendances improved but were countered by more frequent spring, summer and autumn absences which were marked with the ubiquitous 'Returned to work at home'. To compensate, pupils often continued their education well into their late teens and Alex O'Neill of Lower Scolbow was still enrolled at the age of eighteen. Under Master John Bonar, these periods of extra tuition extended from December to March when there was little farm work to be done at home.

The school roll also gives some indication of the destination for those pupils who did not see their future in agriculture. Francis Warwick left to learn grocery at the age of seventeen in 1865. Eliza Warwick left in 1869 to 'learn the art of dressmaking in Antrim'. Two pupils of the same age named James Warwick attended Ladyhill in the 1860s and were distinguished in the rolls as Scolbow Upper and Scolbow Lower. Lower Scolbow James left school at the age of eighteen on grounds of ill-health but Upper Scolbow James was noted to have 'gone to Carrickfergus' in 1863 at the age of twelve. This was to pursue a higher level of education and live with his uncle, the Rev James Warwick, a Presbyterian minister living in Carrickfergus. A surviving letter sent by the Rev James to his brother Charles in Upper Scolbow records the unfortunate pupil going home to 'let the tailor get his measure for his clothes and for a day or two to recruit, as I am afraid that his health won't stand the sea air – as you can see by his right eye he is a little inflamed.' The tailor referred to was most likely Arthur Warwick.

The Rev James Warwick spent his clerical career at Joymount Presbyterian Church in Carrickfergus, of which he was the first minister. Not all his energies were devoted to clerical duties and, in his letter to his brother of 1865, one of these interests becomes apparent. After commenting on his nephew's attainments at Latin, he asks Charles 'Have you got any additional spare cash that you could lend me, £30 or £40 if I were to buy another vessel? I have thoughts of buying another but I might be deficient a little...'. This interest or obsession with shipping had earlier come to my notice when I was looking for details of a ship captain from Antrim in the records of Lloyds of London which are held in the National Maritime Museum. There, I was astounded to find a reference to James Warwick of Scolbow (*sic*) House, Carrickfergus who was being prosecuted in 1867 for a breach of rules relating to insuring a ship. This interest in shipping extended to the harbour of Carrickfergus and the Rev Warwick's obituary records 'there was no more enthusiastic advocate of the scheme [to build new harbour works] or eloquent exponent of its advantages'. The same obituary recorded his 'frank and cordial manner, Presbyterian convictions but catholic interests'.

Despite this, there was a rougher side to Warwick's character. When he proposed to establish Sullatubber National School in Carrickfergus, he fell foul of the senior Presbyterian minister in Carrick, the Rev James White, who had presumed to take the lead in education matters in the town. White's objections to Warwick's application to establish a National School are said to have led to Rev Warwick to arrange for the building of a terrace of houses opposite the manse of the Rev White, blocking out his view. Whatever the truth behind this allegation, the plans for this building project survive in the Public Record Office and show that the Rev Warwick had purchased one of the houses. Another of the Rev Warwick's requests to his brother Charles in his letter of 1865 shows evidence of a meanness of spirit and almost brutality in his assessment of some of the women of his native district. Writing that his servant would soon be leaving, he asks his brother if he 'knew a respectable, quiet, well conducted woman who would answer [as a replacement], if none about you, there might be one about where Andrew lives that would answer as it is a backward, out of the way place and few requiring servants there – If she did not know much she would soon learn – She must be a Presbyterian or Protestant of some sort'.

said he would 'law' witness out of Scolbow

REPORT OF EVIDENCE WILSON VS. LATIMER 1899

Clachan life can appear attractive with images of self-reliance and neighbouring co-operation, attributes undoubtedly strengthened by the close ties of family and kinship which characterised 'villages' such as Upper and Lower Scolbow. Leaving aside the image of Bonar Thompson living on the slender means of his spinster aunt while his father John Bambridge disowned him but lived in comparative comfort in the next house, there were ample opportunities for friction to develop, especially as the houses and cottages sat cheek by jowl. So it was in Scolbow, where some houses were separated by a lane of around ten feet wide – narrower than found in the back-streets of Victorian Belfast. Examination of the *Ballymena Observer* in the late nineteenth century provides ample evidence of many rural disputes in the countryside revolving around four themes: interfering with land drainage, rights of way or trespass and attempts by outraged fathers to obtain maintenance payments for the unplanned pregnancies of their daughters. Solicitors in Ballymena had a reputation for encouraging complainants to resort to law and they developed an entertaining line in cross-examination which filled many newspaper columns. But even by the litigious standards of Mid-Antrim, the vigour with which two Lower Scolbow families pursued a dispute from 1897 to 1899 was remarkable. It involved visits to Petty Sessions, Quarter Sessions and the County Assizes. These visits did not come cheap, for they required the services of two solicitors, two Queen's Counsel, two supporting counsel, a civil engineer and a professor of chemistry. All to be paid from the resources of two twenty acre farms.

James Latimer and his family moved to Lower Scolbow in the mid 1890s and soon took exception to a drain which flowed into their house in wet weather. The drain ran from a stack-yard where his neighbour John Wilson kept pigs. Latimer's attempts to block the offending drain led to violence, both verbal and physical. Blows were exchanged, a graip fork produced and a rafter employed as a weapon during a running battle which lasted throughout an afternoon between the extended Latimer family on one side and John Wilson, Alex and Mary Ellen O'Neill on the other. The Latimers received small fines. At another court Wilson sought redress for the blocked drain, but won only small damages. Battle then resumed, when names were called, blows exchanged and stones thrown, after which John Wilson received a small fine. Latimer's chickens soon took centre stage and were found dead after trespassing on Wilson's manure heap. They, so the chemistry professor found, had been poisoned by ground match heads – a poison common, it was alleged, in the west of Ireland but not in Ulster. Latimer's daughter alleged she heard the crime being hatched in Wilson's byre but Latimer failed to win his case. Wilson then sued Latimer for slander at the County Antrim Assizes on the Crumlin Road, Belfast where the Judge was outraged at having to hear such a case. The jury were also not impressed for they awarded Wilson a farthing in damages.

For time speeds swiftly nowadays bearing us fearfully to join the anonymous hosts which throng oblivion

BONAR THOMPSON

The twentieth century saw continued depopulation at Scolbow. Farms which had remained intact throughout the nineteenth century, began to be amalgamated into larger units – a process summarised in the chart of farms from 1810 to 1970 (Figure 5). Charlie Warwick died in 1894 and left his farm to his daughter Eliza Clark of Ballynoe. Eliza's brother, James, who had gone to his uncle James in Carrickfergus for his education, had pre-deceased his father at the age of thirty-three. Sam Clark farmed his wife's inheritance as an out-farm for about twelve years before selling to 'Big Margaret' Warwick of Upper Scolbow in 1915. In 1899 another farm house was vacant and was pulled down when William Barber left, the land becoming an out-farm of the MacAlonans who lived in neighbouring Carnearny and had the tenancy of it from Lord Massereene since 1838. Jane O'Neill sold to James Hay of Upper Scolbow in 1909, who then sold this land to William Wilson of Lower Scolbow in 1921. The Latimers ended their brief, but eventful, stay in Lower Scolbow in 1919 giving way to their Montgomery neighbours in Lower Scolbow.

After 1945 William Wilson sold his expanded farm to Sam Montgomery of Marymount in Antrim thus ending a Wilson connection with Scolbow which had endured for around 250 years. The Warwick connection in Upper Scolbow had ceased a decade earlier when Sam Warwick left Scolbow. James Hay now owned a large farm in Upper Scolbow of 105 acres, having bought the 86 acre farm of James Warwick who had left by 1911. Although married, James Hay had no children and, on his death, his farm passed to Sam Montgomery of Marymount, near Antrim, who now owned all of the land which had formerly been farmed from Upper Scolbow. Sam Montgomery and his son William did not move to Scolbow but farmed the land as an out-farm.

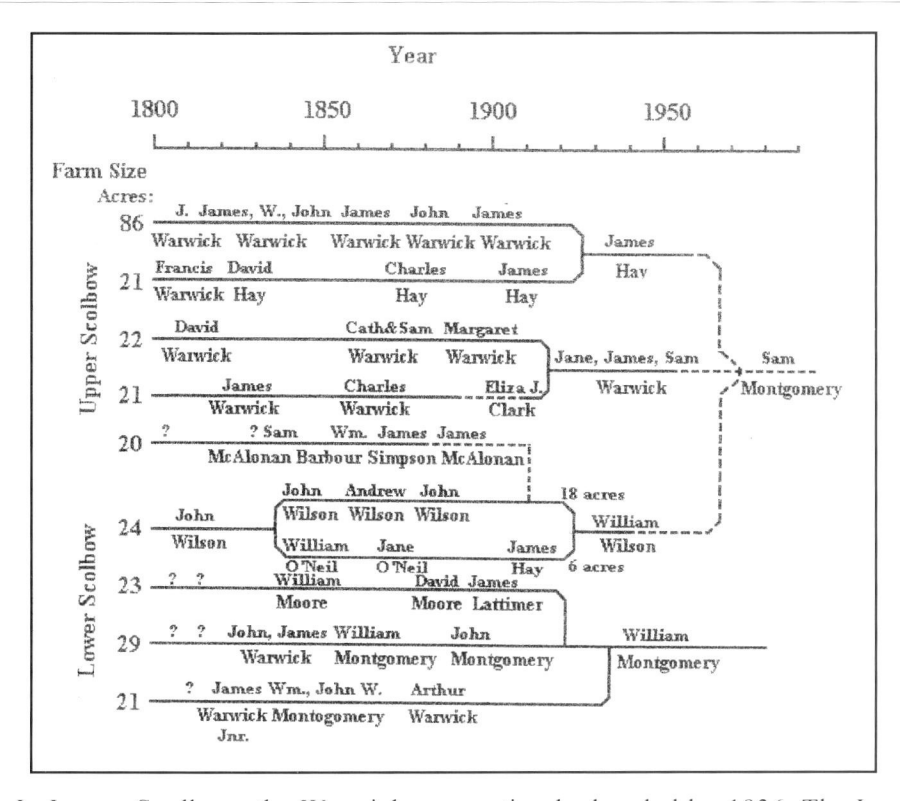

In Lower Scolbow, the Warwick connection had ended by 1936. The Lower Scolbow farms were now owned by a separate and unrelated Montgomery family descended from William, who moved from Ballywoodock when his relation John Montgomery of Lower Scolbow died. His son, also William, continued to farm, albeit from a modern house which faces the county road rather than in the Lower Scolbow clachan. He never married and, when he died in 1997, his nephew, also William Montgomery, took over the farm. He now lives there with his family. At the same time the other William Montgomery, who now owned Upper Scolbow, let the land to his name-sake in Lower Scolbow. Thus something has happened which has not occurred since well before the first Hearth Money Rolls in 1666; Scolbow is farmed in 1998 as a single farm unit.

At the end of the period of population decline, new housing came to Scolbow – not in the traditional clachan settlement but along the Ballynoe Road where it passes through Scolbow. This public road obtained its name in the mid 1970s as part of the road naming initiative promoted by the Royal Mail and local councils. It is a reflection of the decline of Scolbow at that time, that the road was not given the name by which it was known previously – the Scolbow Road – the road which went to Scolbow. The location of the new housing in Scolbow owes much to planning regulations rather than familial attachments to the townland, as Scolbow marks the end of the Antrim green belt. Beyond its imaginary line the regulations governing new houses are less stringent.

Why the decline which has led effectively to the oblivion of both Upper and Lower Scolbow? Given today's economic climate for agriculture, the whole townland could not support more than two economically viable full-time farms and there are good reasons to suppose that this may be a bit optimistic. In part the decline must be chance, for if James Hay had had a family, his family farm could have survived in Upper Scolbow. Other reasons for the decline have been proposed. Samuel Bell analysed changes in population in Scolbow and neighbouring townlands and found that the population decline was greatest at higher altitudes. In other words their harsher climate and remoteness from services such as schools, public transport and shops made them less attractive places to live. Even in 1901 there was some evidence to support this for the households in Scolbow had a curiously marginal or discordant air to them: only two of the nine consisted of the conventional nuclear family unit, with husband and wife and children living under the same roof.

The trials associated with having James Hay as a neighbour played their part. He and his wife were remembered fondly by some for their hospitality, but James left behind a reputation as a difficult neighbour. Despite being a Justice of the Peace he was once found wrestling on the road. He took one of his neighbours to court over a disputed drain while another gave Hay as his reason for his selling out. The right-of-way past Upper Scolbow to farms in Carnearny passed the well which served Upper Scolbow. Despite being marked as an *Old Road* on a 1831 farm map and *Public Road* on an 1858 map, Hay did not grant passage rights easily and on occasion tried to insist that cattle should only pass when led by a halter. A man working on the Hay house is reputed to have asked Mrs Hay if she had had a family. Replying in the negative, she asked did the questioner not think that two Hays were enough.

So in 1998 the Scolbows are quiet. The passing years have seen the progressive destruction of former homes so that only the roofless ruin of Big Margaret Warwick's home still stands. The varied assortment of farm buildings recorded in the censuses of 1901 and 1911 are mostly gone. Their destruction was required to accommodate the needs of modern farm machinery, cattle houses and silos, or maliciously, as happened in 1994 when a fire was lit in the deserted home of James Hay. Hedges, which carefully subdivided the arable ground, have been uprooted since 1970 – again to meet the needs of modern farming. Beech trees planted in the late 1800s along field boundaries at the top of the townland are succumbing to the blast of the wind. What survives are the imperfect accounts of Bonar Thompson and the memories of those who trace their roots to Scolbow. When you ask about Scolbow, a smile may flicker across their faces for they too can find sympathy with Robert Craig of Pittsburgh who concluded a letter of 1842 to his sister 'Long Peggy' Warwick of Scolbow with this epitaph:

I will ever remember Scolbow and its boys and the hill.

ACKNOWLEDGEMENTS

In presenting this brief history I am conscious of the assistance which I have received from the following: the late William R. Clark provided information relating to the family of his ancestor Charles Warwick of Scolbow and copies of farm maps, apprentice indentures and letters relating to the Rev James Warwick. Also now deceased is Nelson Montgomery of Dunadry who provided access to privately-held material as did Norman McKee of Templepatrick. Andrew Warwick Allen provided information on his Warwick family background. The family of the late John Bell of Ladyhill made available his unpublished BA honours dissertation on farming in Scolbow. His son David made available the death-cards reproduced here and his other son Samuel provided his A-level project on settlement patterns around Carnearny. Dr Pat McKay advised on the derivation of Scolbow and references to Scolbow in early seventeenth century inquisitions. Robert Bonar at the Presbyterian Historical Society provided access to the work of Robert Magill. Dr Conor Smyth of Queen's University, Belfast created Figure 3 using ESRI Arcview 3.0a GIS.

REFERENCES & SOURCES

PUBLISHED MATERIAL

CARLETON, S.T. (1991) *Heads and hearths: the hearth money rolls and poll tax returns for Co. Antrim.* Public Record Office of Northern Ireland, Belfast.

FOY, R.H. (1991) *Bonar Thompson: the old days at Carnearney.* Antrim & District Historical Society, Antrim.

JOYCE, P.W. (1995) *The origin and history of Irish names of places Vol II.* Facsimile reprint of the original edition, Edmund Burke Publisher, Dublin.

REEVES, WILLIAM (1847) *Ecclesiastical antiquities of Down, Connor and Dromore.* Facsimile reprint 1992 by Braid Books & Moyola Books.

SPIERS, S. (1985) Schools in Sullatober *Carrickfergus & District Historical Journal*, 1, 20.

PRIVATELY HELD UNPUBLISHED MATERIAL

Dayspring mishandled. Incomplete auto-biographical manuscript by Bonar Thompson (held by R.H. Foy).

Maps of farm owned by James & Charles Warwick in Upper Scolbow 1811, 1831 & 1858.

Some Clarks. Unpublished family history manuscript by W.R. Clark 1985.

Indenture of 1867 binding John Gawn of Carnearney, Co. Antrim as apprentice tailor to Arthur Warwick of Scolbo for 6 years.

Letter October 1865 from Rev James Warwick to Charles Warwick Upper Scolbow.

Letter August 1842 from Robert Craig of Baltimore to Margaret Warwick of Scolbow.

Letter September 1836 from Matthew Wilson, Pittsburgh to Elizabeth Wilson, Ballyno.

Rate Collector's Books for 1932 and 1936 Antrim Rural District Council.

Ladyhill National School Rolls held by North-Eastern Education and Library Board.

PUBLIC RECORD OFFICE OF NORTHERN IRELAND

D/597/2 Down Survey Map of Parish of Connor

D/597/2/18 Down Survey - areas and description of Parish of Connor

D/562/206 Massereene Rents to come 1701.

D/562/210 Massereene rent roll 1705

D/562/991 Massereene duty book 1733

D/1592/2 Lease dated 1696 of the Territory and Manor of Connor in the County of Antrim containing sixteen towns

D/1739/3/15 Chancery brief Lord Massereene vs Lord Ferrard containing list of Connor tenants and rents in 1838

D/2946/2/1-8 Antrim Poor Law Union Workhouse Register 1843-

Val/12D/1/44C Valuation Map Connor

Val/2B/1/8A Valuation Book Connor

Val/12B/1/13A-E Valuation Revision Books Connor

Fin/5A/83 Tithe rental 1835

PRESBYTERIAN HISTORICAL SOCIETY OF IRELAND

MANUSCRIPT VOLUME C1837 ENTITLED

Names of seat-holders and their families and also names etc. of such individuals as belong to the [Mill Row] congregation but have no seat. Extracted from the records of the parish and other documents by the Revd. Robert Magill.

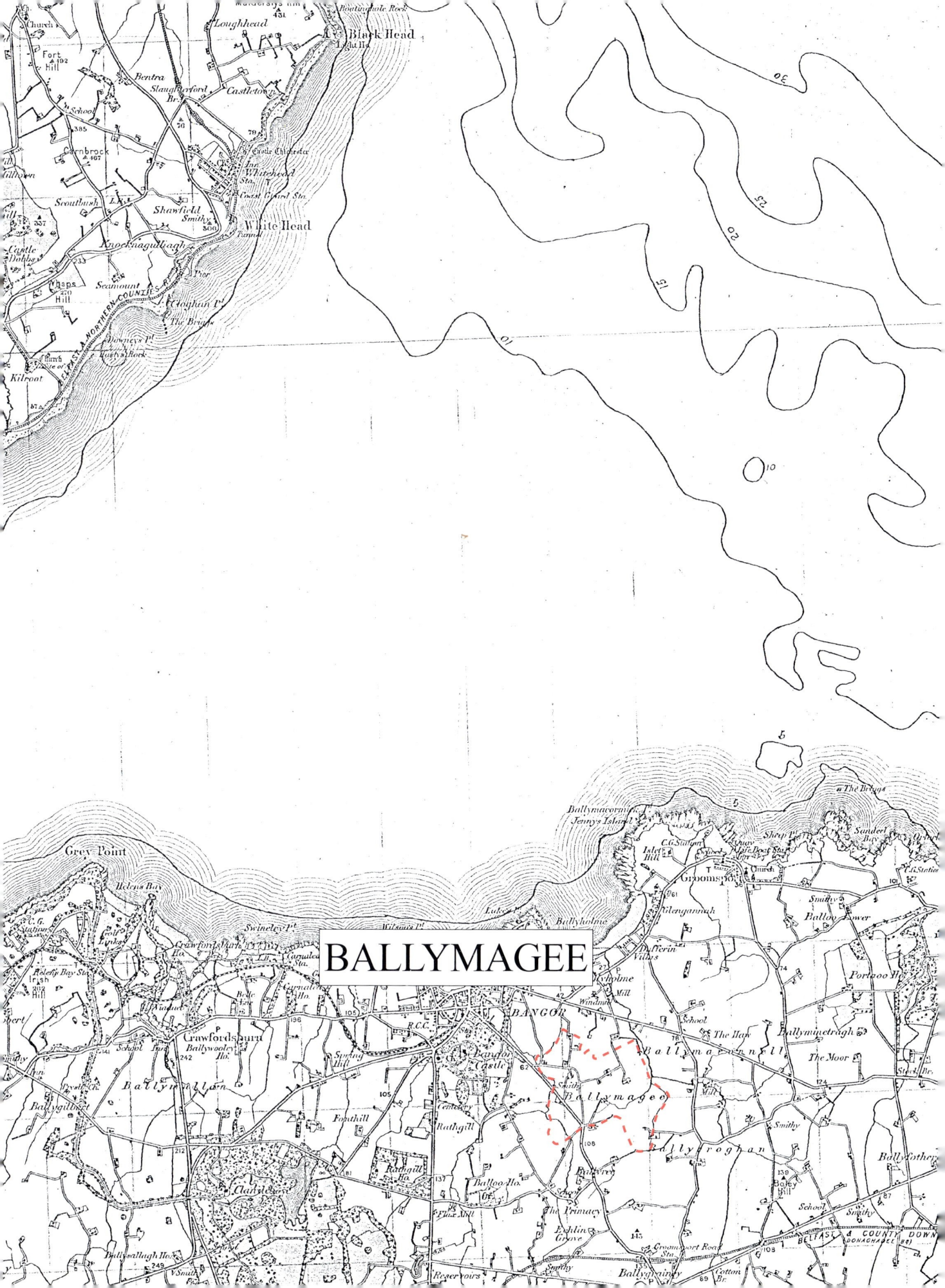

BALLYMAGEE

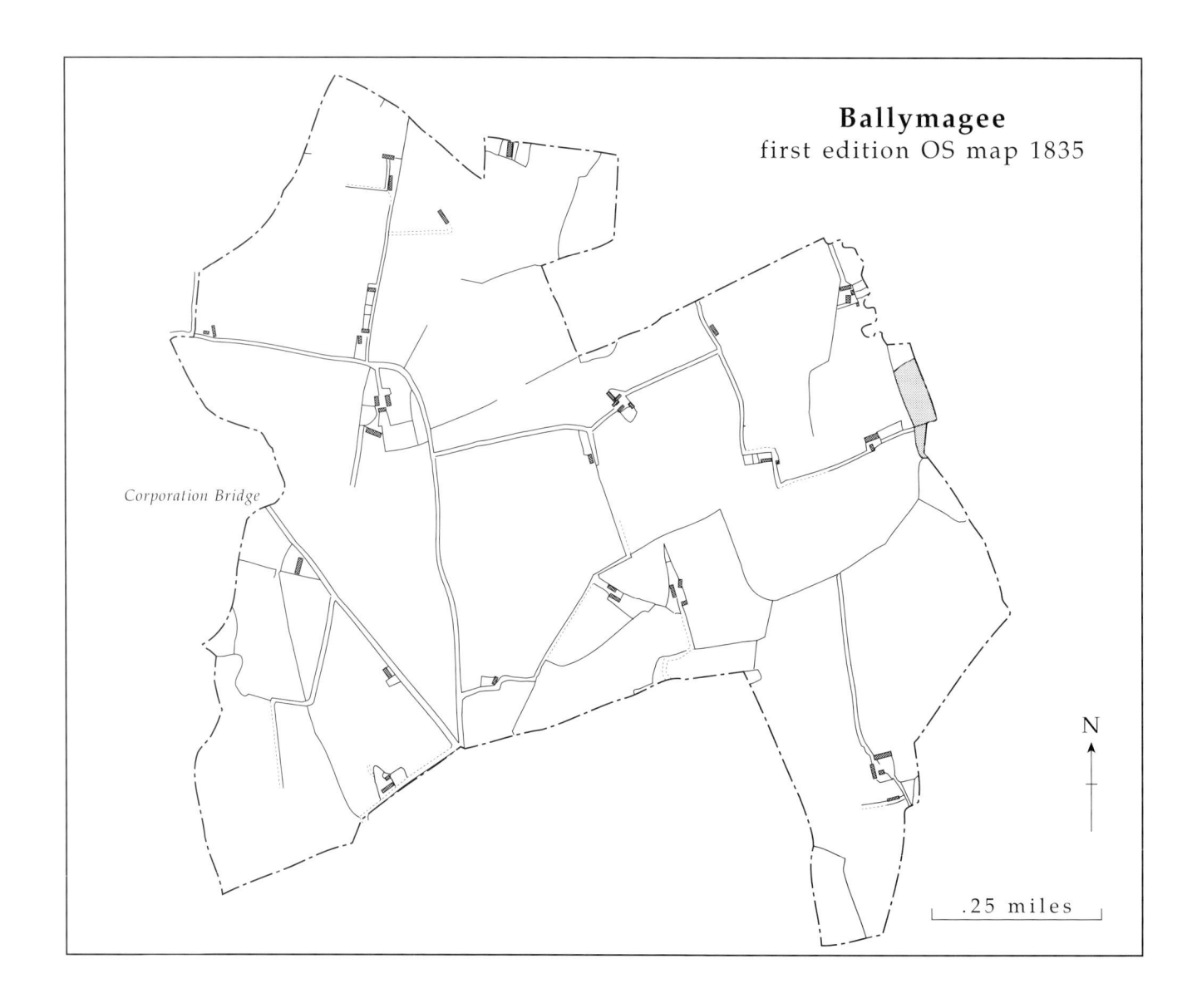

Ballymagee
first edition OS map 1835

Corporation Bridge

N

.25 miles

BALLYMAGEE

SANDRA A. MILLSOPP

Today the townland of Ballymagee is almost completely covered in housing and is cut in half by the section of Bangor Ring Road that runs eastward from the Gransha Road roundabout. It also contains a portion of Bangor Golf Course. The peripheral location of Ballymagee has had an important effect on its history. It lies on the outskirts of the town of Bangor, near enough to be affected by the town but far enough away to withstand its encroachment until the twentieth century. The development of the local road network fixed its character of small family farms for more than two centuries. Its recent history illustrates some aspects of the absorption of a traditionally agricultural townland by an expanding town, a common phenomenon in the late twentieth century.

An unusual feature of Ballymagee, and clearly of other townlands on the estate secured and developed in the early seventeenth century by the original planter, James Hamilton, was the leasing of much of the property on favourable leases to substantial middlemen whose families continued to dominate the district into the twentieth century. For much of this time Ballymagee was divided among three estates and so there could be no single overall plan for its development.

LOCATION

Ballymagee sits on a low hill overlooking Bangor town and bay. Small streams mark several of its boundaries with neighbouring townlands. Although there is no bog left in the townland, marshy land occurs at several spots along the eastern boundary.

Ballymagee is one of over thirty townlands that made up the historic parish of Bangor on the southern shore of Belfast Lough. Until the Reformation these townlands belonged to the monastery of Bangor which had been founded by St. Comgall in the 550s. Ballymagee lies immediately to the south-east of the central townland, known as Corporation, which contains the original borough of Bangor. Elsewhere in Ulster townlands so close to the town were often divided into small fields called townparks because they were let only to the townspeople. Ballymagee, however, was divided into compact farms leased to tenant farmers and until the early twentieth century it retained its agricultural character.

The earliest large-scale estate maps depicting Ballymagee were drawn by Thomas Raven in 1625. They show that it was divided into farms that appear on two separate maps and are difficult to reconcile with the first Ordnance Survey map of 1834.

EARLY HISTORY

Ballymagee has no significant prehistoric remains. It first appears as an entity in documentary sources in 1603 when it was stated to be part of the possessions of the last Abbot of Bangor Monastery which had passed into the ownership of the Crown. The name of the townland is generally taken to mean 'Magee's townland', implying that someone called Magee had once resided there as tenant of the abbey. Several other Bangor townlands also incorporate the names of individuals: Balloo, Ballyfotherly, Ballygilbert, Ballyleidy, Ballymaconnell and Ballymacormick. When James Hamilton made a will in 1616 he referred to several tenants with Irish surnames living on his Bangor lands and asked that they should not be replaced by Scots as long as they remained dutiful servants of the Hamilton family. This may also suggest the presence of tenant farmers on the abbey lands before the Reformation.

ESTATES AND THE CREATION OF FARMS

North Down was not part of the official plantation as the area had already attracted the interest of the Scots. In 1605 King James I granted to his fellow Scot, James Hamilton, the lands of the Abbey of Bangor, including the townland of Ballymagee. The Hamiltons later became Viscounts Clandeboye and earls of Clanbrassil. Ballymagee was among the lands which passed by marriage to the Ward family of Castleward in 1710. By the early nineteenth century some of the Bangor property had passed to a junior branch of the Wards, who lived in Bangor, and by the twentieth century it had again passed through the female line to the Binghams, barons Clanmorris. Ballymagee was, however, among the portions of land which were retained by the main branch of the Ward family whose head had the title of Viscount Bangor.

Sir James Hamilton, later first Viscount Clandeboye, rented out most of his lands in Bangor parish, including Ballymagee. He was, however, wary of making fee farm grants except to members of his family. The maps of 1625 produced for Sir James Hamilton by Thomas Raven, show Ballymagee divided into at least four portions. The major portion, called Wilestown, consisted of 187 acres out of a total of about 285 acres, 3 roods, 20 perches. Ballymagee was typical of the townlands that lay close to the town of Bangor, for they were broken up into portions whereas the more remote townlands were let intact. Ballymagee was

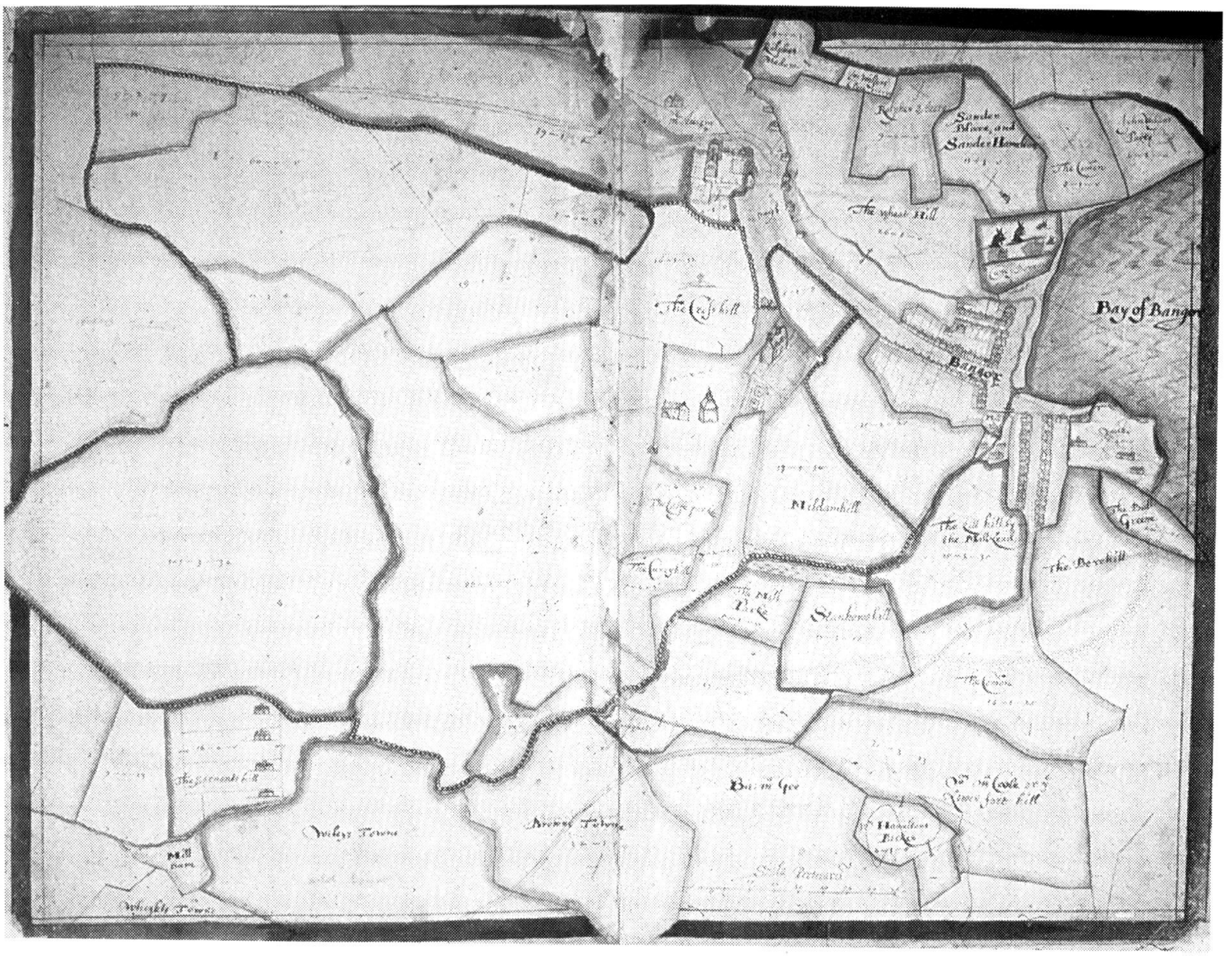

Bay of Bangor
Bangor
The Berehill
The Comon
Sanders Blaue, and Sander Hamilton
The whest hill
The Mill Park

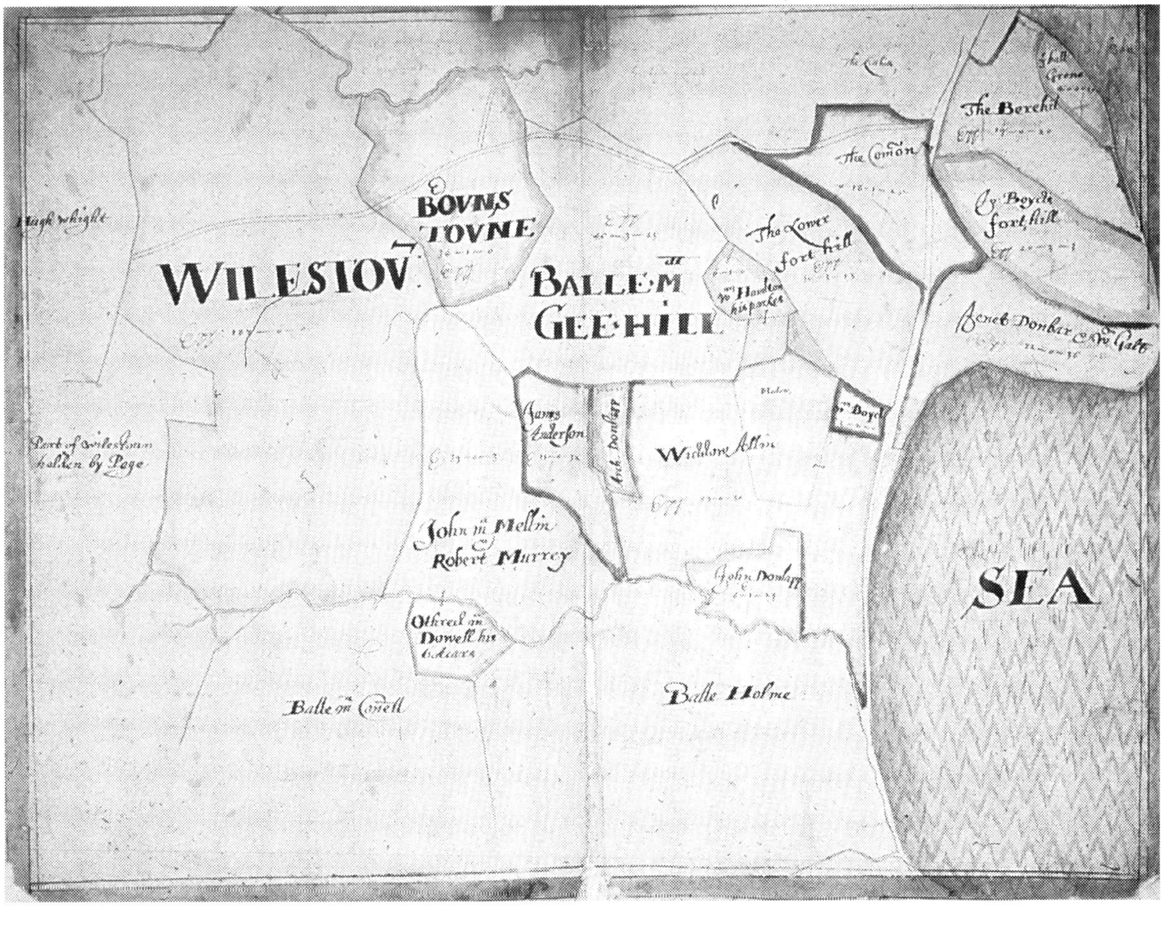

WILESTOV
BOVNS TOVNE
BALLEM GEE HILL
SEA
The Berehill
The Comon
The Lower fort hill
Hugh whight
Part of Wilestoun holden by Page
James Anderson
Widdow Allin
John M. Mellin
Robert Murrey
John Donlapp
Balle Holme

divided into at least two holdings and the larger one leased to the Maxwell family.

In 1674 the Earl of Clanbrassil, then head of the Hamilton family as grandson of Sir James Hamilton, gave Robert Maxwell a fee farm grant of property in the townlands of Groomsport, Gransha, Ballygrainey, Balloo and Ballyholme with mills at Ballyholme and Ballymaconnell. Robert Maxwell's grant included two parcels of land, one of 88 acres and the other parcel of 168 acres in Ballymagee. This was done at a time when fee farm grants were becoming much more common on the estate. The Maxwell family also had land at Finnebrogue near Downpatrick and held it and their Bangor property until the twentieth century. The principal residence of the Maxwell family was at Finnebrogue but in the nineteenth century they built Groomsport House where some members of the family, by then called Perceval-Maxwell, lived. They were, however, never resident in Ballymagee.

A Clanbrassil estate rent-roll dated about 1681 confirms that Robert Maxwell was the principal Hamilton tenant in Ballymagee. It also mentions another tenant, Alex McMechan, who held 60 acres on a forty-one year lease from 1673. This land appears to have passed to Alex Hamilton who held 60 Irish acres or 96 statute acres at a rent of £10 on a one year lease about 1713, according to an appendix to the Clanbrassil rent-roll. In 1716 Hugh Whyte obtained a lease of 120 acres of Ballyree at £4 per annum and 70 Cunningham acres of Ballymagee at £2 per annum. The next surviving rent-roll of the Ward family dating from 1739, records that Mr Whyte was paying £6 for land in Ballymagee and Ballyree. The Whytes had links with Ballyree, but not Ballymagee, in 1681. As no other tenant is mentioned in connection with Ballymagee in 1739, it is almost certain that Whyte had taken over the original McMechan/Hamilton holding. Although the Whyte family intermarried with local families of minor gentry, little is known about them. By the time of the Tenement Valuation of 1860 they had left Ballymagee and a Mrs Whittle held 96 statute acres, let to four tenants.

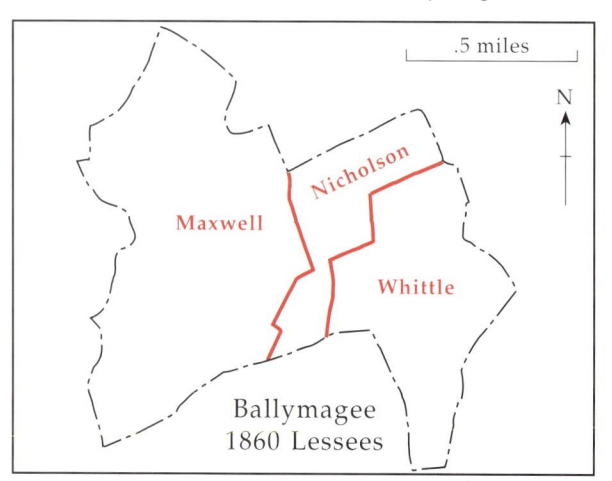

Ballymagee 1860 Lessees

The major landholders in the townland sublet their holdings from an early date. Many rentals and leases surviving for the Maxwell estate, contain information about Ballymagee. These indicate that the Maxwells restricted their leases to substantial tenants. For much of the eighteenth century only two or three tenants' names appear in the rentals associated with Ballymagee. One must, however, take into account the habit in rentals of using the name of a single townland to identify an individual without naming his other properties. Without sight of the original leases it is not possible to identify exactly all those who held land in Ballymagee. A surviving lease does confirm, however, that the principal Maxwell tenant from the 1750s was Patrick Cleland (buried in Bangor Abbey), who held 135 acres of Ballymagee. His wife was the daughter of Hugh Whyte of Ballyree and widow of William Nicholson of Balloo: both these families had connections with

Ballymagee. Cleland's lease for three lives was renewed until it expired in 1842, by which time it was held by his relative, James Rose-Cleland of Rathgael (a neighbouring townland). On the expiration of this lease the Maxwells did not relet the holding to a single tenant: the rentals identify twelve tenants. Although the collection of rents might present greater problems, the Maxwells would enjoy a higher income from their lands. It would appear that they took over the Cleland sub-tenants because some of the names of the new tenants appear in connection with the townland before 1843 in wills, on gravestones, and in the Townland Valuation of 1835. Thus a major change of policy was implemented by the largest landlord in the townland on the expiration of the Cleland lease which had run for over eighty years without any increase in rent. By the time of the printed Griffith Valuation in 1860, the Maxwells had eight tenants holding between them more than 190 statute acres of the townland.

According to *Burke's Landed Gentry of Ireland* the Nicholson family had been associated with Ballymagee since the early seventeenth century, although they did not appear there as tenants of the Hamilton estate in the Clanbrassil rent-roll of 1681. A lease of 1739 from Robert Maxwell to William Nicholson refers to a lease originally granted in 1699. The lands leased included 34 acres of Ballymagee, land in Ballyholme and 120 acres of Balloo. The Nicholson family was still associated with Ballymagee at the time of the Townland Valuation when they had five tenants with just over 50 acres. Their principal holding, however, lay not in Ballymagee but in Balloo.

Only one lease granted by the Whyte family has been traced. In 1786 William and Robert Russell leased 9 acres and 15 sq perches Cunningham measure for twenty-one years or the lives of the two lessees. The lease also mentions the names of tenants whose land was contiguous to that of the Russells: James McClean, James McMicken, and William Pollock, but gives no indication of whose tenants they were. No map has survived to show the layout of the subtenants' holdings at this date.

Another source of information about subtenants, at least the better-off among them, can be wills. Several from Ballymagee appear in a list of Down Diocesan Wills. The earliest names are members of the Nicholson family dating from 1665 to 1839. From the eighteenth century also are Ferguson and McCree and from the early nineteenth century Campbell, Clark, Colvill, Kelly, McCracken, and Russell. The gravestones in Bangor Abbey, too, record individuals from Ballymagee, mostly from the nineteenth century: Andrews, Campbell, Cleland, Colville, Erskine, Gray, Nicholson, and Russell. The Tithe Applotment Book does not mention Ballymagee: indeed, almost all the townlands of the parish of Bangor appear to have been tithe free. The Townland Valuation of 1835 should be a source of names but unfortunately the low value of the farmhouses in Ballymagee eliminated the majority of them. Those mentioned are Henry Russell, Thomas Williamson, Miss Sarah Jackson, Thomas McClean, Robert Robinson, and John Kelly. In 1866 the Nicholsons were contemplating the sale of their

BALLYMAGEE, PARISH OF BANGOR, UNION OF NEWTOWNARDS   VAL/1B/31
COUNTY OF DOWN
SURVEYED BY VALUATORS 9 SEPTEMBER 1835

		QUANTITY	RATE PER STATUTE ACRE	AMOUNT
1	Arable on clay soil, part of moderate depth, part rather shallow, stiff and cold subsoil	26a 1r 29p	15s	£19 16s 5d
	Also cold meadow	1	10s 9d	10s 9d
	Also cold pasture	1	7s	7s
	Also water	1		
	Also waste at house	2		
2	Arable chiefly a good clay soil good depth, about a third a soft loamy soil, bad subsoil, all lies pretty well	29 3 24	16s	23 18s 4d
	Also cold arable and pasture	1 2	10s 3d	15s 4d
3	Arable, chiefly light and part uneven clay soil, part with bad subsoil	21 1 5	14s 3d	14 19s 8d
	Also very light arable knolls	1	7s 9d	7s 9d
	Also waste at house	2		
4	Arable, chiefly a good strong clay soil, good depth, lies well, part undulating surface	27 3 28	16s	23 0s 9d
	Also rocky knolls	2	7s 6d	3s 9d
	Also waste at houses	30		
5	Arable, about quarter deep and good, remainder rather shallow and indifferent soil, clay part uneven	24 1	16s 6d	20 0s 1d
	Also waste at house	1 20		
6	Arable, a clay and loamy soil, part of modate depth, part shallow with rocky knolls	18 3 31	16s	15 3s 1d
	Also light arable knolls	1 1	9s 9d	12s 2d
	Also rocky and furzy portion	1	1s 3d	3d
7	Arable, a very good clay soil, chiefly deep, about three-fifths hilly and very much exposed, good subsoil	29 2 21	19s 6d	28 17s 9d
	Also waste at house	2		
8	Arable, chiefly a good clay soil deep, about a third shallow and uneven with rocky knolls all well sheltered	26 0 36	18s	23 12s
9	Arable, chiefly a strong deep clay and loam, part rather shallow with bad subsoil	17 1 36	18s 6d	16 3s 3d
	Also quarry hole	10	2s 3d	1d
	Also waste at house	1		
10	Arable, chiefly indifferent dark brown soil, with bad subsoil, part a clay soil very uneven and interspersed with rock	25 0 3	15s	18 15s 3d
	Also light arable rocky knolls	1	8s 6d	8s 6d
	Also strip of rocky and furzy pasture	2	1s 3d	7
11	Arable, a good clay and loamy soil, part rather hilly part deep, part moderately so	35 2 22	16s 6d	£29 8s
	Also waste at house	1 20		
12	Arable, chiefly a good clay and loamy soil, part deep, part moderate depth, gravelly	9 3 31	15s 6d	7 14s 1d
	Also light arable	2	8s 6d	4s 3d
13	Arable, chiefly a clay soil, good depth, about a third soft and shallow moory	16 1 35	16s	13 3s 6d
	Also light arable	1	7s 6d	1s 10d
14	Arable, one half good clay soil, good depth, remainder shallow, uneven, and indifferent; part a soft loam with bad subsoil	27 1 24	15s 6d	21 4s 8d
	Also cold moory light and uneven arable	2 1	10s 6d	1 3s 7d
	Also rocky pasture	1 2	5s 3d	7s 10d
		353 2 25		£281 9s 9d

HOUSES (pp 134-5)
  1 Henry Russell   1B   51.5 feet long, 18 feet broad, and 6.5 feet high
1 2 Thomas Williamson   1A   29.5 feet, 22 feet, 13 feet [2 storeys]   £3 18s
2 3 Miss Sarah Jackson   3B   67 feet, 20 feet, 8 feet   £5   2s
  4 Thomas McClean   3B   55 feet, 17.5 feet, 6 feet
  5 Robert Robinson   1B   36 feet, 16.5 feet, 7.5 feet
  6 John Kelly   3B   49 feet, 16 feet, 6.5 feet

TOWNLAND VALUATION (1835)
Although Ballymagee lies on rock, there is a good depth of clay soil over much of it. Cultivation of this abbey land for several centuries had got rid of almost all the gorse and the moory patches so that 95 per cent of the total acreage of Ballymagee was valued at more than 14/- (70p) per acre – WHC

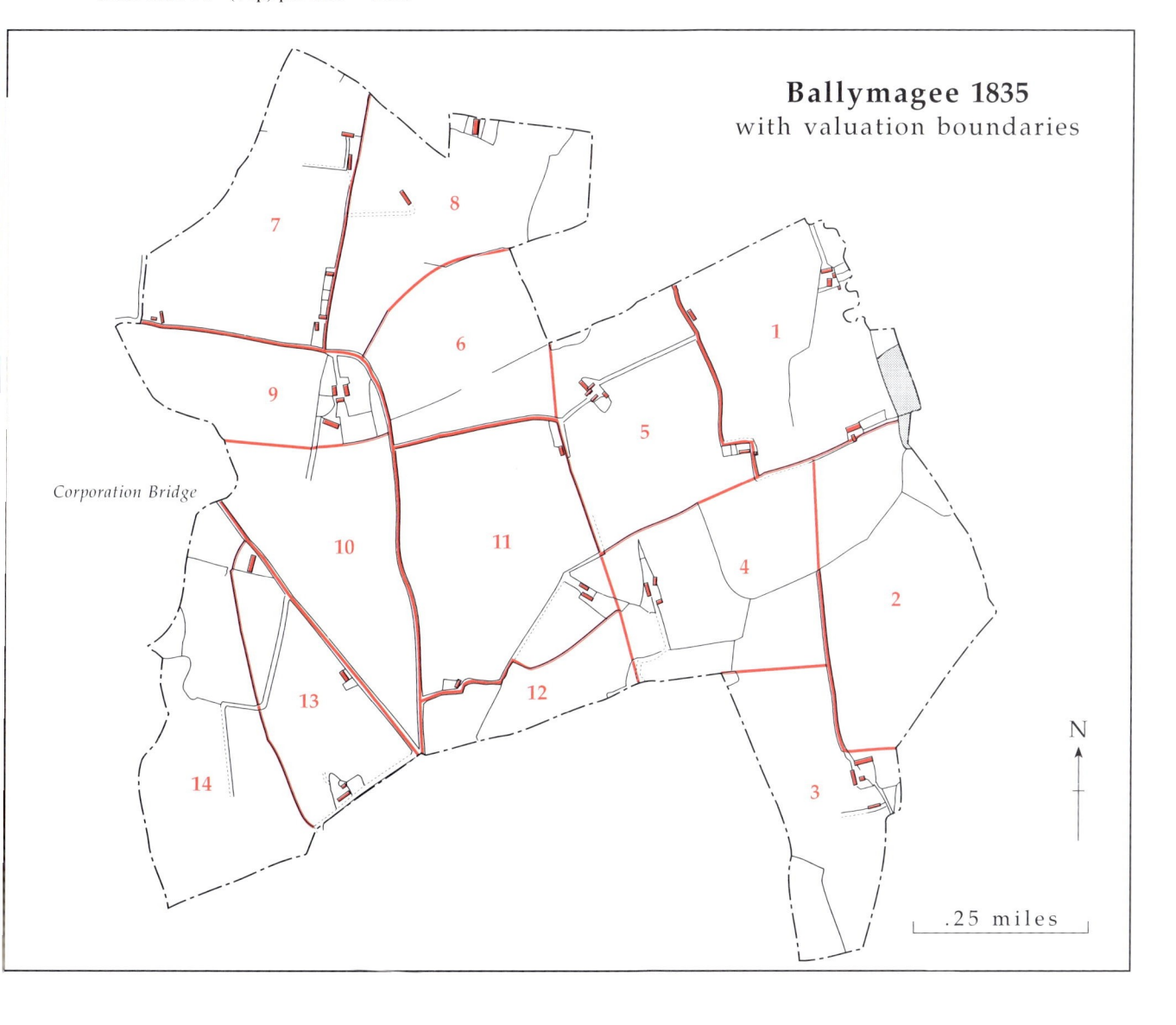

Ballymagee 1835
with valuation boundaries

Corporation Bridge

.25 miles

No. and Letters of Reference to Map.		Names.		Description of Tenement.	Area.	Rateable Annual Valuation.		Total Annual Valuation of Rateable Property.
		Townlands and Occupiers.	Immediate Lessors.			Land.	Buildings.	
		BALLYMAGEE. (*Ord. S.* 2.)			A. R. P.	£ s. d.	£ s. d.	£ s. d.
1		William Erskine,	John W. Maxwell,	House, office, and land,	11 2 35	13 0 0	2 10 0	15 10 0
2		David Hanna,	Same,	House, office, and land,	7 2 20	8 0 0	1 10 0	9 10 0
3	a	Thomas Williamson,	Same,	House, offices, and land,	35 3 20	38 10 0	8 10 0	47 0 0
—	b	William M'Cormack,	Thomas Williamson,	House and sm. garden,	—	—	1 0 0	1 0 0
—	c	Archibald Moorehead,	Same,	House and sm. garden,	—	—	1 0 0	1 0 0
—	d	William Bruce,	Same,	House and sm. garden,	—	—	0 15 0	0 15 0
4	a	Thomas Williamson,	Mrs. Whittle,	Office and land,	28 3 25	33 0 0	0 15 0	33 15 0
—	b	Thomas M'Neely,	Thomas Williamson,	House,	—	—	1 10 0	1 10 0
—	c	John Collins,	Same,	House,	—	—	0 15 0	0 15 0
—	d	Robert M'Cammon,	Same,	House,	—	—	0 15 0	0 15 0
5		Alex. Montgomery,	John W. Maxwell,	House, office, and land,	43 2 10	47 0 0	4 10 0	51 10 0
6		David Andrews,	Same,	House, office, and land,	34 1 0	33 5 0	4 5 0	37 10 0
7 A — B	a }	Mary Colven,	Same,	{ House, office, and land, Office and land,	18 0 3 13 3 35	20 0 0 13 10 0	3 15 0 0 10 0	} 37 15 0
—	b	James Colven,	Mary Colven,	House and sm. garden,	—	—	1 5 0	1 5 0
—	c	Alexander Colven,	Same,	House,	—	—	1 0 0	1 0 0
8		John Boyd,	John W. Maxwell,	Land,	17 3 25	18 10 0	—	18 10 0
9		Andrew M'Clean,	Robert S. Nicholson,	House, office, and land,	23 0 5	26 5 0	2 0 0	28 5 0
10	a	William Martin,	Same,	House, offices, and land,	2 1 18	3 0 0	1 10 0	4 10 0
—	b	Unoccupied,	William Martin,	House,	—	—	0 15 0	0 15 0
11	a	William Hueston,	Robert S. Nicholson,	House and land,	5 0 10	5 15 0	1 5 0	7 0 0
—	b	Robert Hueston,	William Hueston,	House,	—	—	0 15 0	0 15 0
12		John Martin,	Robert S. Nicholson,	House and land,	5 2 35	6 5 0	1 10 0	7 15 0
13		James Russell (*King*),	Same,	House, offices, and land,	15 0 18	15 5 0	2 5 0	17 10 0
14		Hugh Neill,	John W. Maxwell,	House, office, and land,	8 0 1	10 0 0	1 15 0	11 15 0
15	a	Nathaniel Russell,	Mrs. Whittle,	House, office, and land,	31 3 30	34 0 0	2 10 0	36 10 0
—	b	Agnes Russell,	Nathaniel Russell,	House,	—	—	1 0 0	1 0 0
16		Samuel Barr,	Mrs. Whittle,	Land,	25 1 35	27 15 0	—	27 15 0
16	a	Henry Stinson,	Samuel Barr,	House,	—	—	0 15 0	0 15 0
—	b	Letitia M'Connell,	Same,	House,	—	—	0 15 0	0 15 0
—	c	James Rowley,	Same,	House,	—	—	1 0 0	1 0 0
—	d	Unoccupied,	Same,	House,	—	—	0 15 0	0 15 0
17		James Russell,	Mrs. Whittle,	House, office, and land,	10 1 25	10 15 0	1 15 0	12 10 0
				Total,	338 3 25	363 15 0	54 10 0	418 5 0

BALLYMAGEE

TENEMENT VALUATION (1861)
Compare the column of Immediate Lessors with the previous columns of Occupiers: the whole townland divided between three Immediate Lessors: John W. Maxwell, Robert S. Nicholson, and Mrs Whittle. The Tenement Valuation enables us to distinguish between their respective properties.

Comparison of this map, which indicates the field boundaries, with the original map of 1835 reveals that some fields on the northern boundary had since been transferred from Ballymagee to the neighbouring townland of Ballyholme.

Note that Thomas Williamson, the largest farmer in Ballymagee held (3) from Maxwell and (4) from Mrs Whittle, while he lived in a good house on (3). The Valuation Revision Lists record that by 1880 the Williamsons had acquired (7), (16) and (17) and by 1900 (9), (10) and (14). In 1903 they sold the farm in the south-east of Ballymagee comprised of (4), (9), (10), (16), and (17) to James McKeen – WHC

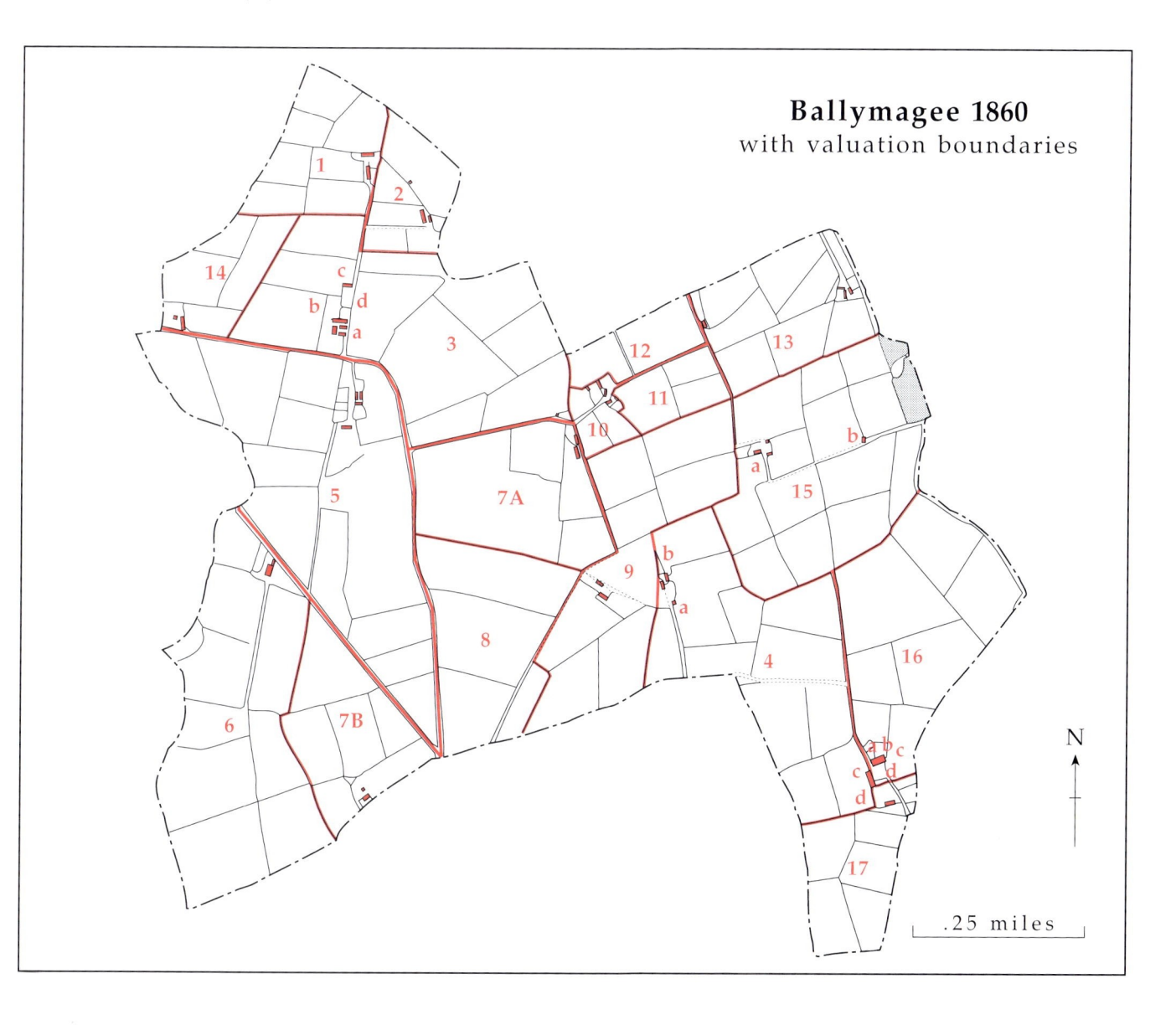

Ballymagee 1860
with valuation boundaries

.25 miles

property. A detailed document (T/662/294) prepared on this occasion shows that their tenants were John Martin, William Houston, Jane Martin, Hugh Bell, and James Russell. Several of these names are familiar from other sources such as the Tenement Valuation.

Some evidence also exists about the type of leases granted in Ballymagee. The Maxwells had held a fee farm grant from the Hamiltons since 1674. In 1716 Hugh Whyte paid the Hamilton estate £502.10s. for a fee farm grant of 120 Cunningham acres of Ballyree at £4 and 70 Cunningham acres of Ballymagee at £2. The Nicholsons held their land from the Maxwells according to their lease of 1739 for a term of three lives: on the death of any of these lives another life could be inserted on payment of £13.13s. within nine months. Other subtenants held a variety of leases including one for three lives and another for two lives or twenty-one years in the eighteenth century. In the nineteenth century examples of subtenants' leases range from yearly tenancies to a one hundred year lease granted in 1864. The tendency was to give better leases to the more important tenants. It is also clear that by the mid nineteenth century the landlord was no longer prepared to grant long leases of large areas to middlemen but favoured instead more direct grants of smaller areas to the occupying farmers.

COMMUNICATIONS

The major road links of Bangor traditionally have been west to Belfast, south to Newtownards and east to Donaghadee and the Ards Peninsula. None of them pass through Ballymagee. High Street, one of the two main thoroughfares in the town, was known as Ballymagee Street from the seventeenth century to the beginning of the twentieth. It led to the Donaghadee Road from which a road branched off to Ballymagee. Farmers in the townland had access to another important route. The Raven map of 1625 shows a road running south-east from Bangor towards Ballygrainey and the Great Bog of Gransha: no road ran through the bog as it was not drained until the eighteenth century. The same road is shown on the first Ordnance Survey map of 1834 linked to the farmsteads by lanes and tracks. This pattern remained intact for many years and provided access to both the bogs at Gransha and the mills at Ballymaconnell and Ballyholme. Then the development of housing in the 1980s and 1990s added many new roads to the townland while some of the older roads became mere laneways, raising local controversies over rights of way.

The most significant road development in the Bangor area in the 1960s was the creation of the ring or circular road to take traffic away from the centre of the town. As a result Ballymagee now includes a major roundabout and a section of the east Circular Road running from SW to NE through the townland. For the first time, therefore, the townland has acquired a major route but at the expense of being cut in two. This project was mooted first in a town-planning booklet in 1945 although the suggested route differs slightly from the road actually constructed.

POPULATION

The Raven maps of 1625 feature only four houses on 'Sarvants hill', which suggests a population of at least twelve. In the census of 1659 'Ballyneghee' is stated to have had ten inhabitants of whom nine were either English or Scots.

```
CENSUS RETURNS FOR BALLYMAGEE
                INHABITANTS                    HOUSES
          MALES   FEMALES   TOTAL    INHAB  UNINHAB  BUILDING  TOTAL
   1841   107  +  110  =  217         41  +    2   +    0   =  43
   1851   103  +  111  =  214         38  +    1   +    0   =  39
   1861    83  +  102  =  185         29  +    0   +    0   =  29
   1871    61  +   67  =  128         23  +    2   +    0   =  25
   1881    39  +   39  =   78         15  +    2   +    0   =  17
   1891    24  +   36  =   60         14  +    1   +    0   =  15
   1901    37  +   25  =   62         11  +    2   +    0   =  13
   1911    38  +   28  =   66         12  +    1   +    0   =  13
```

Not until 1841 are detailed census figures available for the townland. By then the population was 217 living in 41 houses. The Great Famine left little impact as the population lost only three people and three houses. During the next thirty years, however, it shed as many as 136 people and 22 houses. These excessive losses can be explained only by the removal of cottiers and the Valuation Revision Lists for the years 1866-1882 confirm this by noting the demolition or conversion of cottier houses. They reveal that some farmers, especially Erskine and Montgomery, were improving their buildings and that some of them, notably Williamson, were buying up the smaller farms and consolidating them. It is interesting to note that the number of men in the townland fell to 24 in 1891 but recovered, whereas the number of women fell and did not recover: it may be related to a decline in employment opportunities in textiles. Weaving, first of linen and later of cotton, had been an important industry in the parish but had given way early in the nineteenth century to embroidery work put out by entrepreneurs in the towns of Newtownards and Bangor. The 1901 census returns record that of the eleven households six were headed by farmers, three by labourers, one by a mail guard and the other by a housekeeper. After the 1911 census most of Ballymagee was subsumed into the town of Bangor with its system of wards and so the census figures can no longer be used to study changes in Ballymagee. Within living memory, however, the townland has been submerged by housing.

Standards of education seem to have been good in the parish of Bangor. Figures in the 1851 census show that literacy rates in the rural portion of the parish were high, especially for men: two-thirds of the male population could both read and write. Until very recently the townland of Ballymagee did not have its own school but its children attended schools in Bangor town, Ballymaconnell, or at the Primacy in Ballyree. Surviving registers from these schools contain surnames found also in the rent-rolls and valuation and census records for Ballymagee.

The four resident adults who could neither read nor write according to the 1901 census, were all servants.

During most of its history Ballymagee did not have its own church. The nearest places of worship were within walking distance in the centre of Bangor. By the mid-nineteenth century some people at least from Ballymagee were attending Ballygrainey Presbyterian Church which stands at the Six Road Ends and was reached by the Gransha Road passing through Ballymagee. According to the 1901 census ten of the eleven households in Ballymagee were Presbyterian and the remaining one Methodist. Among the servants were three Roman Catholics and one Church of Ireland as well as Presbyterians. In the third quarter of the twentieth century Ballycroghan Presbyterian Church has been built in response to suburban development.

HOUSING

By the 1920s residential housing appeared in the west of the townland. Older Bangor residents can remember the wooden bungalows that for a time graced Williamson's Lane (now Fairfield Road). By 1994 private housing, largely middle class, had spread over most of the townland. Virtually all traces of farm buildings have gone. Even the farm in the south-west corner sports a modern bungalow as the building of the ring road meant the demolition of the old farmhouse.

FARMING

As we would expect, farming was the most important male occupation in the rural portion of Bangor parish. Oats and barley are the main crops mentioned in seventeenth and eighteenth century sources and there were both water and wind mills in the neighbouring townlands of Ballyholme and Ballymaconnell.

The 1850 agricultural census returns for the District Electoral Division indicate a pattern of intensive agriculture. In that year, for example, more than sixty per cent of its 17,019 acres were under cultivation so that harvest-time around Bangor must have been very busy. There were more than four thousand acres of oats, fifteen hundred acres of wheat (which had displaced barley to less than three hundred acres), a thousand acres of potatoes and a thousand acres of turnips. Against this there were 261 acres of peas and beans but only 121 of flax. This would suggest that on the 339 acres of Ballymagee the mix of crops would have been some 80 acres of oats and 30 of wheat as well as 20 each of potatoes and turnips but only 2 or 3 of flax.

COMMUNITY

Although Ballymagee might seem too remote to have been affected by national events, evidence has survived about the participation of some of its inhabitants in the 1798 Rebellion. Archibald McClean was accused of having sworn in a member of the United Irishmen (D/714/3/27) and William Russell took part in the rising. PRONI holds three documents relating to his involvement (T/3055/1-3). The first is a lease of 1786 from Hugh White to Robert and William Russell of 9 acres and 15 square perches in Ballymagee for twenty-one years or the lives of the lessees, at a rent of 7/6 per acre. The second document is a will made in 1798 by William Russell, farmer of Ballymagee, as he was about to leave the kingdom. His brother, Archibald, was to have half the farm and the rest was to go to his sister, Margaret, on condition that she would remain free of 'all encumbrances of any person' but take care of their mother who was to get her living from the farm and meat and clothing for her life. Russell also mentioned his hope to return home. The reasons for his concern are revealed in the third document, a petition to the Lord Lieutenant begging pardon for his involvement in the 1798 Rebellion. According to this account he had gone into Bangor with some boys from the neighbourhood. When they asked him to be their leader, he agreed, not realising the danger. He does not mention his role in any events in the rebellion. He begs forgiveness, especially for the sake of his mother who is now likely to die. Unfortunately there is no other evidence about his fate. The Russell family certainly remained farmers in the district for many years to come.

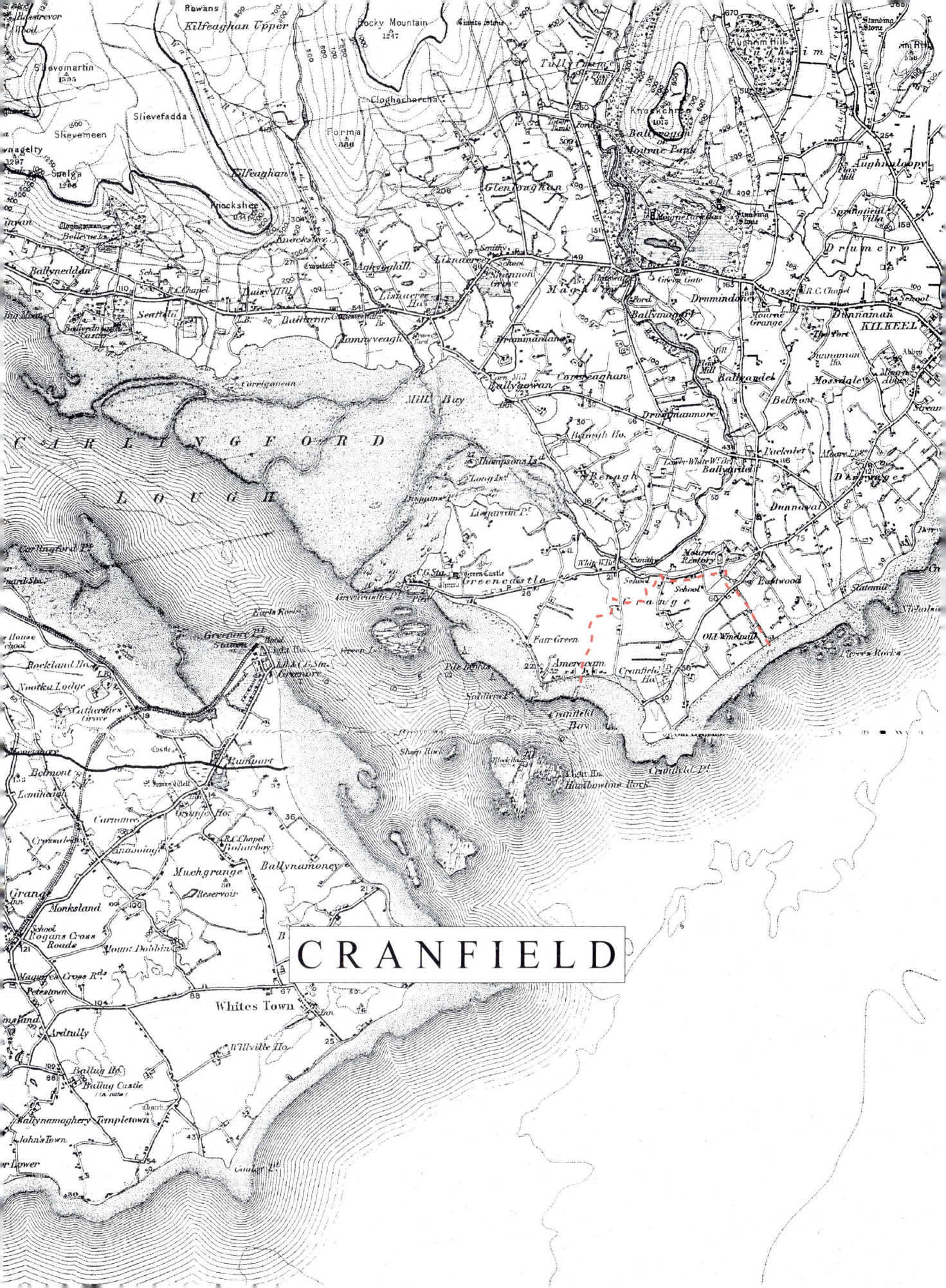

CRANFIELD

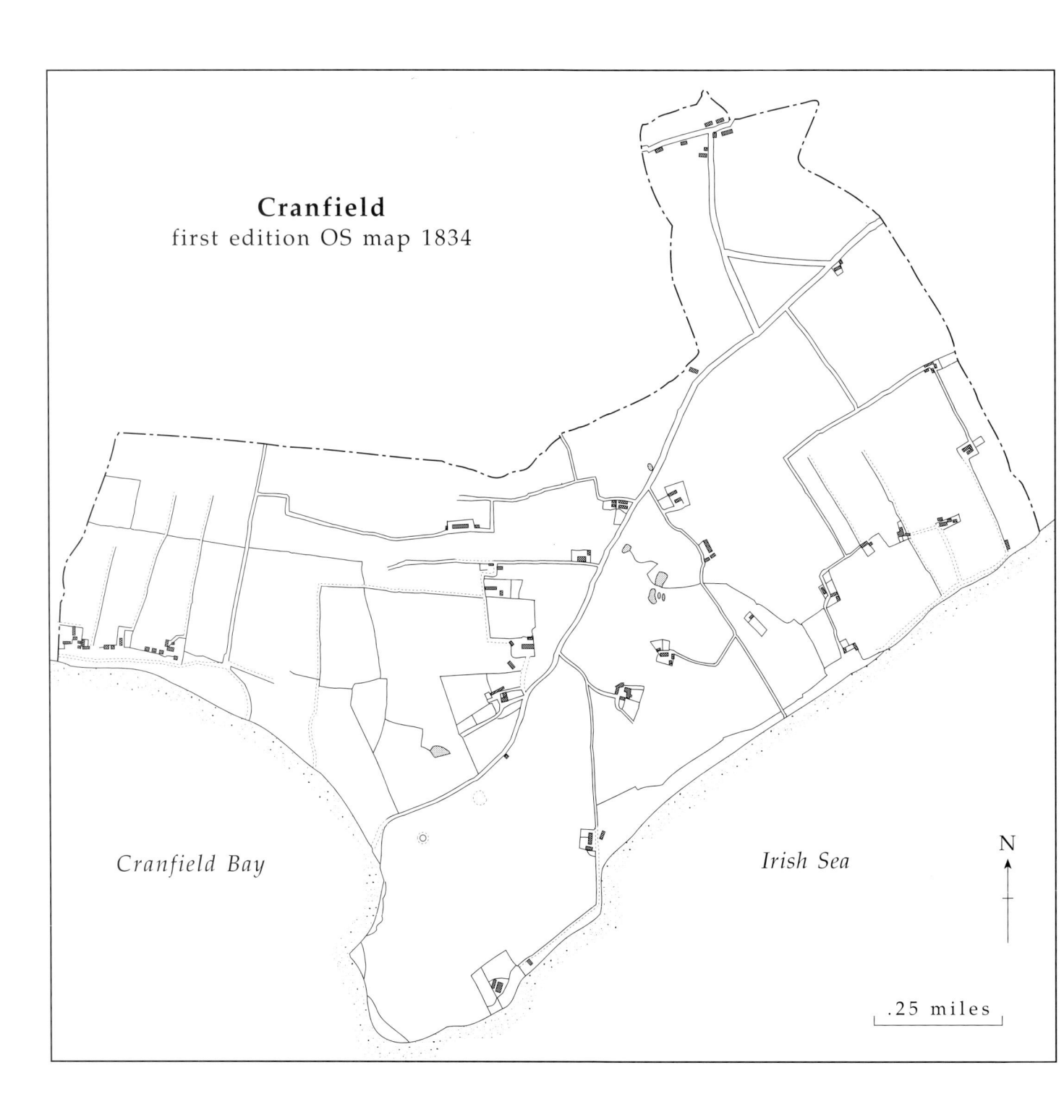

Cranfield
first edition OS map 1834

Cranfield Bay

Irish Sea

N

.25 miles

CRANFIELD

H. S. IRVINE

Cranfield (486 acres) is the most southerly townland in County Down, at the northern side of the entrance to Carlingford Lough. The Lough bounds it on the south-west and the Irish Sea on the south-east, so it is open to easterly gales from the Irish Sea and westerly ones sweeping in from the Lough. Much of the surface is quite flat, though some land slopes up to small hillocks. The soil is fertile, mostly a brown loam underlain by sand, though the western end is less fertile, the subsoil being a stiff clay. The history of the townland has been much influenced by its soil and its coastline, particularly because of its position at the mouth of the Lough.

This study does not consider the story of Cranfield after the mid nineteen-twenties, as it then began to undergo a series of major changes to its surface. Initially a strip of sand banks was developed into a nine-hole golf links. During the 1940s the Greencastle aerodrome extended into Cranfield and after the war the large sand deposits were quarried for building sand. Then too the links was replaced by a caravan site. This was to be the forerunner of other sites. This period of the townland's history merits a study of its own.

The name Cranfield (Creamhchoill – 'Wood of wild garlic') suggests that at least part of the townland was once wooded. There is no memory of this today, and the only trees now are those surrounding a few houses. Little is known of Cranfield's early history. That it was occupied by man in the distant past is evidenced by the remains of a rectilinear mound some seventy feet wide and at least one hundred and fifty feet long. This contains deposits of charcoal, animal bones, marine shells and shreds of 'souterrain' style pottery.

Cranfield was granted by Muirchertach Mac Lochlain to the Cistercian abbey of Newry in 1157, a grant confirmed by the Norman Hugh de Lacy in 1237. Lying alongside the townland of Greencastle with its Norman manor and castle, it must have shared with it its periods of dominance and weakness, being fought over intermittently for most of three centuries. In 1506 it was granted by Henry VII to Gerald, 8th Earl of Kildare and his wife Elizabeth as part of the 'Manors and Lordships of Greencastle and Mourne'. After the Geraldine rebellion it passed to the Englishman Nicholas Bagenal in 1552. Before this, in 1540, Cranfield, with eight nearby townlands, was tenanted by Robert Brabazon.

The recoverable history of Cranfield, as of many townlands, is largely the history of how its land has been managed by its owners and farmed by their tenants. As early as 1333, when the Cistercians were the landlords, there is mention of its being divided into quarters, which would suggest that a considerable area was being farmed. By 1663 the Bagenals, introducing British tenants, let the entire townland to Richard Houston, who sub-let to tenants like William Moore, a settler from the Isle of Man. In 1713 the Needhams, successors to the Bagenals, divided the townland into 'thirds', one of which included the area known then as Turble Bradagh. (Today this area is still known to some as the Turble). These 'thirds' were in the hands of Grizill Houston and John Raymond, who sublet most of their land, and James Wahop (Wauchope) who farmed his 'third' himself. The Needhams were heirs to the Bagenal policy of increasing the number of British tenants on their Mourne estate after the experience of the latter losing their lands to the Jacobites during the Williamite Wars.

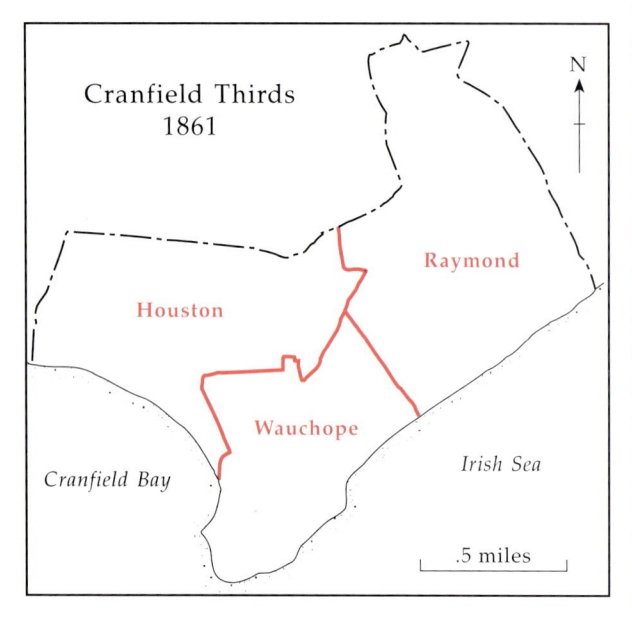

With no extant estate records from 1713 to 1813, it is difficult to reconstruct the history of these 'thirds'. The Wauchope 'third', stretching inland from Cranfield point, was sublet and divided in the eighteenth century into three farms because the sons, entering the Customs and serving further south, were non-resident. The Raymonds sub-let most of their 'third' until their lease fell in 1779. The Houston 'third' may have been divided between two tenants at some time in the mid-eighteenth century, for two leases fell in in 1796 and 1802. Both almost certainly sublet. Map I shows the area contained in each of the 'thirds'.

It was perhaps with the division into 'thirds' that the present road network began to develop. The main road from Kilkeel gave direct access to all three 'thirds'. It ran roughly parallel to the Irish Sea coast through the original Raymond 'third', to the large farms of the Wauchope 'third'. In fact in 1860 it ran direct to the McIlwaine farm at Cranfield House and on to the east end of Cranfield Bay. Off it a side road passed Moore's Hilltop farm and on through the Annett farm to the site of the first lighthouse and, later, the coastguard lookout. Somewhat further north another side road gave access to the Raymond house and farm and later to the windmill, before continuing to the Irish Sea coast. The remaining access lanes to small farms clearly evolved from tracks along the edges of fields. In the 'Raymond' third these eventually extended to the sea, while in the 'Houston' third they served farms to the west of the Kilkeel road and some eventually continued till they met the main road from Mill Bay and Newry, which ran to the west end of Cranfield Bay. At least two of these were used, in the late nineteenth century, as short cuts taken by farmers when going to Newry markets. The Kilkeel road served all three of the 'thirds' of Cranfield, but whether it was an ancient track which influenced the boundaries of the 'thirds' or whether the boundaries of the 'thirds' influenced the route taken by the road is not clear.

When the Wauchope leases fell in 1789 and 1795 the Needham Estate took that 'third' into its own hands and renewed the leases of the three farmers. When the lease of the Raymond 'third' fell in 1779 John Raymond was given a lease of seventeen acres and it seems likely that his former tenants were retained, if they were solvent. The Houston 'third' appears to have had new leases granted to existing tenants in 1796. There was no longer a Houston farming in Cranfield.

In 1779 the Needham Estate gave leases to joint-tenancy farms. These were probably already in existence, created by the Raymonds. One was apparently held at will, another was for three lives and yet another for forty-one years and three lives. Two leases were for thirty-one years, the maximum legal lease for Catholics in 1779. Two were partnerships between two farmers, but in other cases the leases are described in vague terms (e.g. 'Samuel McKee & Co.' and 'Bryan McBrinn & Co.'). These farms varied from fourteen to thirty-three acres. Such partnership farms were not uncommon in Mourne until the early nineteenth century. In 1813 the rents of farms ranged from £0.33 to £0.56 per acre (a number held on leases dating back to 1779, before the price inflation of the French Wars); by about 1880 they ranged from £0.80 to £0.96 per acre. Until at least 1900 the estate records used Irish acres, but here all are converted into statute acres.

The pattern of large farms established by 1800 was continued for at least a century. The three large farms of the Wauchope 'third' continued until after 1900, and the fifty-seven acre Davidson farm on the former Raymond 'third' in 1800 was still largely in being in 1900. However some changes did occur. A Coffey farm of twenty-five acres was subdivided equally amongst four sons before 1830 (See 1861 Valuation Map). An earlier example appears in 1813 when Matthew and Bernard Cleary each held five and a half acre farms. The process went into reverse by 1830 when Bernard Clarke (a variant of Cleary) was in possession of the combined farms. Subdivision, however, seems to have been rare in Cranfield.

The farm census of 1803 throws an interesting light on the economic relationship between some tenant farmers and their relations. William Coffey was tenant of twenty-six acres, but the stock and crops on the farm were apportioned equally to William, David and Widow Coffey. Presumably these were two brothers and a widowed mother. The stock and crops of John Cunningham's farm were likewise divided equally between him and Widow Cunningham (presumably his mother). More unexpected was that Charles Magin, Thomas George and John Doran, who were separate tenants of the estate, all had the same quantities of crops but differing numbers of stock. It is not clear how this arrangement is to be explained.

It will be clear that as a result of the Famine and agricultural movements in succeeding years, the structure of farming in Cranfield must have been affected. The number of farmers fluctuated. The numbers recorded as owning stock and crops in 1803 was thirty-one. By 1830 the number rose to forty-three, but declined to thirty-five in 1862. In 1895 the total was thirty-three. This is what would be

TOWNLAND VALUATION (1834)

Cranfield is the most southerly townland in County Down, and its point marks the northern entrance to Carlingford Lough. The land is in general fertile with a strong, brown, sharp loam over a rather hungry red sandy subsoil. Some parts of it were rather exposed while others were uneven. Note how the valuers used the main road to divide the townland whereas in 1713 Needham, the landlord, had leased it in three divisions to the families of Houston, Raymond, and Wauchope respectively – WHC.

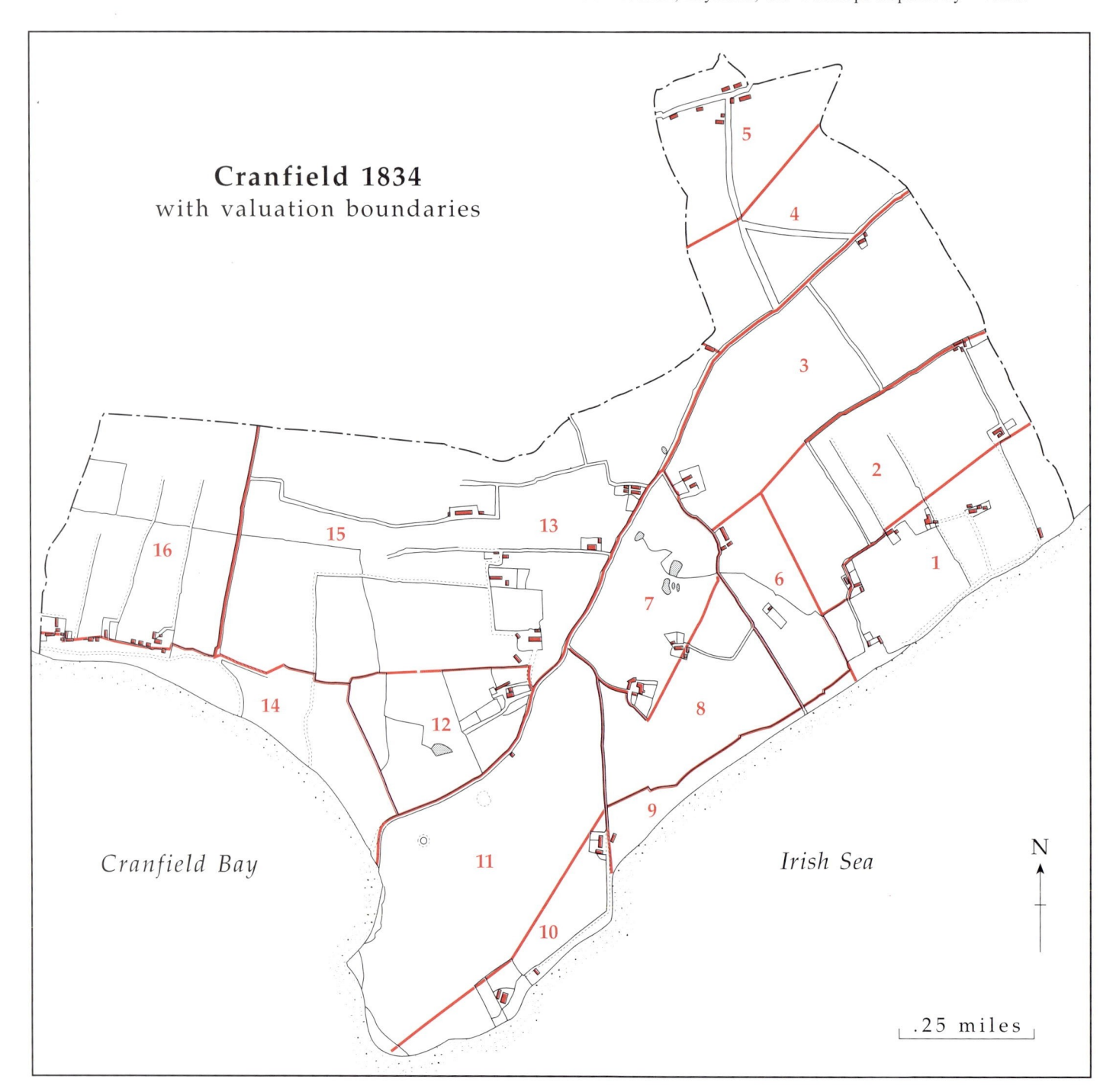

Cranfield 1834
with valuation boundaries

Cranfield Bay

Irish Sea

N

.25 miles

CRANFIELD, parish of Kilkeel, half barony of Mourne, County Down
VAL/1B/ 390A p 121, 30 December 1834

1	Dark sandy and moory soil mostly shallow on open red sandy and gravelly subsoil ⅙ good	} 28a 2r 19p	@	13s 9d	£19 13s 5d
	also steep sandy pasture bank adjoining seashore	3a	@	7d	1s 9d
	also waste at houses	1r			
2	Arable about medium depth of sharp brown soil on hungry red sandy clay subsoil	} 32a 3r	@	16s 6d	27 0s 4d
	also shallow moory arable and light knolls	4a	@	12s	2 8s
	also waste at houses	29p			
3	Arable medium depth of brown sharp and soft soil lying well on hungry subsoil	} 42a 1r 14p	@	16s 6d	34 18s 6d
	also light knolls and shallow arable	4a	@	13s	2 12s
	also waste at houses				
4	Arable ⅔ medium depth ⅓ shallow sharp brown soil on red open sandy clay subsoil	} 20a 3r 30p	@	15s 6d	16 4s 6d
5	Mostly deep and tolerably strong sharp brown on red sandy clay subsoil, a little exposed	} 14a 2r 10p	@	17s 6d	12 14s 10d
	also light shallow gravelly and moory arable	6a	@	13s 6d	4 1s
	also gravel pit and waste at houses	30p			
6	Chiefly dark sandy and moory arable on red sandy subsoil ° tolerably good	} 10a 3r 30p	@	15s	8 3s 10d
	also better arable	3a	@	19s 6d	2 18s 6d
	also waste at houses	20p			
7	Arable mostly very uneven surface ˜ good deep soil ¾ light	} 17a 2r 20p	@	15s	13 4s 4d
	also waste at houses	30p			
	also marsh and rushy pasture	2a	@	1s 9d	3s 6d
8	Deep dark sandy loam lying with part strong on (°) open red sandy clay subsoil	} 20a	@	19s	19
	also sandy arable	4a	@	10s 6d	2 2s
9	Sandy and gravelly bank about ⅓ pasturable	8a 2r	@	9d	6s 4d
10	Deep sandy arable tolerably strong	10a 1r 35p	@	17s 6d	9 3s 2d
	also gravelly pasture belonging to Ballast Office	3r 20p	@	1s 3d	1s 1d
	also arable gardens	1a 2r 20p	@	19s	1 10s 10d
11	Generally good deep sharp brown loam mostly lying on sandy clay subsoil	} 41a 3r 39p	@	21s 6d	45 2s 9d
	also exposed light sandy moory + clayey arable	7a	@	15s 6d	5 8s 6d
	also marshy pasture and gravel banks at seashore	3a 2r	@	1s 6d	5s 3d
12	Arable ⅓ deep ⅔ medium depth of strong sharp soil about ° lying irregular and ° exposed	} 14a 2r	@	18s 6d	13 18s 3d
	also bog meadow and moory arable	3a	@	12s	1 16s
	also sandy pasture	3a	@	2s 9d	8s 3d
	also waste at houses	20p			
13	Arable chiefly light sandy soil and subsoil some good generally uneven part steep and exposed	} 34a 2r 30p	@	14s 9d	25 11s 7d
	also good arable north and south of lot	18a	@	20s	18
	also waste at houses	20p			

14	Sand banks + sandy pasture about ⅓ of the latter	20a 2r	@	6d	10s 3d
15	Stiff shallow clay arable lying flat on stiff blue + yellow clay subsoil some moory arable and also bog pasture	} 46a 3r 29p } 1	@ @	10s 9d 2s 9d	25 4s 5d 2s 9d
16	Arable ⅔ medium depth of strong dark soil ° shallow and stiff chiefly on clay subsoil also waste at houses	} 42a 0r 19p } 1r	@	15s 6d	32 12s 10d
		474a 1r 33p			344 19s 5d

HOUSES

[When the valuers began to assess the buildings in Cranfield they must have examined at least eleven and they pencilled the numbers 5 to 11 against six of them, probably those assessed at more than £3. When the assessment level was raised from £3 to £5, five of them were renumbered in red ink: this is the first number in the following table and it is followed by the original pencil number (in brackets) because some valuation books contain information about these smaller and poorer properties. Editor]

	(5)	Robert Davidson	house and offices	
2	(6)	Joseph Moore	house and offices	£5 12s
4	(7)	Mr Robert Moore	small house and offices	£6 3s
5	(9)	Ballast Office stores		£13
3	(10)	Reverend John McIlwaine	house and offices	£9 11s
1	(11)	Coast Guard station		

Exemptions
Ballast Office stores   2a 2r   £1 11s 11d   £13
Coast Guard station houses   £4

                                                 Patrick Daly   James Deering   James Donnelly

TITHE APPLOTMENT (1830)

The small farms held by individuals with the same surname, as recorded in this document, indicates that many families had been subdividing farms among their members. Although their holdings were small, they were able to supplement their incomes from the sea. At the same time, however, there were four families who had managed to maintain more substantial farms of between 25 and 32 Irish acres (40 to 51 statute acres) and it is interesting to see that their houses were valued in 1834 (see above) – WHC

Tithe Applotment of Cranfield, parish of Kilkeel, Half Barony of Mourne,
FIN/5A/171 by John Moore & John McKnight, 12 February 1830

TOWNLAND	ACREAGE	QUALITY	AVERAGE PER ACRE	AMOUNT OF COMPOSITION
1 Addley William	5 2 18	2nd	1s 11.5d	10s 11d
2 Byrne Bernard	8 0 22	1st	2s 3.75d	18s 10d
3 Byrne James	3 3 26			9s 1.5d
4 Chesnut Arch + partners	7 0 10	2nd	1s 11.5d	13s 8d
5 Chesnut John	4 1 34			8s 9d
6 Clarke Bernard	6 2 37			13s 1d
7 Coffey Agnes (widow)	3 3 34	3rd	1s 6.5d	6s 2d
8 Coffey Eliza (widow)	3 3 34			6s 2d
9 Coffey Hugh	3 3 34	2nd	1s 11.5d	7s 8.5d
10 Coffey Isaac	3 3 34			7s 8.5d
11 Coffey James	4 2 16	1st	2s 3.75d	10s 8.5d
12 Coffey Samuel	10 1 0	2nd	1s 11.5d	19s 10d
13 Commrs of Ballast Office	1	1st	2s 3.75d	2s 4d
14 Commrs of Customs	2 0		1s 2d	
15 Cunigan Felix	3 3 37	2nd	1s 11.5d	7s 9d
16 Cunigan John sen	1	1st	2s 3.75d	2s 4d
17 Cunigan John jun	3 3 12	2nd	1s 11.5d	7s 5.25
18 Davidson Robert	32 0 27	1st	2s 3.75d	£3 14s 5.5d
19 Doran Edward sen	1 2 12			3s 8d
20 Doran Edward jun	3 0 5	2nd	1s 11.5d	5s 10.5d
21 Forsythe Robert	7 3 30			15s 4.5d
22 George Margaret (widow)	2 0 37	1st	2s 3.75d	5s 2.5d
23 George Philip	4 1 35			10s 4d
24 Harrold Daniel	34	2nd	1s 11.5d	5.5d
25 Moore Joseph	14 0 32	1st	2s 3.75d	£1 12s 10.5d
26 Moore Mary (widow)	11 3 10			£1 7s 4d
27 Morgan Arthur	5 0 16	4th	1s 1.875d	5s 11d
28 Murray Alexander	1 1 8	1st	2s 3.75d	3s 0.5d
29 McArdle John	1 1 18	3rd	1s 6.5d	2s 2d
30 McIlwaine Rev John	28	1st	2s 3.75d	£3 4s 9d
31 McKee Alexander	2 2 7		5s 11d	
32 McKee Edward sen	2 2			5s 10d
33 McKee Edward jun	2 1 35			5s 9d
34 McKee John	2 2 15	1st	2s 3.75d	6s 1d
35 O'Neill Tully + brothers	8 1 8	2nd	1s 11.5d	16s
36 Quinn Hugh	5 2 34	1st	2s 3.75d	13s 3.5d
37 Raymond Catherine	5 0 24	3rd	1s 6.5d	8s 0.5d
38 Raymond James	1 2 23			2s 8d
39 Raymond John	1 2 0			2s 4d
40 Raymond Sarah	1 3 22			3s
41 Rodgers Arthur	3	1st	2s 3.75d	6s 11.5d
42 Rodgers Mathew	3		2s 3.75d	6s 11.5d
43 Sibbett Thomas	9 1 0	2nd	1s 11.5d	17s 10.5d
44 Small Robert M	25 1 33	1st	2s 3.75d	£2 19s 6d
	265 1 13			£28 5s 4.5d
				out of £800

expected – a rise from 1803 until the Famine time and a fairly swift decline in the decade and a half after it.

There was some realignment of farm sizes over the period 1830-1895:

TABLE 1

CHANGES IN FARM SIZE: PERCENTAGE OF THE ACREAGE OCCUPIED BY EACH SIZE OF FARM, AS USED IN THE 1841 CENSUS

ACREAGE

	0–5	5–15	15–30	30–
1830	11	42	14	33
1862	4	43	11	42
1895	5	39	28	28

Clearly between 1830 and 1895 the area occupied by farms of 0-5 acres more than halved within a decade and a half of the worst Famine year. Over the entire period the percentage occupied by 5-15 and 30+ acre holdings declined slightly, but the very real increase, by a factor of two, was in the area occupied by the 15-30 acre farms.

TABLE 2

CHANGES IN POPULATION AND HOUSING IN CRANFIELD, 1841-1926

YEAR	'41	'51	'61	'71	'81	'91	'01	'11	'26
Pop.- Male	189	155	136	134	88	104	99	112	87
Female	228	200	143	145	104	87	83	85	83
Total	417	355	279	279	192	191	182	197	170
Per cent Female	54.7	56.3	51.2	52.0	54.2	45.5	45.6	43.1	48.8
Per cent Cumulative Pop. Decline		14.9	33.1	33.1	53.9	54.2	56.4	52.8	59.2
Inhabited houses	74	60	51	50	38	38	40	40	32

What was happening to the population while these changes were taking place?

The best estimate is that in the barony of Mourne the population rose by between thirty and thirty-nine per cent between 1821 and 1841. Probably much of this was absorbed by families moving onto moorland not previously farmed, but it is still likely that there was a considerable increase in Cranfield. The two decades following 1841 were years of quite severe population decline, followed by a decade of stability in the 1860s. The 1870s saw a severe decline, bringing the cumulative loss since 1841 up to fifty-four per cent. Thereafter, despite a small increase in the 1901-1911 period, the movement was slowly downwards. By 1926 the population was only forty-one per cent of the 1841 figure. The severe decline in the 1871-1881 decade caused the census enumerators to note that 'The decrease is attributed to emigration.' The reasons for this may have been delayed emigration from the previous decade or the agricultural depression at the end of the period. Since the number of inhabited houses fell by twelve, or twenty-four per cent of the total, it would seem that a number of complete families left. Tradition has it that at some stage Mr. Henry, the Kilmorey land agent, decided that many cottiers should be turned off the townland and that their houses were unroofed. Some are believed to have moved into Kilkeel. It is said that the Rector of Kilkeel intervened and insisted that Henry should find them other housing – some had apparently been sheltering under upturned boats. It seems, in view of the decline in the numbers of houses, that this action may well have taken place in this decade, and that the drastic fall in population may have been due to a combination of the farming depression and the activities of Mr. Henry. These years saw the disappearance of eighty-seven persons from a population of two hundred and seventy-nine.

TABLE 3

TABLE SHOWING CUMULATIVE POPULATION DECLINE in the Townlands of Cranfield, Ballinahatten and Greencastle and the Barony of Mourne, 1841-1891.

YEAR	CRANFIELD	BALLINAHATTEN	GREENCASTLE	MOURNE
1841	-	-	-	-
1851	14.9	14.4	14.0	15.0
1861	33.1	33.1	14.8	19.7
1871	33.1	43.9	15.5	22.6
1881	53.9	52.1	21.0	28.1
1891	54.2	53.1	21.9	33.2

Consider the decline in two neighbouring coastal townlands and in the barony of Mourne as a whole. Clearly the experience of Cranfield and Ballinahatten townlands were remarkably similar except for the decades 1861-1881. The factors which caused a decline of ten per cent in Ballinahatten in the 1860s, a decade before a similar loss in Cranfield, remain a mystery. Both lost over fifty per cent of their populations between 1841 and 1891. Greencastle lost only just over twenty per cent in the same period. All three had much good arable land. Table 4 illustrates the decline in density of population in the three townlands underlines the extent to which Cranfield and Ballinahatten were depopulated so rapidly over the half century. Further work is needed to explain why Greencastle, with its generally similar quality of land, was so much more successful in retaining its population. Perhaps it had a smaller cottier population initially.

The post-Famine changes in farming obviously affected the lives of the people and their desire or capacity to remain in Cranfield. Before these changes are considered it is necessary to look at the special circumstances obtaining in Cranfield which would also influence their decisions to remain or to leave. Cranfield's position at the entrance to Carlingford Lough was an important

TABLE 4

TABLE SHOWING THE NUMBERS OF PERSONS PER HUNDRED ACRES 1841-1891

YEAR	CRANFIELD	BALLINAHATTEN	GREENCASTLE
1841	86	90	66
1851	73	77	57
1861	57	60	56
1871	57	50	56
1881	39	43	52
1891	39	42	51

influence upon its life and population. The erection of a lighthouse just east of the Point in 1803 and transferred to Haulbowline Rock in 1823, introduced to the townland at least three lightkeepers and their families. In 1813 a coastguard station was established and continued in operation until 1882. There seem to have been always at least six officers, often with families, during these years, which would indicate at least a total of fifteen people. From 1813 to 1882 the lightkeepers, coastguards and their families probably varied between twenty-five and forty persons. Were it not for the departure of the coastguards to Greencastle in the 1880s, the 1891 census would have shown a rise in population. In 1901 the lightkeepers and their families accounted for eleven per cent of the population. The population figures must at times have been distorted as men with large families were replaced by single men and vice versa.

Certainly from the 1850s a number of the smaller farmers were part-time fishermen. From that time also, and probably for many years before, six men rowed the pilot boat which took the local pilot out to vessels entering Carlingford Lough. All of these were small farmers. So was the pilot. They lived in a closely knit community. The farms belonging to the pilot and his crew in the 1860s are shown on the 1861 Valuation map 11, 13, 15, 16, 17 and 18. When their boat was lost in 1866, six of the seven on board were drowned and three of the farms were left with no son to succeed.

There seems to be no way of finding when this practice of combining farm ownership with activity at sea originated, but it was probably a custom dating into the eighteenth century. Until at

Irish Lights lightkeepers' houses (porch, garage and lean-to added recently)

least the 1930s the farms along the shore kept a punt at the back of the beach and a Rogers and two Morgan families, still holding small farms, fished engined thirty-foot skiffs from Cranfield Bay, near Charley's Rock. At least one skiff carried potatoes across the Lough to Greenore. During the Famine the capacity to earn an off-farm income and to secure food must have enabled some small farmers and their families to stave off starvation. For others and cottiers unable to go to sea the shores provided the possibility of gathering whelks and other shell-fish.

The position of Cranfield Point at the entrance to Carlingford Lough influenced the lives of its people in other ways also. In 1842 the number of coastwise vessels (i.e. those arriving from British and Irish ports) entering the Lough for Newry was 1,498, to which should be added those in the foreign trade. It was because of this volume of trade that there was employment for coastguards, lightkeepers and pilots, with their attendant boatmen.

There was also a further intermittent employment for the male population. Because of the dangerous approach to the Lough, especially by the old southern channel, and the further risks within, there were, especially in winter, frequent strandings of sailing vessels, most of them near Cranfield Point. In one spell of storms in November 1852 four vessels were wrecked on or near the Point. These disasters provided timber and other salvage for the local people and also employment, for cargoes saved from the ships often had to be unloaded from badly damaged vessels and carted, usually to Newry, for sale. An example was the *Orissa* which in 1845 struck the Bar while bound from Liverpool to Bombay with a £20,000 cargo. She drove ashore rudderless in Cranfield and her cargo was unloaded and carted to Warrenpoint. Such events must have provided welcome employment in the stormy half of the year for small farmers and labourers, but especially for farmers who had horses and carts. Towards the end of the nineteenth century, as steamers began to displace sailing vessels as bulk carriers, and as the improvements were made to the approach to the Lough, many fewer wrecks took place, reducing the employment obtainable from this source. Nevertheless, the access to extra sources of income for the small farmers must have enabled them to accumulate small stores of capital which agriculture alone could not have provided.

In 1841 two-thirds of the inhabited houses were occupied by farmers. The remaining twenty-four, or one in three of the total, must have been occupied by non-farmers or by brothers of farmers whose land they helped to work. In 1862, omitting the lighthouse keepers and the officer in charge of the coastguards, there were only thirteen houses occupied by persons who did not have land. By 1895 the proportion of householders who were non-farmers had declined to one in seven. The disappearance of the non-farmer element of the population continued in the Famine time until at least 1895. Presumably a considerable number of the 1841 non-farming householders had been farm labourers/cottiers, of whom most would probably have been employed in the three or four largest farms or by widows. By 1901 there were only two labourers over twenty-one years, one of whom was a householder. The other, and five youths aged fourteen to twenty, were living-in as labourers on farms ranging from seven to over forty acres. The remaining labour needs were met by farmers' sons or unmarried brothers and by wives and daughters. Other householders included the lightkeepers and coastguards. What other occupations were represented earlier in the nineteenth century is unclear. Before the Famine there was a blacksmith, but he moved into a neighbouring townland. There must also in the early years have been a miller and probably a kilnman. Some may also have been fishermen or weavers. By 1901 only one man described himself as a fisherman, one as a carpenter and one as a gardener in Ballinahatten townland.

The proportion of males to females from 1841 seems to have varied (see Table 2) but for some reason by 1891 the proportion of females fell below fifty per cent for the first time and remained so until the end of the period. Clearly women were finding it increasingly difficult to find employment or personal fulfilment in Cranfield. Social pressures were on them to leave, as in the case of three sisters who emigrated to Australia when their brother brought his bride to the family home. Employment, other than in housekeeping and helping on the farm, was hard to obtain. In 1901 five women described themselves as seamstresses or dressmakers, one as a spinner (aged fifty-eight) and two (under twenty-one) as servants. Some, in earlier years, probably earned a meagre living as knitters of socks and other garments, but such opportunities must have been much reduced by late in the century.

The decline in population must largely have reflected the changes which took place in farming. Until the late eighteenth century there is no detailed knowledge of farming in Cranfield. The 1803 farm census gives some indication of production at a time when prices were considerably above mid-eighteenth century levels but not at peak Napoleonic War levels. Probably taken in December 1803, or even January 1804, when livestock which could not be fed over the winter had been sold in the October fairs, only nine farmers out of thirty-one had more than one cow. Oats constituted fifty-eight per cent of the four hundred and fifty-five barrels of cereal crops, the remainder being barley. The presence of a windmill in Cranfield in the late eighteenth century argues for a fairly high acreage under oats then in the area and almost certainly into the next century also. Potatoes were clearly being produced for the market, almost a thousand large sacks being still on the farms, one man having almost a quarter of the total. Some flax must also have been grown. Only William Halyday, on one of the large farms of the former Wauchope 'third', had a wholly arable farm. Every farm save one supported a horse, and twenty-four had one of the old solid-wheeled cars. Their replacement later in the century by the Scotch carts must have cut substantially the amount of carting time required.

The acreage of three of the four large farms was 161 acres, so it is possible to compare the stock and crop levels on them with those of the other farms, though these included a large farm of unknown extent. The stocking rates of all types of livestock, including horses, per hundred acres on the large farms was from a quarter to a third of that on the rest of the farms. The large farms were producing much higher rates of crops, save oats, than the others as Table 5 shows.

TABLE 5

RATES OF STOCKING AND CROP PRODUCTION per hundred acres on large farms and the remainder, 1803.

	LARGE FARMS	REMAINING FARMS
Horses	2.5	9.2
Cars	2.5	6.5
Oats (Barrels)	40.4	60.9
Barley (Barrels)	56	31.3
Hay (Loads)	33	17.8
Straw (Loads)	118	99.7
Potatoes (Sacks)	295.6	152.3

It must be concluded that the large farms were employing the small farmers to do considerable amounts of carting, and perhaps also ploughing, for them, or else that the small farmers were keeping horses for which they had little farm work. It is clear that the larger farms were concentrating on crop production, and probably selling hay and straw in addition to their potatoes and cereals.

Unfortunately indications of how the balance of arable and pasture altered later in the century are lacking. There is no proof that there was a large swing away from arable to pasture farming – which might have reduced the demand for farm labourers. There was in the nineteenth century, and perhaps earlier, traditionally an influx of harvesters into Mourne from the Cooley peninsula of County Louth at the time of the corn and barley harvests, which would seem to argue that arable farming continued to be important for much of the nineteenth century. Certainly Cranfield and Ballinahatten were noted for their potato growing into the present century. The competition for wrack to manure arable, and especially potato, land is a measure of the extent of such land. So important was the wrack that in 1885 farmers were charged 2s. 6d. (12.5 p) for each acre of their farm to cut wrack from the shore and to 'gather the inblown wrack from the 1st of May to the 29th September in each year' – the total paid annually to the landlord was equivalent to the rent of a forty-five acre farm.

The adoption of new Scotch carts and improved implements such as ploughs, reapers, drills and threshing machines must have reduced the demand for labour on the larger farms and accentuated the decline of the labouring or cottier class. The introduction of these would have been slow on most of the farms of less than fifteen acres. In 1862 these accounted for forty-seven per cent of the townland, so old labour intensive methods must have died slowly.

The passing on of farms to sons was at times a fraught business. Sometimes the eldest son inherited the land, but this was not always a foregone conclusion.

Wills must have been made by most of the farmers, but few appear to have been probated. Presumably the desires of the testator, once put in writing, were generally accepted by the family. Once the farmer died, the son who succeeded to the farm often had to make arrangements for the rest of the family. Payments had to be made to brothers who might wish to emigrate – three brothers went to Australia in the 1890s because there was no land for them. There is the example of the son who decided to marry and had to provide for the emigration to Australia of three sisters before he could bring his bride to the house. Often a widow had to be provided for in the house for the rest of her days. In at least one case the farmer apparently made arrangements with the Estate for the farm to be divided, with his widow becoming tenant of almost half the farm, which upon her death was reunited with the son's part.

Early in the nineteenth century two brothers worked a farm and divided stock and crops equally between them and their widowed mother. Then too, a Coffey farm was divided equally between four sons on the father's death. In other cases, where there was no son to succeed, a son-in-law might do so. The farm might pass to a daughter until she married. The son succeeding to the farm might find himself responsible for providing a dowry for his sister. One example was that of a young lady who took with her a seven-acre field for five years. Tradition has it that it was difficult to secure its return at the end of the stipulated time! Faced with all these settlements to be made, some who succeeded to the farms felt that the succession was a doubtful privilege. A constant worry for some was that a brother who remained at home and worked on the farm might marry and provision would have to be made for him.

Underpinning the whole economic and social life of Cranfield were the outlets for much of its products. Possibly from Norman times a fair and markets had been held in Greencastle. Certainly in the patent granted to Arthur Bagenal in 1613 he was given the privilege of holding one fair a year and a weekly market, held on Friday. Later a second fair was held. These must have been a useful outlet for Cranfield farmers in days when transport was extremely difficult. It is not known when the markets ceased to operate, but almost certainly when the Needhams procured the right to hold a weekly market and monthly fair in Kilkeel. Despite the competition from Kilkeel, the Lammas Fair continued to be held on the Fair Green in Greencastle up to the end of the nineteenth century, by which time it appears to have been a big social occasion for farmers all over Mourne, from others further inland and for many who came across the Lough from the Cooley Peninsula in County Louth. It was probably the social aspects which enabled it to survive for so long. Most farmers in Cranfield were not more than a mile and a half from the Fair Green, so the fairs must have played an important part in their economic and social life.

Certainly by the nineteenth century the monthly Kilkeel fairs had taken away much of the trade from Greencastle. The building of a combined Market and Courthouse in Kilkeel about 1800 must have signalled the Kilmorey intention to replace Greencastle as the market centre. The Cranfield farmers would have

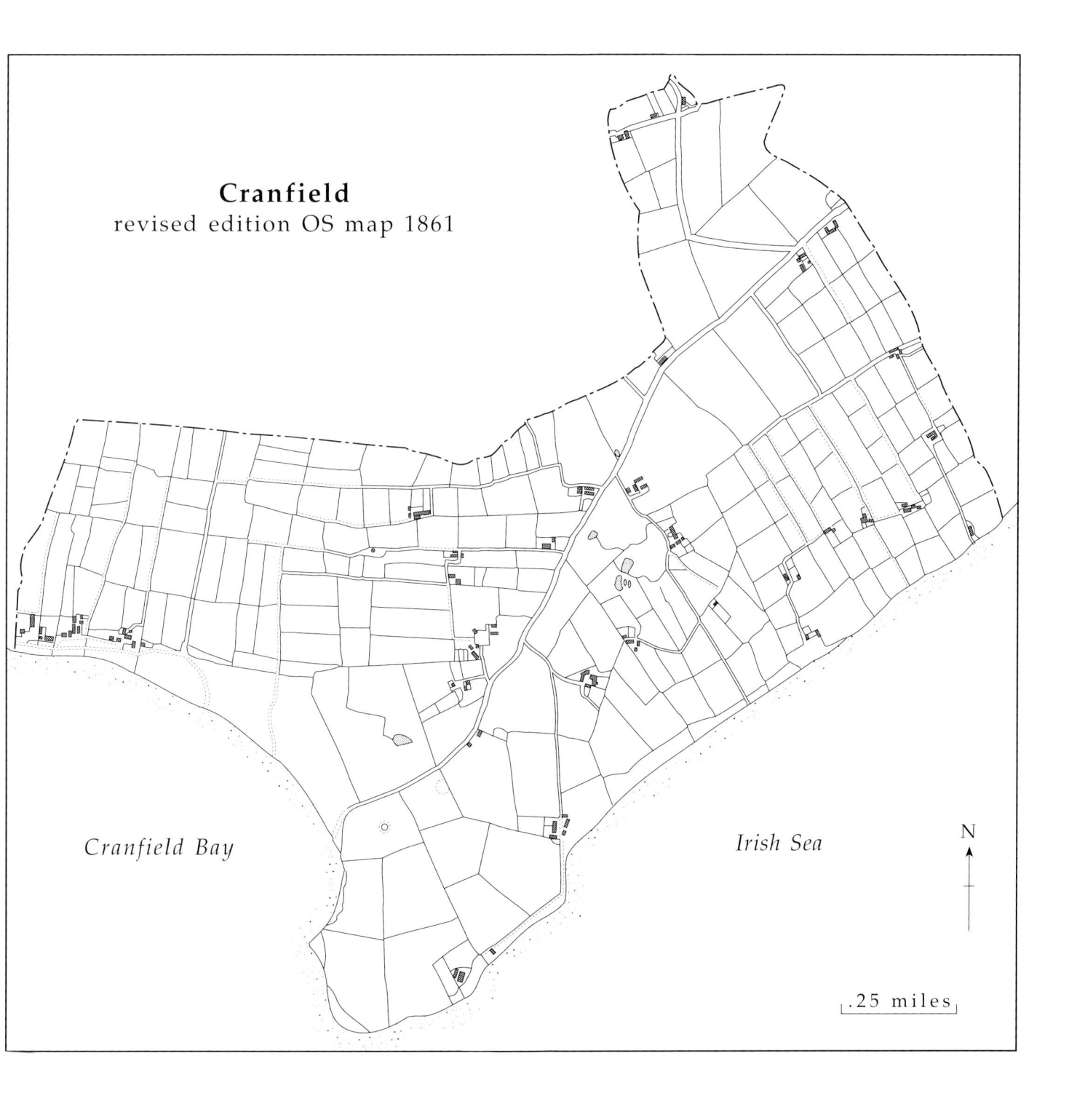

CRANFIELD

Cranfield
revised edition OS map 1861

Cranfield Bay

Irish Sea

N

.25 miles

TOWNLANDS IN ULSTER

TENEMENT VALUATION (1861)
Comparison of the names of the families listed here with those of the 1830 Tithe Applotment list indicates that many families had been subdividing their farms especially in those 'thirds' held by Houston and Raymond. Many of these holdings had become very small, although it should be remembered that the Tithe Applotment acres are Irish acres and so need to be multipled by 1.6 for conversion into statute measure, as used in this valuation. If families made a practice of subdividing their farms among their families, they ran the risk of losing their social standing. In the Wauchope 'third', by contrast, there are only four farms and they are still quite substantial. Note also that all the farms were held from the landlord and there was no longer any subdivision – WHC

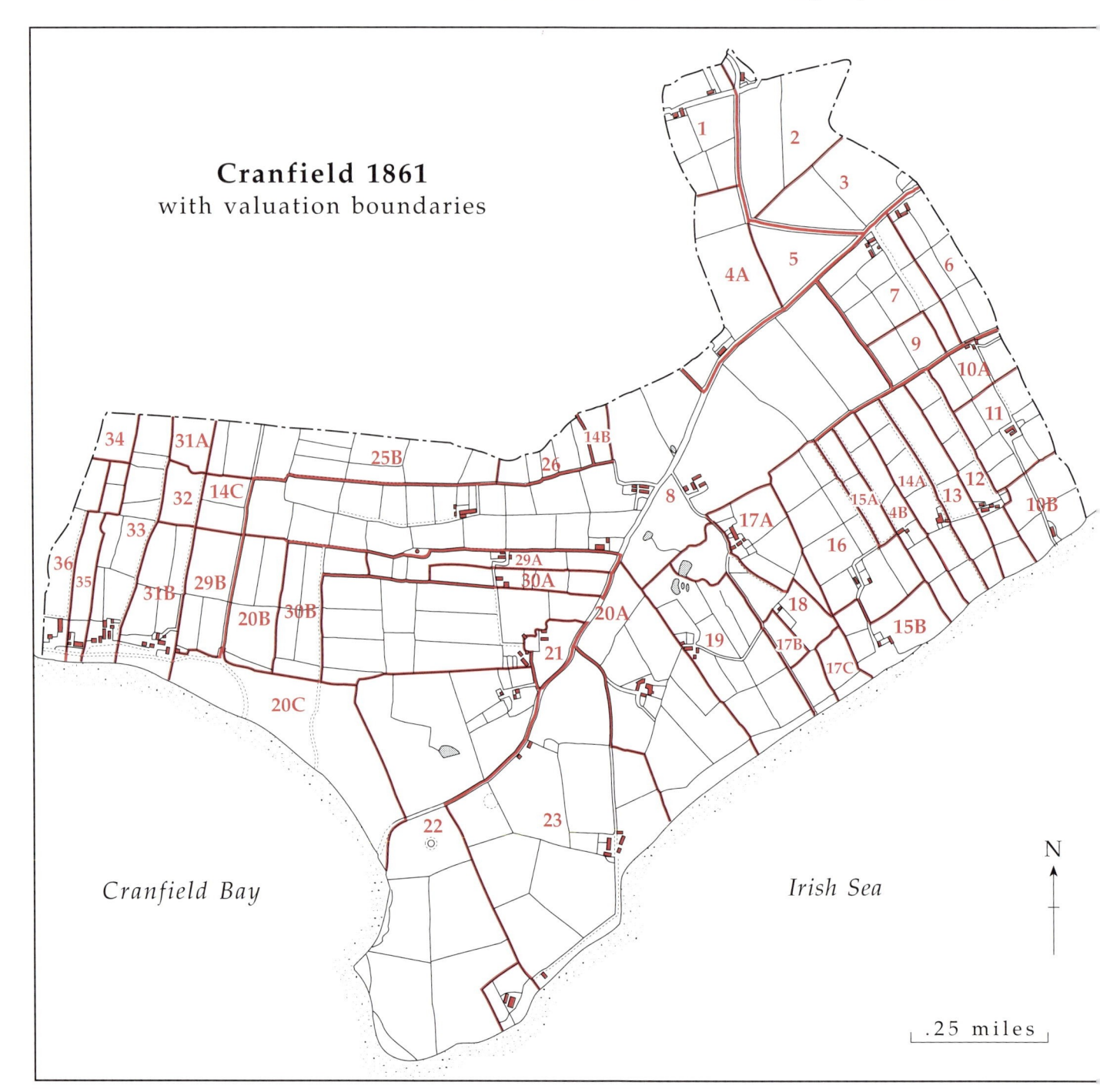

Cranfield 1861
with valuation boundaries

Cranfield Bay

Irish Sea

N

.25 miles

No. and Letters of Reference to Map.	Names. Townlands and Occupiers.	Names. Immediate Lessors.	Description of Tenement.	Area.	Rateable Annual Valuation. Land.	Rateable Annual Valuation. Buildings.	Total Annual Valuation of Rateable Property.
	CRANFIELD. (Ord. S. 57.)						
1 a	Edward Doran,	Trustees of the Kilmorey Estate,	House, offices, and land,	7 3 25	6 15 0	2 10 0	9 5 0
— b	Ellen Rogan,	Same,	House and sm. garden,	—	—	0 15 0	0 15 0
2	Rev. John Forbes Close,	Same,	House and land,	12 3 15	12 15 0	1 5 0	14 0 0
3	Rev. John O'Neill,	Same,	House, office, and land, House (in progress),	9 0 30	8 15 0	1 10 0	10 5 0
4 A — B	Elizabeth Coffey,	Same,	House, offices, & land,	9 3 15 6 0 35	9 5 0 6 5 0	— 1 5 0	} 16 15 0
5	Thos. Cunningham,	Same,	Land,	5 0 5	5 0 0	—	5 0 0
6	Thos. Cunningham,	Robert Davidson,	House, offices, and land,	6 3 25	6 10 0	4 10 0	11 0 0
7	John Burns,	Same,	House, offices, and land,	9 3 30	10 0 0	4 10 0	14 10 0
8	Robert Davidson,	Trustees of the Kilmorey Estate,	Land,	40 0 20	43 10 0	—	43 10 0
9	Nicholas Burns,	Robert Davidson,	Land,	3 1 15	3 10 0	—	3 10 0
10 A — B	Nicholas Burns,	Trustees of the Kilmorey Estate,	House, offices, & land,	4 1 30 6 0 25	4 10 0 5 5 0	2 0 0 —	} 11 15 0
11	Henry Coffey,	Same,	House, offices, and land,	7 2 0	6 10 0	2 0 0	8 10 0
12	David Coffey,	Same,	House, offices, and land,	6 1 30	6 0 0	2 0 0	8 0 0
13	Ann Coffey,	Same,	House, offices, and land,	6 3 30	6 0 0	1 0 0	7 0 0
14 A — B — C	Hugh Coffey,	Same,	House, offices, & land,	6 1 30 1 1 25 2 2 25 2 3 0	6 5 0 1 5 0 1 15 0 3 0 0	1 15 0 — — —	} 11 0 0
15 A B a — b	Hugh Morgan, Edward Morgan,	Same,	House, offices, & land, House, offices, & land,	— —	— —	1 0 0 1 0 0	} 4 10 0 } 4 10 0
— B				5 3 25	4 0 0	—	
16	John Chesnut,	Same,	House, offices, and land,	13 1 15	13 15 0	2 0 0	15 15 0
17 A a B C	John Shields,	Same,	House, offices, & land,	5 2 5 1 1 15 2 1 0	5 10 0 1 0 0 1 15 0	1 0 0 — —	} 9 5 0
— A c	Samuel Raymond,	James Raymond,	House,	—	—	0 10 0	0 10 0
18 17 A b	James Raymond,	Trustees of the Kilmorey Estate,	House, offices, & land,	8 3 20 0 1 30	8 5 0 0 10 0	— 1 5 0	} 10 0 0
19	John Cunningham,	Same,	House, offices, and land,	14 2 20	14 0 0	1 15 0	15 15 0
20 A a — B — C	Joseph Moore,	Same,	House, offices, and land, Land, Land, Right of collecting and taking seaweed from shore,	45 0 5 7 0 35 16 3 10 —	41 5 0 5 15 0 2 5 0 —	9 10 0 — — —	} 58 15 0 20 0 0
— A b	Edward Doran,	Joseph Moore,	House and sm. garden,	—	—	2 0 0	2 0 0
— c	Patrick Morgan,	Same,	House and sm. garden,	—	—	2 0 0	2 0 0
— d	James Scott,	Same,	House and sm. garden,	—	—	1 10 0	1 10 0
— e	Peter Troke,	Same,	House and sm. garden,	—	—	2 0 0	2 0 0
— f	Arthur Patterson,	Same,	Ho., office, & sm. garden,	—	—	2 0 0	2 0 0
21	William Woods,	Trustees of the Kilmorey Estate,	House, office, and land,	2 2 10	2 15 0	8 10 0	11 5 0
22	James M'Ilwaine,	Same,	House, offices, and land,	48 2 0	44 0 0	11 0 0	55 0 0
23 a	Charles Annett,	Same,	House, offices, and land,	41 0 20	38 10 0	8 0 0	46 10 0
— b	John Galer,	Charles Annett,	House and sm. garden,	—	—	2 10 0	2 10 0
— c	Coast-Guard's watch and boat house,	(See Exemptions.)					
24	Light-house keeper's houses, store, & land,	(See Exemptions.)					
—	Trustees of the Kilmorey Estate,		Half annual rent of Light-house, &c.,	—	—	—	0 14 0
25 A — B	Margaret Coffey and Sisters,	Trustees of the Kilmorey Estate,	House, offices, & land,	4 1 15 14 0 20	4 10 0 10 0 0	3 0 0 —	} 17 10 0
26	William M'Kee,	Same,	Land,	3 2 15	3 10 0	—	3 10 0
27 a	John M'Kee,	Same,	House, offices, and land,	8 2 30	7 0 0	3 0 0	10 0 0
— b	William M'Kee,	Same,	House, office, & garden,	0 1 5	0 5 0	1 15 0	2 0 0
28	Thomas Sibbit,	Same,	House, office, and land,	15 2 0	12 10 0	3 0 0	15 10 0
29 A — B	John Knox,	Same,	House, offices, & land,	5 2 0 6 0 0	5 0 0 5 0 0	2 0 0 —	} 12 0 0
— a	Elizabeth Rogers,	Same,	House and sm. garden,	—	—	0 10 0	0 10 0
30 A — B	James Chesnut,	Same,	House, offices, & land,	2 3 0 7 1 0	3 10 0 5 0 0	3 10 0 —	} 12 0 0
31 A — B a	Terence Quin,	Same,	House, office, & land,	2 0 25 7 3 10	1 5 0 5 5 0	— 1 5 0	} 7 15 0
B b 32	Isabella Doran,	Same,	House, office, & land,	0 0 20 2 1 10	0 5 0 1 10 0	0 15 0 —	} 2 10 0
33 a	Thomas George,	Same,	House, office, and land,	11 0 20	8 5 0	1 15 0	10 0 0
— b	William Kenmure,	Thomas George,	House,	—	—	0 10 0	0 10 0
— c	Margaret Kennedy,	Free,	House,	—	—	1 5 0	1 5 0
34 36 b	Ellen Cunningham,	Trustees of the Kilmorey Estate,	House and land,	2 0 0	1 5 0 0 15 0		} 2 0 0
35 a	Patrick Rogers,	Same,	House, office, and land,	4 2 10	2 15 0	1 5 0	4 0 0
— b	Alexander Chambers,	Patrick Rogers,	House,	—	—	0 15 0	0 15 0
— c	John Farrelly,	Free,	House,	—	—	1 10 0	1 10 0
36 a	Patrick Sloane,	Trustees of the Kilmorey Estate,	House, office, and land,	5 0 25	3 10 0	1 5 0	4 15 0
			Total of Rateable Property,	473 3 25	416 5 0	110 5 0	547 4 0
			EXEMPTIONS:				
23 c			Coast-Guard's watch and boat house,	—	—	4 0 0	4 0 0
24			Light-house keeper's houses, stores, & land,	2 1 35	2 0 0	14 0 0	16 0 0
			Total of Exemptions,	2 1 35	2 0 0	18 0 0	20 0 0
			Total, including Exemptions,	476 1 20	418 5 0	128 5 0	567 4 0

transferred their business from Greencastle quite quickly, as buyers would have been attracted to Kilkeel by the weighing and storage facilities. Recognised drovers were employed by them to walk the cattle to Newry after the fairs. At some time during the nineteenth century, or perhaps earlier, some at least of the Cranfield farmers carted produce to the Newry markets to obtain the enhanced prices there. This involved a journey of seventeen miles which entailed an early start, often at 2 a.m., and a return to the farm almost twenty-four hour hours later. It is probable that such journeys were uncommon until the farmer had a spoke-wheeled scotch cart.

For a considerable period Cranfield people regarded Warrenpoint as their port. From the late eighteenth century emigrants from the townland must have walked there to embark for the United States, while smacks must have provided passages, mostly to Liverpool. By 1823 the first Warrenpoint steamer service to Liverpool was inaugurated, later replaced by a Newry to Liverpool sailing. Newry was the town with which they did business, travelling by long car. Some, when the railway arrived in Warrenpoint, joined the train there to continue to Newry.

The opening of the London and North Western Railway's passenger and cargo service from Greenore to Holyhead in 1873 provided a very convenient route to and from England, for passengers and goods were carried across to Greenore by paddle steamer from the Railway pier at Greencastle.

The emergence of townland shops is not well remembered. In the 1880s the Pattersons certainly ran a well-patronised general shop. They went by horse and cart to Newry, setting off at one a.m., taking farm produce to market, then buying stock for the shop and returning about one a.m. the following morning. Later there was Kennedy's small shop described as 'six foot by six' which stocked necessaries and then McManus's and Forsythe's. The only public house still remembered dated back to the 1870s – The Wild Goose Lodge. Kilkeel shop records show that in the 1890s farmers were, often on market or fair days, buying drinks, tobacco and general groceries. Sometimes they got small loans of a few pounds from the shopkeeper, which were usually repaid on their next visit to town.

These developments made movement and an awareness of the world more widespread than a century before. This awareness had also been encouraged by the provision of a National School education available to all in the adjacent townland of Lurganconary, which probably replaced a hedge school. Under Catholic management, it was attended by all creeds until the Presbyterians built their own National School in Cranfield in 1892. It was in the 1890s that, in response to the atmosphere of the times, the Cranfield Orange lodge was established. It became a bonding factor in the life of much of the Protestant section of the population. All of the Protestants worshipped in Kilkeel, though Presbyterians had devotional meetings in members' houses in the 1880s. After 1892 these were transferred to the new school. Catholics had to travel to Massforth until the opening of the chapel in the adjacent Grange townland in 1925. Occasions when almost the entire adult male population of the townland gathered were when the inblown wrack had to be divided on the beach. Men who helped each other at flax-pulling or at calving times then kept wary eyes on each other.

Some families were more aware than others of the townland as a community, particularly those which were long-established. Others moved in as tenant farmers and sometimes were gone in a generation. Some of them were too busy trying to establish their families and they were mostly interested in their own land and in trying to acquire more. Some of them would move to other townlands if a better farm became available. For many, relatives were in the United States, Canada, Australia and Britain. Cranfield was only part of their world.

Having described the kinds of people and their situations in life in Cranfield, it is needful to conclude with some indication of the housing which sheltered them. The first definite information on the housing was recorded by the valuation field officers in 1835. They recorded details of twelve of the most highly valued dwellings and accompanying outbuildings. The large farmers all had slated dwellings, but so had James Coffey on a seven-acre farm and Francis Annett. So also had the Coastguard Officer's house and store. The other five farmers all lived in thatched cottages of the kind that were common in Mourne until quite recently. They were mostly between forty and fifty feet long, about sixteen feet in depth and with walls just over six feet high. Presumably the houses which were not recorded were all thatched. Some must have been pretty miserable. Since there were seventy-four inhabited houses in 1841, there were probably about seventy in 1835. Six of these were slated, or almost nine per cent of the total.

The next detailed account of the housing stock was recorded in the 1901 Census. Table 6 shows the accommodation available in the housing stock in that year.

TABLE 6

THE NUMBERS OF HOUSES OF EACH SIZE, BY NUMBERS OF ROOMS, for thatched and slated dwellings, showing the numbers of inhabitants in each group.

Rooms	1	2	3	4	5	6	7	8+
Thatched								
Nos. of Houses	1	5	9	1	-	-	-	-
Inhabitants	2	21	36	3				
Slated								
Nos. of Houses	-	4	4	6	2	2	1	3
Inhabitants	-	12	11	39	10	17	8	19

The thatched houses represented thirty-four percent of the total housing stock and housed forty-one per cent of the population. They accommodated on average 1.47 persons per room. The slated ones averaged 1.0 persons per room. However, if two large houses with nine persons in thirty rooms were not counted, the remaining slated houses averaged 1.24 persons per room. Two of the two-roomed thatched houses, with five and two persons respectively, had mud walls, but the remainder were of stone.

Clearly the housing stock had declined in numbers since 1835, but the number of slated houses had risen from eight to fifty-eight per cent of the total. The great majority of houses were still the long, low cottages, few two-storey houses having been built. One of the two-roomed houses is illustrated. Now ruinous, the view is from the rear, as the front is overgrown. Occupied in 1862 by John Galer and belonging to the large Annett farm, it was then valued for the Poor Rate at £2.10s. (£2.50). At that time small thatched cottages were rated at as little as 10s. (50p). When the Census was taken in 1901 the occupier was Edward Doran (77) a labourer; his wife Ellen (85); and Richard their son (56), a gardener. The cottage was occupied until at least 1940 as a summer cottage. By today's standards many houses were overcrowded. In 1901 the worst example of this was a three-roomed thatched house which was home to a farmer (58) who farmed four acres; his wife (56); his brother (70); four sons aged 27, 25, 20, 14; and a daughter of 16. The brother was a widower who also was described as a farmer, as were the three eldest sons. One can only imagine the poverty in which the family lived. Many other houses might have been as overcrowded had people not emigrated. The census places on record the conditions in which all too many of the people described above lived in Cranfield until well into the twentieth century.

John Galer's House (1862)

Still occupied site of Raymond's house of 18th century

ACKNOWLEDGEMENTS

Special thanks are due to Mr. Albert Patterson, Cranfield, for much valuable information and discussion.

SOURCES

PUBLIC RECORD OFFICE OF NORTHERN IRELAND
D/654/A2 Farm Census of County Down, 1803
D/1268/1/1 (1813); D/1657 (1895) Kilmorey Estate Rentals
D/619 Box 2 Bagenal Estate Rentals, 1688; 1714
Fin/5A/171 Tithe Applotment Books

PUBLISHED

BELL, J. People and the Land. Belfast, 1992
CRAWFORD, W. H. The Significance of Landed Estates in Ulster, 1600-1820. Irish Economic and Social History. Vol. XVII (1990)
CULLEN, L. M. The Emergence of Modern Ireland, 1600-1900. London, 1981
DUBOURDIEU, REV.J. Statistical Survey of the County of Down. Dublin, 1802
FITZPATRICK, D. The Disappearance of the Irish Agricultural Labourer, 1841-1912. Irish Economic and Social History VII (1980)
GAILEY, A. Changes in Irish Rural Housing, 1600-1900. in O'FLANAGAN, P., FERGUSON, P. and WHELAN, K. Rural Ireland 1600-1900: Modernisation and Change. Cork, 1987
KENNEDY, L. and DOWLING, M. W. Prices and Wages in Ireland, 1700-1850. Irish Economic and Social History Vol. XXIV (1997)
KENNEDY, L. and OLLERENSHAW, P. An Economic History of Ulster, 1820-1939. Manchester, 1985
MAYNE, D. 19th Century Coastguard Stations in Mourne. 12 Miles of Mourne VII (1996)
McCAUGHAN, M. and APPLEBY, J. (Eds.) The Irish Sea: Aspects of Maritime History. Belfast, 1989
O'GRADA, C. Ireland Before and After The Famine. (2nd. Edition) Manchester, 1993
O'MAINNIN, M. B. Place-Names of Northern Ireland. Vol. Three. County Down III The Mournes. Belfast, 1993
TURNER, M. Livestock in the Agrarian Economy of Counties Down and Antrim from 1803 to the Famine. Irish Economic and Social History XI (1984)

DRUMSKINNEY & MONTIAGHROE

DRUMSKINNEY & MONTIAGHROE

JOHN B. CUNNINGHAM

INTRODUCTION

The townlands of Montiaghroe and Drumskinney lie at a height of about 400 feet above sea level close to where Fermanagh, Tyrone and Donegal meet. These townlands lie in a damp upland area between the Bannagh River and the Termon River. Here the latter river forms the political boundary of Northern Ireland.

The landscape is that of steep drumlin slopes, peat bogs, rushy pasture, hay meadows and some reseeded silage grassland. There is an ever increasing number of serried blocks of conifer plantations.

Both these townlands are bisected by the road from Kesh to Castlederg. From the hills of Scraghey which is just inside County Tyrone and about eight miles from Castlederg to about two miles from Kesh the road is known as the Seven Mile Straight. In a straight line the road goes directly up some very steep hills and seems to be a Grand Jury road dating to some time after 1765.

HISTORY AND TRADITION BEFORE THE FAMINE

This part of Fermanagh was Maguire territory prior to the Plantation and was confiscated after the flight of the Irish Earls in 1607. The most powerful local chieftains in this area were Muldoon, McCaffery, Monaghan and McGoldrick.

This area lay on the ancient pathway between the Erne and the valley of the River Foyle and megalithic tombs, standing stones and stone circles are tangible evidence of the occupation of the area by Neolithic and Bronze Age peoples.

Drumskinney Stone Circle which is in State Care is the most famous prehistoric landmark in the area but is only one of the ancient features of the locality. Four other stone circles close by and the 'Giants Grave' at Tawneydarragh testify to the long history of settlement here.

These may have been built here on account of the density of population in the area or its religious significance or indeed the simple availability of suitable stone. Certainly there are many small cliffs or outcrops of freestone rock, known locally as 'spinks', which naturally divide into large regular rectangular boulders. These lend themselves to becoming the raw material for stone circles. Of the five identified in these two townlands the only one of this system of stone circles that has been excavated is that in Drumskinney townland while the others lie in Montiaghroe.

Central Ulster and Leinster are the two main areas of stone-circle building in Ireland. Those in the south are generally made up of a small number of large stones while those in the north have a large number of smaller stones.

Drumskinney stone circle is a not quite circular ring of upright stones some 12.8 metres across and made up of 39 stones with a small round cairn or mound at the side. The highest stone is about four foot high and one foot nine inches wide and nine inches thick. There is a line of 24 stones, 7.6 metres long called an alignment to one side of the circle and associated with the cairn. No one has been able to decide if this alignment points in any logical astronomical or geographical direction but it certainly does not follow any of the cardinal points of the compass. Perhaps some definite information will have to wait until all of the circles are excavated when it may be possible to see that all of them together make some coherent historical statement.

In the nearby townlands of Tawneydarragh and Dromore Big there are two megalithic burial chambers. Neither are complete but the massive nature of the stones used in their building are mute testimony to the power and organisation of the people who erected them in their day.

These tombs may or may not have contained the cremated remains of a great chieftain but some certainly were simply the last resting place of women or children. Some theorise that rather than burial places these megalithic tombs were in the nature of gigantic markers of ancient tribal boundaries and that their occupants were in the nature of sacrifices rather than honoured remains of glorious rulers.

ESTATES AND CREATION OF FARMS (TENANTS AND COTTIERS)

This part of Fermanagh is in the Barony of Lurg and this was granted to English Undertakers in the Plantation, most of whom were from Norfolk or Suffolk in East Anglia. Two Blennerhassett brothers from near Norwich obtained three estates between them. One was eventually centered near Belleek, the second near Kesh and the third which included the Drumskinney area never developed a central village or growth area. This area has continued to lack a central focus down through the centuries and has been fragmented into numerous small areas owned by various landlords including Archdall, Johnston, Barton, Irvine, Brooke and Lowry.

Drumskinney must have been of much greater extent in the past as the first Ordnance Survey maps note a subdenomination called Drumskinney North which would seem to include the modern townlands of Tullynashammer (Shammar's Hill ?), Tievaveeny (The hillside of the mine), Lugmore (Great Hollow) and Meentullyclogh (the smooth hill of the stones). It is probable therefore that ancient

Drumskinney has been much sub-divided into six modern townlands.

In the earliest Plantation records Drumskinney or Montiaghroe does not appear at all and seems to be subsumed under the title of 'the half quarter of Gortnegullion which comprised the two estates of Gortnegullion and Dromore.' In the Hearth Money Rolls of 1665 the inhabitants of Gortnegullion are named as Bryan McGrath and Ternan O'Murrise while in Dromore there was Pattr O'Muldune, Edmond O'Managhan and Cahill O'Muldune.

The townland of Montiaghroe which contains 272 acres is described thus in the Ordnance Survey Name Books in the 1830s.

> MONTIAGHROE... The red bog. It is owned by Mr Johnston and has 46 inhabitants mostly Roman Catholics. It is leased for 3 lives or 31 years and one of the lives is gone.

This Johnston family based at Aghagriffin near Ederney was one of the original Johnston families expelled from the Borders of England and Scotland and forced to Ireland at the time of the Plantation of Ulster.

Drumskinney which contains 290 acres is described as follows:-

> DRUMSKINNEY... the ridge of the knife, where a...... (undecipherable) threw away his knife. There are 34 inhabitants chiefly Roman Catholics. Proprietor Mr H. Vaughan Brooke.

This is the Brooke family of Brookeborough, County Fermanagh. Lord Brookeborough in recent times was Prime Minister of Northern Ireland.

By the time of Griffith's Valuation in the 1860s James Johnston was in possession of Montiaghroe and among his tenants were James Taylor and Thomas Graham who leased 26 and 64 acres respectively. Thomas Graham had four sub-tenants on his property, Catherine Magee, Jane Curran, Thomas Scollan and Robert Taylor. These occupied houses only. These would seem to be farm labourers and survivors of the cottier class which was decimated at the time of the famine. The relatively large farms are also an effect of the famine. Landlords consolidated holdings as the population fell and set the newly 'squared' farms to the most solvent tenants.

The representatives of John Graham, who had died recently, held 109 acres and had two sub-tenants, Jane Magee and Michael Fitzpatrick, who held houses and small gardens. The final tenant in the townland was John Monaghan who leased 71 acres. Later this farmhouse acted as the first post office in the area. These Monaghans were known as 'the Jacks' to differentiate them from the numerous other Monaghans in the locality. The Roman Catholic Chapel of Montiagh and its graveyard occupied a section out of the farm of Thomas Graham. The school here at the edge of the graveyard had not yet been built.

Drumskinney at the time of Griffith's Valuation was owned by the representatives of James Daniel. Caroline Daniel then inherited and soon after John G. Irvine of Killadeas became the owner of the townland. The first two holdings which are beside Drumskinney Crossroads were held between five Monaghans. The first consisting of 38 acres between Edward Monaghan Senior and Patrick Monaghan and the second of 54 acres between James Monaghan, Edward Monaghan Junior and Thomas Monaghan.

There has been an Edward Monaghan among the Monaghans of the Cross from time immemorial and the name may well go back to the Edmond O'Managhan of the Hearth Money Rolls and further into the mists of time.

Holding number three of 6 acres was taken by Henry Muldoon and partly sublet to James Martin who had just a house on the farm. Edward McHugh had a farm of 24 acres and Hannah Monaghan had a house on the property.

Edward Monaghan Senior held property number five which contained 30 acres but although it had offices there was no house on the property number five. Terence Monaghan held 21 acres and an Edward Monaghan who is not designated as either Senior or Junior, held property number seven which consisted of a house, offices and land amounting to 25 acres. James McHugh held 39 acres on his own while John and Bernard Monaghan held 12 acres between them. The final property of 33 acres was held by James Monaghan who let a house to William Johnston.

DEVELOPMENT OF THE ROAD NETWORK

The Grand Jury road which bisects this area in a straight line is linked to two older roads on either side: the road from Ederney to Castlederg and that from Pettigo to Castlederg. It joins them at the top of Scraghey Mountain. As a road it seems to have had little effect other than to open up the area. The crossroads at Montiaghroe with its Roman Catholic Chapel, school, post office and Methodist meeting house looks as if it might have developed into a little village but lack of a sufficiently powerful local landlord or any form of economic development probably thwarted this possibility.

The major market towns for this area always have been Castlederg and Pettigo. The villages of Kesh and Ederney would have featured when these towns had a fair but now only Castlederg is still important. Castlederg, the castle on the Dearg river meaning red river is locally known as 'Gearg'. Pettigo has been in decline ever since the setting up of the Border in 1922 apart from the Second World War when smuggling became a major local industry.

> **Roadbuilding**
> Mr Roderick Grey has passed away. In July 1878 he was appointed Fermanagh's first ever County Surveyor. He was born in Dublin in March 1822. He is responsible for many of the present roads in Fermanagh. He built the new road between Kesh, Ederney and Lack as the old road went over the hilltops. He also built the seven mile straight road from Kesh to Scraghy via Tubrid and rearranged the road from Belleek to Enniskillen. He caused this last road to be brought down to the lakeshore.
> *(Impartial Reporter,* 24 January 1924)

POPULATION GROWTH AND DECLINE

Today the population is thinly spread and getting more so by the year. The Protestant population has tended to move away to the perceived greater security of Kesh, especially those who serve on the security forces, and as a result their local school, known as Drumskinney No 1 Primary School, is on the verge of closing.

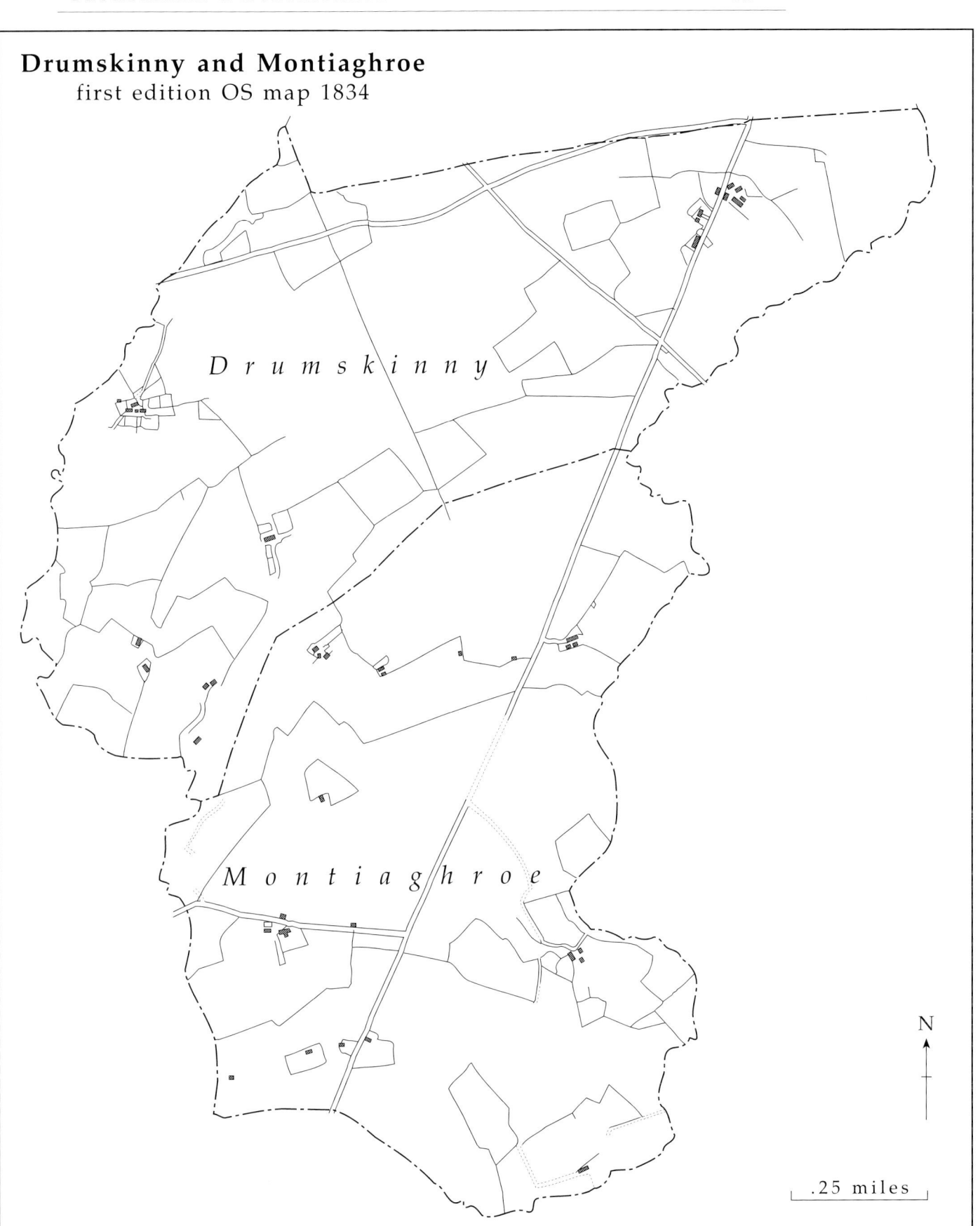

Drumskinny and Montiaghroe
first edition OS map 1834

The local Maintained School, Montiagh School, otherwise known as Drumskinney No 2 Primary School, closed in 1972 in a reorganisation which brought the local Catholic children to the village of Ederney. (There was great rivalry in some areas in the past as to which school had been designated No 1 in the locality. Many almost waged war in an effort to be known as the local No 1 school.)

```
DRUMSKINNY & MONTIAGHROE census returns

YEAR            INHABITANTS                    HOUSES
           MALES  FEMALES  TOTAL      INHAB. UNINHAB BUILDING  TOTAL

DRUMSKINNY
1841        39 + 46 = 85              17 + 1 + 0 = 18
1851        33 + 38 = 71              14 + 3 + 0 = 17
1861        41 + 43 = 84              16 + 1 + 0 = 17
1871        32 + 31 = 63              14 + 0 + 1 = 15
1881        40 + 26 = 66              12 + 1 + 0 = 13

1891        25 + 20 = 45              12 + 0 + 0 = 12
1901        18 + 19 = 37               9 + 2 + 0 = 11
1991        25 + 20 = 45               9 + 2 + 0 = 11
1926        13 + 16 = 29               7 + 1 + 0 =  8
1937         6 +  9 = 15               6 + 1 + 0 =  7

1951           na  = 33                  na    =  8
1961        21 + 21 = 42               6 + 0 + 0 =  6
1971        20 + 14 = 34               7 + 0 + 0 =  7
1981        22 + 16 = 38               8 + 0 + 0 =  8
1991        15 + 12 = 27               7 + 0 + 0 =  7

MONTIAGHROE
1841        29 + 36 = 65              13 + 1 + 0 = 14
1851        27 + 26 = 53              10 + 1 + 0 = 11
1861        21 + 26 = 47              11 + 1 + 0 = 12
1871        23 + 20 = 43               8 + 1 + 0 =  9
1881        15 + 26 = 41               9 + 2 + 0 = 11

1891        17 + 18 = 35               9 + 2 = 0 = 11
1901        11 + 12 = 23               5 + 1 + 0 =  6
1911        16 + 17 = 33               7 + 0 + 0 =  7
1926        11 + 14 = 25               6 + 1 + 0 =  7
1937        15 + 10 = 25               7 + 2 + 0 =  9

1951           na  = 20                  na    =  7
1961         9 +  9 = 18               4 + 0 + 0 =  4
1971         9 +  5 = 14               4 + 0 + 0 =  4
1981         7 +  7 = 14               4 + 0 + 0 =  4
1991         6 +  8 = 14               3 + 1 + 0 =  4
```

According to the Census figures this area did not suffer a great deal during the time of the Famine of the 1840s if these figures tell the whole story.

The most numerous family names in this neighbourhood include those of Monaghan, Gormley and McHugh. The Monaghans are descendants of the 'manaig' who were lay workers on the lands of the ancient monastery of Lough Derg and their numerous nicknames include 'the Unas, Brinies, Jacks, Bafflers, Bogmans, Dubhs, Vickeys, Dalys, the Cross Monaghans and the Bush Monaghans'.

This area suffered one of its greatest population reductions in recent times in the 1960s. In a bid to enlarge itself the town of Irvinestown had built a great number of houses for which there was no local demand and these houses were filled with people from the Montiagh and Scraghey areas. This policy emptied farms and houses in this countryside and led directly to the huge amount of afforestation in the area.

The closing of border roads over the past twenty five years has added to the isolation of this locality and accelerated the drift of people from the area.

TITHE APPLOTMENT RETURNS

DRUMSKINNY & MONTIAGHROE, parish of Drumkeeran, diocese of Clogher, 1833

MONTIAGHROE

382 John Graham	64 acres	@ 4.75d
383 Edward Graham	43a 2r	@ 4.75d
384 Harry Magee	21a 2r 20p	@ 4.75d
385 John Tailor	26a	@ 4.75d
	155a 0r 20p	@ 4.75d = £3.1s.5d

DRUMSKINNY

435 Rick Magee & Magolrick	9a	@ 5.75d
436 Jo Monaghan & Shannon	9a	@ 5.75d
437 Mick Magee	20a	@ 5.75d
438 Tom Moffitt	20a	@ 5.75d
439 Harry Monaghan & E McCue	20a	@ 5.75d
440 Turlough Bawn & sons	10a	@ 7.2d
441 Edward & James Monaghan	17.5a	@ 7.2d
442 Wm Monaghan & sons	22.5a	@ 7.2d
443 James Monaghan	10a	@ 7.2d
	138a	= £3 13s 5d

Even in the 1833 Tithe Applotment returns the contrast between the land-holding patterns in these two townlands is very marked. Montiaghroe had been divided already into the four distinct farms shown on the 1859 Tenement Valuation map. Drumskinny in 1833 still contains examples of partnerships so that the land-holding pattern is difficult to translate on to the 1859 Tenement Valuation map. The 1868 redivision of much of the townland suggests that the process of sorting out holdings had not ended, although the farms had been separated as far as the estate office was concerned – WHC

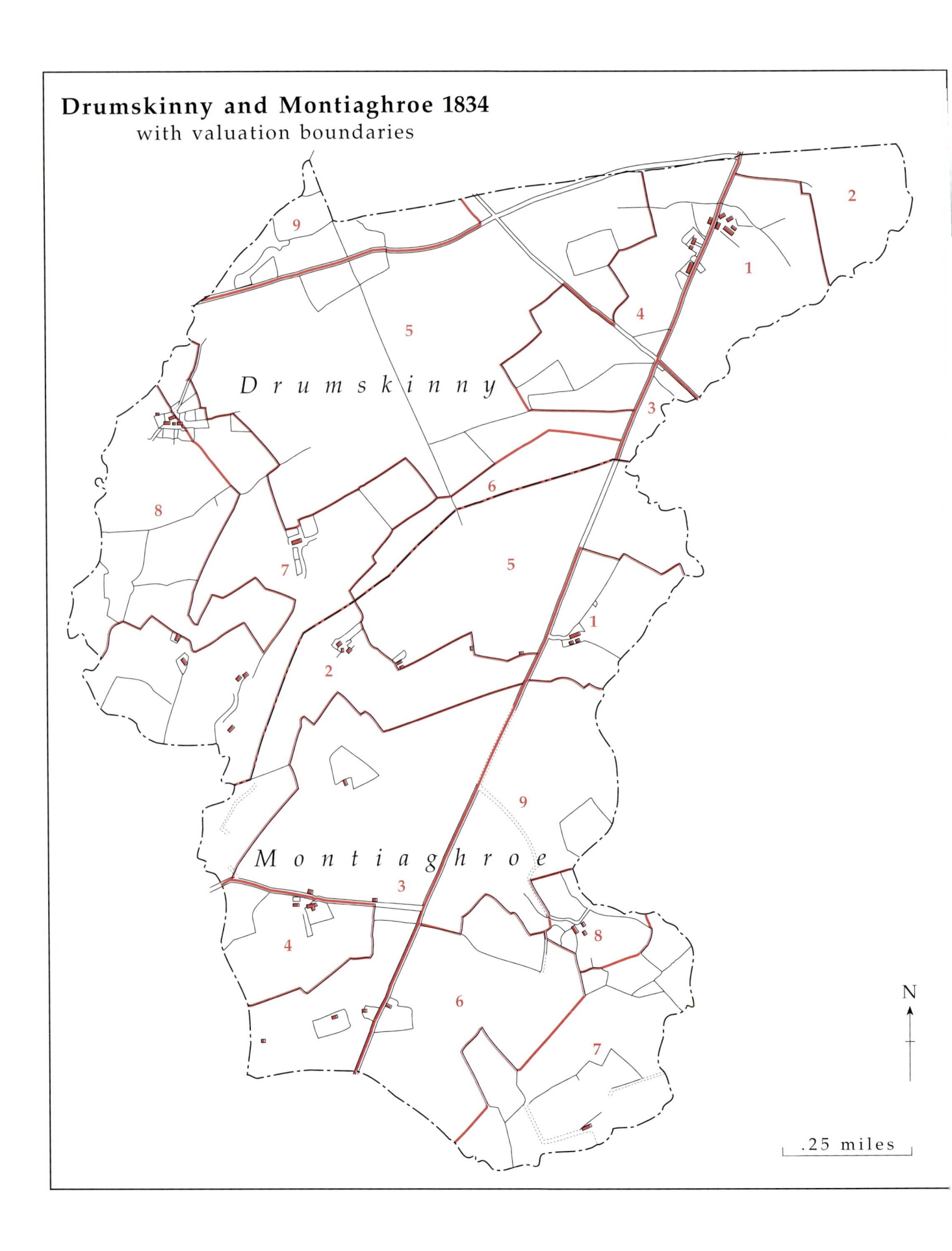

Drumskinny and Montiaghroe 1834
with valuation boundaries

Drumskinny

Montiaghroe

.25 miles

N

DRUMSKINNY & MONTIAGHROE: 24-5 November 1834, VAL/1B/416A & B:

DRUMSKINNY

#	Description	Area	Rate	Value
1	Mixed arable part rather deep, lies well	23a 2r 23p	@ 10s 3d	£12 2s 4d
	also boggy arable	1a	@ 3s 6d	3s 6d
2	Bog	10a 0r 9p	@ 3d	2s 6d
	also arable boggy	1a 2r	@ 7s	10s 6d
	also green pasture	3a	@ 1s 6d	4s 6d
3	generally rather good flat lying meadow by roadside	2a 3r	@ 11s	1 10s 3d
4	flat moory cold arable	28a 1r 9p	@ 6s 3d	8 16s 10d
	also broken pasture on bog	1a	@ 1s 3d	1s 3d
5	Mountain pasture, a few spots reclaimed and in progress of reclaiming	97a 0r 38p	@ 4s 6d	21 17 6d
	also turf bog	5a 3r	@ 2d	11d
6	Turf bog	11a 0r 14p	@ 2d	1s 8d
7	Moory boggy land cold shallow arable	50a 2r 39p	@ 6s 3d	15 17 1d
	also dry heathy pasture	5a	@ 6d	2s 6d
8	middling kind of clayey arable part steep and some flat	24a 2r 19p	@ 10s 3d	12 12s 4d
		10a 2r	@ 1s 4d	14s
9	Boggy arable and pasture	12a 1r 8p	@ 4s 9d	2 18s 4d
	also rocky and broken bog	2a	@ 9d	1s 6d
		289a 1r 39p		£77 17s 6d

There are no houses in this townland worth £5 per year

MONTIAGHROE

#	Description	Area	Rate	Value
1	Part moory arable with sandy subsoil part rather deep lies well and convenient	12a 1r 8p	@ 8s 6d	5 4s 6d
	also soft boggy arable	1a	@ 4s 6d	4s 6d
2	Cold shallow arable and boggy pasture	27a 1r 21p	@ 6s 3d	8 11s 1d
	also heathy pasture	1a 2r	@ 1s 6d	2s 3d
3	Heathy pasture bog	57a 0r 32p	@ 9d	2 2s 10d
	also improved arable	5a	@ 4s 6d	1 2s 6d
4	Rather cold, but chiefly moory arable	15a 1r 7p	@ 8s 6d	6 9s 11d
5	Bog	41a 0r 28p	@ 3d	10s 3d
	also pasture	1a 2r	@ 8s 9d	13s 1d
6	Bog	22a 1r 29p	@ 2d	3s 8d
	also arable	11a 2r	@ 6s 3d	3 11 10d
7	Pasture on bog	20a 3r 1p	@ 1s 4d	1 7s 8d
	also lately reclaimed arable + green pasture	14a 2r	@ 5s 9d	4 3s 4d
8	Good clayey arable with clay subsoil part rocky	6a 2r 4p	@ 14s	4 11s 4d
	also steep pasture	1a 1r	@ 4s	5s
9	Dry knolls heathy pasture	31a 0r 25p	@ 5d	12s 11d
	also coarse meadow	2a	@ 6s 3d	12s 6d
		272 1r 35p		£40 9s 2d

There are no houses in this townland worth £5 per year

Valuators: W A Williamson   Francis O'Callaghan   John McCann

> DRUMSKINNY & MONTIAGHROE
> Townland Valuation (1834). Both Drumskinny and Montiaghroe lie across the 13 miles long straight road that links Castlederg in west Tyrone with the shores of Lower Lough Erne. In them the road rises from 350 feet to 500 feet on its way north. Both the climate and the altitude limited tillage to subsistence and so most of the land was rough grazing for hill cattle. Even in this valuation less than one tenth of the 560 acre was valued at more than 50p (=10/-) per acre. The Tithe Applotment Returns of 1833 indicate family farms. – WHC

CHANGING FARMING PRACTICES.

In the past few years the production of milk in this area has almost ceased apart from a few producers. Suckler cow herds predominate with an increase in sheep rearing also becoming evident. The greatest change of all is the march of conifer plantations across this countryside which parallels a similar huge expansion of forestry across the border in Donegal. The Lettercrann and Pettigo forests in Donegal are now among the largest in Ireland. Deer are becoming relatively common. At present no one can match the price the forestry are willing to pay for farms adjacent to land which is already planted.

THE COMMUNITY AND ITS TRADITIONS

The building of Montiagh Chapel in Montiaghroe townland and later the school beside it provided a focus in the area. The Chapel was built about 1840 under the direction of Rev. James Owens C.C. on the site of an old Mass garden. In penal times mass was also reputed to have been said in the little glen to the east adjacent to Tievenavarnog. The parishioners quarried the stones locally and drew them to the site. According to one report the chapel was to be built on the other side of the road but after the foundations were laid out it was decided to move to the present site. If it had gone ahead as originally planned it would have interfered with, if not entirely destroyed, the stone circle there. This chapel was intended, as was Bannagh Chapel, to be a Chapel of Ease for Magheraculmoney Parish centered in the village of Ederney or Ederney Bridge as it was once known.

The previous place of worship in this area was at the foot of the steep hill in the townland of Edenticromman. Some traces of it are still to be seen at the fork of the road to Scraghy and to Gortnagullion Cross. It was a small thatched building. A guess at the date of erection of this church is given in McKenna's history of Magheraculmoney Parish as the middle of the 1700s. Close by was a well which gave its name to the adjacent townland of Tubrid. The local Church of Ireland was erected in 1774 in this townland with money provided by the Vaughan Charity. The church was built beside the Charitable Charter School for Protestant orphans for which this charity was originally set up.

In 1902 a Methodist Meeting House was erected at Montiagh Crossroads. The building was constructed of corrugated iron and had a congregation of between ten and twenty for the monthly service. The nearby bridge in the direction of Pettigo is marked on the first Ordnance Survey maps as Meeting House Bridge.

Montiagh School stood in a corner of the graveyard adjacent to Montiagh Chapel and as a teacher there for two years I viewed, on a daily basis, a vista of headstones, leaning, sagging and slowly subsiding, their stark and final outlines softened only by the luxuriant grass of summer, the leaves of autumn or the occasional fall of snow. As a result of this experience I consider myself an authority on seasonal change in the Irish graveyard.

Some evidence of the time I taught the children of the locality still hangs from the large beech trees which line one side of the graveyard. The nestboxes we made together still provide homes for the small birds. In many cases I have acquired lifelong friends from among the parents and children. I have fished the little streams and lakes and tramped the rushy fields of winter with dog and gun. Sadly, in an excess of clerical enthusiasm the little two-teacher school was removed in 1989 and now some of the elders of the locality sleep where once I endeavoured to keep their offspring fully awake.

So there are two schools of identical name in this locality and Drumskinney No 1 was in Drumskinney townland while Drumskinney No 2 was actually in Montiaghroe. To confuse the geographer even more Drumskinney No 1 has now migrated to the townland of Dromore Big just across a little stream from its townland of origin. If it is possible to add any more confusion to this situation the school is actually in a subdenomination of Dromore Big known locally as Meenmore.

Drumskinney No 1 P.S. originated with an application for assistance to the Commissioners of National Education on the 1st January 1852. The correspondent for the school was John Monaghan, a farmer of Drumskinney. According to the report of the Inspector who visited it the school was established in November 1851. The schoolmaster was Thomas Gallagher who was aged nineteen and had previously taught in Gushedy School. The Inspector reported that he was not a competent teacher, that the school accounts such as the roll books were not properly kept and that therefore there was no proof of the average attendance.

The schoolhouse was damp and measured 30ft x 18ft. It had three new writing desks. The school hours were from 10 until 3.30 and there was an attendance of twenty boys and fourteen girls. The school fees were a shilling a quarter and all who were unable to pay were admitted free. Five-sixths of the locals were poor. The local Protestant clergyman did not approve of the National School System but thought that the school would be of use to the people of the area. The Inspector was obliged to call with all the local clergy and get their views on the National School System: if they approved this helped the application but the Commissioners were not bound to heed their opinions.

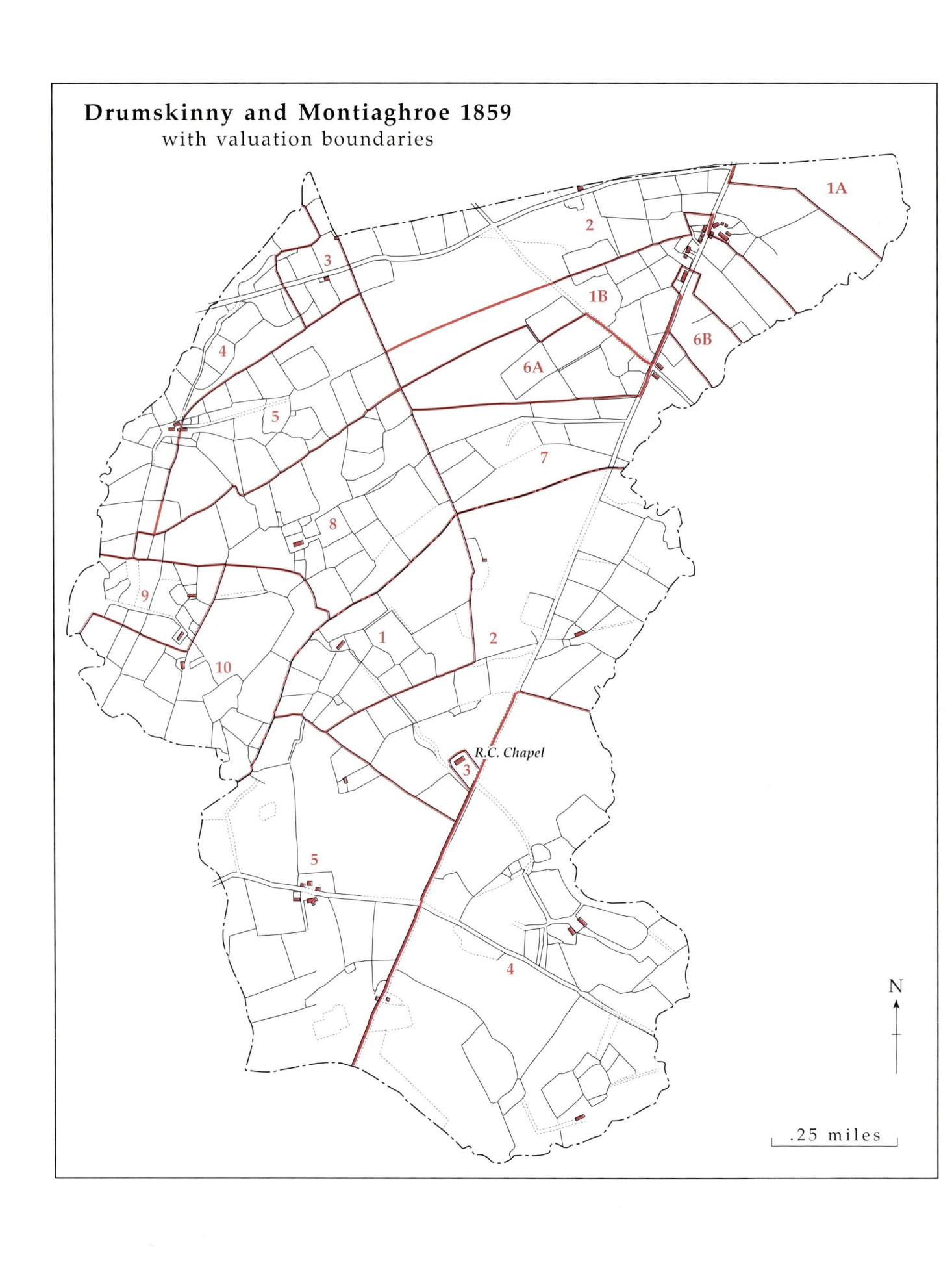

Drumskinny and Montiaghroe 1859
with valuation boundaries

PARISH OF DRUMKEERAN.

No. and Letters of Reference to Map.	Townlands and Occupiers.	Immediate Lessors.	Description of Tenement.	Area.	Rateable Annual Valuation. Land.	Rateable Annual Valuation. Buildings.	Total Annual Valuation of Rateable Property.
	DRUMSKINNY. (Ord. S. 1.)						
1 A a	Edw. Monaghan, sen.	Reps. James Daniel,	House, office, & land,	10 3 29	0 15 0	—	6 5 0
b	Patrick Monaghan,		House, office, & land,	—	—	1 5 0	6 0 0
– B				28 2 10	9 5 0	1 0 0	
2 a	James Monaghan,	Same,	House, office, & land,			1 0 0	5 15 0
b	Edw. Monaghan, jun.,		House, office, & land,	54 1 5	14 5 0	0 15 0	5 10 0
c	Thomas Monaghan,		House, office, & land,			0 15 0	5 10 0
– d	National School-house,	(See Exemptions.)					
3 a	Henry Muldoon,	Reps. James Daniel,	House and land,	6 3 25	2 10 0	0 10 0	3 0 0
– b	James Martin,	Henry Muldoon,	House,	—	—	0 5 0	0 5 0
4 a	Edward M'Hugh,	Reps. James Daniel,	House, office, and land,	24 3 0	9 10 0	1 0 0	10 10 0
– b	Hannah Monaghan,	Edward M'Hugh,	House,	—	—	0 10 0	0 10 0
5	Edwd. Monaghan, sen.,	Reps. James Daniel,	Offices and land,	30 2 35	9 15 0	0 5 0	10 0 0
6 A				17 1 0	5 10 0		
– B a	Terence Monaghan,	Same,	House, offices, & land,	4 3 10	2 10 0	1 0 0	9 0 0
7	Edward Monaghan,	Same,	House, offices, and land,	25 3 35	7 5 0	3 0 0	10 5 0
8	James M'Hugh,	Same,	House, office, and land,	39 3 10	11 0 0	0 15 0	11 15 0
9 a	John Monaghan,	Same,	House, office, & land,	12 0 25	1 15 0	0 5 0	2 0 0
b	Bernard Monaghan,		House, and land,		1 15 0	0 5 0	2 0 0
10 a	James Monaghan,	Same,	House, office, and land,	33 3 20	8 10 0	0 10 0	9 0 0
– b	William Johnston,	James Monaghan,	House,	—	—	0 5 0	0 5 0
			Total of Rateable Property,	290 0 4	84 5 0	13 5 0	97 10 0
			EXEMPTIONS:				
2 d	. . . .	Reps. James Daniel,	National School-house,	—	—	1 10 0	1 10 0
			Total, including Exemptions,	290 0 4	84 5 0	14 15 0	99 0 0
	LUGMORE. (Ord. S. 1.)						
1	Terence Cleary,	Reps. James Daniel,	House, office, and land,	23 2 25	6 5 0	0 10 0	6 15 0
2 a	Felix Monaghan, sen.,	Same,	House, office, & land,	15 3 5	3 0 0	0 10 0	3 10 0
b	Patrick Monaghan,		House and land,		1 10 0	0 10 0	2 0 0
3	Felix Monaghan,	Same,	House and land,	22 3 35	3 0 0	0 10 0	3 10 0
4 a	Patrick Monaghan,	Same,	House, office, & land,	44 1 20	6 15 0	0 15 0	7 10 0
b	Terence Monaghan,		House and land,		2 5 0	0 10 0	2 15 0
			Total,	106 3 5	22 15 0	3 5 0	26 0 0
	MEENTULLY-CLOGH. (Ord. S. 1.)						
1 a	Hugh Doonan,	Reps. James Daniel,	House and land,	12 2 34	4 10 0	0 15 0	5 5 0
– b	Francis Doonan,	Hugh Doonan,	House,	—	—	0 10 0	0 10 0
– c	Daniel M'Gowan,	Same,	House,	—	—	0 10 0	0 10 0
2	William M'Hugh,	Reps. James Daniel,	House, office, and land,	11 2 30	4 10 0	1 0 0	5 10 0
3	John Monaghan,	Same,	House, office, and land,	27 0 5	10 0 0	1 10 0	11 10 0
4	William Monaghan,	Same,	House, office, and land,	39 0 30	9 15 0	1 5 0	11 0 0
			Total,	90 2 19	28 15 0	5 10 0	34 5 0
	MONTIAGHROE. (Ord. S. 1.)						
1	James Taylor,	James Johnston,	House, office, and land,	26 1 30	6 5 0	1 10 0	7 15 0
2 a	Thomas Graham,	Same,	House, offices, and land,	64 2 5	10 15 0	0 15 0	11 10 0
– b	Catherine Magee,	Thomas Graham,	House,	—	—	0 5 0	0 5 0
– c	Jane Curran,	Same,	House,	—	—	0 5 0	0 5 0
– d	Thomas Scollan,	Same,	House,	—	—	0 5 0	0 5 0
– e	Robert Taylor,	Same,	House,	—	—	0 5 0	0 5 0
3	R. C. Chapel and yard,	(See Exemptions.)					
4 a	Reps. John Graham,	James Johnston,	House, offices, and land,	109 2 10	15 15 0	2 0 0	17 15 0
– b	Jane Magee,	Reps. John Graham,	House and sm. garden,	—	—	0 5 0	0 5 0
– c	Michael Fitzpatrick,	Same,	House and sm. garden,	—	—	0 5 0	0 5 0
5	John Monaghan,	James Johnston,	House, offices, and land,	71 0 5	15 15 0	5 0 0	20 15 0
			Total of Rateable Property,	271 2 10	48 10 0	10 15 0	59 5 0
			EXEMPTIONS:				
3	. . . .	. . . .	R. C. Chapel and yard,	0 3 25	0 10 0	10 0 0	10 10 0
			Total, including Exemptions,	272 1 35	49 0 0	20 15 0	69 15 0

> TENEMENT VALUATION (1860)
> Three-quarters of Drumskinny was held by the Monaghan family from James Daniel. The largest landlord in the district, John G. Irvine of Irvinestown, became the direct landlord in 1865 and by 1868 a redivision of much of the townland was made between the tenants, although it was already held in compact farms. The intention may have been to help the extended Monaghan family to sort out their respective properties: John and Bernard made a further exchange in 1896.
>
> In Montiaghroe in 1865 when John Monaghan (5) bought James Taylor's farm (1) he held almost 100 acres of the 270 acre townland. In the same year the heirs of John Graham (4) sold out to Christopher Loan while Thomas Graham (2) sold to John Johnson: in 1896 the Loans bought the Johnson farm. Their immediate landlord sold the townland to the tenants in 1879. – WHC

We get a later glimpse of the school when an application was made for an assistant teacher's salary for this school on January 11th, 1875. The one room of the school measured 32 ft x 16 ft x 11° ft. The Principal teacher was Mr Thomas Gallagher, aged forty-one (if he was nineteen in 1851 he should now be forty-three). The application for a salary for an assistant was made on behalf of Miss Jane McDermott, aged sixteen years who had been a Junior and Senior Monitress in Enniskillen Convent School for six and a half years from 16th July 1868 until 31st December 1874.

There were 86 male and 48 female children on rolls and the average attendance for the past six months was only 34 male and 16 female children. The Inspector was told that the attendance would have been much higher but that a mission had been held in the parish for a period of three weeks the previous July. On inspection Miss McDermott was found to be a competent teacher.

The schoolmaster had a house and land adjacent to the school. Master Gallagher was succeeded as headmaster of the school about 1880 when Mr Johnston Brimstone assumed the office. Like most other schools of the time this school catered for children of all religions.

HOUSING

Most of the houses, 'riz and slated', seem to have had this work carried out just after the First World War. The war had provided great prosperity in the locality as indeed did the Second World War. Relatively few joined up to fight. They preferred to stay at home and grow as much food as possible. The Fermanagh loyalist newspaper, the *Impartial Reporter,* commented on the scarcity of recruits from the Kesh area.

> **Recruiting**
> Lt Knight and his party got 24 recruits on their last visit to Pettigo where 7 recruiting parties before this got none. Donegal was the worst county in Ireland for recruiting as only 500 had enlisted from 21,000 of recruitable age. Kesh is the poorest Unionist area for recruiting in County Fermanagh. There were only six enlisted when recruiting took place at the last Kesh Fair day. Mr McHugh [Nationalist chairman of Fermanagh County Council] had spoken in favour of it. *(Impartial Reporter,* 3 June 1915)
>
> There is widespread apathy for recruiting in Kesh. One old farmer with seven sons at home has sent none of them to war and will send none of them until he sees the nationalists enlist first. 'Why fight Germany the only Protestant country in Europe?' The newspaper thinks that the real reason is the prosperity brought by farmers getting between 50% and 80% more for their produce and shopkeepers are getting their bills paid. The shops will hold on to their shop boys and the farmers to their sons and labourers. *(Impartial Reporter,* 11 November 1915)

Another indicator of the wealth generated is to be seen in Tubrid Graveyard where the number of headstones erected in the ten years after the war is very noticeable. Today many of the older farm houses have been abandoned in favour of the bland bungalows which dot the landscape.

More of the houses in the locality simply removed their thatch and reroofed with galvanised iron. A ceiling was then erected inside to prevent condensation and keep the house warm.

COMMUNITY

Today in the townland of Montiaghroe and Drumskinney the social centre of the area is THE CROSS, a public house owned (according to the recently deceased Andy Cullion who was aged eighty-three) by the Monaghan family for seven generations. It stands at the crossroads, hence its name. The hill overlooking it is known as Monaghan's Hill and it seems to have been a centre of entertainment for a very long time. The sites of several cockpits are to be found on the hillside and horse racing was also carried on here as evidenced by the following song.

DRUMSKINNEY RACES

> All ye men of this nation who loves recreation,
> I'll ask your attention I won't keep you long,
> Gay lads and gay lasses whose beauty surpasses
> All human creation, give ear to my song,
> In praise of all races I'll sing a few verses,
> You won't find their equal go search where you will,

For the flight of Kildare it would never compare,
With the Drumskinney Races round Monaghan's hill.

In the month of December it's well I remember,
The sportsmen came here from the county Tyrone,
And to give them the pleasure and run for the treasure,
That's there in abundance it's very well known,
And without hesitation and just for recreation,
Our Fermanagh sportsmen assembled likewise,
When they all joined together like birds of a feather,
Those dear people and horses would dazzle your eyes.

Now a brave Irish soldier was there as reporter,
And he was instructed to aid on the field,
And in all combination each man to his station,
Unto his appointment for daring to yield,
For crowds were advancing and horses were prancing,
And jockeys were mounting to start in a prize,
All our hearts were excited and greatly delighted,
The cheers of rejoicement did ascend to the skies.

I have rambled for pleasure I won't be outmeasured,
In different places abroad I have been.
But Drumskinney Races exceeds all those places,
For pleasure and pastime that ere I have seen
It being well situated and so elevated,
The scenes you could see a great distance around.
Grand accomodation and good regulations,
Was kept on the racecourse by men well renowned

And let you be friend or stranger, you are free from all danger,
When you come to the sport, just arrive at the Cross.
You'll be kindly greeted and very well treated,
And grand entertainment for both man and horse.
And should you feel weary of a journey so dreary,
Just go down to the parlour and sit at your ease.
They can treat you right handy to a glass of good brandy,
All gin, wine or rum or whatever you please.

Now to make a conclusion excuse my intrusion,
Perhaps my recitation your patience annoys.
So come fill up your glasses and drink to your lasses
Long may they live single our sports to enjoy.
Pray don't be offended it's not that I intended,
So I'll bid you goodbye and I lay down my quill.
May your future be pleasing until our next season,
When we'll all meet again on Monaghan's Hill.

There is no prospect of industry coming to this area but tourism may play an increasing role. There is little employment in farming other than for the farmer himself and those who live here travel to Irvinestown, Enniskillen or Castlederg to work. It is about seven miles from the top of Scraghey mountain to Pettigo on the old road. One local peering into the future was of the opinion that there will soon be a forestry gate at Scraghey and another at the edge of Pettigo and there will be nothing but conifers in between. The same grim prospect may well be in store for Drumskinney and Montiaghroe.

POSTSCRIPT

Since the paramilitary ceasefire at the end of 1994 things have changed dramatically along the Border about Drumskinny and Montiaghroe. Cratered roads have been filled in and tarmacked while economic and social ties disrupted or discontinued for the past twenty-five years have been restored. The Cross pub has customers once more coming a couple of miles from Lettercran in Donegal instead of fourteen miles around via Pettigo. Castlederg mart is now fourteen miles nearer. Commuting to work is much easier too. However, it is not just the restrictions of the last twenty-five years that have been lifted. The Customs are gone! The customs patrols who regularly made the passage between north and south as difficult as possible. A sense of freedom has come to this countryside that has not been experienced since the 1920s, never mind the 1970s. People who have not lived through these times don't understand the feeling of elation and liberty.

GALLON

of Strabane

rte of this Baronie

- carna
- metnocran
- Cauagsi
- cassu
- garuag
- Shagnegallorne
- Shagnebesi
- tledougs
- drome sker
- trentamadm
- loughes
- tcadane
- agttoslas
- darbrogs
- lebaden
- dirikalon
- liglea
- lisne
- titterbrat
- tullane dala
- Corigg
- Aterdala
- Crigsduffe
- galla
- Clogbogall
- newton
- corncran
- dt fross
- fagberna
- publet
- auanschab
- foysm
- nilla
- urtags
- tricnowtra
- tricnbulskan
- encighter
- loaskeags
- C'amis
- leagbar
- Mourne flu.
- Jarge flu.
- dan
- olan

GALLON

W.J. BRADLEY

INTRODUCTION

The presence of a surprisingly large number of clusters of houses in the townland of Gallon Upper – the most numerous in any townland in the north of Ireland – was drawn to the attention of geographers by Dr Desmond McCourt in his research work on rundale in the 1950s.[1] Such an observation alone would make Gallon worth studying, but its history is even more interesting as the story of a native Irish community on a major Plantation estate. From the time of the Plantation up to the years of the Great Famine the three townlands of Gallon were part of a very large estate which passed by marriage in the eighteenth century from Sir William Stewart (later Lord Mountjoy) to the Gardiner family which eventually became the Earls of Blessington. As the records of this estate are held by the National Library in Dublin, more details of its history will have to await the processing of the collection by archivists. In the meantime this account of Gallon will rely on traditional knowledge and on other records which are available for many townlands, such as the Valuation records and census returns.

LOCATION

The townlands of Gallon Upper, Gallon Lower and Gallon Sessiagh[2] lie between two and three miles north-north-east of Newtownstewart in the parish of Ardstraw East, County Tyrone. Gallon Upper and Gallon Lower are traversed by a county road (known today as Gallon Road) which runs directly from Glenock Catholic Church, on the Newtownstewart-Plumbridge road, up to the Strabane-Plumbridge road. Gallon Sessiagh is served by a spur of the road from Newtownstewart to Douglas Bridge: the Sessiagh Road ends at a cluster of houses in the middle of the townland. Gallon Sessiagh can be reached from Gallon Upper and Gallon Lower by the use of private lanes (nowadays little better than paths) about two miles apart, fording the Sessiagh Burn.

The three Gallon townlands lie along the flank of the hill which overlooks the junction of the Owenkillew and Mourne rivers. The lowest ground, around the junction of the Crosh and Sessiagh Burns in Lower Gallon is 62 metres (250

On Bodley's map of Strabane barony Galla is surrounded by mountains

Gallan
first edition OS map 1834

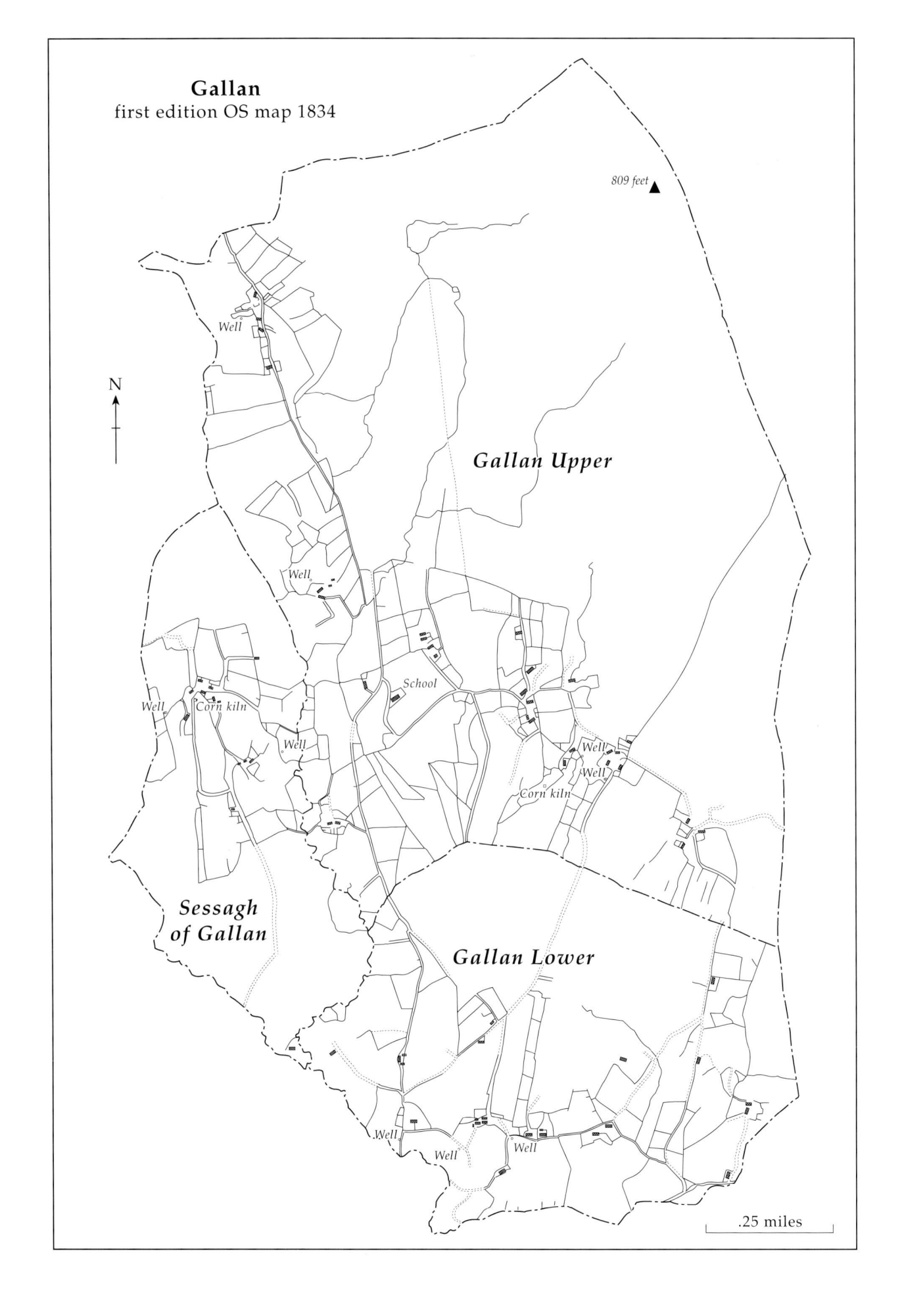

809 feet ▲

Gallan Upper

Sessagh of Gallan

Gallan Lower

N

Well
Well
Well
Corn kiln
Well
Well
School
Well
Well
Corn kiln
Well
Well
Well

.25 miles

feet) above sea level while the highest point is Gallon Tops, in Gallon Upper, at a height of 244 metres (809 feet).

Clusters of dwellings survived until recent times at seven locations in Gallon Upper known as Meenawiddy, Meenaheap, Meenatumigan, Aghnahassan, Aghnaglarig, Crockatore and Magherabrack.[3] There were two clusters of dwellings in Gallon Sessiagh, while in Gallon Lower the dwellings were dispersed along the county roads.

EARLY HISTORY

The word 'Gallan' in the Irish language is usually translated to mean a standing stone. The standing stone which probably gave the whole district its name is located at Crockatore in Gallon Upper; there is another standing stone in the adjoining townland of Shannony East. In Gallon Sessiagh there is also a small stone circle about nine metres in diameter which is nowadays almost submerged in the bog. Turf cutting and land reclamation work at Meenawiddy in Gallon Upper have uncovered an ancient hearth and the remains of timber walls as well as the remains of an ancient field system.[4] A burial cist was discovered near the standing stone in Shannony East and there are two portal tombs in the adjoining townlands of Glenock and Crosh.[5] There is also a well-preserved cashel in Crosh and the site of another in Gallon Upper is marked on recent Ordnance Survey maps.

Three miles east of Gallon, in the townland of Corrick, are the ruins of a monastery reputed to date back to 563 AD, while two miles to the south is the site of the fifteenth century Franciscan monastery at Pubble, which operated until the early 1600s. In Gallon Sessiagh there is a 'children's burial ground' known locally as 'the Dowth', which may have been the site of an ancient church. All that is visible today is a circular mound with a diameter of 25 metres, overgrown by bushes and mature trees. Local people still have a superstitious dread of interfering with these trees or of even entering the place. Older residents affirm the existence of a sweathouse[6] which was situated along a burn near Aghnahassan. They also recall the veneration of a 'holy' well near the standing stone at Crockatore.

In the fourteenth century, Harry Aimhreidh (Avery) O'Neill, the local king, build a castle on the hillside to dominate the valley where the Owenkillew, Strule and Mourne rivers meet. The ruins of this castle are a well-known landmark to this day. In the late fifteenth century a successor, Niall Conallach O'Neill, built another castle about a mile away, close to an important ford on the river Mourne. The settlement which grew around the new castle became known as Lisglas or Baile Nua (Newtown, later Newtownstewart). The last Gaelic chieftain of the area, Turlough Luineach O'Neill, occupied the castle at Baile Nua intermittently from 1567 until his death in 1595.

Among the Irish families who lived in this area at that time were O'Neill,

McAnaly, McCawall, McHugh, McKindry, McNamee, O'Criggan, O'Crossan, O'Cullenan, O'Feghan, O'Gormley, O'Gornery, O'Mulcrew, O'Murragh, O'Mellon, O'Quinn and O'Skeagh.[7]

A number of these names could still be found living in Gallon until recently; in fact McNamee is the most common name in Gallon at the present time.

ESTATES

The district known as Galla (Gallon) was part of the estate granted in 1610 by King James I of England (James VI of Scotland) under the scheme for the Plantation of Ulster to James Chapham, an 'old and faithful servant';[8] 'Galla' is shown on Josias Bodley's map of 1609 to be almost surrounded by mountains. In 1620, when Sir Robert Newcomen bought the estate from Chapham, he found much of the land already let to Irish tenants. Newcomen was succeeded in 1629 by his son-in-law Sir William Stewart (d.1647) who obtained a new patent from the crown in 1629 for the manor of Newtownstewart.

Under the new patent, only one quarter of the townlands on the estate could be leased to Irishmen so the Irish were restricted to certain named townlands as well as 'the several mountains belonging to said several townlands known by the names of Slewtryn (Bessy Bell mountain) and Gallagh al'Escheeve'. This suggests that 'Gallagh al'Escheeve' was the name applied to the entire upland area north east of Newtownstewart: an area which would have been used for summer grazing by the native Irish inhabitants of the river valleys before the Plantation.

As a result of the new restrictions on granting leases to Irishmen in the valleys, it is likely that many Irish families established homes around this time at the most promising locations on the hillsides. Gallagh al'Escheeve would have eventually been divided into the townlands which we know today as Lisnafin, Legfordrum, Tullyherin, Shannony East, as well as Gallon itself. Newtownstewart people still consider people from these townlands as Gallon men and women.

The leasebooks and legal documents which are presently held in the Blessington estate archives[9] could be of great assistance in establishing the dates when these new townlands were established. The first reference to Gallon Sessiagh ('Sessiagh of Gallon) so far discovered appears in a marriage settlement of 1696 which has been preserved in these archives.

A legal agreement, held in the Registry of Deeds, Dublin, records the transfer of the entire townland of Gallon in 1724 from Torlagh O'Crigan of Gallon to Edward Crigan of Gallon and Claud Crigan of Augher. The property was transferred from Edward and Claud Cregan to Daniel Conway of Strabane in 1731:

> All that whole townland of Gallan upper, lower and half sessiagh or what other name or denomination the same is known, called or divided into as it is now marched and meared[10]...

The wording of the lease suggests that Gallon had been split into three distinct townlands, Gallon Upper (952 acres), Gallon Lower (543 acres), and Gallon Sessiagh (205 acres) and that the boundaries had, at that stage, already been defined and marked. These boundaries are shown on the first Ordnance Survey map which was produced in the 1830s.

An examination of this map, together with the comments of the government valuators and their assessments of the value of each portion of land, reveals that even if the original settlements had developed on communal lines (ie extended family units) at some time in the past, the landlords, either directly or through middlemen such as Conway or O'Cregan, had intervened to impose their own structures.

By the 1850s tenants had been allocated parcels of land laid out as fields, containing a variety of soil types, from meadow pasture through arable land to mountain grazing. In many cases these parcels of land were held in partnership between two or more tenants.

The *Statistical Survey of County Tyrone* (1802) provides valuable insights into agricultural developments of the time:

> The farmers throughout Lord Mountjoy's estate, chiefly in the barony of Strabane, are making rapid strides in the point of enclosure, generally small, from one to six acres.

Another of its comments is especially relevant to Gallon:

> Exposed aspects require enclosures to be small, the better to secure shelter, and wet swampy land must always be improved by small enclosures.[11]

A major feature of these townlands both on the Ordnance Survey maps and the estate maps of the Baird estate drawn by R.H. Nolan in 1852,[12] is the patchwork quilt pattern of small fields.

McEvoy pointed out that the construction of the fences around the fields varied. In Gallon Lower they were generally solid earthen dykes on a stone base planted with hawthorn and fronted by ditches, but in the lower parts of Gallon Upper there were fewer hawthorns on the dykes. In Gallon Upper the ditches were replaced by walls of stones which had been cleared from the fields to expedite cultivation.

In February 1851 Gallon Upper and Gallon Lower, together with the neighbouring townland of Tullyherin, were sold as individual townlands of the Blessington estate for £4,950 by the Encumbered Estates Court to Daniel Baird, a merchant from Derry. In the following May he bought the townlands of Deerpark, Rakelly, Croshballinree, Grange and Newtownstewart for a further £26,050 and called his whole new estate 'the Manor of Newtownstewart'.

Gallon Sessiagh was sold separately to James and George Aiken of Dunderg, near Coleraine. Griffith's Valuation of 1859 shows that all the farms in Gallon were held directly from these landlords, although sometimes they were still held in partnerships with other tenants. It is also possible to distinguish the cottiers' holdings because each of them was recorded as holding 'a house and garden' from one of the farmers.

BROGAN.
29„2„29

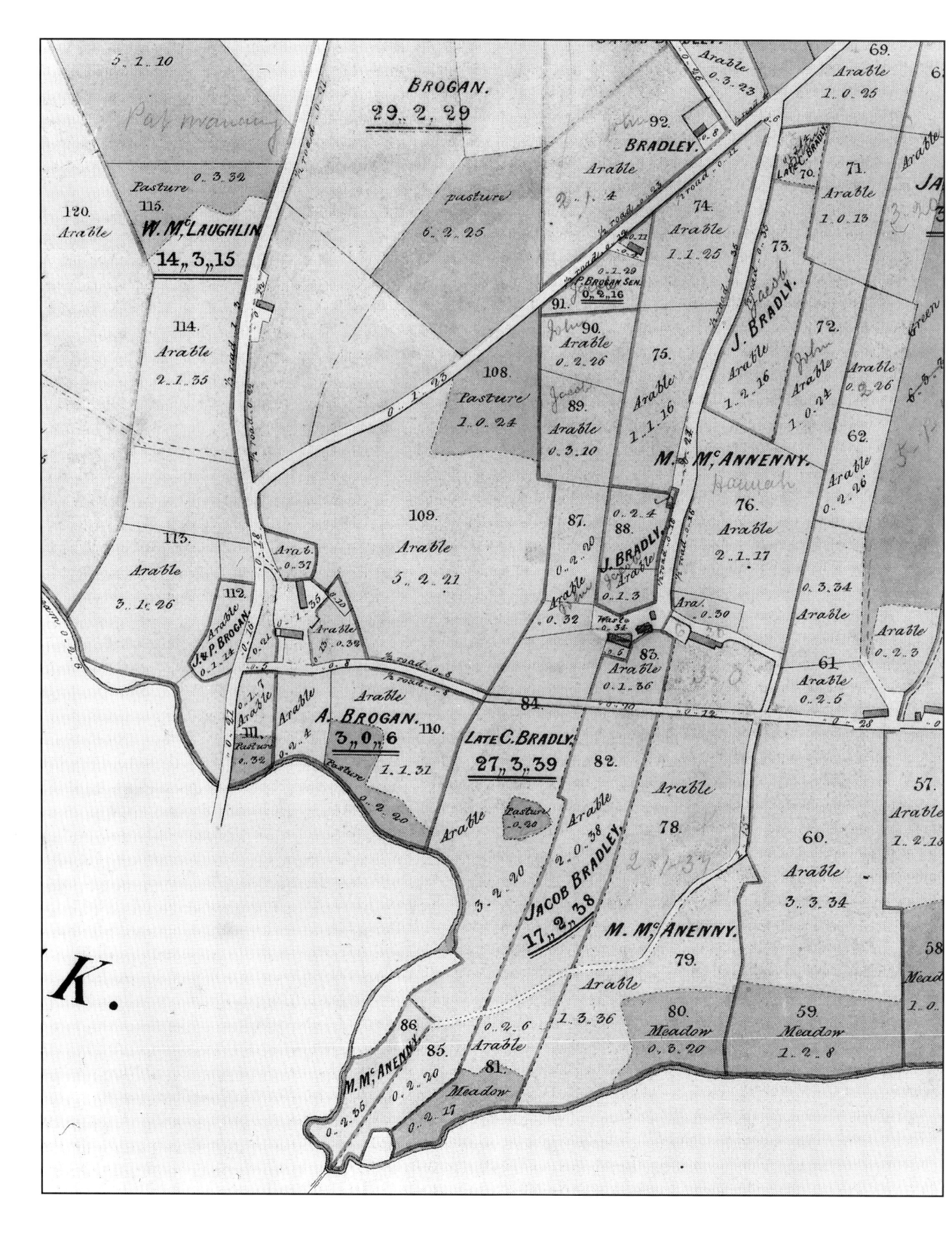

W. M^cLAUGHLIN
14„3„15

A. BROGAN.
3„0„6

Late C. BRADLY.
27„3„39

JACOB BRADLEY
17„2„38

M. M^cANENNY.

BRADLEY

M. M^cANENNY.

J. BRADLY.

M. M^cANENNY.

K.

No.	Type	Measure
		5„2„10
120	Arable	
115	Pasture	0„3„32
114	Arable	2„1„35
113	Arable	3„1„26
112	J & P. BROGAN Arable	0„1„14
111	Pasture	0„3„32
	Arable	0„2„4
110		1„1„31
	Pasture	0„2„20
86		
85		0„2„20
81	Meadow	0„2„17
		pasture 6„2„25
108	Pasture	1„0„24
109	Arable	5„2„21
	Arab.	0„37
	Arable	0„0„34
	Arable	0„32
82	Arable	2„0„38
	Arable	3„2„20
79	Arable	1„3„36
	Arable	0„2„6
92	Arable	3„1„4
91 P. BROGAN SEN.		0„2„16
90	Arable	0„2„26
89	Arable	0„3„10
87	Arable	0„2„20
88 J. BRADLY	Arable	0„2„4 / 0„1„3
	Waste	0„34
83	Arable	0„1„36
78	Arable	
80	Meadow	0„3„20
74	Arable	1„1„25
75	Arable	1„1„16
76	Arable	2„1„17
	Ara.	0„30
69	Arable	1„0„25
70 Late C. BRADLY		
71	Arable	1„0„13
73	Arable	1„2„16
72	Arable	1„0„24
62	Arable	0„2„26
	Arable	0„3„34
61	Arable	0„2„6
	Arable	0„2„3
57	Arable	1„2„13
60	Arable	3„3„34
59	Meadow	1„2„8
58	Mead	

GALLAN TITHE APPLOTMENT: parish of Leckpatrick, April 1834
FIN/5A/19B p21. (Although the printed page provided columns to record three qualities of land, the commissioners chose to use a wider range.)

UPPER GALLON

Edward & Owen Quinn & McCristal & Devlin: 42 acres.2 roods.0 perches. [10 @ 10s, 10 @ 6s, 22.2.0 @ 3s] Annual Value £11.7s.6d. Amount of tithe 14s.9.5d

Patrick Sen. & Jun, & Michael Devlin: 61a.2r.20p. [10 @ 10s, 40 @ 3s, 11.2.20 @ 6d] AV £11.5s.10d. Tithe 14s.8.5d

John & Manus & Neal Sen & Jun, & James McColgan: 84a.3r.0p. [14 @ 10s, 40 @ 5s, 30.3.0 @ 6d] AV £17.15s.4d. Tithe £1.3s.3.5d.

Charles McColgan: 21a.1r. 0p. [12 @ 12s, 9.1.0 @ 5s] AV £9.10s.3d Tithe 12s.4d

James & John McAnelly: 53a.0.33p. [8 @ 10s, 10.0.33 @ 4s, 35 @ 9d] AV £7.7s. Tithe 9s.7.5d

A McAnelly & John Brogan: 40a.1r.17p. [20 @ 10s, 10 @ 6s, 10.1.17 @ 4s,]+ 71 acres of mountain @ 9d AV £17.14s.7d. Tithe £1.3s.2.5d

F. McLaughlin, John McCrory, B.Devlin, B.McCulla, James & Ann Kelly: 31a. [12 @ 10s, 19 @ 4s]+ 86 acres of mountain @ 6d AV£11.17s.6d. Tithe 15s.5d

M & Owen & James McGarvey, E & M Hagan, 36a.1r.30p. [10 @ 10s, 26.1.30 @ 4s]+ 86 acres of mountain @ 6d AV £12.8s.9d. Tithe 16s2.5d

Michael & Neil Sen & Jun McNamee, 7a.2r.35p @ 10s AV £3.17s.2d Tithe 5s.1d

Brine, Ellen, Owen Sen & Jun, James, Charles & Bernard McNamee, 22a.2r. @ 10s.+ 137a. @ 6d. AV £14.13s.6d Tithe 19s3d

Neal, Owen, Dennis, David McNamee & Hugh McCurristel, 15a 2r. @ 10s.+ 137a. @ 6d. AV £11.3s. 6d. Tithe 14s.7.5d

TOTAL: £8. 8s.7d

LOWER GALLON

Dennis Morris, 6a.0r.8p. [5 @ 10s, 1a.0r.8p. @ 6d.] AV £2.10s.6d. Tithe 3s.2.5d

Phill Quinn & C.Brogan, 28a.0r.6p. [16 @ 10s, 12a.0r.6p. @ 1s.] AV £8.12s. Tithe 11s.2.5d.

P.Quinn, A.Brogan & William Cassidy, 29a.3r.14p. [10 @ 12s, 12 @ 6s, 7a.3r.14p @ 1s.6d.] AV £10.3s.8d. Tithe 13s.3d.

H. & Charles Bradley & James McConnell, 86a.0r.8p [16 @ 12s, 30 @ 5s. 40a.0r.8p. @ 1s.] AV £19.2s. Tithe £1.5s.2d.

James Hutchinson, 32a. [8 @ 10s, 10 @ 5s, 14 @ 9d] AV £7.0s.6d. Tithe 9s.1.5d.

John McLaughlin, 19a.3r.3p. [6 @ 10s, 8 @ 4s, 5a.3r.3p. @ 9d.] AV £4.16s.4d. Tithe 6s.3.5d.

Daniel & James McLaughlin, 70a.3.16p. [16 @ 12s, 30 @ 6s, 24a.3r.16p @ 1s.] AV £19.16s.10d. Tithe £1.5s.8.5d.

John, Thomas, James, William & Charles Hutchinson, 57a.3s.10p. [20 @ 10s, 20 @ 6s, 17a.3r.10p @ 1s.] AV £16.17s.10d. Tithe £1.1s.11.5d.

TOTAL: £5.15s.11d.

Extract from R. H. Nolan's map of Lower Gallan 1852 (PRONI).'

> GALLON SESSAGH
>
> John Morris & Dennis McNally, 64a.3r.30p. [10a @ 10s, 20 @ 5s, 34a.3r.30p @ 1s.] AV £11.14s.11d. Tithe 15s.4d.
>
> E. Quinn & James Morris, 10a.3r.17p @ 2s. AV £1.1s.8d. Tithe 1s.4d.
>
> Edward Quinn, 2a.0r.17p. @ 12s. AV £1.5s.3d. Tithe 1s.7d.
>
> Charles Devlin, 13a.3r.9p. [6a @ 10s, 7a.3r.9p @ 2s.] AV £3.15s.6d. Tithe 4s.10d.
>
> James McAleer, 6a.3r.18p. [4a @ 10s, 2a.3r.18p @ 7s.] AV £3. Tithe 3s.11d.
>
> Edward & Owen Quinn, 6a.2r. [3a @ 8s, 3a.2r. @ 4s.] AV £1.18s. Tithe 2s.6d.
>
> Widow Morris & Thomas McMenamin, 47a. [6a @ 10s, 16a @ 6s, 25a @ 6d] AV £8.8s.6d. Tithe 11s.
>
> Dennis Morris, 5a.1r.20p. [1a @ 5s, 4a.1r.20p @ 6d.] AV 7s.2d. Tithe 6d
>
> John Bradley & Brine Morris, 28a. [3a @ 4s, 25a @ 6d.] AV £1.4s.6d. Tithe 1s.7d.
>
> D. Morris, 7a.3r.22p [5 @ 12s, 2a.3r.22p @ 8s.] AV £4.3s.0d. Tithe 5s.4d.
>
> John Bradley, 8a.0r.24p [4a @ 10s, 4a.0r.24p. @ 8s.] AV £3.13s.2d. Tithe 4s.10d.
>
> AREA:173a.2r.16p. TOTAL: £2.12s.9d

> This Tithe Applotment distinguishes the partnership groups and the individuals who held leases on the Blessington estate in 1834. There is a strong relationship between kin groups and the several house clusters, especially in Upper Gallon. This is confirmed by the maps made by R. H. Nolan in 1852 and later for the Valuation Office in 1859. It is also clear that new fields were still being made as the farmers worked to reclaim the mountain moorland – WHC.

In 1932, the Maturin Baird estate was vested under the Land Purchase Acts and sold directly to the tenants.

POPULATION

It is probable that the population figure of 522 persons recorded for Gallon in the 1841 census represented the peak reached before the Great Famine. (This may be an over-estimate because the figure of 98 women in Gallon Lower against 65 men in 28 houses seems improbable: did 39 of them really disappear before 1851?). Gallon Upper had 291 persons living in 50 houses, Gallon Lower 163 persons in 28 houses and Gallon Sessiagh 68 persons in 13 houses.

Although it is unlikely that Gallon escaped the effects of the Great Famine, its population loss was much lower than that for County Tyrone in general: a total of only five houses out of ninety-one disappeared between 1841 and 1851. Indeed, the number of inhabited houses in Gallon Upper increased from fifty to fifty-five during the Famine. Strangely enough, such increases sometimes did occur,

GALLAN Census Returns

YEAR	INHABITANTS MALES FEMALES TOTAL	HOUSES INHAB UNINHAB BUILDING TOTAL
UPPER GALLAN		
1841	147 + 144 = 291	50 + 10 + 0 = 60
1851	141 + 159 = 300	55 + 5 + 0 = 60
1861	129 + 121 = 250	48 + 4 + 0 = 52
1871	111 + 101 = 212	43 + 3 + 0 = 46
1881	101 + 92 = 193	42 + 2 + 0 = 44
1891	91 + 91 = 182	39 + 1 + 0 = 40
1901	67 + 69 = 136	28 + 6 + 0 = 34
1911	57 + 45 = 102	24 + 4 + 0 = 28
1926	54 + 45 = 99	25 + 1 + 0 = 26
1937	56 + 42 = 98	26 + 0 + 0 = 26
1951	na = 95	na = 25
1961	42 + 49 = 91	21 + 0 + 0 = 21
1971	39 + 42 = 81	19 + 0 + 0 = 19
1981	26 + 25 = 51	17 + 4 + 0 = 21
1991	26 + 20 = 46	15 + 0 + 0 = 15
LOWER GALLAN		
1841	65 + 98 = 163	28 + 4 + 0 = 32
1851	41 + 59 = 100	22 + 2 + 0 = 24
1861	52 + 57 = 109	23 + 0 + 0 = 23
1871	49 + 52 = 101	21 + 0 + 0 = 21
1881	36 + 41 = 77	15 + 1 + 0 = 16
1891	26 + 25 = 51	13 + 0 + 0 = 13
1901	22 + 28 = 50	12 + 0 + 0 = 12
1911	22 + 27 = 49	11 + 1 + 1 = 13
1926	17 + 18 = 35	11 + 1 + 0 = 12
1937	19 + 22 = 41	11 + 0 + 0 = 11
1951	na = 29	na = 8
1961	12 + 15 = 27	8 + 1 + 0 = 9
1971	9 + 6 = 15	8 + 0 + 0 = 9
1981	6 + 6 = 12	4 + 2 + 0 = 6
1991	3 + 2 = 5	3 + 0 + 0 = 3
GALLAN SESSIAGH		
1841	39 + 28 = 67	13 + 1 + 0 = 14
1851	30 + 19 = 49	9 + 0 + 0 = 9
1861	24 + 29 = 53	8 + 0 + 0 = 8
1871	21 + 22 = 43	8 + 0 + 0 = 8
1881	25 + 22 = 47	9 + 0 + 0 = 9
1891	16 + 16 = 32	7 + 0 + 0 = 7
1901	16 + 19 = 35	6 + 1 + 0 = 7
1911	17 + 15 = 32	5 + 2 + 0 = 7
1926	15 + 14 = 29	5 + 0 + 0 = 5
1937	9 + 14 = 23	4 + 0 + 0 = 4
1951	na = 17	na = 4
1961	2 + 3 = 5	2 + 1 + 0 = 3
1971	11 + 8 = 19	3 + 0 + 0 = 3
1981	1 + 1 = 2	1 + 2 + 0 = 3
1991	2 + 2 = 4	2 + 0 + 0 = 2

mainly in the poorest townlands where a strong community spirit still survived. Over the twenty years following the Famine, however, Gallon Upper lost almost a third of its population, as well as twelve houses, representing almost a quarter of the housing stock. In contrast, both Gallon Lower and Gallon Sessiagh maintained both their levels of housing and population for another decade or two before both housing and population began to suffer substantial losses. The Valuation Revision Lists contain references to cottier houses being taken down or dismantled by farmers who owned them: it would appear that the cottier class suffered most severely during the Famine and its aftermath.

The census figures indicate also that the average number of persons per dwelling fell from more than 5.5 to 4.4 within fifty years: even if family sizes were not decreasing it would appear that more young people were leaving home while families of unmarried older people were dying out. By 1911 all three Gallon townlands had lost almost two-thirds of their population and more than half of their housing stock.

The population of the three townlands remained relatively stable between 1911 and 1958. This was probably because of the availability of cheap, though extremely basic, housing in the area and the lack of better houses elsewhere. The situation remained static until the early 1970s, when the Northern Ireland Housing Executive embarked upon an ambitious house-building programme, allocating new houses to families in greatest need. Within a few years almost all the rented houses in Gallon had been abandoned by their tenants in favour of modern accommodation in Newtownstewart or further afield.

The second half of the twentieth century had seen a dramatic reduction in the number of Gallon's inhabitants employed in agriculture. Twenty-seven individuals still own farms in Gallon but less than half of these are owner-occupiers. Almost all the farmers supplement their incomes with other employment.

EMIGRATION

After the Great Famine many inhabitants of Gallon emigrated in search of work and a higher standard of living. The most popular destinations were Britain and the United States, although a few individuals ventured as far as Australia. Families such as the McLaughlins, Brogans and McGarveys settled in Philadelphia and San Francisco.

Denis Morris, who farmed in Gallon Upper, had sufficient resources to send his children, both boys and girls, to secondary school in Derry and Strabane. Three of them went on to became priests and nuns who ministered in England and the United States.

Some individuals who had emigrated in the early part of the present century later returned to Ireland with sufficient money to buy farms. Jack McConnell returned from the United States in the 1950s and bought Robert Hill's farm in Gallon Lower. Willie Bradley returned from Australia in the 1920s and bought a

Willie & Charlie Bradley with their wives, Margaret and Annie c.1926. The Bradley brothers had recently returned from Australia

Mary Bradley, Mary Quinn, Annie Quinn and Kathleen Bradley: the photograph was taken the day before Mary Quinn emigrated to Philadelphia

farm in Gallon Sessiagh. His brother Charles bought another farm near Omagh about the same time.

However, finding work remained a problem for those who remained in Gallon. Until the First World War some women found employment doing out-work for factories in Strabane or Derry. Many boys and girls from impoverished families, sometimes as young as eleven years of age, were hired out to work with larger farmers. These children could only attend school during the winter months and some remained illiterate. Men who were not employed on the home farm had to be satisfied with manual work wherever they could find it.

The expansion of linen production at Sion Mills after 1914 provided work for some Gallon people, mostly women. Local farmers supplemented their incomes during the 1920s and 1930s by taking out contracts to maintain the county roads. The outbreak of the Second World War led to improved employment opportunities in Britain.

The introduction of free grammar school education, following the Education Act of 1947, gave Gallon's children an opportunity to improve their prospects of employment. In the last forty years many have gone on to third level education and have found employment in medicine, commerce and education. Unfortunately, such employment of necessity often means living in towns and cities. Those who remain in Gallon depend mainly for their incomes on farming, labouring or related activities.

Pat McAnena's cottage

HOUSING

The first Valuation in the 1830s recorded that there were no houses in Gallon valued at more than £3. This is not surprising as the vast majority of houses were of the traditional style with only one or two rooms, built of local stone and thatched with flax or barley straw. The houses usually had two windows in the front and one or two in the back but no back door. A feature of all traditional houses in Gallon was the 'outshot', an extension of the kitchen built into the back wall near the fireplace.

According to the Tenement Valuation of the 1860s none of the farmhouses was

Top:
The Morris farmhouse at Meenawiddy
Bottom:
Hill's farm with the special barn for his thresher

worth more than £2. In 1891 John Bradley of Gallon Lower completed what was to be the last house built in the traditional style in Gallon. Unusually, he slated the roof. His house was valued at £1.2s. Meanwhile, Robert Hill had his valuation increased to £2.15s when he raised part of his house to two storeys, slated the roof and built new outhouses; the renovated house had six rooms with five windows to the front. Hill's and Bradley's were the only two slated dwelling-houses recorded in the census of 1901. It is interesting to note, however, that many farmers were erecting new outhouses at this time, often two-storey barns, which housed the horses and cattle on the ground floor and had space for storing grain, hay and straw upstairs in the loft.

A one-roomed house with tin roof

Most of the houses mentioned in the 1901 census were still inhabited until the 1970s with only minor modifications. In general, thatched roofs were replaced by corrugated iron or asbestos sheeting. Porches were added to the front of some houses to reduce heat loss. By the 1930s clay floors had been replaced by paving stones or concrete. Only two new houses were built in Gallon in the first half of the twentieth century. Henry Bradley of Gallon Lower built a two-up, two-down house on his marriage in 1926 and doubled its size in 1946. Charles McNamee of Magherabrack built another two-up, two-down house in the 1930s.

The need for a reliable and plentiful water supply on those farms which produced milk led a few farmers to install water pumps as early as the 1930s. By the late 1960s most farmers had a private water supply to their farmyards.

However, it would appear that Gallon's farmers did not always put a high priority on the modernisation of their dwelling houses. As late as the 1960s very few houses had indoor sanitation and in the absence of mains electricity only one householder, John McNamee, had a supply of electricity from his generator. Most

CONDITION OF HOUSING IN GALLON 1958 AND 1994[13]

HOUSEHOLDER IN 1958   N   O/T   DESCRIPTION IN 1958   HOUSEHOLDER IN 1994   N   O/T   DESCRIP. IN 1994

GALLON UPPER
MEENAWIDDY AND MEENAHEAP

Householder 1958	N	O/T	Description 1958	Householder 1994	N	O/T	Descrip. 1994
Seamus Morris	2	O	Two storey, iron roof	Peggy Morris	1	O	Improved
Bernard McColgan Sen	3	O	Two storey, slated	B McColgan	2	O	Renovated
David Devine	8	T	Trad. iron roof	Vacant	-	-	Derelict
James Gilchrist	2	T	Trad. iron roof	-	-	-	Down
Vacant (late JJ Devlin)	2	-	Trad. thatched	-	-	-	Down

AGHNAHASSAN AND MEENATUMIGAN

Householder 1958	N	O/T	Description 1958	Householder 1994	N	O/T	Descrip. 1994
John McAneny	4	O	Trad. thatch/iron roof	Pat McAnena	1	O	Improved
Charlie McColgan	3	O	Trad. iron roof	-	-	-	Derelict
				Charles McColgan Jr	3	O	New house
Charlie Quinn	7	O	Trad. thatched	Sean Devine	6	O	Renovated
Gallon School	-	-	Purpose built, slated	-	-	-	Vacant
Vacant (late McCrory's)	0	-	Two storey, slated	-	-	-	Down
				G McGuigan	3	O	New house
Neil McNamee	4	O	Trad. iron roof	John McDermott	3	O	Renovated
				Mary McNamee	4	O	New house

AGHNAGLARIG, BLACKDYKE AND CROCKATORE

Householder 1958	N	O/T	Description 1958	Householder 1994	N	O/T	Descrip. 1994
Willie Ashenhurst	5	T	Trad. iron roof	-	-	-	Down
Neil Kelly	10	O	Trad. improved	Willie Patton	3	O	Renovated
Bessie McLaughlin	1	O	One room iron roof	-	-	-	Derelict
Willie McClure	4	T	Two storey, slated	-	-	-	Derelict
				Damien McNamee	6	O	New house
				Tommy McNamee	5	O	New house
				Robin Stewart	4	O	New house
Lila McCallion	6	T	Trad. iron	-	-	-	Down
Michael O'Brien	1	O	Trad. thatched	Sadie McNamee	2	O	Renovated
John McNamee (Jr)	9	O	Trad. improved	-	-	-	Derelict
John McNamee Cottage	9	T	Government c.1914	Charlie McNamee	1	O	Renovated
Willie McGillian	1	T	Trad. asbestos	-	-	-	Derelict
Paddy Tracey	6	T	Trad. asbestos	-	-	-	Derelict

MAGHERABRACK

Householder 1958	N	O/T	Description 1958	Householder 1994	N	O/T	Descrip. 1994
Vincent McNamee	5	O	1 up 1 down slated	-	-	-	Derelict
				Vincent McNamee	3	O	New house
Charles McNamee	4	O	Trad. thatched	-	-	-	Derelict
Charles McAnena	1	O	Trad. iron	-	-	-	Derelict

GALLON LOWER

Householder 1958	N	O/T	Description 1958	Householder 1994	N	O/T	Descrip. 1994
Jack McConnell	3	O	Two storey farmhouse	-	-	-	Derelict
Vacant (M McAnena)	-	-	Two storey farmhouse	-	0	O	Part renovated
Neil McAnena	4	O	Enlarged, iron roof	John McNamee	4	O	Renovated
Vacant (Donegan's)	-	-	Trad. thatched	-	-	-	Down
John McAnena	1	O	Trad. thatched	Pat McAnena	1	O	Trad. thatched
John Devine	1	O	One room, iron roof	-	-	-	Vacant
Paddy Maguire	10	T	Trad. slated	-	-	-	Derelict
Henry Bradley	11	O	Two storey, slated	John Bradley	0	O	Renovated
Mickey McAnena	1	O	Trad. thatched	-	-	-	Down
Minnie McLaughlin	1	O	Enlarged, slated	-	-	-	Derelict
Bella McGurk	2	O	Trad. thatched	-	-	-	Down

GALLON SESSIAGH

Householder 1958	N	O/T	Description 1958	Householder 1994	N	O/T	Descrip. 1994
Alice Morris	1	O	Two storey, slated	-	-	-	Vacant
Maggie Quinn	5	O	Trad. iron rood	Aidan McNamee	3	O	Renovated
Mary Bradley	4	O	Enlarged, iron roof	Michael Maguire	4	T	Renovated
				Anne McNulty	1	O	New house
				Gary Drum	3	O	New house

O = Owner, T = Tenant, N - Number of occupants

of the other homes depended on an oil or a tilley lamp to light the kitchen where the family congregated at night: light in other rooms was provided by candles. Only a few houses had bottled gas for cooking and light.

The widespread renovation of old houses in Gallon had to wait until the 1970s. The introduction of generous improvement grants enabled householders to enlarge their houses and install indoor sanitation and mains electricity. A comparison of surveys into the condition of houses in 1958 and 1994 illustrates the changes made in the intervening thirty-six years.[13]

There were thirty-four inhabited houses in Gallon in 1958; twenty-five were owner-occupied and seven were rented out to tenants; a further three houses were vacant. Twenty-three houses were built in the traditional Gallon style: of these eight were thatched, two were slated and the remainder had either iron or asbestos roofs. There were nine two-storey houses of which two had iron and the remainder slated roofs. There were two enlarged houses built in traditional style but with an extra room added at a later date. They both had iron roofs.

By 1994 nine of these older houses had been completely renovated and two had been improved by the installation of water, sewage and mains electricity. Nine new houses had been built. Only one house, occupied by Pat McAnena in Gallon Lower, has remained unaltered: it is a traditional Gallon house, with a well-tended thatched roof and dazzling white-washed walls. Pat's only concessions to modernity are a gas-cooker and a telephone.

Many residents hoped that public authority housing would be provided in Gallon. A single labourer's cottage was built at Crockatore in Gallon Upper in 1912 but no more public housing was ever provided nearer than Newtownstewart.

CHANGING FACE OF FARMING

Because detailed evidence about the character of farming in any district in Ireland is rare, we need to turn to the agricultural statistics first collected by the Irish Constabulary for the government in 1847. Thereafter, these farm returns were collected and published for each Poor Law Union. All three Gallon townlands were in the District Electoral Division of Moyle within the Gortin Poor Law Union. In 1850, Moyle contained in all some 7,676 acres, covering 278 farms with 2,808 inhabitants, whereas the three Gallon townlands had 1,505 acres on about 40 farms with 449 inhabitants. Of the 7,676 acres in Moyle 2,908 acres, or more than a third, were under cultivation. This represents a high percentage, especially when the extent of moorland is taken into consideration. The major crop was oats with 2,003 acres and there were 351 acres of potatoes, 186 acres of turnips, 186 acres of flax and 134 acres of meadow and clover. This would suggest that Gallon might have had at least 300 acres of oats as well as 60 acres of potatoes and perhaps 20 or 30 acres each of turnips and flax.

It is surprising to find so much land described in the Nolan estate maps of 1848 as 'arable'; about 200 acres in Gallon Upper and 190 acres in Gallon

Lower. Most of this land, especially in Gallon Upper and Gallon Sessiagh, had been reclaimed from the moor and bog in the previous century. The poor quality of the land and its subsoil is accurately and minutely detailed in the first Government Valuation carried out in the 1830s.

The identification of three limestone quarries and a gravel pit on the first Ordnance Survey map of 1834 indicates some of the methods that were being used to reclaim the land: spreading lime on the moorland to lower its acidity and encourage grass, and spreading loads of gravel on wet bog. The planting of potatoes had proved ideal for breaking up lea ground and keeping it clear of weeds. To maintain its productivity, such poor land required plenty of labour; the spade was reckoned to be more effective for this purpose than the plough.

The acreage of land under cultivation in Ireland reached its peak in 1859 and henceforth began a steady fall, due to the reduction in population and availability of cheap labour. The oat crop continued to be the most important arable crop. The farmers cut the oat crop with sickles or scythes until the introduction of the earliest horse-drawn reapers in the 1860s. The crop was usually threshed using hand-flails and then carted to Scott's mill in Newtownstewart for grinding. At the turn of the century Robert Hill installed a horse-drawn threshing machine in a specially constructed barn at Gallon Lower and for a few years the local farmers carted their oats to Hill's farmyard for threshing.

Russell's steam thresher from Omagh made its appearance in Gallon just after the First World War. It was a heavy and noisy machine that required a dozen men to operate it efficiently. In 1934 Mickey McAnena of Gallon Lower sold his farm and bought the first oil-fired tractor to operate with a threshing machine in the district. In 1936 Charlie (Ginger) McNamee bought a tractor and was fully employed for many years doing contract work among his farming neighbours. The revival of farm prices during the Second World War enabled many farmers to invest in labour-saving farm equipment, such as potato-diggers and mechanical reapers. By the 1960s the tractor had almost entirely replaced the horse for farm work in Gallon.

During the two World Wars farmers had been encouraged to engage in mixed farming, in order to supply the home market with potatoes, oats and vegetables. Mixed farming has declined in Gallon since the 1960s due to the relatively low prices for these crops and the cost of the labour required to grow them.

During the war years there was also a high demand for home-grown flax to supply the local linen industry, due to the dislocation of traditional supplies from Belgium and the Baltic regions. The retted flax was scutched at one of the three scutch mills along the Derg river near Ardstraw. With the resumption of supplies from continental Europe after 1945 the price for homegrown flax collapsed. Local production of flax had ceased entirely by the late 1950s.

Since the early years of the nineteenth century the price of store cattle for the British market had attracted many local farmers. They had a ready market for their animals at the fair days held on the last Monday of each month at

Gallan 1834
with valuation boundaries 1835

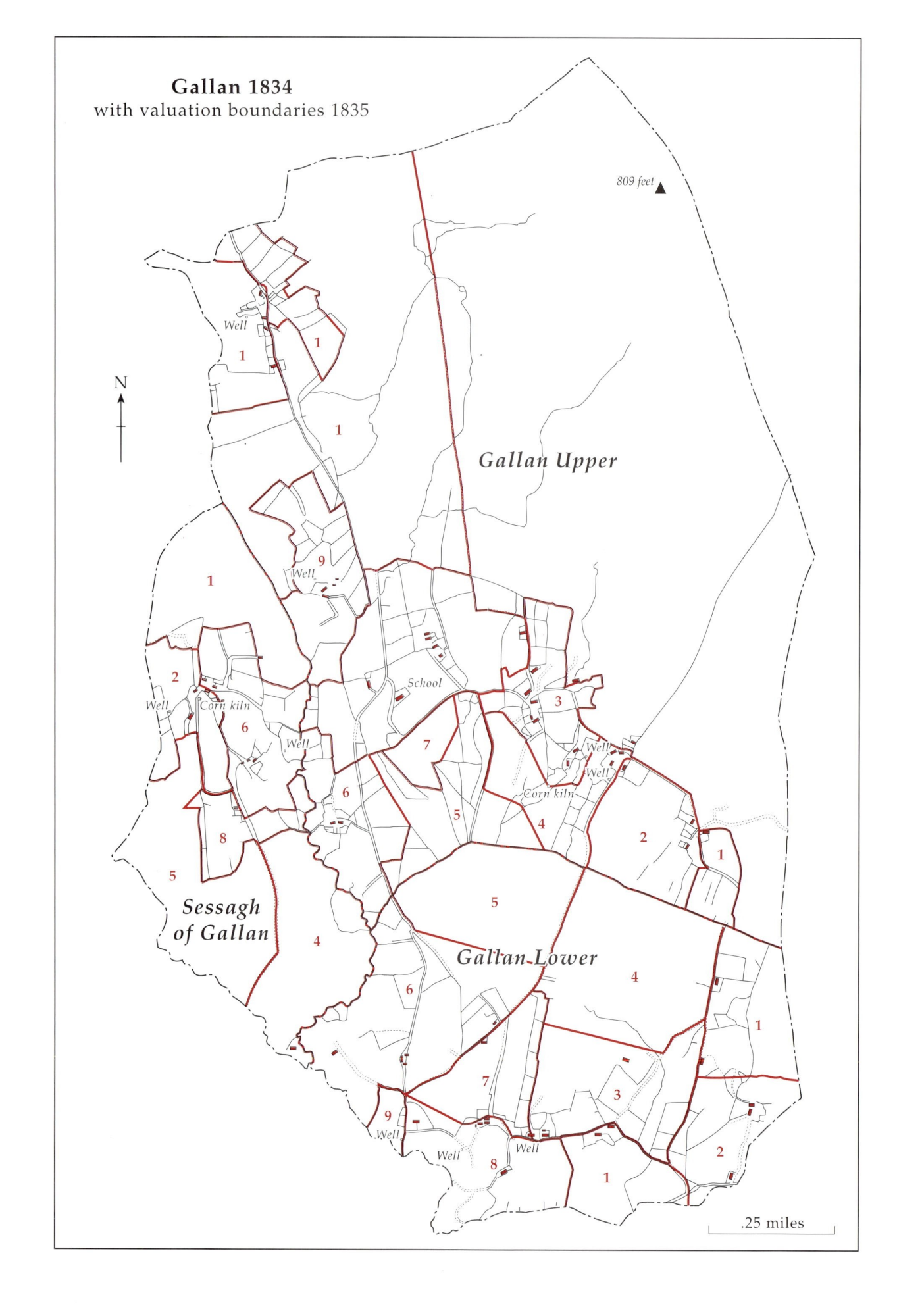

Gallan Upper

Sessagh of Gallan

Gallan Lower

809 feet

.25 miles

Parish of Ardstraw   Val 1B/637A

GALLAN LOWER

NO.	SUBDENOMINATIONS & OBSERVATIONS	QUANTITY	RATE PER STANDARD ACRE	AMOUNT OF LAND £ S D
1	Heathy boggy and green pasture - part of latter reclaimed	27 2.10	1/0°	1 8 7
	Also gravelly and moory arable	2 0 0	7/6	0 15 0
2	Part gravelly part moory arable - with stripes of meadow and pasture	23 0 0	9/6	10 18 6
3	Green & moory pasture one half poor & heathy	29 0 10	0/8°	1 0 6
	Also poor moory arable	3 0 03	5/6	0 16 7
	Also poor moory arable	1 2 0	8/=	0 12 0
	Also poor moory arable	3 3 15	6/6	1 5 0
	Also poor moory arable	5 1 24	9/6	2 11 3
4	Flat tufty soft bog	54 3 05	0/2	0 9 1
	Also coarse green pasture	5 2 0	1/=	0 3 0
5	Coarse tufty, part cut but dry bog	33 3 0	0/2°	0 7 0
	Also good coarse bottom pasture	5 2 0	3/=	0 16 6
6	Part green part moory pasture and cut out bog	41 0 20	0/10	1 14 3
	Also moory arable	2 1 20	4/6	0 10 8
	Also moory arable	6 2 06	9/6	3 2 1
	Also moory arable	8 0 28	11/=	4 9 11
	Also gravelly moor	0 3 0	12/=	0 9 0
	Also moory arable	8 1 08	8/=	3 6 4
7	Medium reclaimed moor on cold clay subsoil	22 1 22	10/=	11 3 10
	Also moory pasture	2 2 0	1/=	0 2 6
8	Fine deep well lying loamy arable, friable clay soil	26 2 30	16/=	21 7 0
	Also good clayey and moory meadow	6 0 0	10/=	3 0 0
	Also quarry pits and adjacent pasture	2 0 0	2/6	0 5 0
9	Well reclaimed moory arable, part steep red sand subsoil	4 0 04	10/=	2 0 3
10	Deep strong arable on gravelly and clayey subsoil	12 2 16	16/=	10 1 7
	Also gravelly arable	2 0 0	10/=	1 0 0
	Also moory meadow and pasture	3 2 0	6/6	1 2 9
	Also bog part being gravelled	2 0 0	0/5	0 0 10
		343 1 21		84 19 0

There are no houses in this townland worth three pounds a year.

GALLAN UPPER

1	Poor moory arable clay subsoil	10 1 22	6/6	3 7 6
2	Shallow gravelly arable on hard gravel subsoil	21 0 29	9/=	9 10 7
	Also poor moory arable and very poor gravelly field	6 1 0	4/6	1 8 1
	Also deep bog pasture	1 2 0	0/6	0 0 9
3	Poor moory rocky and gravelly arable on several small steeps	23 1 0	5/=	5 16 3
	Also moory rocky pasture	4 2 32	1/=	0 4 7
4	Medium gravelly loam on gravel subsoil	22 0 0	10/6	11 11 0
	Also moory arable and coarse meadow	1 0 0	5/=	5 0
5	Coarse meadow on moor, low moor reclaimed, and coarse pasture	32 1 26	5/6	8 18 2
6	Poor moory arable on cold sand subsoil	23 1 28	7/=	8 3 11
	Also bitter gravelly loam	5 0 0	11/=	2 15 0
	Also moor and poorly reclaimed ground	1 2 0	2/6	0 3 9
7	Medium gravelly loam on red sand and gravel	9 1 02	12/6	5 15 9

NO.	SUBDENOMINATIONS & OBSERVATIONS	QUANTITY	RATE PER STANDARD ACRE	AMOUNT OF LAND £ S D
8	Poor moory hilly arable on white & red sand & gravel	56 2 20	6/6	18 8 1
	Also moor partly cut	7 3 25	1/=	0 7 10
9	Medium gravelly and moory arable on red sand and gravel subsoil	32 0 35	8/=	12 17 9
10	Medium clayey and gravelly loam, on sand and gravel subsoil	17 0 15	11/6	9 16 6
	Also coarse low meadow	5 0 00	7/=	1 15 0
	Also poor arable green and heathy pasture	3 0 00	3/=	0 9 0
11	Poor moory arable on sand subsoil exposed	17 3 06	6/=	5 6 8
12	Brown heathy and mixed mountain pasture	174 2 30	0/6	4 7 5
13	Heathy and boggy mountain chiefly dry	478 0 10	0/2°	4 19 7
		954 1 00		£116 8 2

There are no houses in this townland worth three pounds a year

SESSAGH OF GALLAN

1	Heathy boggy mountain pasture	37 1 13	0/5	0 15 6
	Also reclaimed moor and coarse green mixed pasturable verges	3 2 00	2/=	0 7 0
2	Medium gravelly loam with stones on stoney and gravelly subsoil	14 3 20	9/6	7 1 3
	Also poor moory arable and pasture	6 0 00	3/=	0 18 0
3	Poor moory arable chiefly on clay subsoil	15 3 00	6/=	4 14 6
4	Cut bog and good mixed green pasturable verges	41 1 00	0/9	1 10 11
	Also two pieces of moory arable	3 0 00	4/=	0 12 0
5	Chiefly bog about ⅓ mixed, green heathy and rocky pasture	47 0 00	0/6°	1 5 5
	Also green pasture verging stream	3 2 0	2/=	0 7 0
6	Medium gravelly loam, part stony part gravel, with moor on stony and white sand subsoil	17 0 20	9/=	7 14 0
	Also moory reclaimed ground and coarse meadow	5 0 00	6/=	1 10 0
	Also cut mixed green and moory pasture	11 1 00	1/7	0 17 9
		205 2 13		£27 13 4

There are no houses in this townland worth three pounds a year.

TOWNLAND VALUATION (1835)

The three townlands of Gallan lie on the flank of a moory hill used only for summer grazing before they were settled. They contain small pockets of good land each of which could support a family or two. The earliest settlement was probably on the forty acres of good land valued at 16s per acre along the burn at the southern tip of Lower Gallan (8 & 10). Later settlements picked out the land valued between 8s and 12s per acre, notably in Gallan Upper and Sessagh of Gallan. In Upper Gallan note how Meenawiddy, Meenaheap, and Meenatumigan lie along the Sessagh Burn while Aghnahassan, Aghnaglarig, Crockatore, and Magherabrack lie along the 450 foot contour. As population grew more land was brought under cultivation.

The valuators distinguish the value of the land in great detail and comment on the methods and quality of land reclamation: 'bog part being gravelled' (Gallan Lower 10); 'reclaimed moor and coarse green mixed pasturable verges' (Sessagh of Gallan 1); 'moor and poorly reclaimed ground' (Gallan Upper 6). Three limestone quarries and a gravel pit are indicated on the OS maps. – WHC

GALLON

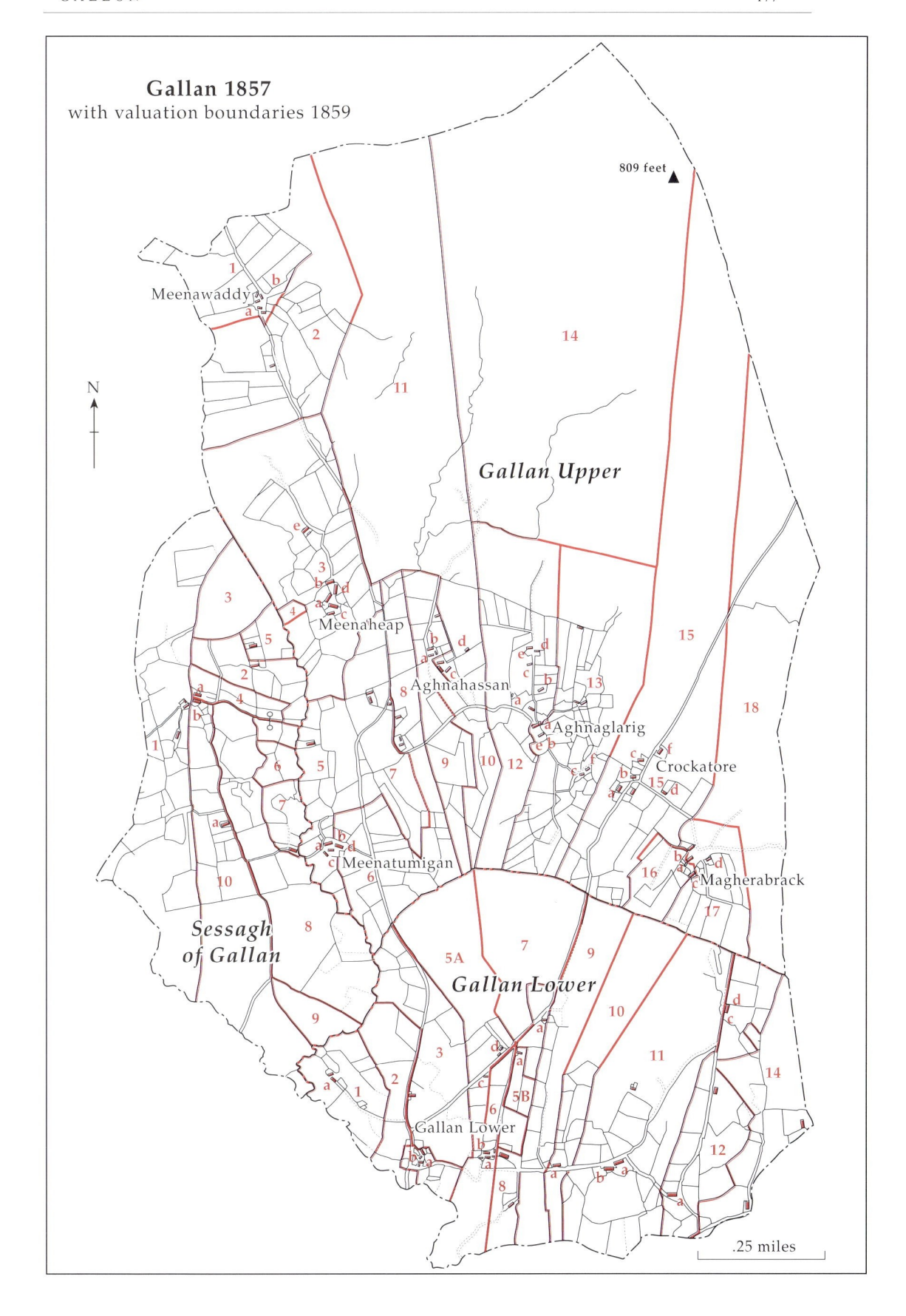

Gallan 1857
with valuation boundaries 1859

Gallan Upper

Sessagh of Gallan

Gallan Lower

Meenawaddy
Meenaheap
Aghnahassan
Aghnaglarig
Crockatore
Meenatumigan
Magherabrack
Gallan Lower

809 feet

.25 miles

PARISH OF ARDSTRAW.

No. and Letters of Reference to Map.	Townlands and Occupiers.	Immediate Lessors.	Description of Tenement.	Area.	Rateable Annual Valuation. Land.	Rateable Annual Valuation. Buildings.	Total Annual Valuation of Rateable Property.
	GALLAN, LOWER. *(Ord. S. 10 & 17.)*						
1	William Hill,	Daniel Baird,	House, office, and land,	15 3 30	5 5 0	0 15 0	6 0 0
2	Patk. M'Ananey (*Jas.*),	Same,	House, office, and land,	14 3 30	5 5 0	0 10 0	5 15 0
3 { a	Patrick Brogan, *(See No. 4.)*	Same,	House, office, & land,	} 30 0 20	{ 5 0 0	0 10 0	5 10 0
	John Brogan, *(See No. 4.)*		Land,		5 0 0	—	5 0 0
4 a	Andrew Brogan,	Same,	House, office, and land,	3 1 0	2 0 0	0 10 0	2 10 0
— { b	John Brogan,	Same,	Ho.,off.,& gar.(*pt. of*),	0 2 20	{ 0 5 0	0 10 0	0 15 0
— —	Patrick Brogan,		Garden (*part of*),		0 5 0	—	0 5 0
5 A { A a	Jacob Bradley,		House, office, & land,		—	0 15 0	{ 6 0 0
	John Bradley,	Same,	House and land,	} 46 2 0	9 10 0	0 5 0	2 0 0
— B { — b				3 1 0	1 0 0	—	
	Michael M'Garvey,		Ho., office, & land,		—	0 10 0	4 0 0
— c	Patk. Brogan (*cottier*),	Free,	House and garden,	0 2 0	0 3 0	0 7 0	0 10 0
— d	Hugh Towler,	Michael M'Garvey,	House,	—	—	0 5 0	0 5 0
— f	Edward M'Connell,	Daniel Baird,	Land,	0 1 20	0 5 0	—	0 5 0
6	Michael M'Ananey,	Same,	House, office, and land,	10 0 20	3 10 0	0 10 0	4 0 0
7 {	Michael M'Ananey,	Same,	Land,	20 1 20	{ 0 10 0	—	0 10 0
	John M'Ananey,				0 10 0	—	0 10 0
8 {	John M'Ananey,	Same,	House, office, & land,	{ 7 3 30	5 18 0	0 17 0	{ 7 5 0
5 A e				0 3 10	0 10 0	—	
9	Elizabeth Hutchinson,	Same,	House, office, and land,	28 2 15	5 18 0	0 17 0	6 15 0
10	Patk. M'Ananey (*Neal*),	Same,	House, office, and land,	28 0 6	3 10 0	0 10 0	4 0 0
11 { a	Daniel M'Loughlin,	Same,	House, offices,& land,	} 70 1 30	{ 7 10 0	1 5 0	8 15 0
{ b	Michael M'Namee,	Reps. Jn. M'Loughlin,	House, office, & land,		7 10 0	0 15 0	8 5 0
— c	John Coll,	Daniel M'Loughlin,	House,	—	—	0 5 0	0 5 0
12 a	John Hutchinson,	Daniel Baird,	House, office, and land,	33 2 10	12 0 0	1 5 0	13 5 0
— b	John M'Namee,	John Hutchinson,	House,	—	—	0 10 0	0 10 0
— c	Hannah M'Crodden,	Same,	House,	—	—	0 5 0	0 5 0
— d	John M'Namee,	Same,	House,	—	—	0 10 0	0 10 0
13	William Hutchinson,	Daniel Baird,	House, office, and land,	9 3 0	5 18 0	1 17 0	7 15 0
14	Samuel Hutchinson,	Same,	Land,	18 1 0	1 15 0	—	1 15 0
			Total,	343 1 21	88 17 0	14 3 0	103 0 0
	GALLAN, UPPER. *(Ord. S. 10 & 17.)*						
1 a	Denis Morris,	Daniel Baird,	House, offices, and land,	34 1 10	10 5 0	1 5 0	11 10 0
— b	Thomas Tanscy,	Denis Morris,	House,	—	—	0 10 0	0 10 0
— c	Patrick Keenan,	Same,	House,	—	—	0 5 0	0 5 0
2 a	Peter Morris,	Daniel Baird,	House, office, and land,	41 0 5	7 15 0	1 0 0	8 15 0
3 { a	John Devlin,		House, office, & land,		{ 0 15 0	—	5 5 0
{ —	Denis Morris,	Same,	Land,	} 60 3 8	13 0 0	—	4 10 0
{ —	Bernard M'Namee, *(See No. 16.)*		Land,		—	—	4 0 0
4 { 3 b	Peter Brogan,	Same,	House and garden,	0 0 20	0 2 0	0 7 0	} 0 15 0
			Land,	0 3 20	0 6 0	—	
3 c	Patrick M'Kenna,	Denis Morris,	House,	—	—	0 10 0	0 10 0
— d	Thomas Traney,	Bernard M'Namee,	House and garden,	0 0 12	0 1 0	0 4 0	0 5 0
— e	Patrick Devlin,	Denis Morris,	House,	—	—	0 10 0	0 10 0
5 { a	Owen Quinn,		House and land,		{ 0 10 0	0 10 0	3 10 0
{ b	John Quinn,	Daniel Baird,	House and land,	} 22 1 20	6 0 0	0 10 0	2 10 0
{ c	Daniel Morris,		Office and land,		0 5 0	1 5 0	
6 { a	James M'Conway,	Same,	House, office, & land,	} 21 0 10	7 0 0	0 10 0	2 5 0
{ b	Edward Rogers,		House, office, & land,			0 10 0	5 15 0
7 a	Charles M'Colgan, *(See No. 8 & 11.)*	Same,	House, offices, and land,	20 2 30	8 5 0	1 5 0	9 10 0
— b	National School-house,	(*See Exemptions.*)					
8 { a	James M'Analley, *(See No. 11.)*		House, office, & land,			0 15 0	4 10 0
{ b	Charles M'Analley, *(See No. 11.)*	Daniel Baird,	House and land,	} 18 1 30	7 15 0	0 10 0	2 10 0
{	Charles M'Colgan, *(See No. 11.)*		Land,			—	2 0 0
9 { a	Charles M'Analley, *(See No. 11.)*	Same,	House, office, & land,	} 19 3 20	{ 4 0 0	0 15 0	4 15 0
{ b	Michael M'Analley, *(See No. 11.)*		House, office, & land,		4 0 0	0 15 0	4 15 0
10 { a	James Brogan, *(See No. 11.)*	Same,	House, office, & land,	} 20 2 0	{ 4 0 0	0 15 0	4 15 0
{ b	John Brogan, *(See No. 11.)*		House, office, & land,		4 0 0	0 15 0	4 15 0
— c	Patrick Brogan,	Same,	House and garden,	0 2 10	0 5 0	0 10 0	0 15 0

PARISH OF ARDSTRAW.

No. and Letters of Reference to Map.	Townlands and Occupiers.	Immediate Lessors.	Description of Tenement.	Area. A. R. P.	Rateable Annual Valuation. Land. £ s. d.	Rateable Annual Valuation. Buildings. £ s. d.	Total Annual Valuation of Rateable Property. £ s. d.
	GALLAN, UPPER—continued.						
11	Charles M'Colgan, James M'Analley, Charles M'Analley, Charles M'Colgan, Charles M'Analley, Michael M'Analley, James Brogan, John Brogan,	Same,	Mountain,	114 1 0	3 4 0	—	0 16 0 / 0 8 0 / 0 4 0 / 0 4 0 / 0 8 0 / 0 8 0 / 0 8 0 / 0 8 0
12 a	James Kelly, (See No. 14.)		House, office, & land,			0 10 0	3 10 0
12 b	Neal M'Namee, (See No. 14.)		House and land,			0 10 0	2 0 0
12	Patrick M'Garvey, (See No. 14.)	Same,	Land,	44 1 20	12 0 0	—	1 10 0
12 c	Susan M'Loughlin, (See No. 14.)		House and land,			0 5 0	1 15 0
12 d	Eliza M'Cullagh, (See No. 14.)		House and land,			0 10 0	2 0 0
12 e	Bernard M'Cullagh, (See No. 14.)		House and land,			0 10 0	3 10 0
13 a	Patk. M'Garvey, sen., (See No. 14.)		House, office, & land,			1 0 0	4 5 0
13 b	Rose M'Garvey, (See No. 14.)		House, office, & land,			0 15 0	6 15 0
13		Daniel Baird,		62 1 0	12 5 0		
13 c	Patk. M'Garvey, jun., (See No. 14.)		House, office, & land,			0 10 0	1 15 0
13 d	Michael M'Garvey, (See No. 14.)		House and land,			0 10 0	2 5 0
— e	Francis M'Bride,	Patrick M'Garvey, sen.,	House,	—	—	0 10 0	0 10 0
— f	William Ward,	Michael M'Garvey,	House,	—	—	0 5 0	0 5 0
— g	Anne Martin,	Patrick M'Garvey, sen.,	House,	—	—	0 5 0	0 5 0
— h	Henry Loane,	Rose M'Garvey,	House,	—	—	0 5 0	0 5 0
14	James Kelly, Neal M'Namee, Patk. M'Garvey, sen., Susan M'Loughlin, Eliza M'Cullagh, Bernard M'Cullagh, Patk. M'Garvey, sen., Rose M'Garvey, Patk. M'Garvey, jun., Michael M'Garvey,	Daniel Baird,	Mountain,	238 0 0	3 2 0	—	0 8 0 / 0 4 0 / 0 4 0 / 0 4 0 / 0 4 0 / 0 8 0 / 0 8 0 / 0 15 0 / 0 3 0 / 0 4 0
15 a	Michl. M'Namee, sen.,		House, office, & land,			0 15 0	4 5 0
15 b	James M'Namee,	Same,	House, office, & land,	122 1 0	10 10 0	1 0 0	2 15 0
15 c	John M'Namee,		House, office, & land,			1 0 0	4 10 0
—	Michl. M'Namee, jun.		Land,				1 15 0
— d	William Beytagh,	Michael M'Namee, jun.,	House,	—	—	0 15 0	0 15 0
— e	Neal M'Namee,	Michael M'Namee, sen.,	House and garden,	0 1 0	0 3 0	0 7 0	0 10 0
— f	Bridget M'Namee,	John M'Namee,	House,	—	—	0 5 0	0 5 0
16 a	Bernard M'Namee, (See No. 18.)	Daniel Baird,	House, office, & land,	12 3 20	3 15 0	0 15 0	3 10 0
16 b	Charles M'Namee, (See No. 18.)		House, office, & land,			0 10 0	1 10 0
17 a	Daniel M'Loughlin, (See 18.)	Same,	House and land,		3 5 0	0 10 0	3 15 0
17 b	Hugh M'Namee, (See No. 18.)	Same,	House and land,		0 10 0	0 10 0	1 0 0
17 c	James M'Namee, (See No. 18.)	Same,	House and land,	15 3 25	1 10 0	0 5 0	1 15 0
—	William M'Ananey, (See No. 18.)	Reps. John M'Loughlin	Land,		1 5 0	—	1 5 0
— d	Ellen M'Namee,	Daniel Baird,	House and garden,	0 1 0	0 2 0	0 3 0	0 5 0
18	Bernard M'Namee, Charles M'Namee, Daniel M'Loughlin, Hugh M'Namee, James M'Namee, William M'Ananey,	Same, Reps. John M'Loughlin	Mountain,	81 2 20	1 12 0	—	0 12 0 / 0 4 0 / 0 7 0 / 0 2 0 / 0 4 0 / 0 3 0
			Total of Rateable Property,	952 3 0	129 17 0	26 11 0	156 8 0
			EXEMPTIONS:				
7 b	. . . .	Daniel Baird,	National school-house,	—	—	0 15 0	0 15 0
			Total, including Exemptions,	952 3 0	129 17 0	27 6 0	157 3 0

card players

TENEMENT VALUATION (1858)

This Valuation map illustrates the landscape at the greatest extent of cultivation. The southern boundaries are defined by streams, one of whose tributaries separates Sessiagh of Gallan from Gallan Upper. Gallan Upper is separated from Gallan Lower by an extensive bog in the upper parts of (5), (7), (9), (10), and (11).

This map and the printed Valuation Book help us to understand how land was reclaimed piecemeal from the waste and made into little fields as the settlements expanded. The 'mountain', or moorland, at (11), (14), and (18) was held in soums for grazing valued at four shillings a soum: the McNamees in (15) had their own arrangement. – WHC

No. and Letters of Reference to Map.	Names. Townlands and Occupiers.	Immediate Lessors.	Description of Tenement.	Area. A. R. P.	Rateable Annual Valuation. Land. £ s. d.	Buildings. £ s. d.	Total Annual Valuation of Rateable Property. £ s. d.
	SESSAGH OF GALLAN—con.						
1	William M'Clintock,	James & George Aiken,	House, offices, and land,	65 2 10	8 15 0	1 5 0	10 0 0
2	Anne Devlin,	Same,	House and land,	11 1 0	3 0 0	0 10 0	3 10 0
3	Anne Devlin, / James M'Aleer,	James & George Aiken,	Mountain,	11 2 8	{ 0 5 0 / 0 5 0 }	— / —	0 5 0 / 0 5 0
4	James M'Aleer,	Same,	House, office, and land,	7 2 20	2 0 0	0 10 0	2 10 0
5	John M'Callan,	Same,	House and land,	4 2 20	0 10 0	0 10 0	1 0 0
6	Owen Quinn,	Same,	Land,	3 2 0	0 15 0	—	0 15 0
7	John Quinn,	Same,	Land,	5 2 5	1 0 0	—	1 0 0
— a	Patrick Quinn,	John Quinn,	House and garden,	0 1 25	0 5 0	0 5 0	0 10 0
8	John Morris,	James & George Aiken,	House, office, and land,	44 3 5	7 15 0	0 15 0	8 10 0
9	William Hill,	Same,	Land,	6 0 15	0 10 0	—	0 10 0
10 a/b	Owen M'Colgan, / Daniel Morris,	Same,	House, office, & land, / House, office, & land,	44 2 25	{ 4 0 0 / 4 0 0 }	0 15 0 / 0 15 0	4 15 0 / 4 15 0
			Total,	205 2 13	33 0 0	5 5 0	38 5 0

Newtownstewart. The coming of the Great Northern Railway in 1860 opened up a market for butter and milk and encouraged many farmers to replace their traditional longhorn cattle with dairy shorthorns, good for both milk and beef. The establishment of a creamery at Newtownstewart in the 1920s ensured a reliable demand for liquid milk. After the Second World War the opening of Nestle's milk-processing plants at Omagh and Victoria Bridge encouraged farmers to build new byres and more hygienic processing facilities on their farms. During the 1950s, however, many farmers became so disenchanted with milk production that now only one Gallon farmer sells milk.

Until the 1960s almost all the farms in Gallon produced pigs and poultry. The weekly sale of eggs provided ready cash to purchase the weekly groceries and often proved a more reliable source of income for the farmer's wife than her husband's longer term enterprises. Many wives reared turkeys and geese for the Christmas market. Pigs too were seen as a cost-effective way of using up leftovers from the farm table. Until the outbreak of myxomatosis, farmers' sons made extra money from trapping rabbits.

During the 1950s and 1960s there was a trend towards more intensive poultry and pig production. Free-range egg production gave way to the deep litter system and the higher standards demanded by the egg merchants meant greater attention to hygiene in the hen houses. At one stage Bernard McColgan's farm was selling 2,500 eggs per week. Pig production also intensified in the 1960s when the leading producers were Tommy and John McNamee in Gallon Upper and Eddie Bradley in Gallon Lower. However, the reduction in prices for poultry, eggs and pork products that occurred during the 1970s discouraged further investment by Gallon's farmers and both activities declined to a shadow of their former selves.

Up to the first half of the present century, sheep production in Gallon was mainly confined to the rough pastures of Upper Gallon. However, following the decline in arable farming since the 1970s more and more land has been given over to the rearing of sheep. This practice has been greatly encouraged by the generous subsidies available from the European Union.

Gallon's householders have been fortunate down through the years in having access to turbary for turf-cutting. Until the 1980s the turf was cut by spade in the traditional fashion. During coal shortages Gallon men earned extra income by selling turf in local towns. In recent years the increasing popularity of oil for home-heating has reduced the number of families winning their own turf. Although the introduction of turf-cutting machines in recent years has taken the drudgery out of turf-cutting, it is regarded today more as a hobby than a necessity.

Modern farming methods and reduced farm incomes mean that small farms are no longer viable. This has led to the amalgamation of smaller farming enterprises into larger units either by outright purchase or by conacre. The numbers of cattle and sheep have increased and the farmers' main crops are now silage and, to a lesser extent, hay in order to feed these animals over the winter. Large silos and sheds have been built to house the cattle and sheep and to store their fodder over the winter months.

COMMUNICATIONS

Although Gallon lies within three miles of Newtownstewart, it is separated from it by the River Mourne. Until 1727, when a stone bridge was built across the river to carry the main road from Dublin to Derry, the people of Gallon would have forded the river near this point; at certain times of the year it would have seemed impassable and they would have been cut off from Newtownstewart. The construction of the stone bridge, together with the opening of the road from Newtownstewart to Gortin must have made Gallon more accessible to all those with business to transact in the town.

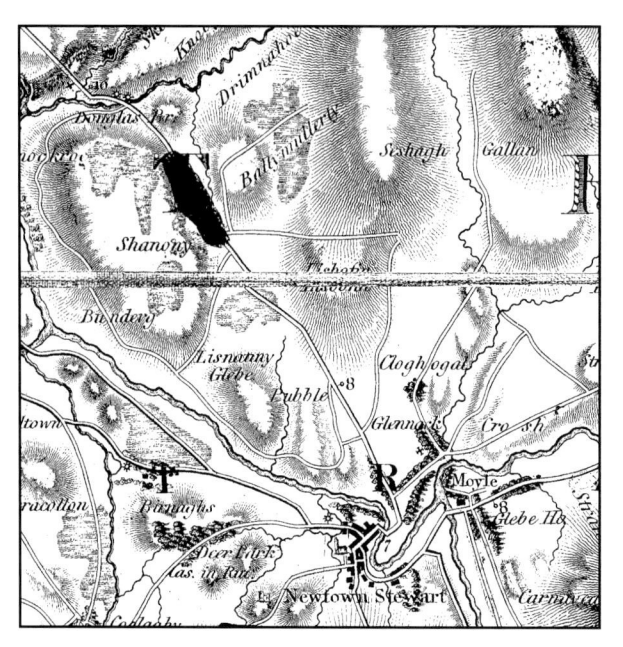

The pace of both bridge and road construction quickened as a result of the Road Act of 1765 which increased the county cess payable by every landholder. The income was used to pay the men who laboured on the roads. As a result, many main roads connecting market towns were constructed with bridges and 'pipes' across the rivers and streams. Landlords encouraged the building of minor roads to open up formerly remote areas in order to encourage settlement. As the roads improved, farmers and dealers began to use the wheel car and, from the early nineteenth century, the big Scotch cart, to transport people and agricultural produce to and from fairs and markets.

The first map of the County Tyrone, produced for the grand jury in 1775 by the McCrea brothers, has not survived. We have to depend on a slightly later map, made by William McCrea and George Knox in 1813.

This map shows a road branching off the main road at Glenock church and terminating in the middle of Upper Gallon, near the site of the school. The first Ordnance Survey map of 1834 shows that this road had linked with another road which came south from the main Plumbridge-Strabane road. Another branch road had opened up through the neighbouring townland of Crosh, while yet another ran through Gallon Lower to meet the road coming up from Glenock church. It is perhaps surprising that Gallon Sessiagh was never linked directly with Gallon Upper by county road; this may have been one of the consequences of the dismemberment of the Blessington estate.

The year 1851 marked the opening of the railway line from Derry to Enniskillen and the construction of another line from Portadown to Omagh in 1860 linked Newtownstewart to both Belfast and Dublin. The improved communications enabled farmers, merchants and cattle dealers to transport livestock and agricultural produce to ports and to import artificial fertiliser and farm implements, such as mechanical reapers. The railway also provided transport for workers commuting to work in the factories at Sion Mills, Strabane or Omagh. After the First World War motor lorries became more common. These vehicles were able to take advantage of the widespread network of roads and lanes to deliver and collect first goods and later animals from remote farms. Two pioneering businessmen who served Gallon were Willie Gallagher of Newtownstewart and Willie Doherty of Mountjoy East who called weekly at farmhouses to buy eggs and to deliver groceries. After the Second World War the delivery of bread by van became commonplace, to such an extent that at one time Gallon was served by different bread vans on four days per week.

Before the age of the motor car Gallon's inhabitants generally travelled on foot or used the farmyard horse and cart if they had to undertake a journey. Only two families kept a pony and trap, the Morris and McColgan families of Gallon Upper. The first motor cars seen in Gallon were owned by visitors, such as the school inspector or the parish priest. Tommy McNamee of Shannony East became the first local man to own a car when he bought his Singer in 1951. During the decades which followed, more and more families purchased cars, so that today all families own at least one vehicle.

THE COMMUNITY AND ITS TRADITIONS

The first settlers in Gallon were farmers and Irish speakers. As they broke in new fields, they gave them names which described the particular character of the field at that time. Many of these field names survive to this day.[14]

John McEvoy noted that the use of the Irish language was already declining in County Tyrone by 1802, although it may still have been spoken in Gallon.[15] The widespread emigration which followed the Great Famine, together with the spread

Glenock Church, Gallon

of elementary education through English, hastened the decline in the use of Irish, so that, according to the census of 1901, only two people in Gallon could speak the language, Jane Kelly aged 38 and Caterine McAnena aged 70. A revival of interest in Irish culture occurred during the last decades of the nineteenth century. Master Crampsie, who was headmaster of Gallon School from 1904 until 1925, included Irish among the subjects which he taught in his night classes.

The fact that the great majority of people of Gallon have always been Catholic, with their own church in the adjoining townland, their own school (from 1831 to 1969) and, for many years, their local shop, along with the absence of public transport, meant that the people of the area developed a distinctive character. Gallon men tended to frequent the same public houses in Newtownstewart, the 'Castle Bar' and McBride's Pub. Gallon men gathered in groups outside Glenock church before Sunday morning Mass to discuss crops and farm prices.

Twice each year, in May and October, householders in Gallon still take turns to hold the Stations. This provides an opportunity for local people to hear Mass in a neighbour's house. The traditional wake still flourishes in Gallon, when friends gather in the home of a bereaved family to sympathise. Games were still played at certain wakes in Gallon within living memory, and 'offerings' were collected at funerals in Glenock until the 1960s: a dead person's standing in the community could be measured by the attendance at his wake and the amount of 'offerings' collected by the priest at his funeral.

During the 1920s and 1930s, Gallon sustained a well-supported football team, which was the match for any team mustered by the surrounding towns and villages. Gallon school won the parish tug-of-war competitions at the annual parish sports during the 1940s. 'Big nights' were frequently held to celebrate weddings or the

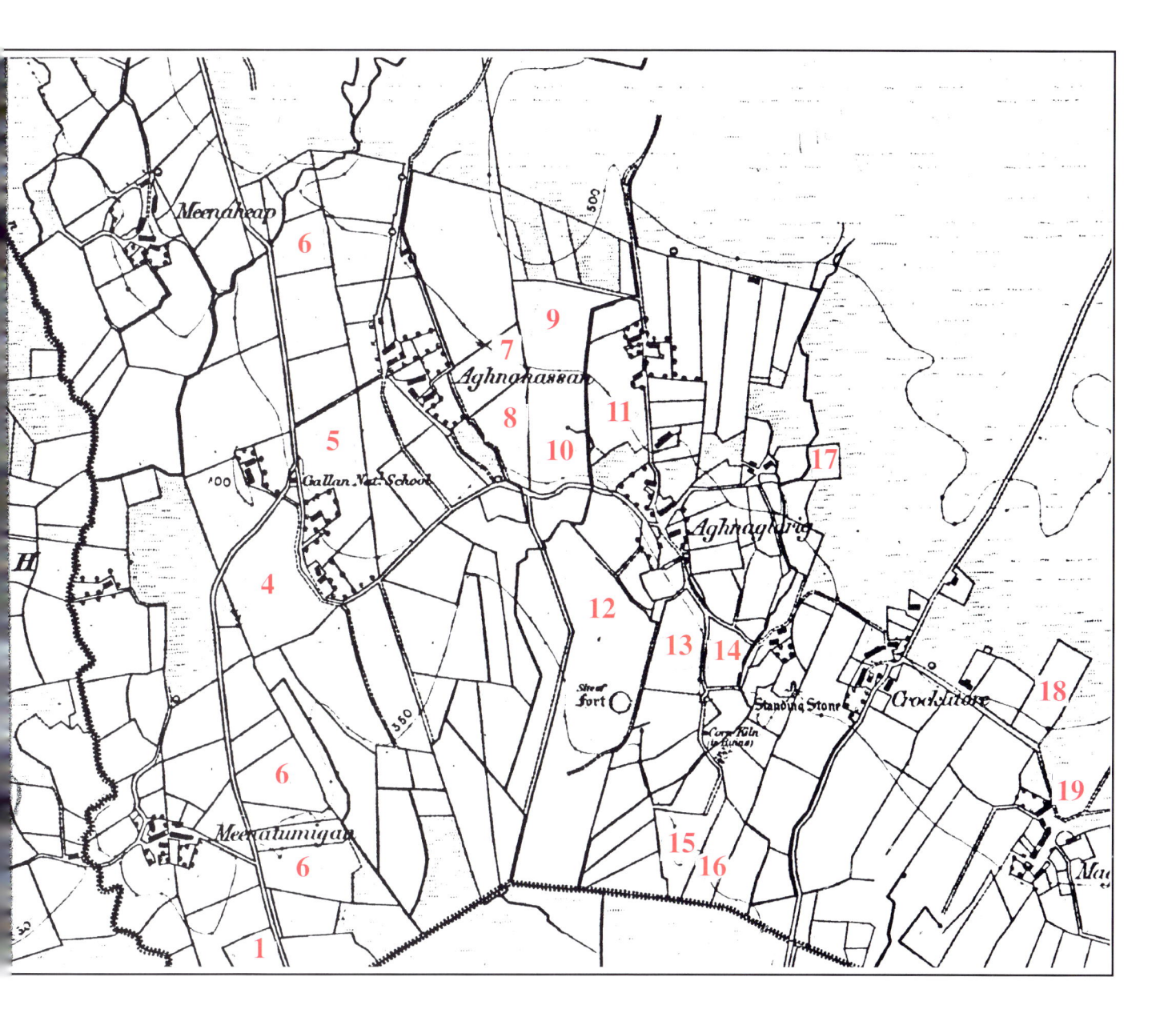

NAMES OF LANDSCAPE FEATURES AND CLUSTERS OF DWELLINGS IN GALLAN UPPER[14]

Aghnahassan: the ford of the pathway
Aghnaglarig: the ford of the planks
Bartymore: the summit of the big house
Clochgare: the short stone
Crockatore: the hill of the well *or* of pursuit

Meenaheap: the smooth place/meadow of the (coarse) grass
Meenatumigan: the meadow of the bushes
Meenawiddy: the meadow of the dog *or* the
Magherabrack: speckled plain
Meenavig: the small meadow

SOME FIELD NAMES (numbered on the map)

1. The scrogg: rocky place
2. Kilnabrae: hill where corn was dried in a kiln
3. Grainne: a gravelly place
4. The School Field
5. The Mass Field
6. The Rap; full of rabbits
7. The Well Field
8. The Spa Field where water was discoloured red by iron oxide
9. Crockraffers: the prosperous hill
10. Parkure: the new field
11. Craggers: stony or barren
12. Banshiks: the marshy pasture
13. Garrowglass: the green garden
14. Crockban: the white hill
15. Crockfada: the long hill
16. Turnaflochan: the hill of the bog cotton *or* the pools of water
17. The Plantings
18. Crockard: the high hill
19. The Lees: the grey shrubbery

return of emigrants on holiday. Music was provided by local fiddlers and singers, such as Hugh Morris and Robbie McClure.

Katie Anne Kelly ran a small shop at Aghnaglarig in Upper Gallon until the 1930s, when Henry Bradley opened his larger premises in Gallon Lower. Bradley's shop enjoyed its heyday during the Second World War when strict rationing was enforced. The introduction of grocery vans and easier access to larger shops in Newtownstewart eventually led to its closure in the 1960s.

For more than a century Gallon school represented an important focus of identity for the community. The first school, with thatched roof and earthen floor, opened in 1831 but was replaced by a new school in 1870. The school reached its highest enrolment of around ninety pupils in the 1890s when school attendance became compulsory. Night classes were held in the school during the early years of the century and the school was also used for concerts and dances. As late as 1952 the Gallon Players used the school to rehearse their very successful production of 'The Whiteheaded Boy' by Lennox Robinson. The school closed in 1969, just one year short of its centenary, its last headmaster being William John Bradley, the author of this essay.

During the last twenty years Gallon has changed in many ways. The population has fallen drastically, especially in Gallon Lower and Gallon Sessiagh, and the number of people gaining a living from the land has decreased even more. Ceilidhing and cardplaying, which were favourite pastimes in former days, have largely died out, due to the coming of television. The older generation find company at weekly bingo and whist drives in nearby towns while the younger folk gravitate towards dances and discos in Letterkenny, Raphoe and Omagh.

Gallon lies within the Sperrin area of Outstanding Beauty; notable scenic spots within easy reach are Corrick glen, Baronscourt forest, Bessy Bell Mountain and the Glenelly valley. The people of Newtownstewart enjoy walking Gallon's roads in favourable weather and the boglands and mountain sides are refuges for a wide variety of plants and wildlife. There are many sites of historic interest within Gallon itself and in adjoining townlands. Less than seven miles away are two very popular tourist destinations, the Ulster American Folk Park and the Ulster History Park. The nearby Mourne and Strule rivers are world-famous for their trout and salmon.

Modern developments have not destroyed Gallon's special charm for locals and visitors alike. Gallon's potential for tourism has not yet been tapped; given favourable circumstances the area could become a magnet for visitors seeking respite from the demands of modern living. Gallon's inhabitants will continue to enjoy a more tranquil existence in beautiful surroundings.

NOTES

1. McCourt, D. (1950). The rundale system in Ireland: a study of its geographical distribution and social relations (Unpublished Ph.D. thesis, Queen's University), p.28.
2. The Ordnance Survey maps spell the three townlands as Gallan Upper, Gallan Lower and Sessiagh of Gallan. In this essay however, the names and spellings used by the inhabitants themselves has been employed.
3. There were at least two other smaller clusters, Blackdyke and Meenavig.
4. The ancient field system in Gallon Upper is similar to that at Ceide Fields, County Mayo. The hearth and timber walls were verified by the Ancient Monuments Division of the Department of the Environment in 1991.
5. Davies, O. and Henderson, W. R. Finds near Newtownstewart, Cist at Shannony East in *Ulster Journal of Archaeology* Vol 4 Part 1 (Jan 1941).
6. A sweathouse was a primitive type of sauna, used in former times for the relief of rheumatism and similar complaints. After a session in the sweathouse the patient completed his treatment by jumping naked into the nearby burn!
7. This list of Irish families is taken from the account of the Inquisition held at Newtownstewart in 1628 and quoted in J. H. Gebbie, (1970) *Ardstraw: Historical Survey of a Parish*. Omagh: Strule Press.
8. There is some disagreement as to the gentleman's name; he is variously referred to in contemporary documents as Clapham, Clephane and Chapham.
9. Blessington estate archives are held in the National Library, Dublin.
10. The transaction described in this document may have been a strategy by the Cregan family to retain their property in case of a 'popish discovery', Registry of Deeds, Henrietta St, Dublin: Book 56, page 136.
11. McEvoy, J. (1991) *A Statistical Survey of Co Tyrone 1802* Belfast: Friar's Bush Press pp. 106-7.

Interior of Gallon School before closure in 1969 with the Principal, W. John Bradley

12 In 1852, Daniel Baird engaged R. H. Nolan of Derry to draw maps of his newly acquired Tyrone properties. They are held in the Public Record Office, Belfast: D/2584/1/1.

13 Population figures for 1958 and 1994 are taken from information collected by W. J. Bradley in 1958 and M McColgan in 1994.

14 The meanings of place-names provoke debate among scholars. This essay wishes to draw attention to the importance of field names in trying to understand how and when those fields were enclosed. We need the services of the Place-Name Project to inform the debate.

15 McEvoy, op cit., p.201.

HOLLYHILL

HOLLYHILL

JOHN DOOHER

The townland of Hollyhill, an area of just over six hundred acres, was largely a creation of the Plantation period when it was awarded as a freehold in the Cloghogenall estate allocated to Sir George Hamilton. Its subsequent history and development became closely identified with the Sinclair family and it was only in the early part of the nineteenth century that this minor estate was laid out in individual farms. The removal of landlord power and control in the early years of the present century may have changed the point of focus in the area but it is remarkable how far the economic and social outlook has remained constant. Hollyhill, like most other rural areas, has certainly experienced change and adaptation but it has also retained much of its earlier shape and structure. This examination will look in more detail at some of those elements of change and continuity.

LOCATION

The townland of Hollyhill is situated approximately three miles north-east of Strabane and near to the village of Artigarvan. The townland is in the shape of a long strip of land rising to the lower edges of Knockavoe mountain and is divided mainly into small farms. There is an absence of woodland in the higher areas, with the notable exception of the planted areas surrounding the Big House, and the district has been cleared of all traces of bog and turf land. The Fowl Glen burn divides Hollyhill from Keenaghan and joins the Glenmornan burn to form a tributary of the Foyle; during the late eighteenth and throughout the nineteenth century this Glenmornan burn acted as feeder to the Strabane canal as well as providing a power source for the numerous mills along its banks. There are no main routes through Hollyhill but it is connected to the surrounding areas and to Artigarvan and Strabane by a network of minor roads. Strabane has traditionally been the market and shopping town for the whole area, though the establishment of the Co-operative Dairy at Artigarvan in 1902 and its later development into a major agricultural store, provided an alternative source of supply for the mainly farming community of Hollyhill.

HISTORY AND TRADITIONS BEFORE THE PLANTATION

Little is known about the area prior to the Plantation of Ulster in the early seventeenth century and there have been no recorded archaeological discoveries there. It is suggested by some local people that there may have been a pre-Christian religious site (Druid's Altar) in the grounds surrounding Hollyhill House and Father Walter Hegarty, in his 1938 survey of the history of Catholicism in the district, identified the location of a Mass Rock or outdoor church dating from Penal times. An area within the estate is labelled on Ordnance Survey maps as Holy Hill and it is quite likely that such identification arose from the oral tradition of the religious connotations of the site.

The existence of other archaeological sites in nearby townlands suggests that Hollyhill may indeed have had a pre-Christian monument. The name Holy Hill appeared on the first Ordnance Survey map and was probably recognised in local tradition at the time.

It is likely that the whole district was covered in pre-Plantation times with woods and shrubbery and this would have made access difficult. Situated as it was on the lower slopes of the mountains meant also that the territory would have been boggy and not very passable, with the result that communication between settlements near Strabane and other parts of O'Neill territory would have used the higher ground and avoided Hollyhill to a great extent. Local folklore, however, tells of Hugh O'Neill passing through the area on his journey from Dungannon to Rathmullan at the time of the Flight of the Earls and the area is also mentioned in a ballad describing the march of Rory O'Hanlon to attack the plantation town of Strabane. The name Hollyhill itself is shrouded in some mystery and its origins appears to have been during the early Plantation period. The district was initially known as Balliburny and was labelled as such in the Bodley survey map of 1609. This probably derives from the Irish *Baile Boirne,* townland of the rocky district, and appropriate to some parts of Hollyhill since the 1834 Ordnance Survey map shows a slate quarry in the area while rock would have been plentiful in the higher reaches of the townland, towards Knockavoe mountain. This latter area is also of some historical renown and it is recorded as the site of a major battle between O'Neill and O'Donnell in the early sixteenth century where, according to the Annals of the Four Masters, the Tyrone men were utterly routed.

In the Civil Survey of 1654/56, following the Cromwellian conquest and examining the ownership of land in Ireland at that time, the district is denoted as 'Belliburny alias Hollyhill' and described as a balliboe of 120 acres Irish measure with a value of £10. It seems clear that the acreage denoted arable land but the most surprising thing here is the complete change of name from Balliburny to Hollyhill, and without any indication of why it occurred. The adjacent townlands or balliboes retained their traditional names and the name Balliburny should not have posed any great problem in being adapted to English. Yet the change took place and henceforth Hollyhill became the standard label.

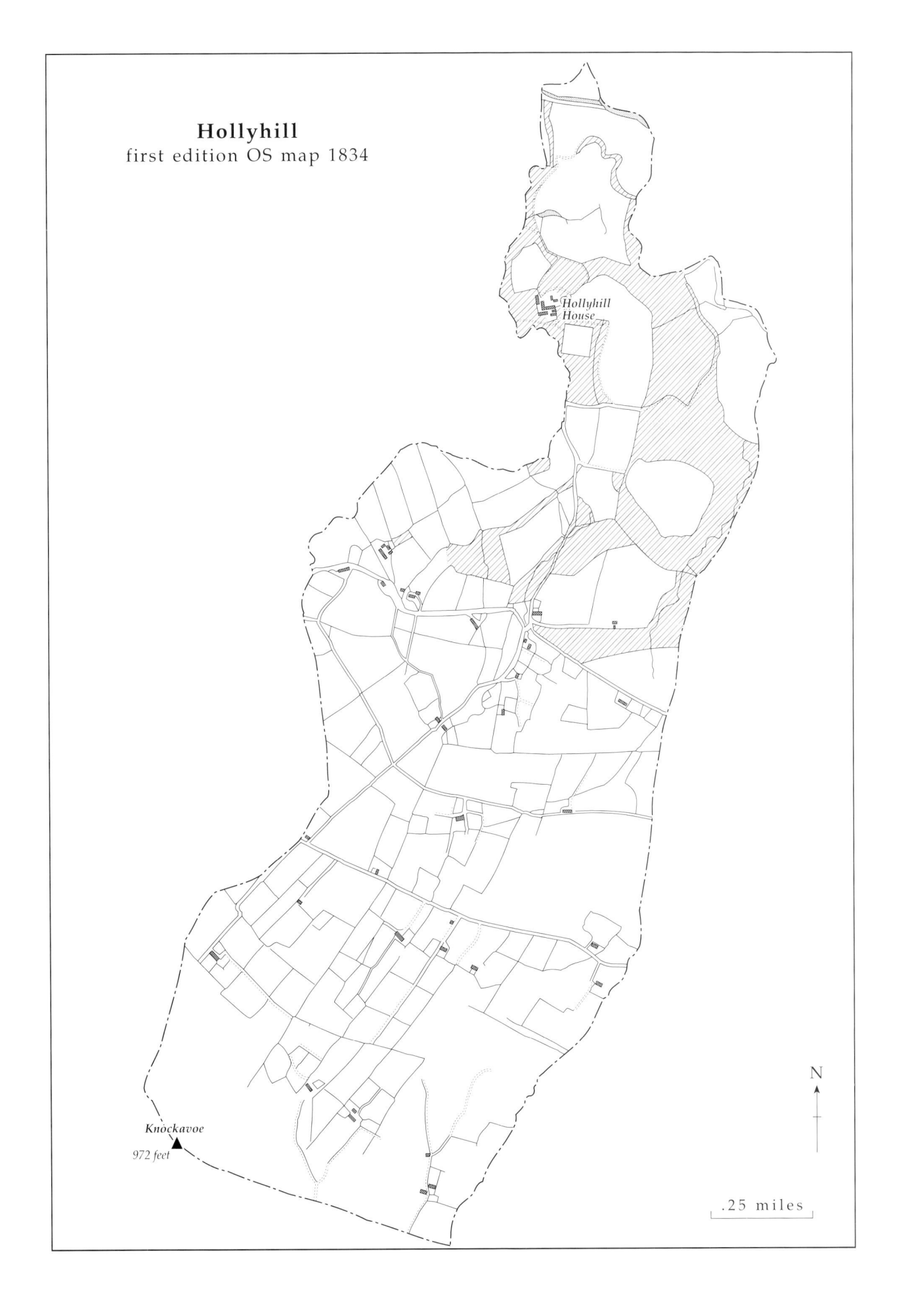

Hollyhill
first edition OS map 1834

Hollyhill House

N

Knockavoe
972 feet

.25 miles

Balliburny lies in the hills overlooking Strabane

LAND OWNERSHIP AND THE CREATION OF FARMS

The district of Hollyhill was part of the Cloghenall estate, parish of Leckpatrick, granted to Sir George Hamilton in the plantation of Ulster. Sir George was brother to the chief undertaker in the Strabane barony, the Earl of Abercorn, and became administrator over a large part of the barony after Abercorn's death in 1618. According to a recent local publication, *The Ulster Plantation in the Strabane Barony* (edited by R. J. Hunter), Sir George was something of an aberration as a plantation landlord, being himself a Catholic and providing refuge and toleration for Catholic clergy escaping from persecution elsewhere. He incurred the hostility and official condemnation of the bishop of Derry, George Downham, and attempts were made to institute punitive action against Sir George and also against Sir Claud, Abercorn's second son and successor to the Strabane estate. No known punitive action came from these protests but they provide valuable information on the local variations in Plantation management and experiences and possibly provide a clue as to why Holy Hill, near the present Big House, became associated in local folklore as a centre for Catholic religious practices.

The Civil Survey recorded that Hollyhill had been granted as a fee farm (freehold) to David Marghee, a Scottish papist, and the same survey examined his claim to a further fee farm in Drumnebuy on the estate of Claud Hamilton. A number of other fee farms had apparently been granted by Sir George Hamilton and this was one method of enticing Scottish settlers to come over to Ulster in

Hollyhill House – a Georgian building with later additions to the rear and side – home of the Sinclair family who controlled Hollyhill until the early twentieth century

the early years of the plantation. Marghee (McGhee) was apparently confirmed in his lands or returned to them in the Restoration, since in 1683 the Hollyhill area was purchased from Captain George McGhee by Reverend John Sinclair. The latter had arrived as rector of Leckpatrick parish in 1665 and appears to have been on easy terms with Bishop Wilde of Derry and with Sir George Hamilton, the chief landowner in the parish and leading representative of the Abercorn interest. Church records show that Sinclair was also installed as rector of the adjoining parish of Camus (Strabane) in 1668 and could thus command the combined income from the tithes and other dues. No doubt this helped him to purchase the Hollyhill farm by 1683 (as recorded in a family history compiled in the latter part of the nineteenth century and forming part of the surviving evidence still available in the former Sinclair house) and to establish the family position in the district. It appears likely that it was at this stage too that the adjoining townland of Keenaghan was purchased since it also was part of the later Sinclair estate but without any separate record of acquisition.

Thus was established the Sinclair ownership of Hollyhill for the next two hundred years and much of the history of the townland in that period was inextricably bound up with the family. There is a paucity of records on developments in the eighteenth century and scattered references in the Abercorn family letters add little to the story. It is clear that the Sinclair family also acquired land near Raphoe in Donegal and they are portrayed at one stage in the Abercorn correspondence as an obstacle to progress because of their refusal to make land available for road-making. In another reference it seems clear that there was a boundary or mearing dispute between Sinclair and Abercorn at the meeting of the townlands of Hollyhill and Artigarvan and it is evident that John Sinclair acted as agent for Abercorn for a period in the 1750s and 1760s. The family also acquired an area of mountainous land on the Tyrone-Londonderry border at Stranagalwilly, in the parish of Learmount, but this would appear to have been for shooting game rather than for any serious agricultural use. Such scattered references, however, contribute little to our knowledge of what was happening in Hollyhill in the period and the historian is left making inferences from other pieces of associated information. Such questions as how the Sinclair family built up their position in the eighteenth century despite owning so little land and how they acquired and lost the Raphoe land are obvious ones that have to remain largely unanswered in this survey. The relative paucity of oral traditions for Hollyhill in the period is also worth comment, though the absence of a settled population in the district until the early nineteenth century may account for the relative silence that surrounds the area.

A map of the Hollyhill farm in the 1740s, drawn by William Starratt, an engineer and surveyor who was employed by Abercorn and other landowners to draw boundaries and organise individual holdings, shows only one other settlement on the Sinclair holding besides the family home. This was a herdsman's house and farm on the south-eastern edge of the estate in the townland of Keenaghan and is said to have been occupied by the Thompson family, one of whose descendants is now the owner and occupier of Hollyhill House.

Much of the district would have been upland grazing and there is ample evidence in the Abercorn correspondence that areas adjacent to Hollyhill were rented out for summer grazing. Farmers from the lowlands in the Foyle basin sent their cattle to be tended during the summer months on the uplands by the people living there – a form of booleying but on a more commercial basis than that practised in other parts of Ireland. Problems arose in 1809-10 when some of these graziers were brought to court for poteen-making and any cattle found on their lands were liable for seizure to pay the fines imposed. This worried many of the lowland farmers and there was a rapid falling off in the grazing arrangement as a result, with a knock-on impact on Abercorn's rental. It is likely that Hollyhill was farmed in a similar manner in the eighteenth century, and there is also evidence in the Abercorn letters that Strabane householders depended on turf from Hollyhill bog in this period. It is clear, therefore, that the estate did manage to provide some income for the Sinclair family despite its relatively uncultivated state. An 1821 survey for the parish of Leckpatrick claimed that 'Mr Sinclair gets six guineas an acre for turf bog but his tenants are not charged with it' while the same report also stated that 'Hollyhill mountain affords a good deal of labour in providing turf for Strabane and their neighbourhoods'.

AN IMPROVING LANDLORD

In the early years of the nineteenth century the management of the estate was taken over by James Sinclair and he was strongly imbued with the ideas of land improvement current at the time. In this period Hollyhill underwent a transformation that was revolutionary in proportion to the lack of developments in the previous century and the role of Sinclair was crucial. He had a history of espousing reformist ideas and had spoken against government excesses at the 1797 Donegal Grand Jury and had equally unavailingly supported a resolution at the Tyrone Grand Jury in April 1810 supporting the admission of Catholics to the franchise. In the famine period of 1817-18 Sinclair had shown considerable concern and had lobbied for government assistance on behalf of the local community; in the late 1830s he was to oppose the introduction of the Poor Law into the area, claiming that poverty was too extensive to be relieved solely by local rates and arguing forcibly for a tax on absentee landlords as a necessary part of poor relief.

It was as an estate manager, however, that he was to make his most significant contribution to the development of Hollyhill estate and the local community. A report by George D. Mansfield on Leckpatrick parish, commissioned by the North West Agricultural Society in 1821, suggested that vast changes and improvements were already under way on the estate:

> ....Considerable portions of the area have been brought from barren and heathy mountains to a certain state of cultivation and improvement. Of these by far the most extensive and most useful have been made on Mr Sinclair's Estate, where many new farms have sprung up in the midst of barren mountains, and comfortable cottages, well sheltered gardens and quickset hedges are seen, where formerly all was one wide waste, the undistinguished abode of the hare and the moor-fowl .... The woods of Hollyhill yielded timber for their houses and farming implements and its nurseries provided quicks and trees for their gardens and fences ....

This report foreshadowed the declining position of linen in the rural economy but stressed that it was at that time still a crucial element for most people: 'the farmer seldom trusts altogether to the profits of his land, but usually calls in the aid of his loom.' Did Sinclair foresee the demise of the domestic linen industry and was this his way of dealing with what would otherwise result in major distress? No doubt his experiences of the famine crisis of 1817-18 had led him to conclude that change was needed in the rural economy and that the estate would benefit in the long run from any improved agricultural production that might accrue.

Education and guidance were considered crucial in such a task and the Mansfield report claimed that Sinclair had established a school on his Hollyhill estate, with support from the mildly proselytizing London Hibernian Society. This must have been a very short-lived establishment as there is no record of it in the report of the Commissioners of Irish Education Inquiry of 1825 nor is it marked on the 1834 Ordnance Survey map. There is, however, some suggestion that the Mansfield survey may have been correct and the present owner of Hollyhill House can point to an area known as 'The School Field' within the grounds of the estate. Sinclair was identified in this period with the establishment of the agricultural school at Templemoyle, near the present day village of Eglinton,

Hollyhill 1834
with valuation boundaries

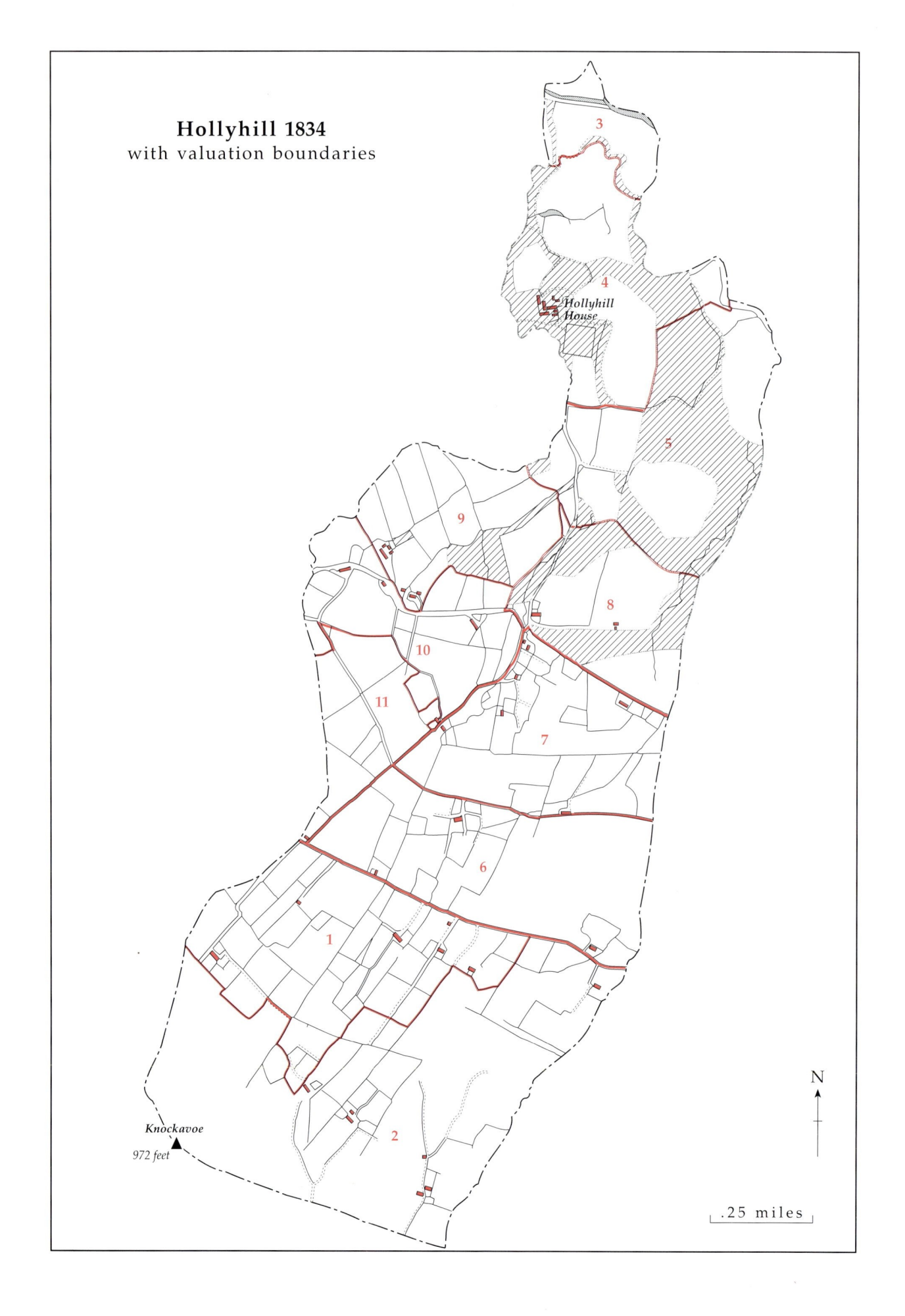

Hollyhill House

▲ *Knockavoe*
972 feet

N

.25 miles

HOLYHILL, parish of Leckpatrick, barony of Lower Strabane, DED of Glenmornan, union of Strabane. Surveyed by valuators 21 September 1833 VAL/1B/640 pp 8,9,50

		QUANTITY			RATE PER STATUTE ACRE	AMOUNT		
1	Reclaimed boggy and moory arable of moderate depth, blueish clay subsoil	62	3	9	6/6	20	8	2
	also heathy mountain pasture in 2 places	10	2		10°		9	2
2	Heathy pasture	114	1	6	10°	4	19	11
	also arable	32	3		6/6	10	12	11
3	Sandy arable part mixed with cold clayey arable flat and well sheltered	13	0	38	15/=	9	18	6
	also planted pasture part stoney and uneven surface	2	1		2/=		4	6
	also waste at house	1	20					
4	Free and partly light arable surface undulating, tops of the hills rather shallow and gravelly,	34	2	4	17/6	30	4	2
	brown gravel subsoil also planted pastures	15			3/6	2	12	6
	also reclaimed moory and boggy arable	6	3		11/6	3	14	3
	also waste at house		2					
5	Clayey and sandy arable, part cold and wet, part moory, surface undulating and tops of hills shallow and gravelly, brown and yellow gravel subsoil	33	0	26	15/=	24	17	5
	Also planted pasture	31	0	37	3/6	5	9	3
6	Heathy mountain pasture, about a quarter well mixed with gorse, brown heath	44	1	35	1/2	2	11	10
	also reclaimed boggy and moory arable in two places	25	2	5	8/=	10	4	4
7	Heathy mountain producing bitter pasture	35	1	6	7	1	0	7
	also reclaimed boggy and moory arable	20	3	8	7/6	7	15	11
8	Moory arable of moderate depth, part steep	22	1	27	9/6	10	12	11
	also planted pasture part heathy in 2 places	16	2	38	2/6	2	1	10
9	Free arable of good depth surface undulating and a small part steep	33	0	16	17/6	28	19	3
	also rough pasture moory and boggy	9	1	9	2/6	1	3	3
10	Cold clayey and moory arable, part wet on a greyish clay and yellow sand subsoil	40	0	35	11/=	22	2	5
11	Heathy and rough pasture	18	2	38	1/2	1	1	10
	also arable	5	0	20	11/=	2	16	4
						£204	1	3
	Deduct for local circumstances 1s per £ from the land					£10	4	0
						£193	17	3

HOUSES

| 1 | William Sigarson | House, spade mill and offices | £7 |
| 2 | James Sinclair | House and offices | £30 |

and helped finance some of the students there; it is likely that these were from the Hollyhill district and his own school may have been a local variant of the Templemoyle Seminary, as it was described by W.M.Thackeray in *An Irish Sketchbook* (1842). There was also a thriving school in the neighbouring townland of Ballee as well as a parish school at Artigarvan in the 1820s and it is probable that the Hollyhill school had a more limited and particular function than the other educational establishments.

The Mansfield report suggested that the improvements and settlements it described took place in Hollyhill but there is considerable evidence to suggest that the initial developments took place in the adjoining townland of Keenaghan and extended from there in the later 1820s and early 1830s to Hollyhill. The Tithe Valuation list of 1827 shows only three occupiers in Hollyhill, while Keenaghan can boast fifty-three holdings, of which only five were under three acres. Thus it appears that it was between 1827 and the compilation of the Ordnance Survey map in 1833/34 that the new farms were settled in the Hollyhill portion of the estate since this map shows most of the townland organised into fields and holdings. There is an absence of reliable information on the terms offered to the tenants on these new farms and where the new occupiers came from. The surnames of landholders in the Tithe List and in the later Griffith Valuation would suggest that many were from adjacent townlands rather than new settlers to the district. Certainly the drawing of farm and field boundaries in the area by Starratt in the 1740s would preclude the possibility that these separate and enclosed farms of the 1820s sprung from communal settlements based on the rundale pattern. They were possibly one landlord's response to a worsening economic situation in his area. Much of the district would previously have been rough pasture and may have been grazed in large tracts, with only limited advantage to either landlord or tenant. Bringing this marginal land under cultivation fitted well with prevailing economic and social theories and offered more substantial future rewards for the owners. A collapsed domestic linen industry and a growing rural population made the search for new methods of livelihood a matter of urgency and a means of escape from the obligation and necessity of perennially supporting the destitute.

A water-powered spade mill had also been set up in the area and this was to provide a source of employment for many years to come. The mill was owned by the Sigerson family and they had moved into the district sometime in the later 1820s from Ardmore in County Londonderry. No doubt favourable terms from Sinclair were influential in establishing the new production base and the intensive cultivation of previous mountain land seemed to guarantee a ready local market. In 1837 Lewis's *Topographical Dictionary of Ireland* mentions two manufactories for spades and edged tools in the parish; the second was probably a further Sigerson-owned mill further up the river in the townland of Gorticrum.

The first valuation of the townland in 1833(VAL/1B/640) looked in some detail at the land and its potential, dividing it into eleven distinct pieces. Those nearest the mountain were denoted as 'reclaimed boggy arable' or 'heathy pasture and arable land' with a relatively low valuation of from six to eight shillings per acre while the farms in the lower reaches near Hollyhill House were worth up to seventeen shillings and sixpence per acre. Grazing land had a much lower valuation than arable while planted areas had minimal assessments.

The growing population in Hollyhill is certainly borne out by the figures from the 1841 Census returns which show a total population of 251 people living in 40 houses, with a further three uninhabited. Most of these families would have been occupiers of land and the figures confirm the evidence of the Ordnance Survey map and valuation records of intensive settlement, carried out with Sinclair's encouragement. It also confirms that there was growing pressure on the land in the pre-Famine period and that previously uncultivated land was being brought into use for food production. This would have been urgently needed in a district like Leckpatrick where the virtual collapse of weaving and the much reduced income from domestic spinning presaged worsening economic conditions. James Sinclair had claimed in evidence to the Poor Inquiry in the middle 1830s that the condition of labourers was not seriously deteriorating in his district but most other witnesses to the investigation had little doubt that prospects had worsened considerably, due in great measure to a rapidly growing population. In his evidence to the Devon Commission hearing at Strabane in 1844, however, even Sinclair had to concede that the condition of the labourers and cottiers was seriously deteriorating and that the small farmers were increasingly relying on their own families for labour, to the detriment of the labourer and the cottier. He further claimed that subdivision and subletting had virtually disappeared in the district, thus reducing further the chances of cottiers acquiring land except by renting previously uncultivated areas. It is likely that it was in this period also that part of Sinclair's upland farm at Stranagalwilly had been brought under active cultivation and it was really only in these mountain areas that additional land was available for the growing population.

How did the Great Famine affect an area like Hollyhill where the landowner had prevented the worst of the subdivision that had been allowed in other parts? The 1851 Census figures suggest that the townland certainly did not escape unscathed and the drop of twenty-eight in the total population, with seven fewer inhabited houses than in 1841, must be at least partly related to the traumatic events of the period.

	POPULATION		
	1841	1851	(% CHANGE)
Hollyhill	251	223	-11.15
Keenaghan	274	240	-12.4
Leck Parish	(4807)	(4139)	(-13.9)

TENEMENT VALUATION (1858)

This valuation map illustrates the outcome of the landlord's project to create farms on the upper part of the townland. It had attracted poor tenants who had had to work hard to create farms to sustain their families. The low valuation of their farm buildings does not indicate prosperity. Note that Montgomery Sinclair held 95 acres of the better land at (11) and (12) for a few years: the term 'caretaker's house' applied to each of the houses on these properties, suggests that the landlord was waiting for more substantial tenants to take these farms. The Valuation Revision Lists record that Mary Sinclair sold to the tenants in 1909. In 1901 Strabane No.1 Rural District Council acquired two sites of just over half an acre each in (10) and (14) to build labourers' cottages and another rood had been taken to build the school by 1911. – WHC

PARISH OF LECKPATRICK.

No. and Letters of Reference to Map.	Names. Townlands and Occupiers.	Immediate Lessors.	Description of Tenement.	Area. A. R. P.	Rateable Annual Valuation. Land. £ s. d.	Rateable Annual Valuation. Buildings. £ s. d.	Total Annual Valuation of Rateable Property. £ s. d.
	HOLLY HILL. (Ord. S. 5.)						
1	William Sigerson,	James Sinclair,	House, offices, spade-mill, and land,	2 3 10	1 15 0	28 5 0	30 0 0
2 a	James Sinclair,	In fee,	House, offices, and land,	186 2 0	98 0 0	40 0 0	138 0 0
— b	George Kilpatrick,	James Sinclair,	House,	—	—	0 10 0	0 10 0
— c	Thomas Kincaid,	Same,	House and offices,	—	—	1 0 0	1 0 0
— d	Bernard Quin,	Same,	House,	—	—	0 10 0	0 10 0
3	Hugh Glackan,	Same,	Land,	1 2 5	0 15 0	—	0 15 0
4	Daniel Divin,	Same,	Land,	4 2 30	2 0 0	—	2 0 0
5	John Quin,	Same,	House, offices, and land,	4 1 35	1 15 0	0 10 0	2 5 0
6	Laurence Kane,	Same,	House and land,	4 1 10	1 15 0	0 10 0	2 5 0
7	Catherine Kane,	Same,	House, offices, and land,	8 0 5	2 15 0	0 10 0	3 5 0
8 a b	James O'Neill, sen., James O'Neill, jun.,	Same,	House, office, & land, House, office, & land,	19 1 10	3 10 0 3 10 0	0 10 0 0 10 0	4 0 0 4 0 0
9	John M'Nogher,	Same,	House, office, and land,	16 2 35	4 15 0	0 15 0	5 10 0
10 11 a	Montgomery Sinclair,	Same,	Caretaker's ho., offs., & ld. Caretaker's ho., off., & ld.	45 2 11 49 0 15	20 10 0 24 0 0	1 0 0 1 0 0	21 10 0 25 0 0
— b	Unoccupied,	Montgomery Sinclair,	House and office,	—	—	0 15 0	0 15 0
— c	John Gallagher,	Same,	House,	—	—	0 5 0	0 5 0
— d	Sinclair M'Farland,	Same,	House,	—	—	0 5 0	0 5 0
— e	Gustavus Kee,	Same,	House,	—	—	0 5 0	0 5 0
12	John Bradley,	James Sinclair,	House, offices, and land,	21 0 30	14 10 0	1 5 0	15 15 0
13 a b	William Tolan, Denis Tolan,	Same,	House, office, & land, House, office, & land,	24 0 30	4 5 0 4 5 0	0 10 0 0 10 0	4 15 0 4 15 0
14 A a — B	Hugh M'Gettigan,	Same,	House, offices, & land,	12 0 5 4 2 30	4 10 0 1 0 0	0 15 0 —	6 5 0
15 A a — B	Robert M'Gettigan,	Same,	House, offices, & land,	23 3 0 5 3 5	8 5 0 2 0 0	1 0 0 —	11 5 0
B a	Unoccupied,	Robert M'Gettigan,	House,	—	—	0 5 0	0 5 0
16	George M'Farland,	James Sinclair,	House, offices, and land,	58 2 30	8 5 0	1 0 0	9 5 0
17	John M'Ateer,	Same,	House, offices, and land,	15 2 35	5 5 0	0 15 0	6 0 0
18 a	Mary Cullion,	Same,	House, office, and land,	15 1 25	5 5 0	0 15 0	6 0 0
— b	Unoccupied,	Mary Cullion,	House and offices,	—	—	0 10 0	0 10 0
19	Edward Hagarty,	James Sinclair,	House, offices, and land,	16 0 25	4 0 0	0 15 0	4 15 0
20	Alexander Ellis,	Same,	House, offices, and land,	16 2 15	4 10 0	0 15 0	5 5 0
21	James Kee,	Same,	House, offices, and land,	33 0 20	5 5 0	0 15 0	6 0 0
22 a	James Cullion, sen.,	Same,	House, offices, and land,	26 3 15	4 0 0	0 15 0	4 15 0
— b	James Cullion, jun.,	James Cullion, sen.,	House,	—	—	0 10 0	0 10 0
23 a	Cecilia Martin, James Cullion,	James Sinclair,	House and land, Land,	13 2 25	1 5 0 1 5 0	0 5 0 —	1 10 0 1 5 0
			Total,	630 3 16	242 15 0	88 0 0	330 15 0

Hollyhill 1859
with valuation boundaries

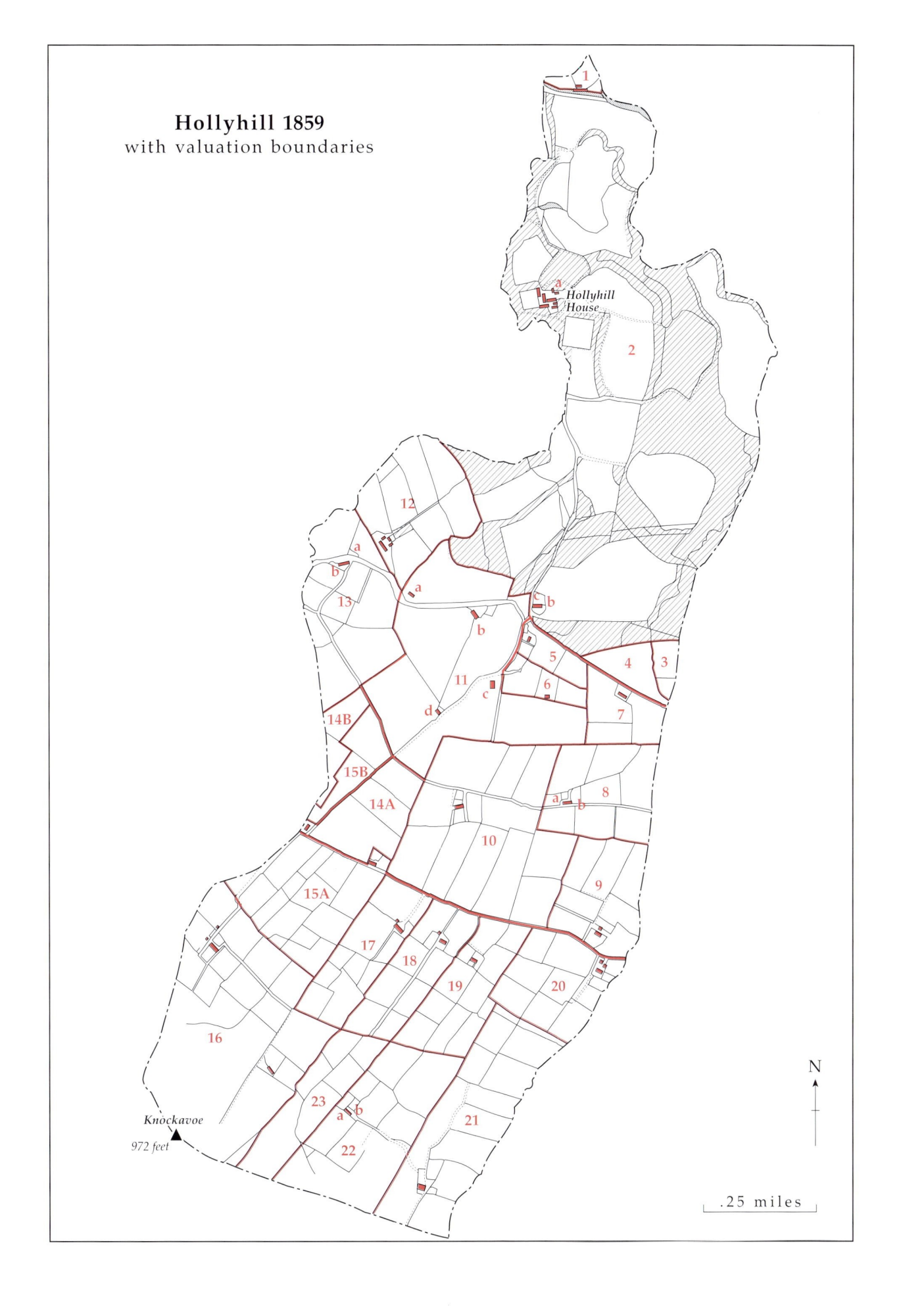

	HOUSES		
	1841	1851	(% CHANGE)
Hollyhill	43	37	-13.95
Keenaghan	48	35	-27.08
Leck. Parish (Rural Portion)	(929)	(752)	(-19.05)

The adjoining townland of Keenaghan had suffered an even heavier loss, both in total population and in the number of occupied houses, evidence that more families were forced to move off the land, but it must be emphasised that such reductions were not exceptional in the circumstances of the time and suggest that the Famine, while dislocating and punitive, did not strike the Hollyhill area very severely, probably because there were comparatively fewer cottiers and holders of very small farms on the estate. It was these, along with the landless labourers, who suffered most severely in other parts of the country from the Great Famine. Many historians have argued that the Famine began a trend of depopulation of rural areas that has continued right up to the present time and certainly the declining population in Hollyhill from 1851 onwards could suggest that it was following the general pattern throughout the country. Some caution, however, should be attached to such generalisations and it is possible that Sinclair and other Tyrone witnesses at the Devon Commission in 1844 were rightly claiming that the reversal of the trend of overpopulation and subdivision had already begun. Thus the Famine may have simply accelerated a trend already in operation. Certainly much of the evidence given to the Devon Inquiry at Strabane in 1844 points to rural depopulation as already well under way.

POPULATION CHANGES 1851–1901

Census totals from 1851 onwards show the continued decline in the population and in the number of inhabited houses in the Hollyhill area. If the number of houses is equated with families, it becomes clear that not only did the number of families living in the district decrease but that the number in each family also decreased since the population fell at a greater rate than the number of inhabited houses. This could be accounted for by increased emigration and later marriages and it would seem, therefore, that Hollyhill exemplified the pattern that was widespread in most other parts of the country in these decades. Yet once again a note of caution should be sounded and a closer examination shows that the rate of population decrease slowed considerably after 1880 and had even marginally increased again by 1911.

	POPULATION	% Change	HOUSES	% Change
1841	251		40	
1851	253	-11.15	33	-17.5
1861	174	-21.97	29	-12.12
1871	146	-16.09	26	-10.34
1881	129	-11.64	24	-7.69
1891	128	-0.77	26	+7.69
1901	133	+3.75	25	
1911	132		26	

Two other points are shown by the figures: the steepest decline in the population was in the decade after 1851 while the largest fall in houses was in the famine decade. It would seem likely, therefore, that it was whole families that were being uprooted in the Famine years while in the post 1851 period it was a case of individuals from within families moving out and looking for new opportunities. The cottier class had all but disappeared by the time the Great Famine ended.

It was the immediate post-Famine generation that had been most strongly affected by emigration and there is evidence of change after 1880. How should this levelling off and partial reversal of a trend be accounted for?

Had prosperity and prospects improved sufficiently to provide a greater confidence in the people and remove the fear engendered by the Famine era? Alternatively it could be claimed that by that stage any surplus in the population had been drawn off and what was left was an aged community and a small number of younger families and prospective inheritors of the family farms. The later nineteenth century continued the rationalisation that had been hinted at in the immediate pre-Famine period with more economic holdings being the guiding principle for many of the surviving families.

FARM CONSOLIDATION

A comparison of householder names in the Griffith Valuation of 1858 with the Census returns of 1901 can be used to show elements of continuity and change in ownership and social structure in the district in this crucial post-Famine period. In the case of Hollyhill these records, along with the regular Valuation updates (VAL/12B/42) appear to show that there was considerable consolidation of holdings and that the houses that disappeared were generally cottier cabins that would previously have housed newly married sons or other related family members. That process of consolidation had begun by 1850 and at the time of the Griffith Valuation there were a number of joint tenancies that was often the prelude to bringing together adjoining farms. By 1901 all of these joint tenancies had disappeared along with the cottier houses that had earlier existed on them.

Farms were no longer supporting more than one household or family group and smaller holdings were disappearing.

CONSOLIDATION AND NEW OWNERSHIP POST-1860				
REF.NO.	OWNER	ACREAGE A.R.P	BUILDINGS £. s. d.	NEW OWNER
13a	Wm. Tolan	24.0.30	0-10-0	John Tolan
13b	Denis Tolan		0-10-0	(1904)
14A	H.McGettigan	12.0.5	0-15-0	
14B		4.2.30		Bernd Devine (1896)
15A	R.McGettigan	23.3.0	1-0-0	
15B		5.3.5	0-5-0	
23.	Cecilia Martin James Cullion	13.2.25	0-5-0	Rob. Cullion Jnr. (1892)
8a	Jas.O'Neill Sen	19.10.10	0-10-0	Jas.O'Neill
8b	Jas.O'Neill Jnr		0-10-0	Jnr. (1869)

There were a number of other holdings that came together in the years after Griffith's Valuation and such changes can be traced in the Valuation records. Two small farms that were without houses (Nos 3 & 4) reverted to the Sinclair estate farm within a few years while another two separate holdings (Nos 5 & 6) came together by 1896 to form a combined farm. In the same year Robert Cullion, junior, gained possession of the farm previously occupied by John McAteer (No. 17) and this was later amalgamated with a former joint holding (No. 23) that had been taken over by Robert Cullion senior, in 1869. These and other changes saw the total number of holdings drop from twenty-three in 1858 to eighteen by 1910.

Clearly such consolidations took place for a number of reasons and with varying results. The valuation records, the 1901 census returns, and oral evidence from the present day can often explain how and why the changes occurred. In the case of Hollyhill it would seem that there was a considerable degree of commercial transfer of ownership and six holdings appear to have been transferred through such sales. Another factor was inheritance or marriage and three farms can be said to have passed to family relatives, probably nephews of the earlier registered owners. In one case a substantial farm that had been identified in the Griffith Valuation as being a caretaker holding (No. 11) in the name of Montgomery Sinclair was transferred to Daniel Murphy before passing to Edward Kirk in 1879 and it seems clear that these changes were commercial transactions rather than inheritance transfers.

There can be little doubt too that such amalgamations and transfers had an immediate impact on former cottier holdings and houses. The result was the disappearance of seven such dwellings in the period between 1860 and 1910, with three of these being removed from the former estate farm taken over by Edward Kirk. It seems likely that there was little demand in Hollyhill district for labourers since most of the farms were small enough to be self-sufficient and the town of Strabane was close enough to provide any necessary seasonal labour and thus the former cottier houses fell into disrepair through disuse. Only those with realistic expectations of inheriting farms or retaining regular employment remained in the area and this allowed the process of consolidation to continue.

THE 1901 CENSUS RECORDS

It was on the Sinclair estate farm that most changes in occupancy took place, with estate workers being replaced for various reasons, and the 1901 Census returns prove very useful in examining the changing work-force and in assessing the labour requirements of a large house at that time. Thus on the estate the census lists such new names as Robert John Dunleavy, carpenter and joiner, James Donaghey, creamery secretary and gardener, James Sharkey, gardener, and George Patterson, spademaker. Sharkey's wife, Mary Jane, also gave her occupation as dressmaker and it is possible that it was her skill that won the family their position on the estate. There were also a number of 'live-in' servants at the big house and these are recorded in the Census returns for the Sinclair household. Samuel McCauley was groom while his sister Rachel was described as a servant. John Harkin, thirty years old, was described as a herd – unusual surely for someone of that maturity – while eighteen year old William McIntyre was returned as a stable help. John O'Donnell was recorded as a carpenter while thirty year old Sarah Hanlon's occupation was given as seamstress. Apart from the McCauley brother and sister who came from County Antrim, the other workers gave their county of birth as Donegal. This might suggest that they had initially come to the district as 'hired' labourers and remained on as paid workers. Significantly only Sarah Hanlon, a member of the Church of Ireland, acknowledged a familiarity with the Irish language but this might not necessarily be strictly accurate as answers may have been provided in the light of how people saw the best prospects for continued employment.

The occupations on the census returns show that there were very few independent craftsmen or trades people in a rural community like Hollyhill. The Sigerson spade mill was one source of non-agricultural labour and this had passed to John McGuinnis, brother-in-law of Dr George Sigerson, in 1897. The mill was clearly less profitable than previously, with the valuation of the buildings being reduced in 1872 and further reduced in 1912. The 1901 census returns show that there were two boarders in the McGuinnis household, both returning their occupations as spademaker. What is surprising is the age of both boarders. John McCann was a forty-six year old bachelor and his companion, James Devlin, was twenty-seven years of age. There might have been expected to be younger apprentices on the holding but surprisingly this does not seem to have been the case. Local tradition suggests that the Sigerson mill had commonly made use of young Donegal labourers in their enterprise and Dr. George Sigerson claimed that he himself had been introduced to the Irish language by listening to the workers at the spade factory. Some of the workers, of course, may have been living in the adjoining townlands or in the small village of Artigarvan like George Patterson, a spademaker living on the Sinclair estate, but it is also likely that the spade mill was approaching its end by 1900 and relied on a relatively small labour force.

HOUSING STANDARDS

The total valuation for Hollyhill changed little in the period from 1860 to 1911 and this would suggest that relatively little development took place in the period. The valuation for the whole townland in 1861 was £330-15 and this had increased to only £334-10 by 1901, though the removal of a number of former cottier houses meant that they were no longer in the rateable totals. A large part of this increase can be attributed to the Sinclair family improvements, with an additional £3 added to the valuation of the big house in the 1870s by the establishment of a laundry room, and a new worker dwelling erected in 1896 with a valuation of £2-10. Few other properties in the district showed valuation changes, with the exception of the spade mill, where the value appears to have plummeted in the period, with two downward revisions. Such a stagnation in development, however, does not necessarily mean poverty in the community since priority may have been given to land acquisition and farm consolidation rather than to housing improvements. In a period when additional land appeared to be fairly readily available it was tempting to reserve surplus cash for that rather than for short term living improvements.

A closer examination of the individual household returns in the 1901 census shows just how limited living standards were, though it would be necessary to compare with other areas in order to assess what was accepted as normal at the time. One major distinguishing feature was the type of roof and it can be seen that there were only six slated houses in the townland as compared to eighteen thatched; and five out of the six belonged to the Sinclair family, with the other belonging to the spade mill. Houses were classified according to size and the number of windows and the table below shows some of the information recorded.

Houses with Slate/Tile Roof		6
Houses with Thatched Roof		18
Single Room Houses		2
Two Roomed Houses		19
Three Roomed Houses		1
More than Three Rooms		2
Houses Classified as	Class 3	15
	Class 2	8
	Class 1	1

Most of the houses were clearly single-storey dwellings and few would have had any of the amenities that are now taken for granted. At the same time there was a relative absence of very poor housing with only two single room cabins which were occupied by no more than two people. It could be said, therefore, that there had been some improvement since the immediate post-Famine period, when there must have been a number of families living in the single room cabins associated with cottiers. The process of consolidation and amalgamation may not have led to noticeable improvements in housing standards but it did manage to get rid of some of the more objectionable houses in rural areas.

The slated bay of the cottage was added to the two-roomed thatched cottage with bed outshot; later the thatch was covered/replaced with corrugated iron

OCCUPATIONS

One other area of interest in the 1901 census returns is the general absence of 'live-in' hired labourers that might have been expected in a farming community. The Sinclair family had a number of labourers but only one of them 'a teenager' that would fit into the category of 'hired' worker. On the holding of James Kee there was a fourteen year old Donegal servant, Owen Boyle, but this was the only case in the whole townland of a young worker from outside the area. It was argued earlier that the farms in Hollyhill generally depended on the labour of the occupying family and the relative absence of live-in hired labour in the census returns supports this.

An examination of the household returns also provides clear evidence that farming was the main activity and only the workers on the Sinclair estate had different designations. Robert Dunleavy gave his occupation as 'Carpenter/Joiner' and we can assume that he was the handyman on the estate. James Donaghey described himself as 'Creamery Secretary and Gardener' while John James Quinn and James Sharkey were simply gardeners. Labourer was the main label attached to adult males who were not landholders but Patrick Giblin was obviously on a higher level, describing himself as 'foreman labourer'. There were three spademakers in the townland returns and the only other clearly defined tradesman was Joseph O'Neill, who described himself as a saddler: no doubt work was available in supplying equipment for the horses on the Sinclair estate as well as for the wider farming community. Unmarried women were generally described as seamstresses and one widow described herself as a 'dealer in tea'. Such specialism seems somewhat out of place in the modern world but the picture of an elderly woman seeking out a livelihood as a door to door salesperson rings true. Local tea-merchants, Devine Brothers, were building up a thriving business at this time and had moved from nearby Glenmornan to Strabane and Lifford in 1895. They had tea-vans distributing supplies through the country areas and it seems likely that Widow Kelly was an independent trader in the same commodity.

CONTINUING CHANGES

In the present century changes in the character of Hollyhill have continued. The transfer of land ownership from the Sinclair family to the occupying tenants appears to have proceeded smoothly in 1908-9 and a considerable number of the nineteenth century family names persist in the area. In other cases they have been replaced by relatives and few of the farms have been transferred to outsiders. There has been little further consolidation of farms and most of the last century's field and farm boundaries remain intact. The major change has been in the management of the farms and there are presently only six full time farmer-occupiers in the townland with five farms leased out to others from neighbouring areas.

A further significant change has been the disappearance of the former landlord family from the area, though the Sinclair name continues in one of the farms. This had been allocated to Rosabel Sinclair, spinster sister of the estate owner, at the time of the tenant purchase and had been renamed Balliburny in reference to the Gaelic name of the district. The farm was later sold to another branch of the Sinclair family and thus the name remains in Hollyhill up to the present. The occupants of the Big House died intestate and the present owner of the remnants of the estate is Hamilton Thompson, a direct descendant of the herdsman who held land in Keenaghan as recorded in the Starrett map of the 1740 period.

Housing in the district in the present century has seen major change with very few of the original farmsteads being now in use and ten having disappeared or lying disused. A number of new houses have been built in the past few years and ten older dwellings have been extensively modernised, including a number of the original workers' houses on the estate. Population figures have fluctuated somewhat with a downward trend being apparently reversed in the past few years.

Caution is necessary, however, in interpreting the figures and the 1981 results are clearly inaccurate both in the total population and in the number of households. This was a period of major political upheaval and a boycott of census returns was being advocated by some groups. It seems clear that part of Hollyhill followed such advice.

In a major sense Hollyhill has lost much of its agricultural character and a large number of houses are occupied by non-farming families or by part-time farmers. The district had boasted a small grocery shop in part of a house up until a generation ago but Cassie McGonnigle's is now only a memory; changing habits and the greater accessibility of transport to neighbouring Strabane have made the rural shop and the mobile grocery van things of the past.

THE SCHOOL & COMMUNITY LIFE

At one period early in the present century Hollyhill could boast of a school and community hall. The school was developed largely through the efforts of Rosabel Sinclair and seems to have won a substantial measure of cross-community support in its early years. It is significant that the same Rosabel Sinclair was recorded in the 1901 census as being competent in the Irish language and it seems possible that the new independent school was her attempt to provide a more diverse education than was standard in the National Schools at the time. She became deeply involved in providing a nursing corps during the First World War and tried her hand unsuccessfully at farming in the post-war period. During the 1920s, however, the issue of education became embroiled with the Border question and the local Catholic parish priest encouraged his congregation to support their own church-run schools. The result was the collapse of Hollyhill school and the end of an educational experiment.

Holyhill school built by Rosabel Sinclair and opened in 1909. It closed in the 1920s

The community hall had a longer life, existing until the later 1960s. It was built for the local branch of the Ancient Order of Hibernians. This was also home for the Hollyhill Band and some of those latterly associated with the hall and band are ready to recount episodes of note in the history of the local A.O.H. and the periodic rivalry that surfaced in relation to the neighbouring Glenmornan band. The rivalry was apparently rooted in divisions within the wider nationalist movement in the post-1916 period and help to explain the separate identity of the Hollyhill-Keenaghan district despite the fact that the people there shared the same church as Glenmornan; shared worship did not necessarily mean a communion of views on social and political outlook. The ending of the outward expressions of dissension in the 1950s and early 1960s was due in large measure to the passing on of an earlier generation and the changing views and needs of the younger people. The organisations, the bands and the halls in both the Hollyhill and Glenmornan areas collapsed and people sought to express their identity and needs in different ways and in less-localized surroundings.

The halls in ruins and the absence of the stirring strains of the marching bands at local sport and social gatherings may be the price that the communities have been forced to pay for progress and change over the past thirty years.

THE SIGERSON LEGACY

A notable figure associated with Hollyhill is Dr George Sigerson, whose father William developed the spade mill and played an active role in the development of Artigarvan. It is claimed that the elder Sigerson provided the land for the building of Artigarvan Presbyterian church and encouraged a number of his workers and acquaintances to make up the numbers necessary to convince church leaders that there was an adequate population for the establishment of a new congregation. Dr George Sigerson was educated at the local glebe school before moving to private schools in Strabane and Letterkenny. He graduated as a doctor in 1859 and combined medical practice with literary pursuits. He became deeply involved in the Irish language movement and in nationalist politics and researched deeply into oral Gaelic poetry. He was prepared to dabble in writing poetry himself and was a prominent figure in the Literary and Gaelic revivals in Dublin in the later years of the nineteenth century. Dr Sigerson claimed that his interest in and knowledge of Irish originated in childhood conversations with hired labourers in his father's spade mill. The surname Sigerson is commemorated in a well-known sporting trophy. The Sigerson Cup, which Dr George donated

---

WM SIGERSON
The manufacture of spades is carried on here for 14 hours a day all the year round. The mill was supplied with two wheels turned by water – one of which blowing two large pair of bellows is 10 feet diameter by 1'6" wide by 8" deep – the water applied at level of axle from a sluice 2 feet deep making the entire fall about 7 feet. MACHINERY C. The other working a large sledge hammer is 12'6" diameter x 3' x 1'1" water applied rather below level of axle from a sluice 2 feet deep – entire fall about 8 feet. MACHINERY B. The threshing mill is also worked by water from a wheel 13'6" x 2'6" x 1', fall 6 or 7 feet used only for the purposes of occupier's own farm.

CAPTAIN JAMES SINCLAIR
Sawing mill used only for farming purposes of Captain Sinclair: wheel 18' x 2'6" x 10". Fall of water 18 or 20 feet overshot. Power applied at top.
PRONI VAL 2B/6/43B (Leckpatrick)

Hollyhill Band (AOH)

in 1911, is still the blue riband competition of Gaelic football among the Irish universities. Sigerson died in 1925 and was buried in Dublin. Much of his poetry is sentimental and there are only scattered references to his childhood home. One easily identified title is 'The Bonnie Brig O'Malezan', associated with the Malison Bridge at Artigarvan.

> O bonnie brig o' Malezan, my heart is with you still,
> And wanders down the rocky ridge unto your rushing rill,
> And sees your trailing ivy sway, the tall trees o'er you wave,
> But your wind's sigh, – it wounds my heart, like a low cry by a grave.
>
> O bonnie brig o' Malezan! 'tis I that loved you well,
> And loved each spot your river roves by moor and mead and dell
> With the great stream far below you, and the kindly mountains o'er
> O bonnie brig o' Malezan – I may never see you more...

Other poems refer to places in the Hollyhill locality and one, *The Church of the Apple Tree*, is associated with a local legend of open-air mass being celebrated in penal times at a particular spot in Glenmornan. The poet claims in a footnote that as a child he was shown the spot by the direct descendants of people who had worshipped there and the legend of the mass-rock sheltered by the apple tree has survived in the oral traditions of the area.

Thus Hollyhill's past. What of its future? It is unlikely that it will re-emerge as a distinct identity and its location and size makes it an unattractive area for community-led regeneration and development. It has managed to retain a sizeable population and there is some evidence of ribbon type housing development taking place. Yet without the Big House it lacks identity and resources and attempts at creating alternative leadership and community interaction have failed. Will it survive best as a rural retreat for those who wish to combine salaried employment elsewhere with part-time farming and associated agricultural activities? Has the Sinclair experiment of developing a self-sufficient and contented peasantry in an area of previously undeveloped land run its course and must it now give way to the harsher reality of changed circumstances and expectations at the end of the twentieth century? History is as much about transitions as about continuity and Hollyhill has epitomised both.

SOURCES

Leckpatrick Parish And Its History by Rev. Walter Hegarty, a commemorative account of 1941

PHILIP ROBINSON, *The Plantation of Ulster* (1984)

R. C. SIMINGTON, ed. *The Civil Survey* Vol 3 (1937)

R. J. HUNTER, ed. *The Plantation of Ulster in Strabane Barony* (NUU 1982)

Sinclair Family Papers in Hollyhill House.

T. W. MOODY AND J. G. SIMMS, eds. *The Bishopric of Derry and the Irish Society of London* (Dublin 1968)

J. H. GEBBIE, *An Introduction to the Abercorn Letters* (1972)

GEORGE D. MANSFIELD'S report on Leckpatrick Parish 1821 in *Ordnance Survey Memoirs Vol 5* ed. A. Day and P. McWilliams (1990)

Second Report from the Commissioners of Irish Education, British Parliamentary Papers, 1826-7, XII, appendix.

S. LEWIS, *Topographical Dictionary of Ireland* (1837)

Evidence given by James Sinclair at Strabane 15 April 1844 in *Report from Her Majesty's Commissioners of Inquiry into the State of the Law and Practice in Relation to the Occupation of Land in Ireland* (*Report of the Devon Commission*), British Parliamentary Papers, 1845, XIX-XXI.

Second Report from the Commissioners of Irish Education, British Parliamentary Papers, 1826-7, XII, appendix.

OWENREAGH

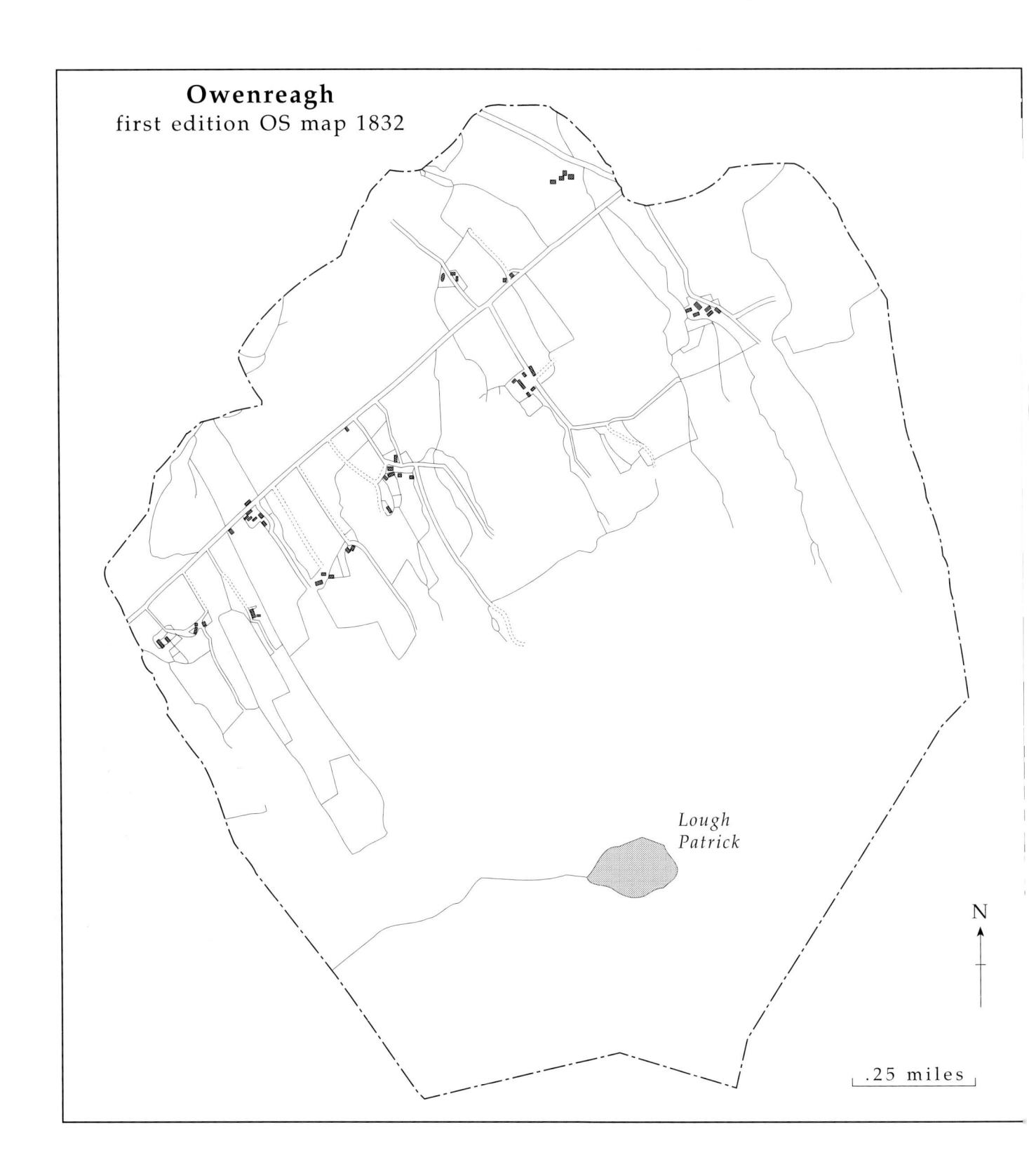

Owenreagh
first edition OS map 1832

Lough Patrick

N

.25 miles

OWENREAGH

GRAHAM MAWHINNEY

OWENREAGH

As I went a-walking one morning in June,
Down by the lands where the wild roses bloom,
And by the meadows and over the brae,
Where the wild whins were blooming by bonny Owenreagh.

My thoughts were of comrades long absent from home,
And of the paths where we used for to roam,
And of the causes which took them away,
From the bonny wild roses which bloom at Owenreagh.

'Tis the soil which is barren and the climate is cold,
And there was but little of silver or gold,
Their pockets to fill or their toil to repay,
Which caused them to wander from bonny Owenreagh.

I fancied them back where the green shamrocks grow,
I fancied them back in the meadows below,
But to the wild whins all abloom on the brae,
They may never return to bonny Owenreagh.

Yet at the same place I have still my old home,
And by the same paths I delight for to roam,
And to think of the comrades so far, far away,
From the bonny wild roses which bloom at Owenreagh.

Yet the roses may wither, but what of the gold?
It is only a moment we have it to hold,
Do riches give pleasure? Does beauty cause pain?
I will wait for the bonny wild roses again.

The Poems of Geordie Barnett – Moyola Books, 1991

Geordie Barnett (1876-1965)

TOWNLAND VALUATION (1833)

Owenreagh lies along the southern side of the River Moyola where it flows through a steep narrow valley. The good arable land is confined to the river banks. Above the southern bank runs the 'new' road from Draperstown to Omagh soon to provide the base for an experimental division of the townland into ladder-back farms – that would provide more scope for the development of family farms. Note that the valuator has deducted one eighth of the valuation 'for local circumstances' and another eighth from the remainder, according to the *Instructions to the Valuators* (VAL/13) – WHC

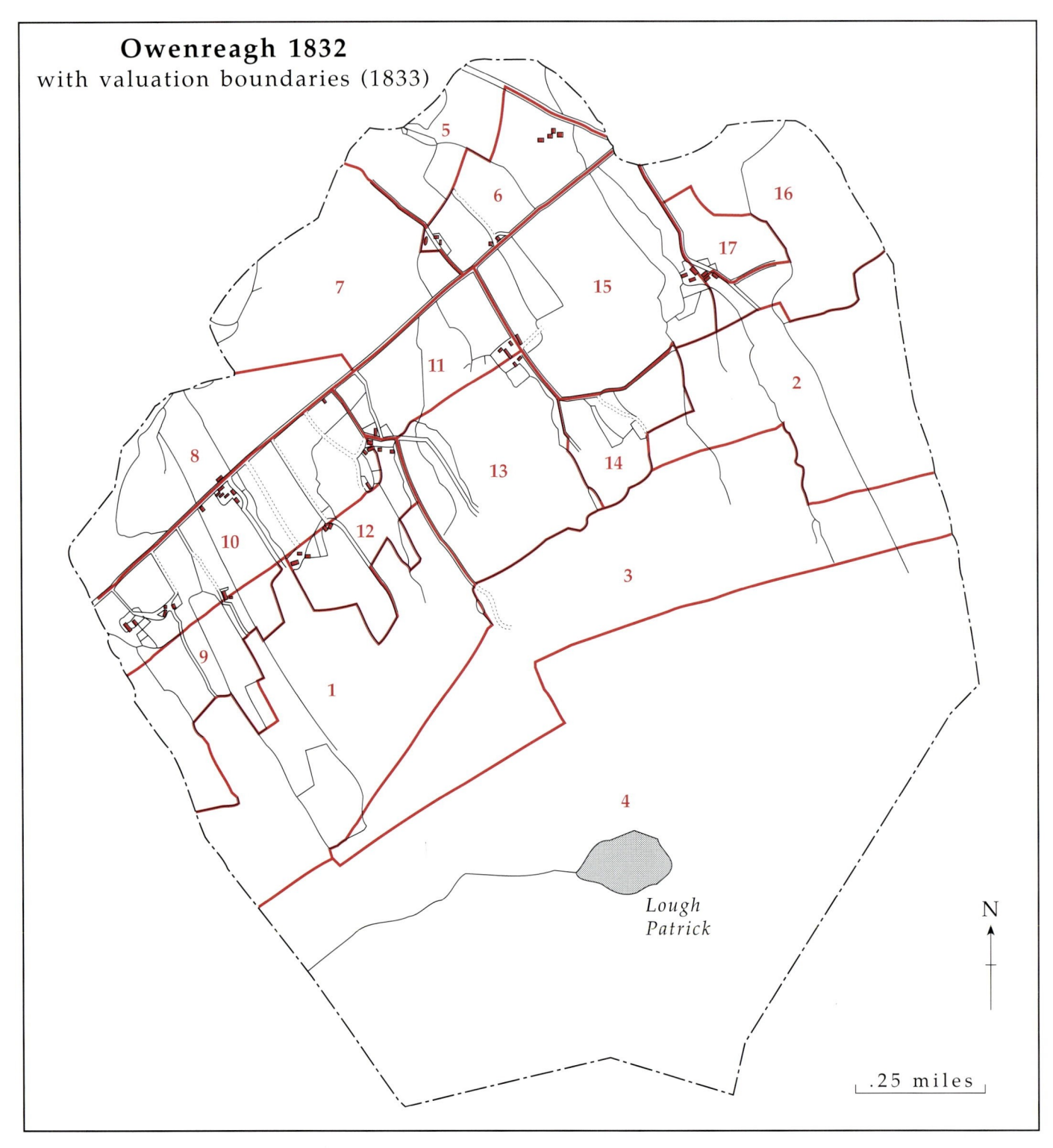

Owenreagh 1832
with valuation boundaries (1833)

Lough Patrick

N

.25 miles

OWENREAGH, parish of Ballinascreen, barony of Loughinsholin, DED of Bancran
(later The Six Towns), Union of Magherafelt   VAL/1B/524

Surveyed by valuators 2/3 July 1833

		QUANTITY	RATE PER STATUTE ACRE	AMOUNT
1	Mountain green pasture	61 1 19	3s	£9 4s 1d
	mountain arable	5	6s	1 10s
2	Green mountain pasture with some shrubs	44 0 26	3s	6 12s 6d
3	Heathy mountain pasture	80 3 06	1s 1d	4 7s 6d
4	Wet bog and mountain	250 0 13	2d	2 1s 8d
	water in Lough Patrick	4 2		
5	Cold and moory arable and meadow	12 3 33	9s	5 16s 7d
	arable	2	13s 6d	1 7s
	cut and green bog and pasture	2 3	3s 6d	9s 7d
	river and gravel strand	1 1		
6	Good arable lies well	16 1 18	15s	12 5s 5d
	meadow	2 1	8s 6d	19s 1d
	waste at house	1		
7	Moory and cold meadow	17 3 23	8s 6d	7 12s
	holms and other arable	9 2	14s 6d	6 17s 9d
	light sandy and rushy pasture	5	4s 1d	
	river and gravel strand	2 1 10		
8	Arable some gravelly	22 2 23	14s 6d	16 8s 4d
	light and sandy arable and pasture	6 2	6s	1 19s
	gravel strand	3		
9	Cold steep and bad arable	17 0 23	7s 6d	6 8s 7d
	bad pasture	1	2s	2s
	cold and bad arable	2	4s 6d	9s
10	Good arable but steep	34 2 9	13s 6d	23 6s 6d
	bad pasture at rowans	1	2s	2s
	light arable top of hill	1	9s	2s 3d
11	Arable gravelly but deep except on the tops of the hills	11 2 36	12s 6d	7 6s 7d
	meadow and moory arable	3 3	9s	1 13s 9d
	moory pasture	1	7s	7s
	bad bog pasture	3	1s 6d	1s 1d
	waste at house			
12	Mountain arable and cold soil	9 0 25	7s	3 4s 1d
	bad cold arable and pasture	3 2	3s 6d	12s 3d
13	Light and cold mountain arable	21 1 9	7s	7 9s 1d
	steep arable	5	10s	2 10s
	bad and light cold arable and pasture	6 3	3s	1 0s 3d
14	Arable very steep and light	9 2 5	7s 6d	3 11s 6d
	steep arable	1	10s	10s
	bad pasture and moor	2	2s 6d	5s

15	Light arable and moory and meadow some	32 0 20	9s 6d	15 5s 2d
	steep arable	8 2	14s 6d	6 3s 3d
	shrubby pasture	2	2s 6d	5s
16	Wet and shrubby pasture	20 3 28	3s 6d	3 13s 2d
	boggy and shrubby pasture	2 2	2s	5s
	cold and light and steep arable	6 2	7s	2 5s 6d
17	Arable light and some steep	6 0 19	10s	3 1s 2d
	meadow and cold arable	1	7s	7s
		759 3 25		£168 16s 8d

Deduct for local circumstances 2/6d per £   21 2s 1d
                                                                                            £147 4s 7d
Deduct one-eighth   18 9s 4d
                                                                                           £ 129 5s 3d

There are no houses in this townland worth three pounds a year.

NB From lot 1 to lot 4 of this townland was valued by the three following valuators:
   John Hampton, Baronial Valuator [no Assistant Valuator listed]
NB From lot 5 to lot 17 of this townland, as also the houses, was valued by the following
   valuators: John Hampton, Baronial Valuator, James Kelly and H Browne, Assistant Valuators

---

OWENREAGH
Both the 1834 religious census and the Tithe Applotment returns of 1825 for the parish of Ballinascreen distinguish between the two neighbouring townlands of Dunernon and Owenreagh and name their respective inhabitants. It is very surprising then to find that the first Ordnance Survey team in 1832 incorporated Dunernon into the much smaller townland of Owenreagh. There is no further mention of Dunernon in the records: it is not even mentioned in the Ordnance Survey name-books which record all the significant place-names in each and every parish. – WHC

These rather melancholy lines written by Geordie Barnett (1876-1965) hint at the loneliness of his native townland and the changes that had taken place there since the days of his youth. The townland is undistinguished to the outsider – it has no church, school, hall, or industry – but to those, like Barnett, who were born and reared on its slopes, every old wallstead evokes memories mingled with handed-down folklore and 'every stoney acre has a name'.

Situated in the parish of Ballinascreen, in the barony of Loughinsholin, in the south of the county of Londonderry, the townland of Owenreagh, together with the neighbouring townlands of Cavanreagh, Glenviggan, Moneyconey, Moyard, and Tullybrick were herenagh or church lands. Most of the remainder of the parish was, from Plantation times, the property of either the Drapers' or the Skinners' Companies of London and so the district comprising these six townlands became known as 'the Sixtowns'. The Sixtowns lies to the south of the parish and takes in the valley of the river Moyola from its source, near the County Tyrone boundary high in the Sperrin mountains, down to the lowlands nearer Draperstown.

The name Owenreagh has been variously interpreted as 'the grey river' and 'the rugged river' and its 760 acres, 3 roods and 32 perches are bounded on the SW by Tullybrick, on the SE by Labby, and on the NW by the Moyola River and Cavanreagh. The road from Draperstown to Omagh runs through the townland taking advantage of the natural valley which was cut into the Sperrin Mountains in the Ice Age. The townland lies along the steep slope between the river at 400' and the mountain plateau at 700' and along this slope, in the 1830s, small farms had been laid out in stripes stretching upwards from the river to the open moorland above. The intention of the landlord, Mr Stevenson of Fortwilliam, Tobermore (who held the land from the Church of Ireland), was to ensure that every tenant had a share of the good land as well as the rough land. Much of this farm pattern is still visible in spite of the ravages of the bulldozer and farm amalgamation. In addition, within the last few years many farmers have reclaimed some of the higher ground for grazing and so the arable/rough grazing boundary has moved further up the hillside. At the head of the slope the land levels out into thousands of acres of bog and heather where the farmers used to cut their peat: in the midst of this mountain plateau sits, rather incongruously, a small lake known as Lough Patrick.

The Moyola valley in ancient times was heavily wooded and the great oak forests of Glenconkyne (between the Sperrin

> RECLAIMING OF MOUNTAIN
>
> The mountainous parts of that subdivision of the above parish [Ballinascreen], locally called the Six Townlands, the property of Mr Stevenson of Fort William, which remained a barren and unproductive waste for centuries back, is at present undergoing irrigation and speedy cultivation by the instrumentality of the proprietor, who, within the last few years, has subdivided the mountains into farms of different sizes and set them out free, or at least at a very trifling annual rent, for a willful period, to such of his tenantry as are able or willing to cultivate them.
>
> A number of these mountain farms are already occupied by many of those of his tenants who formerly held parcels of ground on the lowlands, and are now building farmhouses, office houses and making gardens, small plantings, etc., on these new tenements. They are receiving some assistance of building materials from the proprietor.
>
> This new colonisation will, in a few years, not only become a substantial property to the proprietor, but also enable the cultivators of it to provide their growing family with local settlements, such as their former limited holdings in the lowlands would not afford. It will also give local employ to many of the able-bodied young men who, in the absence of such sources, would be obliged to seek a living or asylum in America or some other foreign nation. Informants William Phillips, Patrick Cassidy and others. 17th November 1836 (p.32).
>
> *(Ordnance Survey Memoirs of Ireland 31, ed. A. Day & P. McWilliams, Belfast, 1995).*

OWENREAGH TITHE APPLOTMENT 1825 (PRONI FIN/5A/43)

		1ST	QUALITY 2ND	3RD	GROSS AMOUNT	AMOUNT COMPOSITION
1	Conway James & Co	3 2 6	3 2 6		7 0 12	8s 1°d
2	Conway Patrick & Co	2 0 25°	4 1 11°		6 1 36	9s 6d
3	Conway Bryan	1 2 19	3 0 38		4 3 17	7s 2°d
4	Conway Thomas & Co	4 3 17	9 2 34.7		14 2 12	14s 3°d
5	Digiany Stephen	1 2 19	3 0 38		4 3 17	7s 2d
6	Hessin Lawrence	1 0 12.3	2 0 25.6		3 0 38	4s 9°d
7	Hagan Patrick	2 0 25.3	4 1 10.6		6 1 36	9s 6d
8	Hanagan Patrick & Co	1 0 12.6	2 0 25		3 0 38	14s 5d
9	Hessin Owen & Co	1 0 12.6	2 0 25		3 0 38	2s 5d
10	Hagan Francis	2 1 28.5	2 1 28°		4 3 17	7s 2°d
11	Hagan Catherine widow	2 1 28.5	2 1 28°		4 3 17	2s 5d
12	McWilliams John & Co	5 2 11	5 2 11		11 0 22	13s 4d
14	Mellon Redmond	3 0 38	3 0 38		6 1 36	9s 6°d
15	Morran Patrick	7 1 6	7 1 6		14 2 12	14s 5°d
					95 3 28	£6 4s 4°d

DUNERNON TITHE APPLOTMENT 1825

No.	Occupier	1st Quality	2nd Quality	Gross amounts	Composition
1	Neal Morian	8.0.15.5	8.0.15.5	6.0.31	17s.1.25
2	McKenady	63.3.6	38.3.21	103.2.27	£3.10s.7.25
3	Henry McCullagh	14.2.12	19.1.30	34.0.2	15s 6.25
4	Thomas Graham	32.1.23	17.3.11	50.0.34	£1. 2s 4
5	John Graham & Co	64.3.6	45.3.33	110.2.39	£2.14s.0.75
				314.3.13	£8.19s. 7.5

[Signed] Robert Foorester
Robert Ferguson

OWENREAGH

(THIS RELIGIOUS CENSUS OF 1834 DENOTED ALL THE RESIDENTS AS ROMAN CATHOLICS)   PRONI MIC 5A REEL 8A

1	Bernard Convery	one family	2 males and 6 females		= 8
2	Patrick Convery	one	1	2	= 3
3	Michael Convery	one	1	2	= 3
4	John(?) Hassan	one	1	3	= 4
5	Stephen Dagney	two	6	3	= 9
6	Thomas Dagney	one	3	3	= 6
7	Francis Hagan	one	2	2	= 4
8	Andrew Morran	one	4	2	= 6
9	Patrick Hagan	one	1	2	= 3
10	Redmond Mullen	one	4	4	= 8
11	Charles Flanagan	one	1	2	= 3
12	Laurence Hassan	one	3	2	= 5
13	John McKeown	one	1	1	+ servant = 3
14	Robert McKeown	one	2	2	= 4
15	Ambrose Conway	one	2	3	= 5
16	Patrick Morran	one	3	4	= 7
17	Patrick Flanagan	one	1	3	= 4
18	Patrick Flanagan	one	2	3	= 5
19	John Williams	one	2	1	= 3
20	Phelix McWilliams	one	3	1	= 4
21	Hugh Lagan	one	2	3	= 5
22	John Conory	one	1	3	= 4
23	Arthur Conory	one	1	2	+ servant = 4
		24	49	59	+2 servants = 110

OWENREAGH was enlarged by the Ordnance Survey by giving it the neighbouring larger townland of Dunernon/Dunarnon. Compare the family names in both the censuses and the Tithe Applotment Returns with the Tenement Valuation.

DUNARNON Census

		FAMILIES			SERVANTS		RELIGION			
Householder		Families	M	F	M	F	Total	EC	RC	Pres.
1	Thos McKendry	1	1	2	3	0	6	3	3	0
2	Thos McVeigh	1	1	1			2		2	
3	Patrick Kane	1	1	4			5		5	
4	Neal Morrow	1	2	3			5		5	
5	James Devlin	1	1	2			3		3	
6	John Graham	1	3	2			5		0	5
7	George Graham	1	4	2	1	2	9		3	6
8	Pat McBride	1	2	2			4		4	
9	Thos Graham	1	3	3	3		9		3	6
10	Henry McCullagh	1	2	1	2		5		5	
		10	20	22	9	2 =	53	= 3	33	17

PARISH OF BALLYNASCREEN.

No. and Letters of Reference to Map.	Townlands and Occupiers.	Immediate Lessors.	Description of Tenement.	Area.	Rateable Annual Valuation. Land.	Buildings.	Total Annual Valuation of Rateable Property.
	OWENREAGH. *(Ord. S. 40.)*						
1	Patrick Kelly,	Reps. John Stevenson,	Land,	1 3 10	0 10 0	—	0 10 0
— a	Martha Bradley,	Same,	House and garden,	0 0 30	0 5 0	0 10 0	0 15 0
2 A a / — B	Francis Cleary,	Same,	House and land,	6 1 25 / 8 0 15	2 5 0 / 0 10 0	0 5 0 / —	} 3 0 0
3 A a / — B	Hugh Lagan,	Same,	House, office, & land,	5 3 25 / 7 2 35	2 5 0 / 0 10 0	0 10 0 / —	} 3 5 0
4 A / — B a / — C	Patrick Flanagan (*Gamekeeper*),	Same,	House, office, & land,	11 3 10 / 3 3 30 / 1 0 25	1 5 0 / 1 10 0 / 0 10 0	— / 0 15 0 / —	} 1 0 0
5 A / — B a	Felix M'Williams,	Same,	House, office, & land,	8 2 15 / 4 2 15	0 15 0 / 2 0 0	— / 0 5 0	} 3 0 0
6	Thomas Steen,	Same,	House and land,	16 2 10	3 0 0	0 10 0	3 10 0
7	John Bradley,	Same,	House and land,	2 1 15	1 5 0	0 5 0	1 10 0
8	Anne Sinclair,	Anne M'Evey,	Land,	1 0 5	0 10 0	—	0 10 0
9	Michael Flanagan,	Same,	Land,	13 0 5	3 0 0	—	3 0 0
— a	Anne M'Evey,	Reps. John Stevenson,	House and gardens,	0 1 5	0 5 0	0 5 0	0 10 0
10 A / — B a	Michael Flanagan,	Same,	House, office, & land,	10 0 10 / 17 0 10	2 10 0 / 3 0 0	— / 0 10 0	} 6 0 0
11 a	William M'Keon,	Same,	House, offices, and land.	35 2 20	9 10 0	1 5 0	10 15 0
— b	Elizabeth M'Keon,	William M'Keon,	House,	—	—	0 5 0	0 5 0
— c	John M'Gonigle,	Same,	House,	—	—	0 10 0	0 10 0
12 { a / b	Edward Hesson, / Philip Hesson,	Reps. Jno. Stevenson,	House and land, / House and land,	10 1 10	{ 1 10 0 / 1 10 0	0 5 0 / 0 5 0	1 15 0 / 1 15 0
13	Anne Melon, / John Melon,	Same,	House, office, & land, / House, office, & land,	19 0 5	2 15 0 / 2 15 0	0 10 0 / 0 10 0	3 5 0 / 3 5 0
14 A a / — B	Michael Flanagan,	Same,	House, office, & land,	12 1 15 / 3 0 12	2 15 0 / 1 10 0	0 10 0 / —	} 4 15 0
15	Patrick Hagan,	Same,	House and land,	1 0 20	0 10 0	0 5 0	0 15 0
16 { a / —	Redmond Melon, jun. / Bridget Hagan,	Same,	House and land, / Land,	23 0 10	{ 2 10 0 / 2 10 0	0 5 0 / —	2 15 0 / 2 10 0
17 A a / — B	John Hagan,	Same,	House and land,	14 0 5 / 2 2 15	2 15 0 / 1 15 0	0 5 0 / —	} 4 15 0
18 A / — B a / — C	Michael Conry,	Same,	House, offices, & land,	5 1 0 / 17 3 15 / 1 0 15	2 15 0 / 5 15 0 / 0 10 0	— / 1 0 0 / —	} 10 0 0
19 A / — B a	Neal Deane,	Same,	House, offices, & land,	1 2 30 / 8 3 10	1 5 0 / 2 0 0	— / 1 0 0	} 4 5 0
20 A / — B / — C a	Thomas Deane,	Same,	House, offices, & land,	2 3 10 / 1 0 10 / 10 3 20	1 15 0 / 0 10 0 / 2 5 0	— / — / 1 5 0	} 5 15 0
21 A / a / — B	Bryan Conry, / John Conry,	Same,	House, office, & land, / House, office, & land,	4 2 15 / — / 9 0 30	2 10 0 / — / 2 0 0	— / 0 5 0 / 0 5 0	} 2 10 0 / 2 10 0
22	Patrick Flanagan (*Gamekeeper*), / Francis Cleary, / Hugh Lagan, / Michael Conry, / William M'Keon, / Michael Flanagan, / Daniel Kelly,	Same, / Same, / Same, / Same, / Same, / Same, / Anne M'Evey,	Land,	3 1 5	1 15 0	—	0 5 0 / 0 3 0 / 0 3 0 / 0 6 0 / 0 12 0 / 0 3 0 / 0 3 0
23 A / — B a / b	George Graham, / Michael M'Bride,	Reps. John Stevenson, / George Graham,	House, offices, & land, / House,	14 0 20 / 94 2 30 / —	7 10 0 / 11 15 0 / —	— / 2 0 0 / 0 5 0	} 21 5 0 / 0 5 0
24 A / — B a / — C / — D	John Graham,	Reps. John Stevenson,	House, offices, & land,	3 1 10 / 11 2 30 / 21 1 0 / 22 0 20	2 5 0 / 6 0 0 / 9 10 0 / 1 0 0	— / 2 10 0 / — / —	} 21 5 0
25 A a / — B / A b	James Graham, / Unoccupied,	Same, / James Graham,	House, offices, & land, / House,	18 3 35 / 43 3 30 / —	10 5 0 / 4 0 0 / —	1 15 0 / — / 0 10 0	} 16 0 0 / 0 10 0
26	Catherine M'Cullagh,	Reps. John Stevenson,	House, offices, and land.	53 3 10	7 15 0	1 5 0	9 0 0
27 A a / — B	Thomas M'Henry,	Same,	House, offices, & land,	38 1 30 / 33 3 30	17 10 0 / 3 10 0	1 10 0 / —	} 22 10 0
28 a	Hicks Hutchinson,	Same,	House and land,	20 0 35	7 10 0	0 10 0	8 0 0
29	Reps. Jno. Stevenson,	Lord Bishop of Derry and Raphoe,	Bog, / Turbary,	70 3 0	0 5 0	—	0 5 0 / 10 0 0
30			Water,	5 1 25	—	—	
			Total,	760 3 32	169 15 0	22 10 0	202 5 0

OWENREAGH 225

This valuation map illustrates the outcome of the landlord's project to create farms. John Stevenson of Fort William, Tobermore, had bought out the fee simple and inheritance of the churchlands known as the Sixtowns of Ballinascreen for £1,591.1s.9d from the Church of Ireland Bishop of Derry on 29 August 1835 under 'An act to alter and amend the laws relating to the Temporalities of the Church of Ireland' (3&4 William IV c.37) passed in 1833 (PRONI D/3622 or /3666). The whole western half of the townland had been redivided into ladder-back farms, giving each tenant a fair share of each quality of land – WHC

Owenreagh 1856
with valuation boundaries (1858)

mountains and Lough Neagh) are well documented. The higher ground would have been the favoured habitat for the farming/hunting people as evidenced by the ancient monuments at Ballybriest, the slopes of Slieve Gallion, and farther to the south-west, the Beaghmore stone circles. Owenreagh has its own stone circle on the high ground overlooking the valley. No physical evidence of the ancient oak forest has survived, as generations of people in this district have struggled against nature to clear the shrubbery and provide grazing for sheep and cattle. There are places where the 'rigs' or 'lazy-beds' can still be seen, usually high up on the hillside where no-one today would consider growing crops. Only field-names and the occasional pile of stones or wallsteads preserve the memory of the poverty-stricken people who lived in these remote parts and scratched out a living from the barren soil.

POPULATION FIGURES

Like many other rural areas, Owenreagh has suffered a dramatic decline in population since the middle of the last century. The population peak before the Famine is clearly evident although there is no folk memory of widespread suffering as a result of the potato failure. Emigration was probably a much more significant factor and there were many families, including my own, where sons and daughters left to start a new life, mostly in America. Letters home encouraged others to come and join them and, in the latter half of the last century, dozens from this townland sailed from the port of Derry.

OWENREAGH, parish of Ballinascreen, barony of Loughinsholin, DED of Bancran (later the Six Towns DED), union of Magherafelt, Magherafelt Rural District, County Londonderry

YEAR	INHABITANTS			HOUSES			
------	MALES FEMALES TOTAL			INHAB UNINHAB BUILDING TOTAL			
1841	87 + 93 = 180			40 + 2 + 0 = 42			
1851	76 + 87 = 163			33 + 1 + 0 = 34			
1861	71 + 79 = 150			33 + 1 + 0 = 34			
1871	54 + 78 = 132			27 + 1 + 0 = 28			
1881	45 + 65 = 110			24 + 1 + 0 = 25			
1891	46 + 68 = 114			24 + 1 + 0 = 25			
1901	37 + 54 = 91 (c)			20 + 0 + 0 = 20			
1911	36 + 46 = 82			18 + 1 + 0 = 19			
1926	27 + 40 = 67			16 + 2 + 0 = 18			
1937	27 + 29 = 56			13 + 1 + 0 = 14			
1951	na = 28			na = 14			
1961	19 + 8 = 27			10 + 1 + 0 = 11			
1971	18 + 19 = 37			12 + 1 + 0 = 13			
1981	11 + 12 = 23			8 + 1 + 0 = 9			
1991	13 + 13 = 26			8 + 0 + 0 = 8			

(c) The decrease is attributed to emigration and removals

The trend of falling population continued throughout the century with the main factor being the drift of farm labourers and small farmers into the rapidly growing market town of Draperstown, three miles to the east. A few farm labourers migrated to England to find work and settled there: for many generations there had been a tradition of seasonal work at the hay harvest and the potato harvest, in southern Scotland and northern England. With the drift away from the land and the amalgamation of small farms, it was inevitable that the number of inhabited houses would decrease.

The derelict Graham homestead

Griffith's Valuation (1859) indicates that the most prosperous landowner in the townland was John Graham. He farmed over 57 acres and his buildings had a rateable valuation of £2.50. The Graham family name is no longer in the townland and the homestead, to which Geordie Barnett referred in an article in the *Weekly Northern Whig* of 7 January 1928, lies derelict.

> In the townland of Owenreagh, at Sixtowns, near Draperstown, in the County Derry, there are two ancient crab-apple trees which have grown to a large size. They flower in May, and the globose fruit ripens in autumn, remaining for a considerable time on the trees. I have gathered quantities in November.
>
> The trees are in a fence along a lane which leads to the farmhouse occupied by the Misses Graham. On the adjoining property, owned by Mrs Eliza Jane Graham, two younger trees of the same kind grow also at a place called the Kiln Hill, and here – Mr Robert Graham of Owenreagh informed me – there grew in his young days a larger and more ancient crab which eventually died of sheer old age. Questioned as to the probable age of the trees, the Misses Graham kindly gave me a great deal of information, which was confirmed and supplemented by that of several of the oldest inhabitants in the district. The story is as follows:-

Portion of the house occupied by the Misses Graham is very old, and is supposed to have been the first farmhouse in the parish to possess glass windows. It was recently repaired and re-roofed, and I had the opportunity of examining the original timbers, which were of native oak and bog fir, and were quite sound except for the portions which rested on the walls. The original owner of this property, Crabtree Farm, was a family named Agnew who came from Castledawson, and who possessed other properties in the neighbourhood. Mr and Mrs Agnew had a family of one son and four daughters. The former died of fever in Owenreagh about 150 years ago.

Nature & Antiquarian Notes – Moyola Books, 1994

Of the twenty-one names listed in 1859, only two, Lagan and Flanagan, still continue in the townland. A few of the other names have been around within living memory, such as McCullagh, Graham and Conry (sic). A look at the corresponding valuation map confirms the existence of numerous very small farms, averaging about ten acres when the five largest farms are excluded. It is not just the small size of the farms that is striking but also the small size of the fields. Anyone familiar with this land today would be surprised at the disappearance of so many of the field and farm boundaries. Where the original small fields do still exist, the field names very often give us a clue to former owners. On my own home farm I was always told that 'Frank's field' referred to a Frank McBride who lived where old wallsteads still exist. These McBrides, who lived far up the hill, were reputed to be very strong men who were able to carry two hundredweight bags of meal from the road to the house (about half a mile) without resting. The valuation of 1859 confirms the existence of this family – Michael McBride was a lessee of George Graham, my great-grandfather.

A cluster of three houses – O'Neill's, Mawhinney's (formerly Graham's), and McCullagh's – existed in the part of the townland known as Dunarnon. When my father, Sam Mawhinney, bought Harry McCullagh's neighbouring farm about twenty-five years ago, he recalled Harry telling him that a particular field was known as 'Barnett's Park'. Nobody had ever heard of Barnetts living in this part of the townland. It wasn't until 1992 that some light was thrown on this mystery. Dr Desmond McCourt, who had been collecting folklore material from George Barnett in the mid 1940s, wrote a piece on his memories of Barnett:

> George also recalled hearing of a former cluster of seven families in Owenreagh called Dunarnon (not marked on the first Ordnance maps of 1835 but located on Sampson's earlier map). The Barnetts had apparently moved there from near Cookstown in the late eighteenth century but some of them, including George's great grandfather, 'Ephriam Barnett the Quaker', were moved to Moneyconey cluster as part of Stevenson's reforms of the 1830s.

Luckily Dr McCourt had recorded this unique bit of oral history before it was lost. The traditions handed down orally take us right back into the mists of time. There is no denying the value of field names and oral tradition!

A noticeable feature on the valuation map of 1859 is the course of the Moyola river which forms one boundary of the townland. In the mid-nineteenth century the river meandered much more and often split up into rivulets. Local people have heard fathers and grandfathers talk of the 'straightening of the river' and there were numerous disputes over who owned the land on either bank as the course of the river was altered.

The stone-arched bridge between Owenreagh and Cavanreagh (Pat Walls's bridge) had not been built in 1859. The Ordnance Survey map suggests that the road crossed over two small bridges as the river there had split into two streams.

1901–FAMILY NAMES IN OWENREAGH: 20 households

Graham 15	M'Cullagh 5	M'Kenna 3	Connery 2	Cuskrin 1
Deane 14	O'Neill 5	Convery 3	Cleary 1	Grey 1
M'Williams 5	Barnett 5	Byrnes 2	M'Closkey 1	Carr 1
O'Hagan 5	Lagan 5	Hasson 2	Connolly 1	M'Guigan 1
Mallon 5	Flanagan 4	M'Namee 2	Bell 1	M'Gonagle 1

1995–FAMILY NAMES in OWENREAGH: 9 households

M'Sorley	10	M'Gregor	4	Flanagan 2
Mawhinney	6	Lagan	4	Devlin 1
Clerkin	5	M'Eldowney	2	

While most of the inhabitants in 1901 could read and write, five out of the twenty heads of households could not sign their name. Eight of the older residents claimed to speak both Irish and English. Almost everyone in the townland had been born in County Derry, with the exception of a few from Tyrone and Patrick McGonagle who was born in Donegal. Patrick recorded, in the most beautiful handwriting, that he was 54 years of age, a widower and a carpenter by trade. He belonged to the Church of Ireland and almost certainly worshipped in the little church of St Anne, just across the river in Cavanreagh. He probably lies there in an unmarked grave. Was the John McGonigle listed in Griffith's Valuation Patrick's older brother or father? Patrick's B1 census form tells us that his house was built of stone and had two rooms and two windows in front, while the B2 form mentions a cow house, a pig house and a turf house. Today all that remains is a heap of large stones high up the hillside on the farm that once belonged to Geordie Barnett and is now Mawhinney's.

On 19 June 1927 Geordie Barnett scribbled on a scrap of paper (which I happened to retrieve) that Robbie Graham had told him that 'old Donald Kelly (Labby) remembered the tanyard (Owenreagh) working and that Andy Clerkin carted oak bark'. This tanyard, owned by the McHenry family, was the only 'alternative enterprise' that survives in the folk memory. In 1859 Thomas McHenry is recorded as owning over 70 acres and the total annual valuation of his rateable property was the highest in the townland at £22. 10s. By 1901 the McHenry name had disappeared from Owenreagh. Thomas McHenry (whose brother Lawrence was Church of Ireland curate in Culdaff, County Donegal, until his death in 1846) died in 1867 and his daughter Margaret married John Graham. Fortunately, many letters and documents relating to these families have been preserved. A booklet published in 1990, containing the autobiography of a grandson of John Graham (also known as John Graham, 1899–1983), contains a fine description of life in Owenreagh in the early years of this century:

> The farm was divided into ten fields. The dividing fences were mostly hawthorn bushes planted close together. These kept the cattle in. Some of the fields were always used for grazing and the others used for crops, which were rotated – one year oats, potatoes or cabbages, then something else the next year. Hay always grew in the same field, and was not planted or sown. It was cut with a scythe, spread out to dry, turned with a rake two or three times, then raked into heaps and later carted to the yard and built into haystacks.

> The dwelling house was two storeys, built of stone, rough-cast on the outside with lime mortar and whitewashed, and it had a slate roof. There was a large kitchen-living room, a parlour (not much used), three bedrooms and a fairly big pantry. Some rooms were papered, others plastered smooth and whitewashed. The kitchen and pantry had concrete floors, the other rooms had wooden floors. There were two fireplaces – a large open fireplace in the kitchen and a small grate in the parlour. Turf and firewood were used for cooking and heating. We always had crickets living in the walls around the kitchen fire. It was nice to hear them chirping and it was supposed to be lucky to have crickets in the hearth.

> An iron bar hung over the fire, about five feet from the floor. This bar could be swung out and from it hung three or four chains. The cooking pots, pans and kettles were hung on these chains and could be raised or lowered on to the fire. We had cooking pots and ovens of different sizes. The pots were round and fairly big, while the ovens were flat, and when cooking meat or a rice pudding, hot coals were piled on the lid so that it had heat all round. The kitchen fire never went out.

At night it was banked up and in the morning it was raked out and it was still burning brightly.

Some of the homes in the district were low, one-storey buildings with thatched roofs, thatched with oat straw. Thatch kept homes cool in summer and warm in winter. Thatching was a skilled trade.

Far from Owenreagh, Moyola Books, 1990

The Thomas McHenry who featured in the 1859 Valuation was a second cousin of Sir John Lawrence, Viceroy of India, and the Lawrence family of Ballinascreen had many distinguished members. [A full family tree appears in *The McHenry letters (1834-46)* published by Ballinascreen Historical Society in 1996.] For a few generations the Graham name dominated their end of the townland and it is interesting to note that Constable Edward Loughrey of the Royal Irish Constabulary who was the 1901 census enumerator, always transcribed the name as 'Grames' which would be the colloquial pronunciation!

In contrast to the comparatively large farm just described, Anne and John Melon (sic.) lived in 1859 on a farm of nineteen acres. This long, narrow strip of land, although much more extensive than most farms in the district, typifies a farm and family about which relatively little is known. I would guess that Anne and John were sister and brother and I presume that John was the grandfather of Maggie Mellon, whom I remember frequently riding a bicycle into Draperstown. Today Mellon's house, like a dozen others in the townland, lies deserted and derelict. In 1901 five members of the family lived there, including the six-year old Maggie. Because the Mellon family have left so few traces this poem by Geordie Barnett may serve as their epitaph:

Mellon's deserted cottage with its tin roof

MELLON'S POTATO GATHERING

It happened to be in November, the truth I'm inclined to be telling,
When the neighbours fore-gathered together to dig up the spuds for Miss Mellon,
I happened to be a near neighbour with a dwelling house down by the road.
So cooks with provisions in plenty took over my humble abode.

Now the kitchen is flagged with big boulders, with paving stones down by the crook,
Where the kettle it swings by the fire as it hangs in that nice cosy nook.
A tractor was digging potatoes and Kelly sat broad at the wheel,
Whilst a lot of fine boys and a damsel were scattered all over the field.

The smell of the tea was enchanting, attracting the folk that passed by,
And my floor was a sight with egg shells as the cooks hurried up with a fry,
The bacon it fizzled and curled and bounced like a ball on the pan,
God help us the bacon's so skinny with the laws that now govern the land.

I sigh for the days that are over when the bacon was deep in the side,
With lard for to keep our joints nimble, and keep out the cold from our hides.
A bicycle squeals when it dries up and a tractor it groans without grease,
And we humans may dry up the same way, till we scarcely are able to sneeze.

So the work it went on in deep silence with never a snatch of a song,
And when that is the way in our country there's something tremendously wrong,
So clod in some wallops of butter that the eggs may not stick to the pan,
And keep up the strength of our farmers lest the last of them fade from the land.

'Old' Geordie and 'wee' Geordie Barnett

Geordie Barnett's grandfather was William McKeon (sic.) listed in the 1859 Valuation as having 35 acres at Owenreagh. McKeon's daughter, Eliza Jane, became the wife of Geordie Barnett, Senior. The second of their nine children was also George, born in 1876. Tuberculosis caused the death of three of the family and when Geordie was only twelve his mother died, leaving a neighbour woman to help bring up the family. Geordie himself was often in ill-health and seldom at school. From the age of twelve he was at home helping his father on the farm. Although he disliked the hard manual work of the farm he had to do as he was told. It was during the long monotonous days digging with a spade, cutting hay with a scythe, or ploughing with a horse, that he developed his lifelong interest in his immediate environment.

Geordie Barnett on the road

... If you had been driving through the Sperrin mountains about thirty years ago there would have have been a strong possibility that you would have met, a few miles outside Draperstown, a small lightly-built man with a small bag hanging on his back. He would have been walking at a brisk pace, head bent downwards and shabbily dressed, complete with heavy wellington boots and a peaked cloth cap. Nothing unusual in that, you might say – the Ulster countryside still abounds in 'characters' and cranks. But Geordie Barnett was neither. He was a scholar, every bit as much as those who sit in the ivory towers of our universities. Historian, archaeologist, botanist, geologist, folklorist, musician and poet, Geordie had spent sixty years studying all aspects of the Sperrins and of him it could be truly said that 'work did not interfere with his education'.

Geordie Barnett's Gortin – Moyola Books 1992

Now the Barnett dwelling lies derelict, just a field length away from the crumbling Mellon house.

In 1901 only two out of the twenty inhabited houses were described as first class, five were second-class and the remaining thirteen third-class. The two first class houses were those of Margaret Grames (sic.) – 'Crabtree Farm' referred to earlier – and Annie O'Neill. Both are now derelict. All of the houses in the townland had non-perishable walls i.e. stones, brick, or concrete, and it would appear that fourteen (seventy per cent) had thatched roofs. If Constable Loughrey returned today he would see little that was recognisable from his visit in 1901! All of the present dwellings are in excellent repair. Almost half of them are new bungalows which have been built within the last decade or two, while the others are old farmhouses that have undergone substantial renovations and extensions. To some extent the trend of migration to the town is now starting to reverse as affluent young people are seeking planning permission to build in the countryside in order to escape from the rapidly growing housing estates.

Some of the farmers in the townland now have other full- or part-time jobs and

The Barnett dwelling

the result of this is that their farming activities are restricted to evenings or weekends. No crops are grown, other than grass which is harvested in the summer as silage. Morrowing still continues and machinery and man-power are often shared between neighbouring farms. The whole farming scene has been vastly transformed in recent years with increased mechanisation and the growth in farm size due to amalgamation.

Relationships in this community continue to be excellent and this has been reflected, in recent years, in the formation of the Sixtowns Community Group which is well supported in its endeavours to promote the social and economic well-being of the area. The quality of the friendships in this district is reflected in a letter written during a visit to New York in 1927 by 'Master' Charles McKenna to his friend and neighbour, Geordie Barnett. The neighbourliness and the exile's longing for news from home shine through this correspondence as McKenna, a Catholic, tells Barnett, a Presbyterian, of his experiences and relays news of others from Owenreagh, known to them both, who have found success on the other side of the world.

Brooklyn, New York, 12 August 1927

My dear George,

Kindly accept my sincere thanks for your two letters – the only ones I have received from home since I left there. I anxiously await another.

Well, to begin at the beginning. Master Orr saw us off at the boat and did everything in his power to make us comfortable for the night. We left Liverpool at 3 and, much to my surprise, I was not seasick for five minutes from I left Belfast till I arrived here. A transatlantic steamer – they just call it a boat – reminds me of a rock or little island in the ocean and is a study in itself. We travelled in what is called the tourist department and **it is** quite good enough for anyone. The food was plentiful and of the best quality and we had a selection of ten different kinds at every meal – just fancy that. The days passed rapidly. There were sports during the day and dancing – yes, and drinking too. At night you make new acquaintances – some very nice people, others, as at home, of a wearying and undesirable kind.

All my relations have met us at the landing stage and whisked us away in two taxis, crossing the Brooklyn bridge on our way. Since then my principal work is sight-seeing. On Sunday last young Tommy Gillespie – one of the boys who lived in 'James Peter's' – motored us 110 miles through the principal streets in New York and yet we only saw a part of this immense city. Yesterday we went up the Hudson River on a pleasure steamer for 60 miles – that is between New York city and Jersey – and I'll never forget the splendour and the sights I saw along the banks on both sides. There were two thousand or more on board and remember 600 more of these boats run every day.

The first man I received a letter of welcome from was an old pupil – Geordie Barnett. He and James – a few days afterwards – visited us here and needless to say we discussed many old time reminiscences. We are invited to Geordie's whenever we can find an opportunity. All, or nearly all, the Sixtowns boys who live around here, came to see us and all admit they have to work hard. One thing has struck me particularly. While all the houses of worship are open on Sundays, work never ceases. The stores are nearly all doing business and the navvies are hard at work on the streets. Generally for a working man it is seven days a week work. Just contrast this with the way work is done in Ireland.

In some respects I like this country, but home is home be it ever so humble. The heat sometimes is oppressive to me but the people who live here say it is quite alright. I have not made up my mind how long I shall stay. Maggie Byrnes, her sister, and Peter Gillespie are untiring in their efforts to make our visit pleasant and happy and I am pleased to say that they have a nice home and are in very comfortable circumstances. Maggie is a wonderful little woman. She has related to me some of her vicissitudes in this country during the past twenty years and it is little less than a miracle she has come out on top. In fact she and Peter are almost independent. Their house at the present moment is worth about six thousand pounds.

Give my regards to your father, to Mary, and to Maggie and her father. I hope the little house is being left severely alone. Kindly keep me posted in all local news.

                Sincerely yours,
                Charles McKenna

PS I wonder if you will be able to decipher this pencil scrawl. I hope you are making use of the two fields of grass.

What sort of weather have you had since I left there? How are Mr and Mrs Sands and baby? And John Bradley (Jamie Ned) is my successor at the collecting on

Sundays. I bet he will not get as many coppers as I did. Has anyone sprayed my plot of potatoes? I trust the little plantation in front of Connolly's will be left undisturbed. How is Jim Barnett? I sincerely hope he is steadily improving.

We all regret not recording more information from parents and grandparents while they were alive, but it is never too late to start. Consider this rather morbid tale from this townland told to Geordie Barnett (and written down by him) on 18 June 1927. The narrator was Pat Mellon (Maggie's father). I am confident that there is no other record of this incident.

> About 65 years ago Paddy Bradley ('Wonnel') found, when cutting peat at the south side of Lough Patrick, human remains beneath about four feet of peat. The body had fair curly hair and dressed only in drugget (half wool and half linen – home spun) underclothing. There was a leather belt of curious workmanship around the neck. There were four or five policemen at McBride's, Sixtowns, at the time. The find was reported to them. They left a policeman named Pat Gallagher to guard the body and sent for the sergeant at Draperstown (their superior). There was a fancy hazel stick with the body. The remains were taken to McBride's barracks. Old Thomas McHenry went to see the remains and said he recognised the belt as that worn by his son at the time of his disappearance. He waked the body as that of his son. It was subsequently buried at the Old Church, Sixtowns. At the inquest a merely formal verdict was passed on account of insufficient evidence of identity and the fact that there was nothing to show how death had occurred.

Producing a series of minor publications relating to the history of this area, has helped, I hope, to preserve some of my heritage. There is, however, much more to be done. This article has tried to illustrate some things which may be done to record the history of a townland.

INDEX

Abercorn, James Hamilton, *1st Earl of*, 194
Abercorn estates, 194-6
Acre, different measures of, 14, 15
Agricultural schools, 197
Agricultural statistics, 25, 26, 59, 108, 172
America, 51, 55, 130, 131, 166, 226
Annual Revision Lists, 18, 20-22, 46, 57, 107, 166, 202, 205, 206
Antrim (*town*), 76, 81
Antrim, Co., 11, 12, 31, 37, 70, 82, 207
 - North, 37, 40
Antrim estate, 38, 42
Arable farming, 59, 60, 124, 125, 172, 201
Archbishop of Armagh's estates, 10
Armagh, Co., 31
 - North, 11, 16
Armoy, 37
Artigarvan, 191, 196, 200, 208
Australia, 49, 51, 55, 124, 126, 131, 166

Bagenal family, 113, 114, 126
Baird estate, 161, 164, 188n
Ballinahatten, 121, 125
Ballybogey, 61
Ballyhenry, 15
Ballymena, 89
Ballymoney, 37, 40, 41, 54, 56, 57, 61, 62
Bands, 62, 212
Bangor, 97, 107
Barley, 59, 60, 107, 124, 125
Barnett, Geordie, 217, 221, 227, 229, 230, 232-4
Beans, 107
Belfast, 51, 55, 82, 182
Blacksmiths, 60, 124
Blessington estates, 158, 160, 161, 182
Boards of Guardians, 21
Bodley maps, 8, 12, 156, 194
Booleying, 196
Bootown, 39, 40, 42, 60
Border, North-South, 140, 143, 153, 211
Boundaries, townland, 9-11
Boyd family, of Forttown, 47, 48, 50, 54, 55, 57-9
Bridges, 30, 182, 229
Britain, 51, 131, 166, 227
Bronze Age, 37, 137
Brownlow estates, 12, 14, 28
Burnside, Alexander, 43, 46, 48, 59

Canada, 51, 55, 131
Carrickfergus, 88, 89
Castlederg, 137, 140, 153
Catholic Church, 62, 108, 130, 139, 140, 142, 146, 184, 192, 194
Cattle, 59, 60, 92, 124, 146, 170, 173, 181

Celibacy, 51, 54, 56, 57
Census, Irish, 1659, 8, 40
Census of Population
 Comparative tables, 51, 81, 107, 120, 142, 165, 205, 226
 - 1841, 20, 21, 81, 120, 201
 - 1851, 20, 107, 201
 - 1861, 20
 - 1891, 107
 - 1901, 21, 22, 50, 52-8, 82, 107, 131, 132, 170, 205-9, 229, 230
 - 1911, 21, 107, 166
 - 1926, 120
 - 1981, 211
Census Office, 20
Church lands, 72-4, 97, 113, 114, 143, 221, 225
Church of Ireland, 108, 146
Civil Survey, 24, 192, 194
Coastguards, 122
Coleraine, 61
Colonsay, 42
Commissioners of Irish Education Inquiry, 197
Conacre, 18, 19, 181
Cooley Peninsula, 125, 126
Corn-mills, 24
Cottiers, 16, 18, 30, 48, 49, 56, 65n, 80-2, 107, 121, 125, 139, 166, 201-207
Cotton, 27, 107
Cromie estate, 42, 43, 64n

Dairy farming *see* Cattle
Death cards, 70, 71
Derry (*City*), 166, 168, 182
Derry, Co., *see* Londonderry, Co.
Devon Commission, 43, 46, 48, 59, 201, 204
Donegal, Co., 31, 137, 153, 197, 207, 208, 229
 - South, 16
Down, Co., 12, 31
 - North, 16
Down Survey, 8, 70, 72
Downham, George, *Bp. of Derry*, 194
Drama societies, 186
Drapers Company, 221
Draperstown, 218, 221, 227, 231
Dublin, 182

Emigration, 51, 55, 70, 81, 121, 124, 126, 130, 131, 166-8, 226, 227, 234, 235
England *see* Britain
English, settlers, 41, 42
Enniskillen, 153, 182
Epidemics, 21
European Union, 29, 181

Fairs, 32, 33, 126, 130, 173, 181

Family farms, 15, 19, 49, 54, 91, 92, 115, 125, 126
Famine, 1840s, 16, 18, 21, 50, 80, 81, 107, 120, 123, 142, 164, 166, 201, 204, 205, 226
Farming, development of, 24-9, 51, 57, 59, 60, 92, 107, 108, 124, 125, 146, 170, 172-81
Farms, creation and development of, 12-20, 32, 48, 49, 76-8, 90, 91, 98-106, 115, 120-9, 138-40, 161, 200, 205, 210, 218, 221, 228
Fermanagh, Co., 31, 137
Fertilisers, use of, 24, 27, 59, 125, 173
Field sizes, 60
Flax, 27, 59, 60, 124, 172, 173
Flight of the Earls, 192
Forestry, 146
Forsythe family, of Forttown, 49, 55, 57, 58
Four Masters, 192

Games, 63, 184, 186
Glynns, The, 40, 42
Grand Juries, 30, 31, 137, 146, 182, 197
Greencastle, 113, 121, 122, 126, 130
Greenore-Holyhead steamship service, 130
Griffith's Valuation, 6, 9, 25, 47-50, 54-7, 76, 87, 101, 139, 161, 200, 205, 206, 227, 230

Hamilton, *Sir* Claud, 194
Hamilton, *Sir* George, 191, 194
Hamilton, James, 97, 98
Hearth Money Returns, 8, 41, 42, 64n, 70, 74, 139, 140
Hedges, 60, 92
Hegarty, *Fr* Walter, 192
Horse racing, 151, 152
Horses, 59, 60, 124, 170, 173
Horseshoes, 63
Housing, 21-4, 57, 58, 107, 131, 132, 150, 166, 169-72, 208-10
Housing Executive, Northern Ireland, 166

Independent Orange Order, 62
Irish Land Commission, 18
Irish Language, 183, 184, 207, 208, 211, 212, 229
Irvinestown, 143
Islay, 42

James I, *King*, 42, 98, 160.

Kesh, 137, 140, 150, 151
Kilkeel, 114, 121, 126, 130
Knox, George, 31, 182

Labourers' cottages, 24, 58, 61, 172, 202
Land Acts, 18, 43, 164
Land measurement, 14, 15
Land Registry, 18
Landlords and tenants, 6, 7, 12, 16-18, 31, 32, 34, 73-8, 98-106, 138, 194-6
Law suits, 89, 90, 92
Leases, 6, 12, 14-17, 49, 74-8, 98, 100-6, ,115, 160, 161, 194, 200, 205, 206, 210
Lendrick, John, 31
Lewis, 200
Lighthouses, 122

Limavady, 54, 55
Linen industry, 11, 16, 17, 25, 27, 30, 55, 107, 168, 173, 197, 200, 201
Liverpool, 130
London Hibernian Society, 197
Londonderry (*City*) *see* Derry (*City*)
Londonderry, Co., 16, 17, 31, 229
Lurgan, 28

Machinery, agricultural, 27, 59, 60, 92, 125, 173
Magill, *Rev.* Robert, 78, 80
Manchester, 82
Mansfield, George D., 197, 200
Markets, 31-4, 126, 130
Marriage patterns, 54, 56, 59, 204
Mass Rocks, 192
Massereene estates, 73-5
Maxwell family, 100-106
Methodist Church, 108, 140, 147
Middlemen, 16, 17, 106, 161
Monaghan, Co., 12, 31
Montgomery, Gabriel, 31
Monuments and Buildings Record, 11
Mountjoy estates, 157, 161
Mourne, 115, 120, 126
Musicians, 186, *see also* Bands

McCrea, William, 31, 182
MacDonnell family, 40, 41
McEvoy, J., 161
McGuinnis, John, 207

National School Registers, 21
Needham family, 114-6, 121, 126
New York, 234, 235
Newry, 114, 130
Newtownards, 107, 166
Newtownstewart, 160, 161, 172, 173, 181
Nolan, R.H., 161, 162, 172, 188n

Oakboy disturbances, 30
Oats, 59, 60, 107, 124, 125, 172, 173
Occupations, 51, 55, 56, 107, 122, 123, 153, 168, 209, 210
O'Donnells, 192
O'Hanlon, Rory, 192
Omagh, 166, 173, 182, 221
O'Neill, Hugh, 192
Oneilland, 24
Orange Order, 62, 130
Ordnance Survey, 7-9, 32, 37-9, 43, 69, 70, 73, 98, 106, 138, 139, 141, 147, 161, 173, 182, 192, 193, 197, 200, 201, 216, 220

Pasture, 59, 60, 124, 172, 201
Peas, 107
Pender's Census, *see* Census, Irish, 1659
Philadelphia, 166
Pigs, 66, 181
Pinkerton Family, of Forttown, 48, 49, 55, 58
Pittsburgh, 70, 92
Place-names, origins of, 37, 70, 72, 113, 159, 169-72, 188n

Plantation of Ulster, 6, 8, 12, 24, 40-2, 75, 98, 138, 139, 160, 191, 192, 194, 221
Poor Inquiry, 1830s, 201
Poor Law Boundary Commission, 25
Poor Law Valuation, 78, 82
Population, 20, 21, 25, 50, 91, 92, 107, 120-4, 140-5, 164-6, 201, 204, 207, 210, 226, 227
Portadown, 55, 182
Portrush, 61
Potatoes, 59, 107, 124, 125, 172, 173, 232
Poteen making, 196
Poultry, 60, 181
Prehistoric remains, 1, 37, 113, 137, 138, 159, 225, 226
Presbyterian Church, 62, 76, 108
Public houses, 130, 151, 153, 184
Public Record Office of Northern Ireland, 21, 24, 31, 89

Rabbits, 181
Railways, 32, 33, 181, 182
Raven, Thomas, 98, 106, 107
Reformed Presbyterian Church, 62
Religious Census, 1834, 220, 223
Revising Valuer's Office Notebooks, 24
Road Act (Ireland) 1765, 7, 30, 182
Roads, 30-2, 61-3, 106, 114, 137, 140, 182, 195, 218, 221
Rocque John, 31
Route, The, 40, 42
Rundale, 6, 17, 48, 78, 157
Rural District Councils, 24

Sampson, George Vaughan, 31
San Francisco, 166
Schools, 62, 70, 82, 88, 89, 107, 130, 140, 142, 146, 147, 150, 168, 183, 184, 186, 197, 200, 211
Scotch carts, 124, 125, 130, 182
Scotland, 227
Scots, settlers, 41, 42, 194
Seasonal migration, 227
1798 Rebellion, 109
Sheep, 59, 181
Shops, 63, 130, 184, 186, 211
Sigerson family, 200, 208
Sigerson, *Dr* George, 207, 208, 212, 213
Sigerson, William, 212
Sinclair family, 191, 195, 196, 202, 203, 207, 208, 210
Sinclair, James, 196, 197, 200, 201, 204, 212, 214
Sinclair, Rosabel, 211
Sion Mills, 168, 182
Skinners Company, 221
Sloane, Oliver, 31
Small-pox, 80
Spade mills, 200, 207, 208, 212
Sperrin Mountains, 11, 221
Standing stones, 159
Starratt, William, 196, 200, 210
Steamer services, 130
Stevenson, John, 221, 225

Stewart, Archibald, 38, 43
Stone circles, 137, 138, 160, 226
Strabane, 166, 168, 182, 191, 192, 196, 201, 202, 204
Subletting, 16, 100, 101, 114, 201
Sweathouses, 159, 187n

Tea merchants, 210
Templemoyle, 197, 200
Tenants *see* Landlords and tenants
Tenement Valuation, 9, 16, 17, 20-2, 46, 87, 100, 105, 106, 128, 129, 150, 169, 177-80, 202, 203, 223, 231, 232
Textiles, 107 *see also* Linen industry
Thackeray, W.M., 200
Thompson, Bonar, 76, 82, 83, 88
Tithe applotments, 17, 45, 46, 54, 55, 76, 101, 118, 119, 143, 163, 164, 200, 220, 222, 223
Topographical Dictionary of Ireland, 200
Townland Valuation, 1830s, 7, 9, 23, 32, 44, 45, 85-7, 101-4, 116-18, 131, 144-6, 169, 173-6, 199-201, 218-20, 225
Townlands, Study of, 6
Towns, 7
Tuberculosis, 21, 80, 232
Turf cutting, 16, 181, 196
Turnips, 59, 107, 172
Turnpike roads, 30
Tyrone, Co., 31, 137, 182, 192, 197, 204, 221, 229

Unitarians, 62

Valuations, 9, 18
Valuation Revision Lists *see* Annual Revision Lists

Wakes, 184
Warrenpoint, 123, 130
Warwick, *Rev.* James, 88
Waters, W. H., 70
Weaving, 11, 17, 30
Wheat, 59, 107
Whyte family, 100
Wilde, George, *Bp. of Derry*, 195
Williamson, James, 31
Women, 82, 107, 168, 210
World War 1, 150, 151, 168, 211
World War 2, 29, 59, 140, 150, 168, 173
Wrack, 125